HAPPENINGS

**BRIEF ACCOUNTS ABOUT PEOPLE AND EVENTS
THAT HAVE AFFECTED MY LIFE**

By

James Juan Spillett

Matt + Family
Hope you enjoy
this Juan Spillett
10/27/15

DEDICATION

To my maternal grandfather, Raymond Madsen Whittier, who I affectionately called "Daddy Pa". He probably affected my life for good more than anyone I have known.

PROLOGUE

Over time, I gradually have come to realize life is largely what we make of it. Time, events, and particularly those with whom we associate greatly influence our feelings and actions. But, it is we who determine how we react and what kind of person we are or will become. This, in turn, determines our destiny.

I have been both blessed and fraught with frequent ups and downs. I have at times strongly felt the influence and power of my Father in Heaven, while at other times I have felt as if I were far removed from Him and His influence. Nevertheless, I have had an interesting and sometimes exciting life. Quite frequently I have been directed away from pitfalls into which I probably would have fallen, if it had not been for the protection or influence of a superior being. My life also has often been spared – for what purpose(s) I do not know.

My life has been one of frequent change. For example, during my youth I attended five grade schools and two high schools, as well as six colleges or universities. My footsteps often were pointed in new directions, some of which were not of my choosing. More often than not these changes afforded me new opportunities and memorable experiences. Someone, it seems, was trying to teach me important lessons. But, perhaps because of my stubborn nature, it often took me much longer than it should have to learn some of life's important lessons. As I grow older, I realize more and more that I still have much to learn.

Frequent changes have brought me into contact with thousands of people, as well as with new cultures and places. These experiences have impressed upon me that ALL people are basically good and the world in which we live is both a beautiful and amazing place– one we should care for and treat with respect.

I have been privileged to travel extensively. I have circled our planet more than a half dozen times and lived and worked on every continent except the Antarctic, which I have visited. I have lived or worked in more than a dozen countries (i.e. Italy, Austria, Uruguay, Paraguay, Ecuador, India, Iran, Chad, Bolivia, Honduras, Mexico, Macedonia and Australia), In all, I have visited more than one hundred countries, and have lived in eleven states, namely: Idaho, Oregon, Utah, Washington, California, Wyoming, Montana, New Mexico, Colorado, Maryland and Texas.

As a result of my travels and associations with people of various countries and cultures, I have been impressed that, regardless of where we live, what language we speak, or to which nationality we belong, ALL of the world's people have far more similarities than differences. We truly are our Father in Heaven's children!

Despite frequent changes and my having lived a somewhat nomadic life, early in life I developed a sense of belonging to a particular place. During my youth, my family and I returned each summer to the family farm in the Rockland Valley of southeastern Idaho, which we called "The Ranch". "The Ranch" provided a feeling of peace and served as a stabilizing influence in my life. Thus, the Rockland Valley represents "home" to me.

Books also have greatly influenced my life. Some of the fondest memories of my youth include the re-living - at least in my mind - what I have read or others have read to me. Frequently, during summer evenings on the farm and after the chores were done, my father and I would sit on the wooden steps of the log house on "The Ranch"; and he would read aloud to me until dark. We read books such as, "Tom Sawyer", "Girl of the Limber Lost", "Call of the Wild", "Baree, Son of Kazan", "Big Smoke Mountain", and others. Because of my favorable and early acquaintance with books, perhaps I can be considered "a book addict". Throughout my life I have avidly read and collected literally thousands of books. Though most of my books were stacked on shelves or packed away in boxes, I considered them to be treasures. Even when funds were tight, which was common during the twelve years I attended various colleges or universities, somehow I still managed to buy some books of particular interest to me. Throughout my life I have been impressed that books are an investment in the future. Although time to read, let alone thoroughly "digest" the books I read, often seems to be limited, I still cherish my books and the time spent with them.

My primary objective in writing "Happenings" is to present, especially to members of my family, brief accounts about some of the people and experiences that have influenced my life. Through reading these narratives, I hope they and others may be able to avoid some of the pitfalls of life and, thereby, live better and more productive lives.

TABLE OF CONTENTS

A STILL SMALL VOICE

"Yea, thus saith the still small voice, which whispereth though and pierceth all things, and often times it maketh my bones quake, while it maketh manifest..."

Doctrine & Covenants 85:6

It had been a fabulous fishing trip. Homer and Karl, two of my maternal uncles, and I had spent almost a week hiking, camping and fishing in the lakes and streams which drain into the East Fork of the Salmon River in central Idaho. We had caught and released trout until our arms literally ached. In fact, the fishing had been so good that we stayed in the backcountry two days longer than we had planned. This was despite our food supply having been exhausted and our having nothing to eat but fish. Our fish diet resulted in joking statements, such as, "Don't you wish we had something besides trout to eat, like say a can of tuna or sardines?" Nevertheless, we had a wonderful time and greatly enjoyed being together in this beautiful, rugged country.

We were tired, sunburned and dirty when we returned from the back country to the old, red Dodge pickup we had left parked near the end of the road along the East Fork of the Salmon River. We threw our packs into the back of the vehicle, beneath a canvas we had stretched over two bowed metal staves. These made the dirty, old truck look somewhat like a modern-day covered wagon. As we slid onto the seat, we remarked to each other as to how good it felt to again sit on something soft, after having spent so much time squatting around a campfire or, at best, sitting on a hard rock or log.

Before starting our journey home, we studied our Idaho road map. After evaluating alternative routes, we decided not to return by the direct route by which we had come. Instead, we decided to follow the road up the Main Salmon River, past Sunbeam Dam, over the Galena Summit, and then down into the Wood River Valley and the town of Ketchum. Thereafter, we would cross the Snake River Plains, which we knew as the "Big Desert". Upon reaching the Snake River, we would follow it upstream until we came to Rock Creek, which we would follow upstream until we entered the Rockland Valley and eventually arrived home.

We stopped at the Sunbeam Dam. Here, fishermen stood in line, trying to catch Chinook salmon. Several of the men with whom we visited indicated that no salmon had been landed that morning. Although two had been hooked, both had "broken free". We observed a good number of large trout swimming in the deep, clear waters adjacent to the dam. We wondered why no one showed any interest in catching some of these nice trout, rather than concentrating strictly upon salmon. We discussed whether or not we should unpack our fishing gear and try to catch some of these large fish to take home. But, we agreed we had eaten more than our fill of trout during the past week and decided to continue our homeward journey.

It was shortly past midday when we arrived in Ketchum. We were hungry and relished the thought of being able to eat something other than fish. We selected a small cafe, which we hoped would not be too expensive for our limited funds. After parking our dilapidated and dust-covered pickup, we entered the eating establishment and sat at a table near the window. We commented to each other as to how strange it seemed to sit at a table and to have such "niceties" as silverware, dishes, and even napkins, let alone have someone else prepare and serve our food. However, after studying the menu provided by the waitress and noting what we considered to be exorbitant prices, we agreed among ourselves, "We're paying dearly for these luxuries!"

As we ate the first meal we had not prepared for ourselves over a campfire in more than a week, we decided to make a short detour to Sun Valley, a ski resort which serves as a year-round playground for the rich and famous. We thought, "It might be interesting to see this famous village and the people associated with it."

We drove to the village of Sun Valley. And, as we circled the grandiose lodge, we rather self-consciously noted the contrast between our dirty, dilapidated vehicle and the bright, shiny, new cars so evident here. We, in our dirty, threadbare clothes and with our sunburned arms and faces, likewise contrasted with the generally well-groomed and stylishly-attired tourists. However, we observed with chagrin that we and our old, dirty truck attracted more attention from others than did the well-dressed tourists and their sleek automobiles. Perhaps giving vent to some of his feelings, Homer repeatedly honked the pickup horn as we drove slowly around the circular drive in front of the big lodge. This resulted in our attracting even more attention.

We returned to Ketchum, after a "quick look" at Sun Valley - a world foreign to what we had known during our lives. Again, we studied our road map and noted a "point of interest", the "Shoshone Ice Caves", north of the town of Shoshone. Remarking to each other about the oppressive heat, particularly as compared to the invigorating mountain air to which we had become accustomed during the past week, we surmised that a visit to the ice caves might be both refreshing and a respite from the hot, dreary desert.

We eventually spied a crude, hand-painted sign alongside the highway. The sign simply stated, "Shoshone Ice Caves" and a crude red arrow pointed toward a rough, dirt and gravel road, which led from the highway into the desert. Thus, turning off from the smooth asphalt highway onto a narrow, tortuous road, we shortly came to a flat, open area that was strewn with broken bottles, rusty cans, and other garbage. Here, another crude sign and arrow pointed toward a footpath. We assumed the refuse-strewn flat served as a parking area for visitors to the caves. Jumping out of the pickup, we raced down the path, vying with each other to see who could reach the caves first. The rugged path, which crossed over rough lava flows, and the oppressive heat of the desert soon slowed our pace to a walk. What a contrast with the mountains where we had spent the previous week fishing! As we walked, we conjectured as to, "How can there be any ice out here – with this heat?"

The path eventually led down into a deep depression in the basalt and then into an open cavern. Shortly after entering a wide-mouthed cavern, the path veered sharply to one side and was replaced by a roughly built, board walkway. In single file, we followed the walkway, going further and further into the gloomy interior. The damp, cool air and the gloom of the cave soon enveloped us. Goose pimples rose on my bare arms and I started to shiver. It didn't seem that cold and I reasoned, "Maybe my shivering is caused by the darkness, rather than the dank cold air." Nevertheless, for some reason I had a feeling of foreboding.

As we shuffled along the board walkway, Homer related how he had heard that the ice in these caves froze during the summer, rather than during the winter. This, he claimed, was due to the insulating effect of the overlying lava flows. In muffled tones, we debated as to whether or not this could be true. As we entered deeper and deeper into the cave, the eerie gloom gradually evolved into pitch darkness. We could not even see our uplifted hands in front of our faces, let alone the walkway upon which we trod. Despite not being able to see, we still continued along the narrow, board walkway. I was in the lead, with Homer and then Karl following closely behind me.

Suddenly, a penetrating "still, small voice" commanded me to "STOP!" With one foot raised in mid-air, I stopped dead in my tracks. Homer pressed hard into my back, almost toppling me forward. "What's wrong?" he inquired, while urging me to continue forward. I started to lift my now firmly planted foot to continue forward when the penetrating "still, small voice" again commanded me to "STOP!" I do not know whether the voice was audible or only in my mind; but it had forcefully commanded me – not once, but twice – to "STOP!"

Sensing my reluctance to continue forward, Homer and Karl queried me as to why I had stopped so abruptly. Rather than tell them about the "still, small voice", I simply said, "I don't know why, but for some reason I'm afraid to go any farther." Homer then offered to lead the way. But, when he tried to shuffle around either side of me, he found the walkway was too narrow for him to pass. Thus, he suggested I spread my legs apart, so he could crawl through and assume the lead position. I spread my legs, and on hands and knees he began to crawl through. However, when only part way through, he suddenly stopped. "What's wrong?" I asked. In a somewhat trembling voice he exclaimed, "There's nothing in front of you!" The narrow, board walkway ended abruptly only a few inches in front of my feet!

The three of us carefully crawled, on hands and knees, along the walkway back towards the cave entrance. We dared not stand and walk, as we had done with such confidence when we entered the cave. After what seemed an almost interminable distance and length of time, the pitch darkness of the cave evolved into an eerie gloom and we gradually could distinguish the forms of each other and the board walkway. Eventually, we could see well enough to stand and walk. We then scurried out of the cave and along the path to our parked vehicle. Upon reaching the pickup, we pawed through our camping gear, until we located a flashlight. Then, after ensuring that the flashlight "worked", we returned to the cavern.

The beam from the flashlight soon revealed that the relatively wide and sturdily constructed walkway shortly reverted into a narrow, rickety catwalk, which was supported by posts embedded into the cave floor. Below the end of the catwalk, where the penetrating "still, small voice" had twice commanded me to "STOP!" there was a sheer icy ledge, which dropped perhaps ten feet into what appeared to be icy water. Furthermore, the beam from the flashlight revealed sheer, icy walls on either side of the cave. These likewise plunged straight down into the water and appeared to be too smooth to offer a handhold or a means whereby one could get out! In front of us, for as far as the beam from the flashlight penetrated into the dank darkness, all we could see was water!

We again retreated to the mouth of the cave. Here, we gathered rocks, which we carried back to the end of the catwalk. First, we dropped a few rocks into the water below. The resounding splashes indicated deep water. Then, with as much force as we could muster – given our precarious position on the narrow catwalk – we threw rocks toward the interior of the cave. All likewise splashed into what sounded like deep water.

We deliberated over and over, "What would have happened if we had continued only a few inches further along the board walkway?" We surmised that our falling into the icy water perhaps would have resulted in our being injured. Given the sheer icy walls surrounding what appeared to be deep, icy-cold water below, "Could we have gotten out?" And, "How long could we have withstood the chill of the icy water. Would we also have become disoriented and lost in the darkness?" Our conclusion was: "It could have been disastrous!"

As we contemplated what could have happened, I offered a silent prayer of thanksgiving for the protection I had been afforded by a "still, small voice". I also vowed that I would strive more diligently in the future to do what I knew to be right – IF I could continue to be protected. I since have realized it is not one's prerogative to bargain with the Lord, but that we should be more submissive in trying to follow His will.

Because of this "happening" in an ice cave in the "Big Desert" of central Idaho and because of subsequent experiences, I am impressed that our Father in Heaven loves each of us. Furthermore, if we will but listen to His "still small voice", He will warn and protect us.

I came upon a song some years ago that epitomizes the workings of a "still, small voice". Subsequently, I had the opportunity to meet the composer. In fact, his daughter, who was serving in the "Peace Corps", lived with my wife and me for a short time while we were living in Chad, Africa.

"Through a still small voice the Spirit speaks to me
To guide me, to save me from the evil I may see
If I try to do what's right, He will lead me through the night
Direct me, protect me and give my soul his light
Listen; listen to the still small voice"
(Bradshaw, M. 1970. "The Still Small Voice"
in Sing With Me. B-92
The Church of Jesus Christ of Latter-day Saints)

"WHAT TIME IS IT?"

"Time is the essence of life." And, "History is a pattern of timeless moments."   **T.S. Elliot**

Table Mountain is an impressive, flat-topped landform located some seven miles west of the town of Rockland in southeastern Idaho. Rarely during my youth did the inhabitants of the Rockland Valley mention this mountain without referring to the "Old Maids" (Dr. Edith Maxwell and her sister Amy) who lived with a "bachelor" (Bob Shear) in a dilapidated old house nestled in a large ravine immediately below the south rim of Table Mountain. They lived in the most humble of circumstances: i.e., they had no electricity, no running water, nor any of the modern conveniences common to most of the inhabitants of the Valley. Their abode consisted of an unpainted, weather-beaten, three-room house, an outdoor "privy", and a small, lean-to shed, which served as a barn. Their spacious "front yard" served as a corral for their livestock, which consisted of a few cows, a flock of sheep and a team of horses. In addition to a quarter section of dry-land wheat ground, which the "Old Maids" leased to a local farmer for a "cost-share" portion of the crops, they owned some surrounding sagebrush-covered rangeland upon which they pastured their animals. Except for the occasional sale of a cow or sheep, they subsisted almost entirely upon the meager income from their dry farm.

Bob Shear would harness their team of horses, hook them up to an ancient buckboard wagon, and make the trip into Rockland at about two-week intervals. There he would purchase staples from the Rockland Mercantile and collect their "General Delivery" mail from the Post Office. While returning home, he also would stop on the bridge over Rock Creek. There, with a bucket attached to a rope, he would fill a large, wooden barrel on the wagon with water from the stream below. This served as their source of drinking water. There was a small spring not far from their house, but Dr. Maxwell claimed the water from it was "unfit for human consumption." Only their livestock used the water from the spring.

Everyone in the Rockland Valley knew about the "Old Maids" and most had seen Bob Shear during his periodic visits to town. However, many in the Valley, particularly the younger inhabitants, had never met Edith or Amy. They only had heard the older residents relate how Dr. Maxwell and her sister had worked unceasingly for many days and nights - ministering to those stricken during the flu epidemic of 1918. Many "old-timers" attributed the "Old Maids" with saving either their lives or the lives of their loved ones during this epidemic that claimed the lives of so many in the Valley. Furthermore, Dr. Maxwell and her sister Amy refused remuneration for their unselfish service. Thus, many still felt indebted to the "Old Maids".

Shortly after the flu epidemic of 1918, the Maxwell sisters retreated to their father's homestead at the base of Table Mountain. Here, they became recluses. Insofar as anyone could recollect, neither ever ventured away from this homestead until Edith's death in 1964. There were a number of stories as to why the "Old Maids" had become recluses. One story accounting for their solitary existence claimed "Edith was involved in a tragic love affair". Another was, "They simply didn't have anywhere else to go." Perhaps the most common was, "Edith had promised her father, while he was on his deathbed, that she and Amy would never leave the family homestead." I never determined which, if any, of these was true.

There likewise were numerous accounts as to how or why Bob Shear joined the Maxwell sisters in their lonely setting sometime during the late 1920's or early 1930's. A common thread in most of these stories was that his father was "well-to-do" and Bob inherited considerable wealth when his father died. Thereafter, he went "back East", where he lived like an aristocrat – attending operas, balls and other social events – until his money was gone. He then returned to the Valley and eventually moved in with the "Old Maids." Oddly, there seemed to be considerable animosity between him and Dr. Maxwell.

Primarily because of the Maxwell sisters' humanitarian services during the 1918 flu epidemic, many of the Valley's residents tried to ensure they always had what they needed to subsist. This was difficult at times, particularly during the not uncommon severe winters in this part of Idaho. Repeated efforts were made to entice the "Old Maids" to move into town, where their needs could more easily be provided. However, Edith and Amy insisted upon continuing their humble, solitary existence at the base of Table Mountain. As a result, it became almost an annual event - during the dead of winter - for some of the Valley's residents to undertake an expedition to Table Mountain to ascertain the "Old Maids" needs. Thus, both they and their livestock survived from year to year.

The winter of 1949 was one of the most severe ever recorded for southeastern Idaho. Except for a few adventurous souls on skis and the almost daily delivery of mail by a ski plane to Rockland, the Valley's residents had virtually no contact with the outside world for most of a two-month period. A common pastime in Rockland's two pool halls was the making of bets as to when the State Highway between Rockland and American Falls would be opened. After road crews had worked from both ends of the highway for two weeks, they finally met and the road was open. Many of the Valley's residents drove their trucks out of the Valley to get coal and other supplies. But, before they could return, another snowstorm "blew in." and the highway was closed for another four weeks.

No school was held during this "state of emergency." After the initial shock of being isolated from the rest of the world, most of us in the Valley decided to make the best of the situation. We began to visit at each other's homes. Evenings often were spent making candy, popping corn, playing games, or simply visiting and having a good time. Despite inconveniences caused by the deep snows and unusually severe weather, there probably was more social activity than usual and most of the Valley's residents experienced an enjoyable winter.

Several people shortly noted that Bob Shear had not come to town for a number of weeks. The Postmaster, Alvin Ralphs, verified that the "Old Maids'" mail had not been picked up for over a month. Thus, some began to conjecture as to what might have happened at Table Mountain. A few even began to discuss how the "Old Maids'" situation might best be ascertained.

Early one clear, cold winter morning, Leonard Hull, Norman Moss and I strapped wooden skis onto our overshoe-covered boots, filled our backpacks with food and the Maxwell Sister's accumulated mail from the Post Office, and started our journey towards Table Mountain. Much of the ample amount of mail for the "Old Maids" consisted of medical journals. I wondered, "Of what value are these journals to Dr. Maxwell, especially given her isolated situation? She never sees anyone, let alone doctors anyone!" Nevertheless, we agreed to carry ALL of their mail.

In route to Table Mountain, we stopped at the Archie Weatherford home some three miles west of town. Archie invited us in, "to get warm and to eat an early lunch." Mostly, I think he just wanted to visit. Prior to our departure he insisted we stop at his place for supper during our return.

It was late afternoon when we finally topped the ridge above the "Old Maids'" humble abode. As we huddled together, trying to catch our breath after the exertion of skiing uphill against a stiff wind, we observed there was no smoke coming from the chimney of the house below. Expectantly, we skied down the hill towards the front of the house. As we approached the old shed, which was little more than some weathered boards nailed to a pole frame, we saw something unbelievable. Inside, standing rigid - like a statue - was a dead horse. I couldn't believe it. How could the animal have died and remained standing? What's more, the dead horse inside the shed appeared to be in better physical condition than the poor horse standing outside. This shaggy animal was so thin you could count its ribs. It appeared to be so weak that it was resting its nose upon the ground and its ears were drooped and its eyes closed. The sheep huddled in front of the house were in even worse condition. They had eaten the wool off from each other's backs and the exposed skin had festered into large, blister-like sores. It was enough to turn your stomach.

Hesitatingly, we glided past the pitiful animals towards the house. On the rickety wooden porch, to the side of the entrance door, were the stacked carcasses of eight or ten sheep. Why had these animals been stacked here? As we approached the porch and dead sheep, we called loudly, "Anyone home? Is anyone there?" There was no answer from within. We unstrapped our skis, leaned them against the house, and tromped onto the narrow, wooden porch. We banged loudly on the door. Still, there was no answer from within. Listening, however, we thought we could hear something moving inside. What was it? What was going on?

We looked at each other, questioning, "Who wants to go in first?" Leonard and I waited for Norman to open the door. He finally opened it and we expectantly peered inside. Lying scattered upon the floor of what served as the kitchen-living room were approximately a dozen sheep. These were in an even more pitiful condition than those we had passed in the yard! Across the room, in front of a large, wood-burning, kitchen stove stood two blanket-covered forms. Edith and Amy were completely wrapped in ragged blankets and huddled over the kitchen range. They were trying to light a fire with pieces of sagebrush they apparently had gathered from the surrounding hills. And, on top of the stove were at least a half dozen cats. It was indeed a sight to behold!

Norman, Leonard and I stood quietly by the door. We did not know what to make of the situation in front of us. Eventually, Dr. Maxwell slowly turned and stared blankly towards us. With no sign of emotion, she quietly inquired, "What time is it? Our clock stopped. We don't know what time it is." What a question! Norman withdrew a watch from his pocket, looked at it, and told Dr. Maxwell the time. She then slowly extended a thin, wrinkled hand from beneath her bundle of blankets, took a round, metal alarm clock from off the top of the warming oven above the stove, and methodically set the hands and carefully wound the clock, before placing it back on top of the warming oven.

Not knowing what else to do, we removed our packs from our backs and started to remove their contents and place them on top of a round wooden table in the corner of the room. The "Old Maids" inquisitively joined us. Dr. Maxwell was particularly interested in the medical journals we had brought from the Post Office. She insisted upon methodically reviewing the "Table of Contents" in each journal, before responding to our inquiries. Amy stood to one side, much like a shy little child. Whenever we directed a question to her, she would look imploringly towards her sister or act as if she had not heard us. Edith appeared to be their sole mouthpiece.

After we had emptied our packs and Dr. Maxwell had thoroughly inspected their mail, she finally appeared ready to answer some of our questions. When we inquired as to the whereabouts of Bob Shear, she explained, "Our cows wandered off in a blizzard a few days ago and he's out searching for them." As to the condition of the animals outside, as well as the sheep in the house, she explained, "We ran out of hay some days ago." And, "The weather has been so bad and the snow so deep, we haven't been able to gather sagebrush for them." As to the sheep inside the house, she stated, "We're treating them with medicine, trying to keep them alive until we can get some food for them." The dead sheep stacked on the porch were those that had died inside the house.

Dr. Maxwell politely answered our questions, but kept glancing towards the clock on the stove and at the stack of mail on the table. It was obvious she was anxious to read the medical journals. Finally, she stated, "It's getting late. You'd better be going, if you're going to make it back to town. Hadn't you?" Thus, we placed our empty packs on our backs and the "Old Maids" escorted us to the door. As soon as we were outside, they quietly closed the door behind us. We strapped on our skis and started back to Rockland.

In route, we stopped at Archie Weatherford's. We related to Archie and his wife Annie our experiences of the day and ate supper with them. After returning to Rockland, we related to others the pitiful conditions we had observed at Table Mountain. As a result, an expedition was organized. Several crawler tractors were used to open the road between Rockland and Table Mountain, and several trucks delivered hay and other supplies to the "Old Maids". Thus, the Valley's residents again saved them and their livestock.

Oleen Stokes, the father of my best friend, "Nick" Stokes, was one of those who drove a truck to Table Mountain. Mr. Stokes suffered from palsy. When first stricken with this malady, only his index finger quivered. Then, his right hand and eventually his entire right arm trembled uncontrollably. When he sought medical assistance, the doctors told him they could not alleviate nor effectively treat his ailment. Finally, he went to the renowned Mayo Clinic. The doctors there prescribed a new medication, which they claimed, would help deter the advance of the malady.

Dr. Edith Maxwell observed the trembling of Mr. Stokes' arm, while the hay and supplies were being unloaded from his truck. She instructed him, "Come into the house. I want to examine that!" She questioned Oleen as to when the trembling had begun and how it had progressed. She then stated, "I think maybe I can help you." She withdrew a prescription booklet from among the medical journals, which were neatly lined up along some shelves on the wall of the house. She then asked Mr. Stokes to spell his name for her and she wrote a prescription for him. "Here," she said, "Take this to the drugstore. I think it might help you." To Mr. Stokes' surprise, he later discovered that the prescription Dr. Maxwell had written for him was identical to that which he had obtained from the Mayo Clinic! Dr. Maxwell's medical journals apparently had kept her abreast of modern-day medicine!

During our return journey from Table Mountain, I pondered over and over the happenings of the day. Dr. Maxwell's inquiry as to, "What time is it?" kept resounding in my mind. Why was the correct time so important to her? What difference would it have made if she had not known even what day it was, let alone the correct time? Didn't she live in a seemingly "timeless" world? Should we be concerned about "What time is it?" How important is time? Or, is it more important what we do with the time we are allotted during mortality?

I eventually concluded, "Time is a MOST valuable asset. Without time, life is of no value and we are nothing." Also, what we do with our time is most important. We can squander or waste it in the pursuit of pleasures or worldly goods or we can use it in trying to help others and to improve ourselves and the world around us. As a model, should we not consider how Jesus Christ used his time on earth? He spent his life teaching and serving others.

Like Dr. Edith Maxwell – the "Old Maid" at Table Mountain – I concluded that we should be very much concerned about, "What Time Is It?"

MR. SNAPP

"Greater love hath no man, than this, that a man lay down his life for his friends." John 15:13

My first meeting with Mr. Snapp was not pleasant. My father had purchased a grocery store in the small town of Helix, Oregon, and our family had recently moved there from off the family farm in Rockland. A newly acquired friend and I were shooting ground squirrels with our .22 rifles in a field near the edge of Helix, when we observed a battered and faded, old, blue Ford pickup moving slowly along the road next to the field. In addition to good numbers of squirrels, the field also contained some sleek, well-bred Black Angus cattle. As we waited for another squirrel to raise its head far enough out of a burrow to afford us a shot, the pickup stopped along the road, next to where we had left our bicycles. A small, bent man, with an over-sized Stetson hat on his head, got out of the vehicle. He examined our bikes and then gazed in our direction, before crawling through the fence and starting to limp towards us. As the diminutive man approached us, a gruff voice inquired, "What do you think you're doing in my field?" We explained, "We're just shooting squirrels." We also added, "We're being careful about the cows." But, an even gruffer voice ordered us to, "Get out of my field!"

Although a newcomer to Helix, I knew the man who ordered us out of his field was Mr. Snapp. He lived through the block from our house and his black and white dog, which invariably rode upon the seat beside him in his ancient pickup, were community "fixtures". Although I had not previously met Mr. Snapp, others had pointed him out and told me a little about him. Mr. Snapp was small in stature, but I eventually learned he was a "big" man in many respects. His back was bowed from many years of hard labor on ranches and farms, as well as from arthritis. His legs were markedly bowed and he walked with a limp. This, he claimed, was the result of "too many years on the back of a horse", and a broken leg, which he suffered when a horse fell on him "many years ago."

Mr. Snapp's gruff voice perhaps resulted from his having smoked a pipe much of his life. Though it was only infrequently lit during the time I knew him, his small, crooked-stemmed pipe almost always dangled from the corner of his mouth. Up close, his gruff voice was offset by a kindly, weather-beaten and wrinkled face, which was accented by a pair of dark eyes. These dark eyes invariably twinkled behind a pair of gold-trimmed spectacles. Despite the years depicted by the lines in his face, his thick mop of hair showed only a few traces of gray. His hair, however, usually was hidden beneath a large, battered and faded Stetson hat.

Mr. Snapp's daily attire consisted of a plain blue work shirt, a Levi jacket, the unbuttoned breast pocket of which usually bulged with a tobacco pouch, and a faded pair of Levi pants, which more often than not were tucked into the tops of his cowboy boots. On special occasions, he would change into a light tan gabardine stockman's suit, complete with a wine-colored, snap-button cowboy shirt, a bolo tie, and a clean, well-blocked Stetson. Mr. Snapp, with his dog sitting beside him in his pickup, was a common sight in Helix, as he drove from his home in town to his nearby farm several times each day to look after his small, but highly prized, herd of purebred Angus cattle.

It seemed I encountered Mr. Snapp more and more frequently after he "kicked" my friend and me out of his field. Neither of us spoke, but it seemed for some reason he was closely scrutinizing me. A few weeks had passed when my mother told me, "Mr. Snapp has been in the store and he wants you to come to his house to see him." I immediately thought, "Something has happened to one of his cows and he's going to try to blame it on me." I told my mother how Mr. Snapp had ordered my friend and me out of his field, even though we'd been careful not to disturb his cows nor shoot towards them. I also told her, "I don't want to see Mr. Snapp. If there's something wrong with any of his cows, it's not my fault." Nevertheless, she insisted I immediately go to Mr. Snapp's house, because "I promised him I would send you." Thus, I reluctantly agreed to go.

I slowly walked to Mr. Snapp's home. I hesitated before climbing the front steps to his large, gray stucco house. After I rang the doorbell, Mrs. Snapp, a rather stoutly-built and pleasant-looking woman, who was considerably larger than her husband, opened the door. I explained, "My mother said Mr. Snapp wanted to see me." She invited me into the living room and said, "Please be seated, while I try to locate my husband."

I nervously waited. I imagined all kinds of accusations that he might try to level against me. "Why did he want to accuse me? I hadn't done anything wrong!" Mr. Snapp shortly limped into the room. I arose and stood stiffly, awaiting his accusations. Instead, he smiled and insisted I "Sit down." He then began to question me. "Do you like animals?" I explained that I did. After further probing on his part, I explained how we had lived on a farm prior to coming to Helix and that I had had a dog, a horse and a number of calves. He then questioned, "What do you want to do or become in life?" I had to admit, "I'm not sure. I haven't decided." He then wanted to know, "What do you like?" This was followed by, "What don't you like?" On and on went the interrogation. What was he getting at, anyway?

Mr. Snapp eventually reached into the small pocket of his Levis and extracted a gold pocket watch. He flipped open the cover, stared intently at the face of the watch and stated, "Guess it's time to go do chores. Would you like to come with me?" "This is it," I thought, "Now he's going to show me what's happened to one of his cows!" Nevertheless, I nervously agreed to accompany him.

Mr. Snapp's black and white dog met us as we descended the back steps of his house. She expectantly wagged her tail, as we walked from the house to the nearby garage in which the old Ford pickup was parked. As soon as Mr. Snapp opened the pickup door, the dog jumped up onto the seat. Mr. Snapp jokingly scolded her and told her to "Get over", so I could get in. She obediently moved closer to him. He explained, "If I leave her behind, she'll sulk for days."

We backed out of the driveway and moved slowly through Helix. It surprised me how almost everyone we passed smiled and waved to Mr. Snapp. He, in turn, cheerfully greeted them. I had thought he was an "old grouch."

We entered a long lane near the edge of town, which led to a neat, white barn and a set of corrals. We stopped next to the corrals and got out of the pickup to inspect what Mr. Snapp informed me was his "pride and joy." It was a small breeding herd of about 25 purebred Black Angus, which were in the corrals. A huge bull placidly stared at us, as it contentedly chewed its cud. Mr. Snapp proudly informed me this was his herd sire and "he weighs in excess of a ton." As we approached the pen, the bull stretched and ambled slowly toward us. Mr. Snapp chuckled and said, "I guess the big boy wants his back scratched." He then administered a liberal scratching to the back of the monstrous animal, while explaining to me how he had developed or selected his prized breeding herd.

We next entered a large corral, which contained about a dozen cows with their young calves. Rather than the animals moving away from us, the cows came towards and even followed Mr. Snapp, while curiously staring at me. The calves, however, stood back and hesitated about following their mothers. "Those," announced Mr. Snapp, "haven't had time to get to know me yet. But, they will!"

Mr. Snapp's open display of affection for his cattle and how they acted toward him caused me to temporarily forget my fears about him accusing me of having harmed one of his animals. My fears returned, however, when he said, "Let's go into the barn. I have something I want to show you." Although I said nothing, I immediately thought, "He's going to show me a sick or injured animal. Then, he'll try to blame it on me! He probably showed me his cows and how much he loves them just to make me feel sorry for something I didn't do!"

We walked through a wide alleyway, which led from the corrals into and through the center of the barn. There were box stalls on either side, which had large gates that could be swung across the alley to direct animals wherever desired. These stalls also contained mangers, which could be supplied hay through overhead chutes leading to a second-story hayloft.

We stopped in front of a stall that held six young heifers. Mr. Snapp opened the gate and motioned for me to enter. He then ordered me to "Take a good look" at the young animals. I closely scrutinized each heifer, looking for an injury or something wrong with them. He then asked, "What do you think of them?" I meekly replied, "They look okay to me." His eyes twinkled as he explained how he planned to show this group of heifers at various livestock shows. "But," he continued, "I'm not as young nor as spry as I used to be. I was wondering if you'd be interested in helping me to train and show these animals."

What a surprise! I couldn't believe it. I'd always loved animals and enjoyed working with them. But, except for a dog, I thought our moving to Oregon had put an end to my doing such. I stood speechless. However, I think my emotions let Mr. Snapp know I indeed was interested in his offer. Looking at the heifers in front of me, I envisioned an entirely different relationship with Mr. Snapp than I previously had imagined. He then exclaimed, "Well, don't just stand there. I've got something else I want to show you!" "What now?" I puzzled.

Mr. Snapp led me to another stall. Then, while pointing to a young bull inside, he asked, "What do you think of him?" I carefully examined the young animal and said, "I think he looks great. Why?" He then explained how he'd been watching me the past few weeks and had decided my being willing, he'd like me to help him train and show his prize heifers. However, he didn't think it fair for me to show only his animals. Thus, "If you're willing and do a good job, I'd like to give you this bull calf – to show as your own." He further explained, "The calf's official or pedigree name is Snapp's Black Boy." Also, "It probably would be best for you to show your calf as a 4-H animal." This would require the bull calf becoming a steer. I later learned "Black Boy" could have been sold as a breeding animal for a much higher price than would be received even for a champion 4-H steer.

Thus began my apprenticeship and lifelong friendship with the gruff old man who had ordered me out of his field the first time we met. I learned a great deal from him, not only about cattle, but also about people and life. For example, rather than forcefully teaching "our" calves to lead, as I previously had done with my calves while living on the family farm in Idaho, Mr. Snapp insisted we simply halter and tie them to the manger each night when we fed them. And, while they were tied to the manger, I should spend time brushing and talking to them. "This way," he explained, "they'll follow you, rather than you having to lead them." And, he was right!

We talked about many subjects as we fed and cared for our animals and while my visits to the Snapps' home became more and more frequent. Mr. Snapp told me about his boyhood and how he came West on his own "to become a cowboy at the ripe old age of fourteen." He told about the difficulties he encountered in "the good old days," as well as about the many good times he had experienced. He never expressed bitterness or remorse for what might have been. Rarely did he speak ill of anyone, no matter what they might have done. Above all, he impressed upon me his firm belief that one usually gets out of life just about what they put into it. Also, most people basically are good. And, if you treat them fairly and with respect, they usually will treat you in the same manner.

Little by little Mr. Snapp's life unfolded before me. I learned how he had followed some of the big cattle drives in eastern Oregon while only a boy. I also learned about some of the mistakes he made, while trying to become a "rough and tough cowboy". Accounts about people who had befriended or helped him were common; whereas, little was said about those who wronged or treated him unfairly. Much credit was given to those who helped get him started and to eventually own his own ranch, which he lost during the "Great Depression" and then had to start over again. Eventually, with the help of others, he became a successful wheat farmer. Although he had swapped cattle ranching for wheat ranching, he claimed, "Next to my wife and family, my first love always has been cattle."

Mr. Snapp decided to "retire" a few years prior to our meeting. He turned his wheat farm over to his only son and he and his wife Grace moved into town. However, he purchased a small, nearby farm, where – at least on a small scale – he could raise cattle. His philosophy was, "A man should keep busy." And, "It's best to keep busy doing what you enjoy most." Although he told me many things about his life, especially his young cowboy days, it eventually dawned upon me that he never spoke about his early childhood or his parents. It was as if his life began when he came West from somewhere back East at the age of fourteen. He virtually worshipped his only son and apparently had given him everything within his power to give. It appeared he also had tried to shelter his son from difficulties or trials such as he had faced during much of his life. As a result, it seemed his son was grossly spoiled. Though Mr. Snapp never stated such, it appeared one of his greatest desires was to see his son become a successful rancher. Although he provided at least two ranches for his son, he quickly went through them and, insofar as I know, Mr. Snapp never had the pleasure of seeing him succeed in any worthwhile endeavor. Because he had been so zealous in making things easy for his son – by protecting and simply giving him things without his having to earn them – Mr. Snapp perhaps accepted much of the blame for his son not being successful. Despite his desires or ambitions for him, I think he eventually realized he had neither his father's ambitions nor his love for animals and the land. This is not to say, however, that Mr. Snapp did not continue to love and try to help him. He took every opportunity possible to praise or to brag about even his smallest achievements. But, as a whole, his son appeared to be too busy seeking the easy or "good" life to realize how much he was hurting his father. It appeared to me, Mr. Snapp had turned to trying to help young people, such as myself, to develop proper attitudes and to pursue meaningful goals in life. I was neither the first nor the last he "took in" and essentially treated as his own. He also always spoke with pride about the accomplishment of "his" boys or girls. Still, I often wondered – with the success he enjoyed through working with other people's children – "Wouldn't it have been great if he could have had similar success with his own son?"

Winter passed quickly. As spring approached, Mr. Snapp and I began making detailed plans as to where and how we were going to show our string of animals. We felt certain we were going to win many prizes. But, my father then announced he was selling the store and we were moving back to Idaho. It appeared Mr. Snapp's and my plans were for naught. He solemnly presented me with "Black Boy". I could take him back to Idaho with me. All he requested was I periodically write to him and let him know how both I and "Black Boy" were doing. Thus, developed a pattern of occasional letters and infrequent visits, which spanned more than fifteen years and instilled in me an abiding love for Ed and Grace Snapp.

"Black Boy" traveled to Idaho with our family's belongings in the back of my grandfather's truck. I eventually showed him in the Power County Fair, where he took top honors. I then showed him in the Eastern Idaho State Fair, where he placed first in his class and I received first place in "fitting and showing". I was even featured on a local radio program. And, Mr. Snapp traveled the more than six hundred miles from Helix to Blackfoot, Idaho – just to see how "his boy" and his calf were doing. Regretfully, I was so engrossed in the showing of my calf and the many activities at the fair that I spent very little time with him during his visit to Idaho. In fact, I later realized I did not even thank him for coming. Of course, Mr. Snapp never mentioned my rudeness.

Thereafter, my grandfather helped me take "Black Boy" to the Golden Spike Livestock Show in Ogden, Utah. This was one of the largest and best-known livestock shows in the Intermountain West. Although "Black Boy" didn't win any major prizes here, he was auctioned off for the then exorbitant price of forty-seven cents per pound. He weighed in excess of eleven hundred pounds! Thus, I was rich beyond my wildest dreams. Many years passed before I began to realize the friendship, guidance and love I received from Mr. Snapp were far more valuable than the money I received from the sale of "Snapp's Black Boy".

Mr. Snapp continued to demonstrate love and concern for me throughout the years. In his periodic letters, he inquired as to what I was doing and what were my goals or ambitions in life. He encouraged and counseled me to always do my best. I sometimes followed paths that he probably did not fully understand. For example, after my military service, I spent two and one-half years as a "Mormon" missionary in South America. Nevertheless, he always continued to encourage me to do my best in whatever endeavor I might be engaged. Most importantly, he always let me know, usually in an indirect way, that he was proud of me and considered me to be "his boy".

I fortunately had the opportunity to return to Helix to visit Mr. Snapp and his wife Grace on a number of occasions. Each visit was memorable. He would insist we visit as many people as possible with whom I had become acquainted during the year my family and I had lived in Helix. Almost invariably when we would visit someone, he would proudly announce, "This is one of my boys. He's come home for a visit!" His wife Grace also treated me royally. She remembered and prepared my favorite foods and delectable meals. We truly had some wonderful times together.

During one visit, Mr. Snapp and I "took in" the world-famous Pendleton Roundup. We didn't miss a single day or hardly a single event during the weeklong celebration. During another visit, we toured the recently completed McNary Dam on the Columbia River. During each visit, we toured the countryside around Helix, looking at and discussing various aspects about the beautiful farms or ranches, crops, and particularly the livestock we saw.

The years passed. I spent two years in the U.S. Army, two and one-half years as a "Mormon" missionary, and several years in various universities. The day before I graduated from Utah State University, I married my wife Carol. We spent that summer in Rocky Mountain National Park in Colorado, where I worked as a seasonal Park Naturalist. Thereafter, we spent a year in Quito, Ecuador, where I was a Fulbright Scholar studying Natural History. It was during this time, while we were in the Galapagos Islands, our first daughter (Cris Tina) was born.

Upon our return to the States, I felt it was time to again visit Ed and Grace Snapp. I particularly wanted to show off my wife and new daughter to them. We debated whether or not we should leave Cris Tina with her grandparents, rather than subject her to the long trip from Utah to Oregon. But, when discussing our proposed visit on the phone with Mr. Snapp, he insisted we must bring her, "So I can judge whether or not you should keep her." He further insisted we stay with him and Grace for as long as possible, "So I can determine whether or not you found the right girl to marry."

We drove from Utah to Oregon. Little did I expect this would be my last visit with Mr. Snapp and Carol's only opportunity to get acquainted with him and his wife, Grace.

After we had visited with Ed and Grace a few days, Mr. Snapp drew me aside and pronounced his verdict concerning my wife and daughter. Regarding Carol, he stated, "You'd better hang onto her. I doubt you'll find one much better." But, concerning our daughter, he claimed, "I've consulted with Grace and we've decided you need to leave her with us – so we can spoil her properly."

As always, Ed and Grace were wonderful hosts. Their years, however, were beginning to take a toll. Though they insisted upon taking us to visit many people and places, it was evident such activities were difficult for them. Their spirits were still young, but physically they were becoming old. No longer could they do many of the things they wished to do. Mr. Snapp even had sold his farm and beloved Angus cattle. He wistfully related to me how he no longer could care for them properly and now he had to be content just "puttering" around his yard and garden, helping his neighbors, and reminiscing about the past.

Carol and I reluctantly bid farewell to Ed and Grace. Our visit with them had been most enjoyable and memorable, but we had to return to Utah and my graduate studies at Utah State University. Only a couple of months later, we received a letter from Grace. She informed us, "Ed has died." She described how, while still in bed, they had talked – before she got up, "To go to the kitchen to prepare breakfast." She then called Ed to come and eat, but there was no answer. Returning to the bedroom, she found him still in bed. Upon touching him, she found he had died during the few minutes she had been preparing breakfast. She also described how he had "the most contented look upon his face – as if he was having a beautiful dream." Grace also told us how Ed had frequently mentioned how happy he had been, because my family and I had visited them. She claimed, he was especially happy because "Juan FINALLY has found a good wife to look after him." And, "Because he now has a family, maybe he'll settle down and I won't have to worry about him any longer."

We held a family reunion the following summer in the Blue Mountains of eastern Oregon. The Blue Mountains are not far from Helix, so we decided to again visit Grace. When she met us at the door to her home, she graciously invited us in and asked us to be seated. She then disappeared into another room. When she returned, she placed a box in my hands and stated, "Here, Ed kept these in a special place. I'm sure he'd want you to have them back." Inside were one of my high school yearbooks, a small gold medal I had won with "Snapp's Black Boy", and an assortment of photographs and letters I had sent to him and he had guarded for many years.

I sent a Christmas card and letter to Grace later that year. I tried to tell her how much I appreciated my association with her and Ed over the years. However, instead of a reply from her, I received a letter from her daughter-in-law. She informed me that Grace had quietly joined Ed shortly after our visit with her that summer.

Ed and Grace were not religious people with respect to some of the connotations many people place upon one "being religious". They rarely attended church or worship services. Insofar as I know, they were not even affiliated with a given church denomination or congregation. Nevertheless, they were some of the most Christian people I have known. Perhaps even without realizing it, they espoused the true meaning of the gospel of Jesus Christ. They were living examples of the "golden rules" of "Do unto others as you would have them do unto you", and "Love thy neighbor as thyself". Throughout much of his life, particularly during the years I knew him, Mr. Snapp truly "laid down his life" for others.

Ed and Grace always seemed to demonstrate concern for me. For example, whenever I would eat a meal with them, they would insist I say a blessing upon the food. This was because they knew I believed in so doing. Also, although a pipe almost always habitually dangled from the corner of Mr. Snapp's mouth, rarely did he light it in my presence – because he knew I did not believe one should smoke. In fact, he repeatedly counseled me, "Don't you ever take up the filthy habit!"

While my wife and daughter and I were visiting with the Snapps, Ed and I were sitting on their front porch talking, while our wives were preparing a meal in the kitchen. Ed reached into his shirt pocket and withdrew a cigar and handed it to me. "Why don't you light this when you wife comes out?' he said. "Then we can see if she really loves you." An odd expression then crossed his face and he quickly retrieved the cigar and said, "No! You couldn't do that! It wouldn't be right! It's against what you believe."

I further realize how truly unselfish and Christ-like Ed and Grace were when I think of the many young people, such as myself, they took into their home and their lives. They imparted much of themselves and their worldly goods to us. Their passing left a void in my life, but I am thankful they were a part of my life. I hope, in some way, I added something to their lives. I also anticipate someday again having the opportunity to reunite with Ed and Grace. I wonder, however, when we again meet, "Will Mr. Snapp still have a pipe dangling from the corner of his mouth?"

THE ARMY AND MY FIRST AIRPLANE RIDE

"War is hell!" Training for war also can be hell.

The Korean War continued unabated and became more and more of a concern to many, especially to me and other young men of my age. One by one my friends and acquaintances were drafted into military service, first to be trained in the "art" of war and then to "defend" their country in that far-off land.

My father had accepted a teacher-exchange position in England. He, my mother and my two brothers (Gary, who was ten, and Val Gene, who was less than a year old) had gone to England, while I remained behind to operate the family farm. I had obtained a loan of $3,000 from the bank to initiate my farming career. With this money, I purchased a 1950 Dodge pickup, a small International Model A Farmall tractor, including some implements (i.e. a two-way, single-bottom plow and a mower), an assortment of tools, and a number of young dairy calves). I planned to raise the calves on "dairy supplement" and milk from the family's sole remaining milk cow.

My long-term goal was to become a cattle rancher. I hoped to achieve this through hard work, perseverance, and by first becoming well established on the family farm. I knew, however, I undoubtedly would have to serve a tour of duty in the military service, unless the conflict in Korea soon subsided.

Many people did much to help me get started on the farm. For example, my Uncle Homer and Aunt Ora Whittier invited me to live with them. This I did, until there arose a misunderstanding, which was not their nor my fault. My grandmother told Ora I had complained about her cooking and homemaking abilities, which I had not. Rather than dispute what had been said, I simply moved into the old log house on the family farm and began the life of a bachelor. Homer and my grandfather, however, continued to help me, primarily by letting me use some of their farm equipment in exchange for my periodically working for them on their farm.

Gene and Gayle Kress invited me to stay with them shortly after I had moved into the house on the ranch. I first became acquainted with them when working on their farm near Roy when I was sixteen and still in high school. Thus began my lifetime friendship with this choice couple and their family. They then were building a basement house in Rockland. Partially to help repay their kindness, I assisted them in the building of their house.

I worked from dawn to dark and often well into the night throughout the summer. I worked mostly on the family farm, but also for my Uncle Homer, grandfather and Gene Kress. The summer and fall went relatively well. I raised eleven calves with milk from the family cow. I fixed or rebuilt almost all of the fences on the farm and harvested good crops of alfalfa hay and barley, as well as changed and greatly improved the ditch irrigation system. Using Gene's crawler tractor, I cleared the brush from the tillable portion of the pastureland and converted it into dry farm cropland. I then planted a crop of winter wheat on this newly cultivated land. Although prospects of my having to serve in the military still loomed on the horizon, my farming situation looked good.

Virtually all of my fellow high school classmates had been drafted into the Army by the fall of 1952. I surmised my being the youngest in my class perhaps was the reason I had not been drafted. Nevertheless, because of uncertainty regarding my pending military service, I met with the Draft Board and inquired, "When can I expect to be drafted?" I also explained, "I need to know my draft status in order to plan the coming year's operation of the farm." The Draft Board members examined their lists of potential inductees and informed me I probably would not be selected for military service for at least another year. They further stated, "If your name comes up while you have crops in the field, we'll defer you until after you have harvested your crops." With this assurance, I invested virtually all I had received from the sale of my crops in purchasing two dozen Hereford feeder calves. These, I reasoned, should return a good profit, after I had fed them throughout the winter, pastured them the following summer, and fattened them in the fall – prior to my being drafted into the military service.

Except for caring for my livestock, I had relatively little to do during the winter. My friends were gone and I was too broke to afford most forms of recreation or entertainment. My Aunt Melba and Uncle Ezra Moore then informed me the Monsanto Chemical Company was opening a new elemental phosphorus plant in Soda Springs, where Ezra was the School Superintendent. They also offered to let me live with them. Gene Kress graciously offered to care for my livestock, while I obtained winter employment with Monsanto. Everything seemed to be going well.

Shortly after I began living with Melba and Ezra and working for Monsanto, I received a notice from the Draft Board. I had to go to Boise for a pre-induction medical examination in December. This startled me. Thus, I again met with the Draft Board and again inquired as to my status regarding military service. The Board members again assured me I would not be called up for military service prior to fall. And, "If your name comes up sooner than anticipated, we'll defer you until after you've harvested your crops."

Early one morning in late February of 1953, after working a graveyard shift at the Monsanto plant, I returned to my uncle and aunt's home. Aunt Melba solemnly handed me an "official" letter. I nervously opened the Government-franked envelope. The enclosed letter began with, "Greetings from the President of the United States..." I had been drafted into the military service and was ordered to report to the induction center in Boise in less than two weeks!

Despite not having slept in more than twenty-four hours, I hurriedly drove from Soda Spring to Pocatello. There, I met with the clerk of the Draft Board, a bitter woman noted for her calloused attitude towards military draftees. I tried to explain, "There must be a mistake. The Board assured me I wouldn't be drafted until fall!" She refused to listen to me and simply stated, "Sorry. You're now in the Army! There's nothing you can do about it. If you wanted to be deferred until after you harvested your crops, you should have done something before now!"

Not knowing where else to turn, I turned to my grandfather. He then was serving in the State Legislature and was well acquainted with each of the Draft Board members. He somehow arranged a special hearing for me with the Board, during which both he and I pleaded my case. The Draft Board modified their decision. I would be deferred until July, but no later! "This", they claimed, "should provide sufficient time for you to sell your livestock and make arrangements for someone to harvest your crops." Regarding their previous commitments to defer me until after I had harvested my crops, they simply stated, "Your name came to the top of the list sooner than we expected. There is nothing more we can do."

I wrote to my family in England and informed them about what had happened. They began to make arrangements to return home early. They would not remain in England until fall, as my father had agreed in his original contract. I continued to work at the Monsanto plant until late spring. I then returned to the farm and sold my livestock for much less than I had expected to receive by selling them in the fall. I harvested a first crop of hay and made arrangements for my grain to be harvested after my departure for the military service. It appeared I would have an excellent crop of irrigated barley. But, because of drought, my dry land wheat crop in the newly cultivated ground would be only marginal.

My family returned home in mid-July and I prepared to enter the military service. On July 28, I took a Greyhound bus from American Falls to the Reception Center in Boise, where I was to be inducted into the U.S. Army the next day. That morning, I went to my Uncle Ray and Aunt Grace Spillett's to bid farewell to them and my cousins, Bob and Ted. Bob and Ted had built a chute system leading from their milk barn into an adjoining corral. After milking the cows each morning and evening, they would run the cows into the chute, place a surcingle on them, and then ride them. This was how they practiced to compete in local rodeos. They had one cow that was an exceptional "bucker". As a special favor to me, they ran this cow into the chute so I could ride her.

After the surcingle was place around the cow. I climbed on board. Then, with a hoot, they opened the gate and turned the cow and me loose. I thought I was riding pretty well, until the cow ran into the corral gate and banged my right leg into a brace panel. I half jumped and was half thrown from off the back of the animal. We examined my leg and couldn't detect any broken bones, though it was scraped and bruised from the knee to the ankle. I then hobbled to the car and was driven to American Falls, where I caught the bus to Boise.

The following morning my right leg was swollen and black and blue from the knee down. I could hardly walk from the hotel, where I and the other draftees had been billeted, to the Reception Center – where, following a medical examination, we were to be inducted into the U.S. Army. Our medical exam involved our first having to take off all our clothes, except our socks, and then stand in line, until a doctor could examine us one-at-a-time. Our being naked did not deter the nurses from repeatedly passing through the room. However, each time before entering they would shout, "Close your eyes. We're coming through!" When some of us turned our backs or tried to cover ourselves with our hands, they simply guff-hawed, "You certainly don't have anything we'd want to see!" Or, "You don't have much to hide, do you?" During one part of the examination, the doctor ordered, "Turn around, bend over and spread your cheeks." When the fellow next to me spread the cheeks of his face, the doctor laughed until he had tears in his eyes. With a rubber-gloved hand, he then gave each of us a rectal exam. After having probed each of us with his finger, the doctor sauntered back along the line, goosing each man with his thumb as he passed. He then announced with a loud voice, "Best looking bunch of A-holes I've seen in a long time!"

While eating breakfast in the hotel restaurant prior to our physical examination, several inductees placed granulated sugar beneath their fingernails. They suggested we do the same, claiming, "You can dislodge the sugar into your urine sample." And, "If you have sugar in your urine, you'll be classified as a diabetic and won't be inducted into the Army!" This ploy apparently didn't work, as the examining doctor shortly announced, "You ALL passed your physical exams with flying colors!"

Before we put our clothes back on and went into another room to be inducted into the U.S. Army, the doctor stated, "If any of you think I missed something or you might have something wrong, which might defer you from military service, let me look at it now." I timidly approached the doctor and, while pointing to my leg, said, "My leg really hurts. Would you look at it?" He glanced at my leg and said, "It does look pretty bad, doesn't it?" He then loudly stated, "Next!" Thus, I hobbled into the adjoining room to be inducted into the U.S. Army.

After a brief induction ceremony, we recruits were taken to the train depot and placed on an overnight train for Seattle, Washington. Upon our arrival in Seattle the next day, we were loaded onto a bus and taken to the Reception Center at Ft. Lewis. There, we were issued Army clothing and assigned quarters.

The following days were a continual round of placement tests, examinations, falling in or out of formations, and of being assigned to "details". "Details" consisted of anything from "policing" or picking up litter (primarily cigarette butts) to helping inventory and stack or arrange in an orderly fashion mountains of supplies. One "detail" we soon came to dread was slaving much of the night scrubbing pots and pans or, worse yet, cleaning grease traps in the mess hall kitchens. We quickly learned not to trust anyone or to volunteer for anything. For example, three of us were assigned a detail to paint the wooden floors in the halls of the Headquarters building. The sergeant in charge of the detail confided in us, "If you'll do a REALLY good job, I'll get the three of you weekend passes, beginning this evening." We worked like slaves and took only a few minutes to bolt down our lunch. We were determined to finish our assigned task as quickly as possible, so we could FULLY enjoy the promised weekend pass. We also took special care to apply the paint just right and not to get it onto either the mopboards or the walls. When we finished, even the sergeant agreed we had done "an exceptionally good job". He then said, "Give me your dog tags, so I can make sure I get your names right on your passes. Eat as fast as you can at the mess hall, get into your Class A uniforms and I'll meet you at 18:00 hours in front of the barracks with your passes."

We were elated. Finally, we were going to get away from the "rat race" called the Army for a whole weekend. We hurriedly ate and dressed in our Class A uniforms, while bragging to our buddies how this "neat" sergeant was getting us weekend passes. We then anxiously waited for almost an hour for the sergeant to appear in front of our barracks. He finally came. But, instead of presenting us with the promised passes, he brusquely ordered us to "Get dressed in your fatigues!" When we asked, "Why?" he told us to, "Shut up! Or, I'll have you on KP all weekend!"

We changed from our Class A uniforms back into our fatigues and then solemnly marched back to the Headquarters building, where we spent most of the night painting the office floors. While we were silently working, one of the colonels we had encountered while painting the halls during the day returned. He looked at us and then asked the sergeant, "Aren't these the same men who were painting today? I thought you promised them weekend passes?" The sergeant's reply was, "Yes sir, they are. But, they weren't ready when I got their passes for them, so I figured they just as well finish the job!"

The platoon sergeant assigned to our barracks took special delight in making us fall into and out of formation. He'd sharply blow his whistle and shout "Fall in!" Then he would time how long it took before every man in the barracks was standing stiffly at attention in his assigned position "in formation". Thereafter, he would inspect us - to ensure all of our buttons were buttoned, our faces clean-shaven, our boots polished, and on and on, while continuously berating, belittling and calling us all the derogatory names he could think of. If he caught a man in violation of the dress code, moving a muscle or even his eyes while he was supposed to be at attention, it meant a minimum of twenty pushups. Even though we fell into formation in less than twenty seconds, it was never good enough. "I want to see blood on the doors when you fall out of the barracks!" he shouted. A few of us made plans to accommodate him. We took positions just inside the barracks building. The second we heard his whistle and harsh voice, we hit the door with our feet. This resulted in the door being torn off its hinges and crashing to the ground in front of the barracks. Rather than please the sergeant, he became enraged. In addition to our having to do innumerable pushups and having to fall in and out of formation for an additional hour, he made each of us hand over to him all we had left of the "Flying $10" we'd received upon our arrival at Ft. Lewis, which was for us to buy toilet articles and to "tide" us over until our first payday – two weeks hence. "This", he claimed, "is to replace the door you stupid #%& bums ruined." We observed, however, the old door was only repaired and put back up. The sergeant simply pocketed our money!

The falling in and out of formation often continued for hours, until some men became so fatigued it was almost impossible for them to stand still while in formation. Their inability to remain statue-like while at attention resulted in the sergeant assigning them more pushups or other tasks; thereby, further aggravating their condition. Once, when we rushed into formation, a thin, young fellow was so fatigued he fainted and fell headlong upon the pavement. The fall broke some of his front teeth and caused both his mouth and nose to bleed profusely. Those next to the prostrate man were aghast and some moved to assist the poor guy. But, the sergeant gruffly ordered them to "Get back into formation!" He then ordered two of us to, "Get that jerk out of here! I don't want blood on my area!" We couldn't believe a man could be so calloused. Despite the many horror stories we had heard about basic training, we were certain it could not be as bad as the harassment to which we now were being subjected. How wrong we were!

We eventually were informed we would not receive our basic training at Ft. Lewis. We would be sent elsewhere. Most would be sent to Ft. Bliss, Texas or to Ft. Sill, Oklahoma for artillery training. Some also would be sent to Ft. Ord, California for infantry training. Most of us were certain conditions at any of these posts would be better than at Ft. Lewis. First, we'd get away from the continuous fog and rain in the Seattle area. Second, we wouldn't be subject to the continual harassment to which we'd been subjected since our arrival. Then, we began to hear rumors about conditions at these other posts. It was reported troops at Ft. Bliss were being housed in tents, rather than barracks. Many had died, primarily from heat prostration. There had been an outbreak of meningitis at Ft. Sill, which had resulted in even more deaths than reportedly had occurred at Ft. Bliss. More and more of us were hoping to be among "the lucky few" to be sent to Ft. Ord in "sunny" California, even if it meant we would be trained as infantry. Regarding the weather at Ft. Lewis, I was there for more than a week before I discovered our company area was only a few hundred yards from Puget Sound. It had been so foggy or rainy since my arrival I had not seen the nearby Sound until then.

Orders were posted on the company bulletin board, which we regularly checked. Finally, there it was! My name was among the "lucky" (?) few to be sent to Ft. Ord for sixteen weeks of basic training. Seventeen of us were being sent on a special flight on Saturday at 12:00 hours. As instructed, we sent our civilian clothes home and packed and repacked our duffel bags. We wanted to be ready for our flight to California. This would be my first airplane ride, as well as the first for many in our "California-bound" group of draftees.

We were taken by bus to the Seattle airport almost two hours prior to our plane's scheduled noon departure. Upon our arrival at the airport, we discovered our plane was a contracted two-engine DC-3, which normally was used as a cargo plane. It was not equipped with any of the niceties of a commercial passenger plane. Seating was in bucket seats, along either side of the plane. There was no hostess, of course, and no in-flight meals.

We anxiously waited, while the pilot and co-pilot boarded and took their places in the cockpit. We then were ordered to board by means of a small ladder. We took our seats and, as instructed, buckled our seat belts. However, after several unsuccessful attempts to start one of the engines, we were ordered to de-plane and assemble on the tarmac alongside the plane, while the mechanics worked on the faulty engine. Twice during the afternoon, when the mechanics thought they had corrected the problem, we boarded the plane and waited for takeoff. But, the pilot was unable to start or keep the engine running. We again were ordered to de-plane and wait, while the mechanics repaired the motor. Finally, the mechanics again signaled the pilot to start the faulty engine. After much sputtering and coughing, the engine finally came to life and we hurriedly were ordered to "Get onboard before the motor stops!"

It was past 18:00 hours when our plane rumbled down the runway and, with a shudder, became airborne. Although I since have taken hundreds of flights and have flown more than a million miles, as well as had a number of "close calls" associated with air travel, this still is my most memorable flight. Besides being my "first airplane ride", it came very close to being my last.

We circled Seattle and then headed for the coast. There, at an altitude of only a few hundred feet, we turned south and followed the coastline. As the engines steadily droned, the newness and exhilaration of being airborne diminished. The sun sank towards the horizon and more and more clouds appeared below. Eventually, because of both clouds and ensuing darkness, we no longer could see the coastline nor the Pacific Ocean. As we became enveloped in darkness, some of us wondered how the pilot would be able to land in the darkness and through the dense clouds or fog below.

A few hours passed before the pilot announced over the intercom, "We're over the Monterey Airport. We'll be landing in a few minutes." Monterey is adjacent to Ft. Ord. We were almost there! Peering through the window behind my seat, I could see a small opening in the dense clouds and some rows of colored lights below. These apparently indicated the airport runway. The pilot literally dived our plane through the opening in the clouds and within seconds the two front wheels of the DC-3 bounced on the runway pavement. However, when I looked out of the window toward the front of the plane, I was shocked to see the form of a large hanger immediately in front of us. I braced for the inevitable crash. But, our plane's two engines suddenly roared and the plane began to shudder violently. The wheels rose off from the runway and we again were airborne. We flew right over the hanger. As I looked down, it appeared that the plane's wheels did not miss the building more than two or three feet. I could not believe it.

When we had gained sufficient altitude, the pilot circled the Monterey area a number of times, but there were no openings in the dense fog through which we could penetrate and land. The pilot shortly announced, "We'll fly to the Oakland Airport, where weather conditions are reported to be suitable for landing."

Our landing at the Oakland Airport was without incident. Our group of seventeen recruits then was placed on a bus and we spent most of the night traveling to Ft. Ord. Following our approximately 04:00-hour arrival at Ft. Ord, we were issued bedding and assigned bunks at the Reception Center. We were not, however, allowed to go to bed. Instead, we were ordered to sit in the Orderly Room. This, we were informed, was "Because it's almost chow time, anyway."

As we sat, waiting until the 06:00-hour "chow time", I stared blankly through the Orderly Room windows into the dense fog outside. With a start, I realized, "The weather here is no different than it was in Ft. Lewis!" It certainly didn't look like "sunny" California! As we waited for our first meal since breakfast the previous day, noises and activities around us began to increase. We began to hear the crack of rifles being fired, the "rat-a-tat-tat" of machine guns and the periodic boom of distant canons. There also was the rattle of "field gear" and the rhythmic thud of boots on the pavement as companies of men "double-timed" past the Reception Center. It was eerie how companies of ALWAYS running soldiers appeared out of the fog and then quickly disappeared into the mist. It was like a scene from Dante's Inferno, which we had read in high school English class. It was unearthly and I hoped I was only dreaming.

We spent most of our first day at Ft. Ord on details, mostly picking up cigarette butts and other litter, similar to what we had done at Ft. Lewis. Late in the day, our group was informed we would be assigned to "I" or "Item" Company of the 20th Regiment for our sixteen weeks of basic training – as soon as the previous trainees cleared the Company area. We also were informed some of the men just finishing basic training in "Item" Company would be flying to Ft. Lewis on the same plane we had flown on to California. Ft. Lewis was the port of debarkation for Korea.

It was late that night before we finally were permitted to "hit the sack" in the Reception Center. We had not slept nor had our clothes off for two days. As tired as I was, I still could not sleep. Over and over I pondered, "What am I doing here? What's before me?" And, "Will I be able to take it?"

Following an early breakfast the next morning, we were marched from the Reception Center to I Company of the 20th. Everywhere one looked there were companies of men in battle uniform. And, they were ALWAYS running! No one smiled. Most wore the grim countenance of fatigue on their faces. Or, was it the countenance of "death"? What kind of life was before me?

I experienced some difficult trials during the almost six months I spent at Ft. Ord. These included a two-week stay in the hospital, because I had pneumonia or what commonly was called "The Ft. Ord Hack". Because my illness caused me to miss two weeks of basic training, I was transferred to "K" or "King" Company and, during my time in this Company, six fellow trainees died or were killed and several committed suicide. We had a Company Commander who had received a battlefield commission and was determined to make "paid killers" out of all of us. He literally was crazy and eventually was institutionalized. Such trials, I believe, taught me some important lessons. For example, I learned I could take much more than I thought I could. I found I was both physically and mentally as good or better than the majority of the men with whom I trained. Above all, I learned life is primarily what one makes of it. Attitude is most important. Also, outward appearances often are deceiving. Large and robust men, who may appear to be very tough, in reality may be "panty-waists"; whereas, others who appear to be puny and frail in reality may be both physical and mental giants. Skinny, little men with whom I trained sometimes were able to withstand unbelievable punishment and refuse to give in; whereas, seemingly strong men often quickly fell by the wayside and readily gave up when faced with adversity. Furthermore, difficulties or adversity often brings out the best, as well as the worst, in men. It often surprised me how – when the going really got tough – just whom you could and could not depend upon.

The first evening we were in "Item" Company the "word" quickly spread. Nineteen men, who had just finished training in I Company, had been killed when the DC-3 in which they were flying to Ft. Lewis had crashed! This was the same plane in which we had almost crashed in Monterey! It could have been us, rather than them! I again had been protected and my life spared. For what reason, I still am not certain.

Each time I board an airplane, which has been frequent during my life, I think about "The Army and My First Airplane Ride". Though I hope I never have experiences such as I had in the army, especially during basic training, I feel these did much to prepare me for life and perhaps served as a "proving ground" for me.

A SPECIAL CALLING

"Behold, there are many called, but few are chosen.And why are they not chosen? Because their hearts are set so much upon the things of this world..."   Doctrine & Covenants 121:34-35

It was an unusually cold and miserable day in January 1954. I was standing towards the end of a long line of disgruntled and complaining soldiers at Camp Darby, Italy. We were lined up in alphabetical order and waiting to be interviewed and then assigned a job and duty station in the U.S. Army's Austrian Command. The drizzling rain had penetrated our overcoats and dampened both our clothing and our spirits.

We had arrived at the port in Livorno (Leghorn) only hours previous. After disembarking from the troop ship in which we'd spent twelve long days, we had not had sufficient time to regain our "land legs". Many men still were suffering from the nausea of seasickness. Because of rough seas during much of our voyage, we had been confined to the cramped, hot and humid, and, more often than not, smelly hold of the ship. Virtually everyone had been seasick for at least a few days. The rocking of the ship, the vibrations caused by its propellers – especially when they came out of the water – and the thud of the ship's hold - when it crashed back into the sea - made it almost impossible to sleep in our cramped, four-tier high bunk beds that were only racks of taut canvas stretched over a pipe frame. Now, as we stamped our feet in the mud, in an effort to get warm, our previous situation onboard ship did not seem to have been much worse than this miserable Italian weather. The uncertainty of where and what duty we might be assigned in Austria added to our discomfort, as well as to our anxiety.

Almost all of us had recently completed basic training. The recently signed "touch-and-go" Korean armistice meant that most U.S. servicemen were still being sent to Korea. Thus, we felt fortunate to have been assigned to Europe and especially to Austria. Only sixteen of the three hundred and sixty-five men in my basic training company had been assigned to the Austrian Command. Furthermore, only four of us were U.S. citizens. The others planned to obtain U.S. citizenship by serving in the Army for two years. Included in our group were two English brothers – whose father taught at the University of California in Berkley, a Norwegian, an Italian – who was determined to stay in Italy, a Lithuanian – who had witnessed and experienced many of the horrors of World War II, a Greek, a Russian – who had served in the Russian Army and had continually chided us for being "panty waists" during our basic training, a German, and an Austrian – who was anxious to return home.

I had read and heard much about Austria, i.e. its friendly people, beautiful mountains, and wonderful winter sports. Besides wanting to learn German, I particularly wanted to learn how to ski and climb mountains. Upon getting to Austria, I was determined to somehow get into both the Command's ski and mountain climbing schools.

Prior to our embarkation at Camp Kilmer, New Jersey, I had purchased a couple of German textbooks. Each day, while onboard the troop ship, I had spent several hours studying my books. I also frequently cornered my German and Austrian buddies and had them coach me in their native tongue. I already thought I would be able to "get by" in German, at least insofar as being able to ask directions while traveling and to negotiate purchases. Given time and practice, I was certain I would become fluent in German.

While standing towards the end of the line and nervously stamping my feet, I heard a booming voice over the loud speakers command, "Spillett! Report immediately – on the double – to the Orderly Room!" I scurried toward the entrance to the building in front of us. Why was my name being called? I paid little heed to the remarks of others, such as, "How lucky can you get?" And, "Why are you getting special treatment?"

Upon entering the building, I encountered two men seated behind a large table, alongside which were cardboard boxes filled with packets containing the personal records of the men in our shipment. The contents of one packet were spread upon the table. I observed my name on some of the papers. I wondered, "What goes? Why are they singling me out?" Several more men were standing on either side. All were intently looking at my records or at me. One of the men behind the table then informed me, "We're considering you for a position here in the 588th Replacement Company. IF you are qualified and selected, you'll be working with us."

I was further informed that the 588th consisted of approximately twenty-five "hand-picked" men, most of whom were college graduates. The Company was part of the Inspector General or "IG" Corps, which was directly under the Commanding General in Austria - NOT the Camp Darby Post Commander. The 588th's mission was to interview and assign jobs to troops who arrived from the States at about twenty-day intervals, as well as to process troops returning to the States from Austria, also at alternate twenty-day intervals. Thus, those in the 588th spent about three out of every ten days processing troops.

The men explained, "Although you've really got to be on the ball and we have lots to do when we're processing troops, we have plenty of free time between shipments. Members of the 588th enjoy special privileges. We don't stand guard duty. We're never assigned KP. We don't participate in most Saturday training sessions. And, most of the time we don't have to stand inspections." Furthermore, they carried overnight passes in their wallets and were free to come and go from the Company and Post, except during "regular" working hours or while processing troops. In short, "You'll be most fortunate IF you are selected to serve in the 588th!"

One of the men then offered me a cigarette. I said, "No thanks, I don't smoke." The men then examined my records some more and a couple of them asked me some questions about subjects I could not relate to being part of a job interview. One fellow then glanced at his watch and announced, "It's time for a coffee break. Let's run over to the snack bar." They invited me to join them and we walked a few hundred yards to the snack bar located in the Company Area. Upon entering the snack bar, we walked to the head of a long line of men waiting to be served. There were a few mumblings from those in the line, but apparently it was an accepted fact at Camp Darby that members of the 588th did not have to wait in lines when they were processing troops. A member of our group then announced, "It's my turn to buy. What will you have?" He then started to take orders. When he came to me he asked, "What do you want, one cup of coffee or two?" When I explained, "I don't drink coffee. Could I just have a glass of milk?" His reply was, "For Hell's sake, what do you do?"

Most of the men in the 588th drank, smoked and did other things I did not do and which were contrary to my religious beliefs. I later learned, at least at the time of my "interview", they knew little about The Church of Jesus Christ of Latter-day Saints or the "Mormons". However, despite the obvious differences in our way of life, they decided to "try me out" in "their company". They informed me I would be given a probationary period of a month. Then, if they didn't like me or if my performance was not satisfactory, I would be assigned a position in Austria. Also, if I did not like the 588th or did not want to remain in Italy, I could choose to go to Austria. Thus began my apprenticeship as the Morning Report Clerk in the 588th.

My duties as Morning Report Clerk consisted primarily of typing a daily, letter-perfect report as to the status of each man permanently or temporarily assigned to the Company. This meant, when we were not processing troops, I had ONLY to account for the twenty-five-men permanently assigned to the 588th. Such a report normally took only a few minutes. However, when we were processing troop shipments, my reports had to ACCURATELY account for upwards of five hundred or more individuals. Thus, my work would vacillate between doing almost nothing to virtually being overwhelmed with lengthy and complicated reports. I soon determined I did not like office work nor did I like the environment at Camp Darby or in Italy.

Liquor seemed to be omnipresent, both at Camp Darby and throughout Italy. The snack bars on Post were little more than beer parlors. Liter bottles of German beer, which contained twelve percent alcohol, sold for ten cents. The Post Exchange or "PX" likewise sold beer and had a "Class VI" liquor store, which sold all kinds of liquor at what the men claimed were "ridiculously low prices". The Servicemen's Club sold both beer and mixed drinks for ten cents each. The Club also adjoined the mess hall, making it convenient for men to "drop in" for a "quick" drink before dinner or to have a drink or two while waiting for the normally long "chow lines" to become shorter. Beer even was sold at the bowling alley, which was next to the gymnasium where evening movies were shown. Similarly, alcoholic beverages were readily available throughout Italy. For example, in nearby Livorno and Pisa there seemed to be a bar on almost every corner. Alcohol was for sale virtually everywhere. Furthermore, water throughout Italy was not potable. Thus, the custom was to drink wine, rather than water, with meals.

Prostitution was recognized in Italy as a legitimate or legal occupation. Livorno particularly was noted for its many "houses of ill repute". When the U.S. Navy's Mediterranean Fleet was in the port, two "Shore Patrol" men were assigned the task of guarding the entrance to each known brothel. - to deter sailors on "shore leave" from entering them. Based on the presence of Shore Patrol guards, my buddy and I counted twenty-six brothels in a two-block area!

There didn't seem to be a decent place in or near Camp Darby where a serviceman could spend his off-duty hours. Therefore, despite the privileges associated with being in the 588th, I decided to go to Austria at the end of my month's probation. I repeatedly told those with whom I worked, "I'd rather be a foot-slogging infantryman in Austria than have a soft job here in Italy!"

When I completed my month's probation, Captain Shelly, the CO for the 588th, called me into his office. He commended me on how well I had performed as the Morning Report Clerk and how the men in the Company liked me and wanted me to stay. He then said, "Some of the men have told me you've decided to go to Austria. Don't you want to stay here?" Although I had firmly resolved to go to Austria and NOT stay in Italy, I heard a voice, which I swear was not mine, say, "Yes, I'll stay!" I couldn't believe it! What should I do? I was so perplexed that I was speechless.

While walking back to the tent, which served as our living quarters, I castigated myself for not telling Captain Shelly, "I don't want to stay in the 588th nor in Italy. I want to go to Austria!" I firmly resolved I'd tell him first thing the next morning, "I've changed my mind. I don't want to stay in Italy. I want to go to Austria!"

When I entered the tent where I bunked, my buddies immediately queried me as to whether or not I had decided to stay in Italy. Reluctantly, I told them, "I told Captain Shelley I would stay." They cheered and said, "We thought you would!" But, I then said, "I've changed my mind. The first thing tomorrow morning I'm telling the CO I want to go to Austria." This I did, but Captain Shelley then informed me, "It's too late! The decisions been made. And, you've agreed to stay in the 588th." He further claimed, "Once you've become accustomed to it here, you'll enjoy it. Think of all the privileges you'll have by staying here"

Days and then weeks passed, but I neither became accustomed to nor enjoyed life at Camp Darby. I resolved to somehow find a way whereby I could get out of Italy. I eventually learned enlisted men, if they met certain qualifications, could apply for Officer's Candidate School ("OCS") and be sent back to the States to train to become an officer. Upon investigation, I found I met the qualifications. Thus, I made application and was accepted for OCS. As a result, a man was selected to replace me as the Morning Report Clerk. But, the CO asked me to "stay on for a few weeks to train my replacement". During this time, I learned those completing OCS had to remain in military service for at least two years after they became commissioned officers. This meant I'd have to spend three years, rather than two, in the Army – IF I completed OCS. I then reasoned, "I have my replacement trained and if I now turn down going to OCS, they'll have no alternative but to send me to Austria." So, just prior to the time I was to be sent back to the States, I told the CO, "I've changed my mind. I've decided not to go to OCS." This assuredly meant I would be sent to Austria!

I had my bags packed and had bid preliminary farewells to my friends in the 588th, with whom I now had worked for several months. I was to accompany the next shipment of troops to Austria. But, just prior to our departure, the CO called me into his office and explained, "The Company needs some temporary help in the Special Orders Department. Would you mind staying and helping for a few weeks?" I felt this was a reasonable request. I also thought, "If I help for a while, maybe they'll give me a better assignment when I do go to Austria." Thus, I accepted the "temporary" assignment..

I worked in Special Orders for several weeks and the workload in the 588th returned to normal. Again, I was scheduled to go to Austria with the next shipment of troops. The 588th then was informed that, for the first time, it would have to "stand" the annual Inspector General or "IG" Inspection at Camp Darby. Furthermore, the Company Orderly was scheduled to take a month's leave during the inspection period. The CO again called me into his office and asked if I'd be willing to spend a few weeks learning the Orderly's job and then filling in for him during the IG Inspection. Thus, I again agreed to remain in the 588th for "just a few more weeks!"

I spent a couple of weeks learning the Orderly's job and he then went on leave. We prepared for and passed the IG Inspection "with flying colors". The Orderly returned and I again packed my bags to go to Austria. I processed with a shipment of troops from the States. We were to board the train the next morning and I was spending my last evening in the 588th visiting the men with whom I now had worked for almost eight months. While we were talking and joking about my new assignment, a telegram was delivered to one of them. He was informed that his mother was ill and not expected to live. Furthermore, the Red Cross had made arrangements for him to IMMEDIATELY return to the States on emergency leave.

The next morning, just prior to my scheduled departure for Austria, the CO AGAIN called me into his office. He explained how the man going on emergency leave lacked only a few months to complete his tour of duty. Therefore, he would not return to Italy or to the 588th. He then asked me, "Would you be interested in filling his position?" However, he cautioned me with "This would be a PERMANENT assignment in the 588th - NOT a temporary one!"

I had by this time developed close ties with many of the men with whom I worked. Despite not liking the environment at Camp Darby or in Italy, I had all but concluded, "There must be a reason for me to stay in Italy." Anyway, I accepted the CO's offer, which was my fourth and final assignment in the 588th.

Prior to accepting my final assignment in the 588th, I had located three "Mormons" stationed at Camp Darby. Two already had returned to the States and the remaining man was not a very active Church member. Because I wanted to associate with men who believed the same as me, I had begun to search the records of the troops we processed - looking for "Mormons" with whom I could visit. Those with whom I worked became aware of what I was doing. And, whenever they encountered a "Mormon" during their interviews, they would either record their names or direct them to me. As a result, I began to meet perhaps a major portion of the "Mormon" servicemen entering or leaving the Austrian Command.

Charley Bartanan, the "Mormon" or LDS Servicemen's Coordinator for the Austrian Command, was stationed in Salzburg, and President Perchon, who presided over the LDS Swiss-Austrian Mission, eventually were informed there was a "Mormon" in the 588th Replacement Company who was contacting the LDS servicemen entering the Austrian Command. Thus, shortly after accepting my final assignment in the 588th, I received a letter from President Perchon. He informed me, "Many servicemen entering the Austrian Command do not know where to contact other members or organized groups of the Church. By the time some of these men eventually are contacted, they often have become inactive. Both Charley Bartanan and I have been earnestly praying that we might find a way whereby LDS men entering the Command could be contacted and directed to other members and organized groups of the Church in Austria." In short, I was the answer to their prayers!

Thereafter, Charley Bartanan made an official request; whereby, I could systematically contact virtually every LDS serviceman entering the Command. I then would inform them of the locations and meeting schedules for Church groups in the areas to which they were assigned and also send Charley their names and duty stations. Thus, these servicemen could be contacted upon their arrival in Austria.

I was selected in the early fall of 1954 to attend a six-week Training, Information and Education ("TI&E") course in Salzburg. I informed Charley I was coming to Austria and looked forward to meeting him. He, in turn, informed me he was one of the instructors for the course. Thus, I soon met Charley. We spent many off-duty hours together in Salzburg and became fast friends. He was truly a remarkable man. Also, for the first time since my arrival in Europe, I had the opportunity to attend and participate in "Mormon" Church services and activities.

Prior to my returning to Italy, Charley insisted upon setting me apart as an LDS Servicemen's Group Leader and assigned me the task of organizing an LDS Group at Camp Darby. I tried to tell Charley, "I know only one "Mormon" at Camp Darby and he's not very active." Therefore, "There's little reason to set me apart as a Group Leader." Nevertheless, Charley persisted and instructed me to "Search out the LDS servicemen stationed at Camp Darby and organize an LDS Servicemen's group there." He also promised, "If you will be faithful and put forth the effort, the way will be opened whereby you will be able to locate a sufficient number of Church members to organize a Group and to conduct regular Church services." But, like the Apostle Thomas, I doubted Charley's promises would be fulfilled.

My busy, but most enjoyable, six weeks in Austria passed too quickly. Upon my return to Italy and Camp Darby, however, I found there had been dramatic changes during my absence. Three new men had been selected and assigned to the 588th. Unbelievably, two of these were "Mormons"! The 588th also had been assigned the task of disbanding the Trieste Command and re-assigning its personnel. As a result, the number of men at Camp Darby had increased by more than ten thousand. Furthermore, the Trieste Command had an organized LDS Servicemen's Group of approximately thirty men. With no effort whatsoever on my part, there already was a functioning LDS Group at Camp Darby!

The Chaplain's Assistant at Camp Darby and I had become close friends prior to my going to Austria. Upon my return, he informed me he had received permission to examine the records of every man on Post – both officers and enlisted men – and to record the professed religion of each man. As a result, he handed me a list that contained the names of fourteen LDS servicemen permanently stationed at Camp Darby. I could not believe it. Charley Bartanan's inspired promises had not only been fulfilled, but also very quickly!

I began contacting the men whose names were on the list the Chaplain's Assistant had given me. Although most were no longer active members, there was a sufficient number to organize an LDS Servicemen's Group and to hold regular meetings. The Group from the Trieste Command initially served as a nucleus, but when its members were shipped elsewhere, our numbers drastically decreased. Still, Charley's promises were fulfilled.

Prior to my going to Austria, I also had received a letter from President Perchon wherein he informed me about a young man from Tennessee who was stationed at Camp Darby. This man had written to him, inquiring as to whether or not he knew of any LDS servicemen stationed in Italy. He was not a member of the Church. But, prior to his entering the military service, he had been contacted by "Mormon" missionaries in the States and he wanted to associate with "Mormon" servicemen and learn more about the Church.

I went to the barracks housing the company to which the fellow from Tennessee belonged. There, when I inquired as to where I might find him, I was directed to the second floor and told he occupied the lower bunk on the left-hand side at the end of a long room. A young man was sitting on a footlocker in front of the bunk to which I had been directed. He was reading a book and when I approached him and asked, "Are you from Tennessee?" His reply was, "Yes. Why?" I then told him about the letter I'd received from President Perchon. He jumped to his feet and heartily embraced me. Thereafter, we became close friends. Although he was not a member of the Church, he had accepted and lived many gospel principles, i.e. he did not smoke nor drink alcoholic beverages, coffee or tea. He also lived a moral life, which could not be said for most U.S. servicemen stationed in Italy. Although we frequently discussed religion, I did not try to systematically teach him the gospel, More often than not we just spent time together; attending evening movies on Post, bowling, or simply eating together in the mess hall.

After my return to Camp Darby from Austria and while attempting to locate the "Mormon" servicemen on the list the Chaplain's Assistant had given me, I encountered the name of a man in the same company as the fellow from Tennessee. Upon inquiring where I could find him, I again was directed to the second floor and the last bunk on the left-hand side of a long room. The man I was looking for occupied the upper bunk and the fellow from Tennessee the lower. They were bunkmates!

As I approached the familiar bunk and asked a man, who was leaning against the wall and smoking a cigarette while looking out the window, "Do you know where I can locate 'so-and-so'?" His reply was, "That's me. What do you want?" I hesitated. It was obvious this man was not living his professed religion. Then, somewhat avoiding my purpose for being there, I explained how I was well acquainted with his bunkmate, the fellow from Tennessee. He then told me how the fellow from Tennessee "is a real swell guy" and how they had been bunkmates for almost a year. When I asked him where he was from, he said, "Tremonton, Utah". I then told him, "I'm a 'Mormon' and we're organizing an LDS Servicemen's Group. Would you like to join us? I've been informed you're a member of the Church." This caused the fellow's face to redden and he quickly extinguished his cigarette. But, he then stiffened and hesitatingly explained, "I used to belong to the Church. But, I'm not interested in religion anymore." Not knowing what else to do, I wrote down the location and times of our weekly meetings and handed it to him. I also invited him to join us, "Whenever you feel like it." Here was a man who had forsaken that for which his bunkmate of almost a year had been searching. I do not know whether or not the fellow from Tennessee knew or ever learned his bunkmate was a "Mormon". For sure, I never told him.

The Lord has told us "...there are many called, but few are chosen.. Because their hearts are set so much upon the things of this world..." (D&C 121:34-35). My "special calling", while stationed in Italy, impressed upon me that each of us has special callings. In fact, we may have many callings and may be called not once, but repeatedly, to fill them. Accepting our callings also might mean we must set aside some of "the things of this world". Still, the acceptance and filling of such callings is up to us.

CHARLEY BARTANEN

"You cannot tell by the wrappings what is inside a package."

Prior to meeting someone, have you ever formed a mental image of them and then – when you met them – found they were not at all like you expected them to be? Such was the case with me and Charley Bartanen.

Charley was the "Mormon" or LDS Servicemen's Coordinator for the U.S. Army's Austrian Command and stationed in Salzburg. Some months after I received my final assignment in the 588th Replacement Company at Camp Darby, Italy, I received a letter from President Perchon of the LDS Swiss-Austrian Mission and then from Charley. They requested that, insofar as possible, I should contact each LDS serviceman entering the Austrian Command and inform them of the locations and schedules for "Mormon" Church services in the areas to which they were assigned and also send Charley the names and duty stations for these men. Thus began my frequent communications with Charley.

Perhaps because of his position as the LDS Servicemen's Coordinator for Austria, I assumed Charley must be an imposing and dynamic individual. I envisioned him to be large in stature, "well-built", athletically inclined, and of a demeanor that would command respect from all who met him. Remarks about Charley by men being processed through the 588th prior to their return to the States further substantiated the mental image I had formed. Some used explicative comments to describe Charley, such as, "A fantastic man!" Or, "One of the greatest guys I've ever known!" Some also expressed appreciation for what Charley had done for them or for others.

I was selected during the fall of 1954 to attend a six-week Training, Information and Education (TI&E) course in Salzburg. I shortly learned Charley would be one of the instructors. When I received a course outline, which listed the instructors, I noted that Charley was only a corporal; whereas, almost all of the instructors were officers. I previously had assumed Charley also was an officer.

His being ONLY an enlisted man further impressed upon me that he must truly be a "human dynamo."

Upon my arrival at the Army post in Salzburg, I inquired of servicemen I encountered, "How can I locate Charley Bartanen?" I shortly was told, "I know Charley Bartanen. I'll take you to him." While my "guide" and I walked across the Post, I asked him, "Are you a 'Mormon'?" His reply was, "No, but Charley Bartanen is." He also added, "You know, Charley's one of the neatest guys I've ever met."

We eventually entered a large barracks building, where a group of men stood in a circle at the far end. They were talking and laughing. As we approached them, I tried to ascertain which might be Charley. Then, when my "guide" introduced him to me, I couldn't believe it. Charley was the shortest and least becoming man in the group. There must be a mistake! He was nothing like what I had imagined him to be. Rather than tall and masculine, he was short and pudgy. Instead of having a distinguished face, his was round and jovial. He even had a bald spot in the middle of his tousled head of hair. In no way did he resemble the Charley Bartanen I had envisioned!

Charley warmly welcomed me to Austria and introduced me to each of the men in the group. Thereafter, during my six weeks in Austria, I spent as much of my free time as possible with Charley. Although his outward appearances were different than what I had conjured they would be, I quickly learned he was a dynamic and remarkable person. Whenever I accompanied Charley, I was amazed at how many people knew and warmly greeted him. This was true of officers and enlisted men alike. Though Charley had many responsibilities and was always busy, he was never too busy nor in too much of a hurry to not greet and "give a good word" to everyone he met. He could visit as congenially with the Commanding General of the Austrian Command as he could with any of the enlisted men. He seemed to exude a love for life and for others. What's more, others seemed to reciprocate in like manner to him.

As Charley and I became close friends, he discussed with me more and more "what we might do to help the LDS servicemen in Italy and Austria." His major concern seemed to be, "What can I do to help others?" Little by little, however, he related to me bits and pieces about his life. He apparently was the only son of an alcoholic and abusive father, who was known as "the town drunk". Because of this father's addiction to alcohol, he and his mother lived in dire poverty and were often beaten by him. However, his father died while he was in his teens and he then faced the responsibility of supporting himself and his mother. But, like his father, he began to drink and was well on his way to becoming an alcoholic when an older man took an interest in him. Through this good man's influence, Charley began to live a better life. Two young "Mormon" missionaries also eventually taught him the Gospel of Jesus Christ and, thereafter, Charley's life dramatically changed for the better.

Charley forsook alcohol and other vices and replaced them with a determination to live the gospel of Jesus Christ to the best of his ability. He changed so markedly that he was asked to serve as a "Mormon" missionary. Although he desired "with all his heart" to serve a mission, he declined the calling. He did not have the means to support his widowed mother, let alone support himself in the mission field. Others, however, stepped in and provided support both for his mission and for his mother. Thus, with great fervor Charley served a two-year mission and determined to dedicate his life to serving God and others.

After serving a two-year mission, Charley returned home to his mother, who he referred to as "one of my greatest loves." Then, he shortly was drafted into the U.S. Army and again had to leave his beloved mother. He frequently mentioned how he longed to return home to be with and to help her. He even numbered the days until he would be discharged from the Army and could do so. Nevertheless, he greatly enjoyed the work in which he was engaged and loved those with whom he associated. There was no doubt in his mind or in the minds of others that Charley was engaged in an important work and was a remarkable asset to the Austrian Command.

My six-week assignment in Austria passed all too quickly. Following my completion of the TI&E course, I obtained permission to attend a weeklong "All-European LDS Servicemen's Retreat" in nearby Berchesgaten, Germany, a half hour by bus from Salzburg. Charley also participated in this "retreat".

As the time for my return to Italy drew nigh, Charley discussed more and more fervently with me "what can we do to assist the LDS servicemen stationed at Camp Darby?" I repeatedly explained to him that during the more than nine months I had been at Camp Darby I had located only three LDS servicemen stationed there. Two of these already had returned to the States and the remaining man was not an active Church member. This did not deter Charley in his concern for the "Mormon" servicemen stationed in Italy.

Immediately prior to my departure from Austria and return to Italy, Charley explained how he "felt impressed" that he should set me apart as an LDS Servicemen's Group Leader. Also, I should be charged with organizing an LDS Servicemen's Group at Camp Darby and conducting religious services each Sunday. I repeatedly reiterated to Charley how I thought this would not be possible, due to a lack of members. Nevertheless, Charley promised me, "If you'll be diligent, the way will be opened whereby you will be able to locate additional LDS servicemen." And, "You'll be able to organize a servicemen's group and hold regular Church services." Thus, I agreed to do my best with regards to whatever Charley asked me to do. He set me apart as a Group Leader. However, I still was a "doubting Thomas" as to his promises being fulfilled.

Following a marvelous week at the Retreat in beautiful Berchesgaten, I returned by train to Livorno, Italy. I could not believe my eyes when I arrived at Camp Darby. Everything had drastically changed! There were troops everywhere! During my absence, the 588th Replacement Company had undertaken the task of demobilizing the U.S. Army's Trieste Command. Instead of the approximately five thousand men normally stationed at Camp Darby, there now were in excess of fifteen thousand. Furthermore, among the Trieste troops there was an active group of about thirty LDS servicemen. Some of Charley's promises already were fulfilled! Three new men also had been assigned to the "hand-picked" 588th and two of these were "Mormons"! One was from Wenatchee, Washington and the other from the town of McCammon in southeastern Idaho, which is not far from my hometown of Rockland. Who would have believed it?

The weeks following my return to Italy were indeed eventful. Regular LDS Church services took place for the first time at Camp Darby. And, these were held in a recently completed chapel. There were two Army chaplains at Camp Darby. The Head Chaplain was a devout Southern Baptist and the other a Catholic priest of Italian descent from New York. A young serviceman from the South, with whom I previously had become a close friend, served as the Chaplains' Assistant. Shortly after my return, he handed me a list of names. "These," he explained, "are the 'Mormon' servicemen permanently stationed at Camp Darby." He then told me how, while I was gone, he had received permission to go through the personal records of all the men on Post – enlisted men and officers alike – and record the religious preference listed for each. Thus, with no effort whatsoever on my part, I now had the names of fourteen LDS servicemen stationed at Camp Darby.

I immediately began to search out the LDS servicemen whose names were on the list. Although some were no longer active Church members or did not want to affiliate with us, there was a sufficient number to organize an LDS Servicemen's Group. Despite my doubts, Charley's promises were quickly fulfilled. The Lord truly works in miraculous ways, His wonders to perform! All too soon the Trieste Command was disbanded and our Camp Darby Group was on its own. Though attendance at our meetings varied from as many as a dozen down to but two, we managed to hold regular Church services until my departure for the States in May 1955.

I continued regular communications with Charley, including reports on LDS servicemen entering the Command, throughout the remainder of my time in the 588th. I looked forward to him also passing through the 588th on his way back to the States – to again be reunited with his dear mother. However, shortly before his scheduled arrival, he wrote and informed me, "President Perchon has requested I re-enlist – so I can continue to serve as the LDS Servicemen's

Coordinator in Austria." As much as Charley loved his mother and wanted to return home to be with her, I could not believe he would honor such a request. But, he did. Thus, I did not have the opportunity to see nor to associate with him again.

Following my return to the States and discharge from the military service, I lost track of Charley. Still, I often think about him, his promises to me, and his faith and diligence in serving God and his fellow men. I wonder where he might be and in what worthy cause he might be engaged. I hope someday to again meet and enjoy his company. Also, I especially hope I never forget the important lessons he taught me, i.e. with faith and determination we can change our lives for the better – no matter how low we have sunk. And, we do not need remarkable physical characteristics to be a dynamic person. Even a short, pudgy and partially bald guy can be a notable force for good. The wrappings do not tell us what is inside the package!

"IT'S A SMALL WORLD"

"All the world is a stage. The stage and play of life remain the same, only the players move on."

Karl, a maternal uncle who is six months younger than me, and I essentially were raised as twins during our youth. We often played and lived together, as well as frequently accompanied my grandfather, who I called Daddy Pa. Karl and I noted that wherever we accompanied my grandfather we invariably encountered someone he knew. It did not matter whether we were on the streets of Salt Lake City, visiting Yellowstone National Park, or camping in the wilds of central Idaho, we always seemed to run into someone my grandfather had previously met.

Daddy Pa was a very friendly and outgoing man. Some family members claimed, "He's never met a stranger." He also had a special talent for remembering names and faces, as well as details about those he met. Nevertheless, it was uncanny how – no matter where we went – he would meet someone he had met previously. Such encounters were so common that, whenever Karl and I accompanied him, we'd jokingly question, "Who do you think we'll meet this time?"

Most people can recall how they have encountered former acquaintances in unexpected places. Such meetings have occurred frequently throughout my life. Not only have I often met previous acquaintances in unlikely places, I also have repeatedly met some people in many different places.

Norman Reese was from Aberdeen, Idaho, a small town about thirty-five miles from my hometown of Rockland. Although Norm was a couple of years older than I, we became acquainted through competing against each other in athletics, both in high school and during summer "church sponsored" softball competitions. Norm also served as a "Mormon" missionary in Tennessee during the time my Aunt Carol also served as a missionary there. Therefore, she likewise knew Norm and occasionally mentioned him in her letters. Still, Norm and I were just casual acquaintances.

Following my induction into the U.S. Army and being processed at Ft. Lewis, Washington, I was sent to Ft. Ord, California for basic training. My basic training, first in "Item" and then "King" Companies of the 20th Regiment, was a nightmare. Days were spent running from one training area to another. We recruits were so tired and worn out that during lectures or instruction periods we concentrated mostly upon trying to keep our eyes open. If we did not, we were punished by having to do innumerable pushups or crawling on our bellies for hundreds of yards over rough, rocky terrain. Worse yet was being assigned "KP" and having to scrub pots and pans most of the night. Cleaning black, sticky cosmoline off rifles or other weapons in the armory also was a despicable task. Sundays, however, were different.

Though we usually were confined to the Company Area and still subject to being assigned "details" or tasks, there were no training sessions on Sundays. It was the only day you had time to write a letter home, to unhurriedly polish your boots and brass, or take care of the details associated with being able to "pass inspection". Most important, at least to me, one could attend church services on Sundays at one of the small chapels scattered around Ft. Ord. During these services you could forget, at least temporarily, the rigors and harassments associated with basic training. At church, you could reminisce about the joys of the past and contemplate the prospect of a better future. It was amazing how virtually every man in basic training at Ft. Ord attended Sunday church services. Some men even checked the schedules on the bulletin board and attempted to attend those services that lasted the longest. Most of these men did not appear to be religiously inclined and probably infrequently, if ever, attended church at home. But, church services now offered a respite from military life.

The men who had expressed a desire to attend specific church services and who had signed up to do so would "fall into formation" in front of the Orderly Room at an appointed time. The lists of names would be read, each man accounted for, and each inspected by the cadre to ensure they were dressed in "proper Class A uniform". The formation then would be marched – in strict military order – to the designated post chapel where the services would be held. Before being dismissed to enter the chapel, strict orders would be given to "Be back in formation IMMEDIATELY following the services!" We then would be dismissed and allowed to enter the chapel in single file. There, we were expected to quietly sit on wooden benches and await the commencement of the services.

Before the services began and before succumbing to a fatigued slumber, as did most men who attended church during basic training, I first would intently study the faces of those in the congregation. I hoped to see someone I knew, especially from home. I wondered, however, given the closely-cropped heads and the fatigue-drawn faces, whether or not I'd be able to recognize former acquaintances. However, on either my second or third Sunday at Ft. Ord, I recognized Norman Reese and he recognized me. Here was someone from home! I don't think either of us even dozed during that service. We were too anxious to discuss news from home.

The final "Amen" eventually was pronounced. Norm and I almost frantically pushed through the milling soldiers towards each other. We heartily shook hands and embraced, as if we were long-lost friends, rather than mere casual acquaintances. Questions gushed from our mouths. "What's happening at home? Do you know so-and-so? What are you doing here?" I learned Norm had been drafted almost immediately after having completed his mission to Tennessee and he would complete basic training a couple of weeks before me. All too soon, we had to join our respective formations and return to our training companies for another long week of arduous training. Before parting, however, we agreed to meet at church each Sunday. And, "Whoever gets there first, save a seat for the other one – so we can talk about home!"

The following weeks of basic training were less difficult, because of my anticipated visits with Norm during church services each Sunday. Both of us could hardly wait to exchange news and reminisce about home. All too soon Norm completed basic training and was shipped out. He didn't even have an opportunity to tell me where he was going. I simply assumed he had been sent to Korea, similar to most troops after finishing basic training. Thereafter, I also finished basic training and was assigned to the Austrian Command, but ended up being stationed in Italy.

Shortly after my arrival in Italy I had the opportunity to attend an LDS Servicemen's Conference or "religious retreat" in Frankfurt, Germany. It was indeed an adventure for a country boy like me to travel alone by train across northern Italy, through Switzerland, to the city of Frankfurt. The countryside, particularly the lush, green valleys backed by the snow-capped Alps, was spectacular. My journey, however, was marred by the nagging thought of, "How will I get to the Army Post upon my arrival in Frankfurt?"

My train finally pulled into the "bahnhof" or train station in downtown Frankfurt. With trepidation, I shouldered my duffel bag, walked through the station and out onto the streets of Frankfurt. I did not know where nor how to find transportation to the Army Post where the conference was to be held. Then, to my great surprise, I saw Norman Reese standing near the entrance to the station. He and one of his buddies, Robert Handley from Phoenix, Arizona, also had come to Frankfurt to attend the conference. Norm and Bob were stationed in Ulm, which is not far from Frankfurt. Fortunately, they were well acquainted with Frankfurt and knew how to get to the Post.

The three of us were inseparable during the religious retreat. In addition to attending the conference, we visited places of interest in and around Frankfurt. The week passed quickly and I had to return to Italy. I thought, "That's probably the last I'll see of Norm till we get back home." As for Bob, "I'll probably never meet him again." How wrong I was!

Following my return to Italy, Neal Torgensen, a buddy from my basic training days at Ft. Ord, and I planned a tour of Scandinavia. Neal was from southern Utah and stationed in Nurenburg, Germany. Prior to being drafted into the Army, he served as a "Mormon" missionary in Norway. Thereafter, he married a Norwegian girl. He encountered difficulties in bringing his bride to the States and, before she could join him in Utah, he was drafted into the Army. Anyway, when we got together for our planned tour of Denmark, Sweden and Norway during the fall of 1954, Neal had been married eighteen months, during which time he had spent only eighteen days with his wife.

I traveled by train from Livorno, Italy to Nurenburg, Germany, where I joined Neal and we took another train across Germany to Denmark – the land of some of my maternal forefathers. Perhaps my Danish kinship gave me a "feel" for many of the "friendly" Danes we met during our stay in the delightful country of Denmark. We then traveled by ship to the coast of Sweden and then by train to Stockholm. After spending a few days seeing the sights in this impressive capital city, we again boarded a train to the northernmost parts of Sweden and to the city of Narvik in northern Norway. We then traveled south along the Norwegian coast by various means; i.e. buses, trains, and boats or ferries. Norway essentially was Neal's second home. He was fluent in Norwegian, well acquainted with much of the country, and had friends or in-laws in many of the towns or villages we visited. We were treated royally everywhere we went. People insisted we stay in their homes, see all the sights in or near their towns or villages, and eat all we possibly could from the bounteous tables they set before us. I had never eaten so many different and usually delicious foods in my life. Neither had I eaten so often. Some days we ate as many as four meals during an afternoon. In short, we had a fabulous time. The only dampening factor was Neal did not have his wife with him. She finally had made it to the States just before he was sent to Europe!

When Neal and I arrived in southern Norway, he decided to spend his remaining leave time with his in-laws. I, in turn, decided to travel by boat to Scotland, where I would visit friends of my parents in Edinburough. Thereafter, I'd visit additional friends of theirs in Manchester, England, before taking in some of the sights in London and Paris - prior to returning to Camp Darby, Italy.

I had a most enjoyable visit with the Gregson family in Scotland. They showed me many sights in and around Edinburough. We took in the Military Tattoo, which is a spectacular music festival presented in the medieval castle overlooking Edinburough. I then traveled by bus to Manchester, where my father taught school on a teacher-exchange program just prior to my entering the military service. I visited and stayed with the most hospitable Devine family, who had been my family's next-door neighbors and close friends.

The Gregsons continually tried to impress me with the "fact" Britain had the biggest, fastest or best of almost everything in the world. For example, they claimed England had the world's largest and fastest trains, as well as the best and fastest cars. When I complimented Mr. Gregson on how nice his English-made car was, he smugly informed me, "This model of automobile was the FIRST in the world to travel a thousand miles in a thousand minutes!" Then, when we passed a Rolls Royce, he inquired, "What do you think of that automobile?" When I stated, "It looks pretty nice." His reply was, "Nice? Why that is THE automobile of the world!"

The Devines, in contrast, were of the opinion that everything in the United States was bigger, better or faster than anything in Great Britain. I tried to explain that, although we did travel at speeds in excess of seventy miles per hour on some of our highways, travel in much of the U.S. was similar to what it was in England. Trains in the U.S. also were similar to those in England.

Following a most enjoyable stay with Mr. and Mrs. Devine and their young son David, I took an afternoon bus to London. I then spent the night in a hotel near Grosvner Square and made arrangements to take a sightseeing bus tour of London the next morning. I arose early, hurriedly ate breakfast, and anxiously awaited the arrival of the tour bus. Upon boarding the bus, I was startled by some shouts and jeers from the rear of the vehicle. There, to my surprise, were Norman Reese and Robert Handley. They too were on leave from their Post in Germany and had arrived in London the previous evening. In short, we spent three glorious days in London, seeing the sights and discussing happenings at home. While in London, we also spent time with Terry Harrup, who was serving as a "Mormon" missionary in England and was stationed just outside of London. Terry was from Norm's hometown of Aberdeen. They had gone to school together. Terry also was Lennie Hunt's boyfriend. Lennie lived in American Falls and was my girlfriend Jeanette's youngest sister!

My time with Norm, Bob and Terry in London passed quickly. After a short visit to Paris, I returned to Camp Darby. Some months later, I was selected to attend a six-week Training, Information and Education course in Salzburg, Austria. While participating in this course, I learned another religious retreat or LDS Servicemen's Conference was to be held in nearby Berchesgaten, Germany. There would be two sessions of four days each. The first session would begin immediately following my six-week training course. Thus, I requested and was granted permission to attend the first session of this retreat, prior to my returning to Italy. Upon completion of my course in Salzburg, I took a bus to Berchesgaten and then checked into a large hotel in this picturesque town. I took my luggage to my assigned room and decided to look for a place to eat dinner. As I entered the hallway, I was greeted with shouts and jeers. There stood Norm and Bob! They also were attending the first session of the conference and had just arrived by bus from Ulm. Furthermore, their hotel room was just two doors down the hall from mine. We again spent four wonderful days together.

Norm, Bob and I had by now become fast friends. Oddly, however, we never wrote to each other. The only time we found out what the others had been doing was during our chance encounters in the most unlikely or unexpected places.

My tour of military service in Italy ended the summer following my get-together with Norm and Bob in Berchesgaten. I then returned to Idaho and worked for a few months before enrolling in Ricks College (now BYU-Idaho) during the fall of 1955. I shortly received a call to serve a "Mormon" mission in Uruguay, South America.

In early January of 1956, I entered the Mission Home in Salt Lake City. Here, I would receive five days of orientation and training before being sent to Uruguay. I had my head down and was charging up some narrow stairs in the back part of the Mission Home, on my way to visit a friend (Carl Barkdahl), who was from American Falls and was going on a mission to Brazil, when I suddenly "plowed" into a fellow coming down the stairs. We grabbed each other, to keep from falling, and then gave simultaneous shouts of joy. It was Bob Handley! He was returning to Germany as a "Mormon" missionary!

We were very busy during our five-day stay in the Mission Home. Still, Bob and I renewed acquaintances and discussed happenings since we last met in Berchesgaten. I learned that Norm had married shortly after returning home from his military service. He and his wife were awaiting the arrival of their first child. Regretfully, I hadn't taken the time to look him up after my return home.

I spent two and one-half years as a missionary in Uruguay and Paraguay and returned home in the early fall of 1958. Thereafter, I enrolled in Brigham Young University (BYU) in Provo, Utah. There were about sixteen thousand students attending BYU, virtually all of whom were LDS or "Mormons". For church services, students were divided into congregations, or "wards", of about four hundred each, based primarily upon where they lived. The first Sunday I attended my assigned ward, I ran into Bob Handley. Similar to me, he had completed his mission and had decided to enroll at BYU. We had been assigned the same ward! Thereafter, in addition to periodic encounters on campus, Bob and I regularly got together each Sunday.

I spent the summer following my academic year at BYU working in Yellowstone National Park. I had determined I wanted to pursue a career in wildlife management. BYU did not have a Wildlife Science Department. Thus, I decided to transfer to Utah State University (USU) in Logan the fall of 1959. Although USU is a State institution, the student body is predominantly "Mormon". As at BYU, the "Mormon" students are divided into wards, primarily on the basis of where they live. The first Sunday I attended church services in my assigned ward I again encountered Bob Handley, Unbeknown to me, he too had decided to transfer from BYU to USU. And, although there were more than twenty student wards at USU, we had been assigned to the same ward. As a result, Bob and I again got together each Sunday - until we both graduated in 1961. Regretfully, I have lost contact with Bob and have not seen him since we graduated

My maternal grandfather died following a family reunion on July 4, 1959. Shortly afterwards, my grandmother moved from Rockland to Pocatello, a distance of about forty-five miles. While visiting my grandmother one weekend, I attended church services with her. When we entered the chapel, there, with a smile on his face and his hand extended to greet me, stood Norman Reese! He and his family, which now consisted of his wife and three young children, were living in Pocatello. They lived only a few houses down the block from where my grandmother lived. Needless to say, Norm and I again renewed our acquaintance.

My grandmother eventually moved from Pocatello and I lost track of Norm. Nevertheless, I frequently remember the many unexpected encounters I had with both Bob and Norm in unexpected places and almost literally throughout the world. Although many years now have passed since I last saw them, I am certain that someday we will meet again and discuss what has happened during the intervening years since we last met. Our many encounters at so many unexpected times and places have demonstrated and thoroughly convinced me that "It's A Small World"!

REVENGE

"Revenge is mine, saith the Lord." "See that no one render evil
for evil unto any man…"   Thessalonians 5:15

The Korean truce had been declared. Still, there was a dreaded
fear that fighting would resume. I was in basic training at Ft. Ord,
California, and our instructors repeatedly tried to impress upon us
"You're being trained to be paid killers!" Their job, they claimed, was
to make us "tough" and to teach us how to "hate" – "So you'll
survive, when the going really gets tough!"

The short nights – we rarely were allowed to sleep for six hours –
frequently were interrupted with forced marches through the "boon
docks" or with harassing exercises, such as repeatedly falling into and
out of formations. This, we were told, was to instill in us a "sense of
discipline". Whereas, "You think you're men. But, you're nothing but
undisciplined sissies!" The short nights, however, became almost
interminable when we had to stand guard duty. The long days were
filled with one training session after another. Although our instructors
repeatedly reminded us, "What we're trying to teach you might save
your life!" more often than not you simply concentrated on just trying
to keep your eyes open, rather than upon what the instructors were
trying to teach.

There was the haunting "boom-de-de-boom-boom" of the drums
and the rattle of steel helmets, rifles and bayonets – the instruments of
war – as we double-timed endless miles from one area to another and
then back again. There also were the unwieldy heavy weapons, such
as the base plate of an 80mm mortar, which we somehow, in addition
to our rifles, packs and other gear, had to carry as we dog-trotted on
and on. This is not to mention the cold, damp and foggy mornings,
which made you shiver uncontrollably. We were not allowed to
button our collars around our necks – in an effort to keep warm when
we were cold. Then, when the cold, miserable mornings were
followed by hot, scorching days, we were not allowed to unbutton or
loosen our clothing to dissipate the heat. There were hurried meals,

innumerable push-ups on the ground and pull-ups on the bars, as well as the burning thirst, which resulted from being rationed to only one-quart canteen full of water for an entire day in the field. Some of our forced runs, under full field gear, were for as much a seven miles without a break. Literally dozens of men would pass out, while still on their feet. They then would pitch forward, forcefully hitting the ground, where they would remain motionless until they regained consciousness. Perhaps the worst was how we were taught to hate. This instilled in us a desire for revenge – particularly against those who were inflicting such misery upon us.

Almost without realizing it, we began to hate those who had drafted us into the Army. We hated the Army and its food, as well as it's innumerable and what usually seemed to be nonsensical rules and regulations. Above all we hated those who "lorded it" over us – especially the cadre who took delight in making us do push-ups until we fell flat on our faces from exhaustion and also made us crawl, flat on our stomachs, across the roughest, rockiest terrain they could find – until our knees and elbows were bruised and bleeding. We hated those who made us scrub and scrub again our ancient, dilapidated, wooden barracks, until they were so clean a white glove would remain unsoiled, no matter where it was rubbed. We hated those who insisted our rifles were not clean, no matter how meticulous we might have been in our efforts to keep them spotless. We even hated our fellow trainees and looked for excuses whereby we could vent our hate by inflicting verbal and physical abuse upon them. In short, we wanted revenge!

One man, for example, shouted accusations that an adjoining bunkmate had stolen a razor from his footlocker. Others nearby did not wait for proof of guilt or even stop long enough to realize the accused man was so young and clean-faced he did not need to use a razor. Instead, they immediately ganged up on the poor guy, rolled him up in a blanket, beat him unmercifully, and tossed him down the barracks stairs. Few words were spoken, except in anger. Then, it suddenly dawned upon us, no longer would it be difficult to kill someone, an act we could not have imagined committing a few weeks earlier. Our instructors apparently had achieved their goal. We had become "trained killers!"

Some men broke under the strain of basic training. It was surprising which men often broke first. Rather than the puny kid in the next bunk, who didn't appear to be old enough to be drafted, it more than likely was the burly, first-string college football player who would sprawl on the floor, kicking uncontrollably and crying, "I can't take it any longer!" Some who "cracked" mentally were sent to the hospital. Two men in our company took their own lives. One shot himself in the head, which is a rather awkward thing to do with an M-1 rifle. The other slashed his wrists with a bayonet and bled to death, while alone in the showers during the middle of the night. In contrast, a short ruddy-faced farm boy – who was not more than five-foot four-inches tall and had been stricken with polio during his youth and had one leg shorter than the other, which caused him to bobble from side to side when running, and whose left arm was much shorter and smaller than the right, which made it difficult for him to properly handle a rifle - would simply grin and bear the difficulties placed before him.

Most of us gradually came to the realization we could take much more punishment then we previously had thought possible. A strong bond of camaraderie began to develop among some of us. We gradually came to realize which men could be relied upon when the going got especially tough. We ascertained which men could not be trusted or who could not withstand the stress or difficulties we faced. Those of us who felt strong bonds of kinship even began to taunt or dare our cadre to "Try to break us, if you can!" or "If you dare!" Others, however, attempted devious ways to avoid or escape the difficulties associated with our rigorous training regime. Simpson was one of these.

Like most men in our platoon, Simpson had been drafted into the Army. He was tall, fair-haired, and fairly well built. Generally speaking, he was a handsome, rugged-looking individual. He was physically much better endowed than most men in our platoon or even in "King" Company. However, Simpson apparently had devised a plan whereby he thought he could avoid much of the harassment to which we were being subjected. He tried various ploys to gain favor with Mendoza, our Platoon Sergeant. Although his efforts occasionally resulted in his being assigned an extra "detail", they eventually began to pay dividends. More and more frequently Sergeant Mendoza would place Simpson in charge of drilling our platoon or directing groups assigned to "details" or undesirable tasks.

Simpson enjoyed giving orders. It also appeared he took special delight in belittling or giving a bad time to those who were smaller or weaker than he. This was despite his dislike for being told what to do or being harassed by others. Nevertheless, whenever Sergeant Mendoza put Simpson in charge, we knew we would have to do more pushups, be subjected to more harassment, and be drilled harder and longer than would have been the case if we were under the Platoon Sergeant's command. This resulted in most of us developing a hatred for Simpson and we began to look for ways to get even with him.

One evening, after a strenuous day in the field, about a dozen of us were selected for a "detail". We were to sweep, mop and clean some classrooms on the far side of the Post. Rather than his taking charge, Sergeant Mendoza put Simpson in charge of our "detail". This pleased Simpson and he insisted we march at attention while we traversed several miles across Ft. Ord. He further insisted we shoulder our brooms and mops as if they were rifles. When he thought he had the attention of others we encountered along the way, he would even command our small "brigade" to "Halt!" He then would proceed to drill us in the manual of arms, with us using our brooms and mops as if they were weapons. Given time, I think he might have devised a special drill for those carrying buckets.

As we entered the classrooms we'd been assigned to clean, Simpson began barking specific instructions to each of us – as if he thought we were not intelligent enough to know what to do or how to do it. I had by this time taken all I was going to take from Simpson. Turning to one of my buddies I said, "I'm going to put this guy in his place. Are you with me?" He said "Yes!" and I grabbed Simpson by the collar, shoved him into a corner, and gave him a good face slapping. Simpson started to shout threats, such as, "I'll have you court-martialed for insubordination!" And, "You'll pay for this!" But, when he saw the rest of the men in our detail backing me up and cheering me on, as well as my countering his threats with statements such as, "You won't live long enough to court martial anyone!" he became meek and submissive.

We gave Simpson to understand he was no better than we. He didn't have to tell us what to do nor how to do it. Also, the quicker we got to it, the quicker we'd be able to get back to the barracks and perhaps even get a few hours of much-needed sleep.

It was amazing how quickly Simpson became one of us. In fact, he worked harder at cleaning the classrooms than any of us. While we sauntered back across Ft. Ord to "King" Company, he even insisted upon treating all of us to an ice cream at the Post Exchange. In meek terms, he stated, "I'll forget everything that's happened tonight, if you will." All of us agreed to do so.

Simpson continued to be one of us for about a week. He then reverted to his prior ways; seeking favor with Sergeant Mendoza and again "lording it over us". Our hatred toward Simpson was rekindled. Some men in our platoon, particularly those who had been on our classroom-cleaning detail, swore, "When we settle the score with Simpson next time, we'll make sure he never forgets he's a 'peon' – just like the rest of us!" Simpson became aware of our animosity towards him and his fear of our retribution was such that he begged Sergeant Mendoza to let him sleep in the Cadre Room with him. When we went on bivouac, he even arranged to sleep in the Officer's Tent. And, during the day, he always made sure he was near Sergeant Mendoza or other cadre. Simpson, however, continued to taunt us with statements such as, "As soon as we finish basic training, I'm going to OCS (Officer Candidate School). I'm not going to remain a 'peon' like the rest of you!"

Our basic training finally came to an end. The approximately three hundred and sixty-five men in "King" Company were shipped in many directions. Most were sent to Korea. Some were sent to various schools or camps for additional training. Others were sent to leadership school. And, sixteen of us were assigned to the Austrian Command. Two of this group, Charles McCoy from Los Angeles and I, ended up in the 588th Replacement Company in Camp Darby, Italy. Simpson was one of a very few selected for OCS.

One of my duties as the Morning Report Clerk in the 588th was calling the roster or names of the men as they disembarked from the troop ships upon their arrival in the port at Livorno, Italy. As I called each man's name, he was required to step forward, salute and shout, "Here, Sir!" - before descending the gangplank from the ship. In this manner I accounted for each man in my daily "morning reports", which were submitted to the Commanding General in Austria.

Troops assigned to the Austrian Command were processed through the 588th and given duty assignments in Austria. After having recently been awarded my corporal stripes, I was calling the roster for another disembarking shipment of troops from the States when I read the name, "Simpson". He stepped forward and shouted, "Here, Sir!" I realized, "Here is my old 'friend' from basic training." I thought, "What can I do to get even with him for the misery he dealt us during basic training – now that he's under my power?"

I looked Simpson straight in the eyes and asked, "What are you doing here? I thought you were going to OCS?" His retort was, "What gave you that idea?" I had to continue calling the roster, but I later pulled Simpson's "Form 20" or personal record from the files and read, "Dropped from OCS for academic reasons". I then surmised, "My old 'friend' from basic training isn't as smart as he thought he was! Why, he's still a 'peon' like the rest of us!"

My hatred for Simpson had somewhat diminished during the intervening months between basic training and his arrival in Italy. Still, I pondered, "What can I do to get even with the SOB?" I finally contrived for Simpson being put on latrine detail. I determined I'd have him scrubbing and polishing latrines in our Company area every possible minute of the day and night during his three-day stay in the 588th. I'd make certain we had the cleanest latrines in the Austrian Command – if not in the entire U.S. Army! Under my direct supervision, Simpson would scrub and polish over and over again the floors, walls, wash basins, and especially the urinals and toilets in each of the six latrines in our Company area. Thus, I sternly outlined to Simpson what I expected him to do while he was in the 588th and under my command. I further iterated to him, "If you don't do what I tell you to do and do it well, I'll make sure you get the worst possible duty assignment in Austria!" With this, Simpson embarked upon his three-day latrine cleaning and polishing detail.

I periodically checked on Simpson, to ensure he did the best job possible and did not "slack off". However, instead of enjoying my revenge and the opportunity I now had to dictate the most menial tasks I could think of for Simpson, I had a feeling of guilt and became depressed by what I was doing. It perplexed me as to why I should feel this way. Why didn't I feel good about getting even? Hadn't Simpson dealt unjustly with me and others during our basic training days? Why didn't I feel good about "getting even"? Like Edmond Dante in the "Count of Monte Cristo", I found revenge was bitter, not sweet. Still, I could not understand why. Then, sometime later, I came upon this passage, "Revenge is mine, saith the Lord." Also, in reading Paul's letter to the Thessalonians (I. Thes. 5:15) I learned we should not return evil for evil to any man. I began to realize my trying to get even with Simpson was contrary to God's law and probably why I did not feel good about seeking revenge.

Hopefully, my seeking revenge against Simpson taught me an important lesson. Namely, no matter what others might do or how wrongfully they might treat us, we should not seek revenge nor try to get even. Revenge or the returning of evil for evil only leads to remorse!

"CHANCE"

"Idleness is the devil's workshop."

His last name was "Chance", but the first time I saw him, I didn't think he had much of a chance in this world. I was temporarily serving as the Company Clerk for the 588th Replacement Company and sitting at a desk in the Orderly Room when two men carried the lifeless form of a man into the room and unceremoniously dumped him on the floor in front of me. One of them said, "This is Private Chance. He's an alcoholic. We were ordered to guard him during the twenty-four-hour train ride from Salzburg to Italy." Although their assignment was to keep him from obtaining alcohol of any kind, in some way – they did not know how – Chance had obtained some alcohol and now was completely inebriated.

The mission of the 588th was to process shipments of troops who arrived at Camp Darby either from the States or from Austria at approximately ten-day intervals. Troops from the States were processed and given duty assignments in Austria; whereas, those coming from Austria were processed either for discharge or re-assignment in the States. Regretfully, there usually were three to eight men in each shipment from Austria who were to be given "368" (Undesirable) or "369" (Dishonorable) discharges from the U.S. Army. Many of the "368's", similar to Chance, were alcoholics. As such, they were considered "undesirable" or "unfit" for military service. The "369's" usually had been convicted of crimes – more often than not sexual offenses.

Private Chance was completely unconscious. Only the whites of his eyes were visible. His whole body was trembling. He apparently had lost control of his bladder and bowels and was making a terrible mess upon the Orderly Room floor. I summoned Captain Shelley (the Commanding Officer of the 588th). When he observed the prostrate form of Private Chance, he demanded an explanation from the two guards. Both men stammered and explained how Chance had escaped their vigil for "only a few minutes." They further claimed, "It would have been impossible for him to have obtained any liquor in such a short time, let alone consume a sufficient amount to account for his present condition." But, he had!

Captain Shelley ordered the two men to sit Chance upon a chair. Their efforts to do so were futile. Chance's limp body simply slid or slumped off from the chair onto the floor. The CO's efforts to communicate with Chance likewise were in vain. It appeared to be impossible to rouse him to consciousness. In desperation, Captain Shelley called the Company Driver and ordered him to take Chance and his two guards to the hospital. He also ordered the two guards, "Don't you let him out of your sight! If you do, I'll hold you responsible for whatever happens!"

The two guards grasped Chance's limp body by the arms and legs. They essentially drug him from the Orderly Room and dumped him into the back of the Company's three-quarter-ton truck. They then were off to the hospital, near the port area in Livorno. "Well," I thought, "That is that!" I was wrong!

Less than an hour later the vehicle returned and the two guards again carried Chance's limp body back into the Orderly Room. The Duty Officer at the hospital would not admit Chance. He claimed his condition was "NOT Service connected." Therefore, he could not or would not admit him into a military facility. Instead of trembling, as previously had been the case, Chance's body now only sporadically twitched. His breathing was rapid and shallow. I feared for his life and immediately summoned Captain Shelley. He agreed with my prognosis. We both felt, if not given prompt medical attention, there was a good chance Private Chance would die. Captain Shelley telephoned the hospital and insisted upon talking to the Duty Officer. His pleas for medical treatment for Chance, however, were to no avail. In desperation, the Captain called the Post Commander. He briefly explained the situation and emphatically stated, "If this man is not given prompt medical attention, he'll probably die!"

The Post Commander promised he would contact the hospital and get back with the CO. The telephone rang a few minutes later and the Post Commander told Captain Shelley arrangements had been made for Chance to receive medical aid at the hospital. Thus, Chance again was loaded into the back of the Company truck and he and his two guards returned to the hospital.

We processed the troops from Austria and shipped them to the States. I had almost forgotten about Chance when he again was carried into the Orderly Room. While he was in the hospital being "dried out", his clothes and money had been taken away from him. Nevertheless, immediately prior to his scheduled release from the hospital and return to the 588th, he somehow had again obtained alcohol. Although unable to stand unassisted, he now was in a better condition than when he had first arrived from Austria. He at least was conscious and could talk more-or-less coherently.

Upon seeing Private Chance's condition and after having interrogated his two guards, Captain Shelley again summoned the Post Commander. Both of them then questioned Chance at great length as to "How did you obtain the 'booze'?" Short of torture, they tried every ploy they could think of to get Chance to tell them how he obtained some alcohol. His guards and those at the hospital were at a loss to explain how he had done it, especially since he didn't have any money. They also claimed he had been out of their sight for "only a few minutes". And, they could not believe he could have consumed a sufficient quantity of alcohol in such a short time to account for his present condition. None-the-less, somehow he had!

Chance resolutely refused to tell anyone how he had obtained the alcohol. Although he was unable to stand without the assistance of his guards, I was impressed by how he looked his interrogators straight in the eyes and stated, "I won't lie to you. But, I won't tell you how I got it either! If I told you how I got it, then I wouldn't be able to get any more. And, if I can't get it anymore, I'll die!"

Despite their threats, Chance refused to tell his interrogators what they wanted to know. The officers shortly realized there was no way they could persuade him to tell them how he had obtained alcohol. They then mutually resolved they would make certain he did not obtain any more, at least while he was at Camp Darby. The Post Commander ordered the two guards NOT to let Chance out of their sight, "Not even for a minute!" They were to guard him twenty-four hours a day. They were to, "Eat with him. Sleep beside him. And, even accompany him when he goes to the latrine!"

Upon hearing the orders given to his guards, Chance pleaded, "I won't make any trouble – if you'll let me have just one beer a day. I think I can make it on that! If I can't have at least one drink a day, I'll go crazy!" Both the CO and the Post Commander refused to listen to his pleas. He and his guards were sent back to the hospital, where Private Chance again would be "dried out".

Chance and his two guards returned to the 588th a few days later. This time he walked into the Orderly Room unassisted. It was the first time I had seen him able to stand on his own. He informed us he had been ordered to remain in the 588th until he could be sent back to the States with the next shipment of troops from Austria, which would be in a couple of weeks. He then would be given an undesirable discharge from the U.S. Army and, as a civilian, would have to "make it on his own".

It was while Chance was waiting for the troop shipment from Austria that I became well acquainted with him and learned how he had become an alcoholic. Formerly a Sergeant, but now a Private, he was born and reared on a farm in the mid-West. He led a conservative and uneventful life as a farm boy. He learned well how to work and was very industrious. Soon after entering the U.S. Army, he became a heavy equipment operator in the Corps of Engineers. He enjoyed his work and worked hard. As a result, he received regular promotions. Shortly after arriving in the Austrian Command, he was made a supervisor. As such, he no longer operated heavy equipment. Instead, it was his responsibility to tell others what to do. He did not like this. He preferred doing the work himself. He claimed the monotony of telling others what to do and not doing the work himself "bored him to death" and "almost drove him mad". Although he claimed he rarely drank even an occasional beer before his arrival in Austria, he started to drink - "to kill the boredom". At first, it was "just a few beers each evening". Before long, however, he was drinking "harder stuff" and more and more frequently. He also began to drink until he passed out. Finally, he realized he was dependent upon alcohol and was unable to cope without frequent drinks, even during the day.

Chance went to his CO and asked to be put to work. Rather than being a supervisor and merely telling others what to do, he wanted to again operate heavy equipment. However, he was told they didn't have such a position for him. He then asked to be transferred to an area where he could do construction work. His request was granted. But, when he arrived in the new area, he again was assigned a supervisory position. His craving for alcohol increased and he no longer could control his drinking habits. Eventually, he was drunk most of the time. This resulted in disciplinary actions being taken. One by one he lost his stripes; he was "busted" from a Sergeant back to a mere Private. Now, he was going to be "busted right out of the U.S. Army!"

Chance repeatedly told me he would give anything if he could quit drinking. He felt, however, his need for alcohol had become such that he could not live without it. He knew he had become an alcoholic, but honestly believed his addiction was such that he no longer could survive without at least occasional drinks.

It so happened that while Chance was assigned to the 588th there was considerable construction work being done at Camp Darby. Observing this, Chance asked to see the Post Commander. Upon meeting with his former interrogator, he begged to be permitted to operate one of the big tractors being used in construction. The Commander questioned him about his physical condition and bluntly told him he didn't think he was any longer capable of physical labor. However, after Chance repeatedly assured him he was "one of the best cat-skinners in the world!" And, "Yes! I'm physically able to operate a tractor." The Commander finally relented and consented to giving him a "chance".

Virtually overnight Chance was miraculously transformed into one of the happiest men I've ever seen. He was like a child with a new toy. In the mornings he couldn't wait to start up "his crawler tractor". His guards almost had to threaten him to get him to stop long enough to eat lunch or dinner. From dawn till dark, he insisted upon spending almost every minute operating "his" tractor. Meanwhile his two guards spent most of their time lounging in the shade of nearby trees, while watching him work. They began to complain. They were tired of doing nothing. One even remarked, "This doing nothing is enough to drive one to drink!"

All too soon a shipment of troops arrived from Austria. When they had been processed, Chance would be sent back to the States with them. He then would be dishonorably discharged from the Army. He dejectedly entered the Orderly Room and earnestly pleaded with Captain Shelley to be permitted "to remain in the 588th and to continue to work on construction at Camp Darby." He explained, "If I can just keep working, I think maybe I can overcome my addiction to alcohol. But, if you send me home and I don't have any work to do, I'll probably end up soused again. Then, all will be lost!"

Captain Shelley explained, "I don't have the authority to change your orders." Somehow, Chance then managed to present his plea to the Post Commander, who, in turn, refused to give Chance another "chance". He claimed, "Orders are orders!" Private Chance "had" to return to the States with the shipment of troops from Austria.

Chance cried like a heartbroken child. He begged each of us to help him to stay at Camp Darby, so he could "keep working" – at least until the construction work had been completed. He was afraid to return home, fearing he would go back to drinking. Work, he felt, was his only salvation.

Regretfully, none of us were able to help Private Chance with his request. When I last saw him, his two guards were literally dragging him into the back of the truck that would take him to the ship for his return to the States. What a marked difference from the first times I saw Chance. Instead of the guards having to carry him, he now was resisting their efforts to do so. And, instead of begging for "just a few beers", he now was pleading to be allowed to work. It was indeed a sad situation.

There was nothing I could do to help Private Chance. Thus, I simply bade a now dear friend farewell and wished him luck. Despite his overpowering weakness with respect to alcohol, many of us at Camp Darby had gained considerable respect for him. He had many admirable qualities, i.e. he was honest, industrious, friendly, and had a sincere desire to again become his own master. He also was a dear teacher. He taught me that alcohol is a formidable enemy, one with which we should not tinker. Furthermore, if we are not actively engaged in a good cause or doing meaningful work, there is a good chance the devil will lure us into his domain. Idleness truly is the devil's workshop!

ONE DRINK IS TOO MANY

"One drink is too many, and a thousand is not enough."
Alcoholics Anonymous

This is the slogan of Alcoholics Anonymous, an organization dedicated to helping people overcome their addiction to alcohol or the "disease" called "alcoholism". Do you believe "One drink is too many"? Or, do you think an "occasional or social drink" doesn't hurt anyone? I believe "One drink IS too many." Let me tell you why.

After having served about nine months in the 588th Replacement Company at Camp Darby, Italy, I had been sent to six-week Training, Information and Education (TI&E) course in Salzburg, Austria. While at Camp Darby, I had located only three men stationed there who were "Mormons" or members of The Church of Jesus Christ of Latter-day Saints. Two of these had returned to the States and the remaining man was not a very active Church member. Thus, upon my return from Austria, I was both surprised and happy to find that two of three new men assigned to the handpicked, twenty-five man 588th were "Mormons".

One of these was a somewhat older fellow from Wenatchee, Washington. He had an M.S. degree from Brigham Young University and had taught school for a number of years. He had married, divorced and then remarried and had a five-year-old daughter. Although he was more familiar with the scriptures and doctrines of the "Mormon" Church than the other fellow, Dean, and me, he apparently had convinced himself that abiding by the gospel principles advocated by the Church was not important – at least not for the present. He repeatedly told us, "You ought to have a good time NOW, while you're young! There will be plenty of time to repent when you get older!" He particularly chided Dean for being a "goody-goody" and for "not being one of the guys."

In contrast, Dean had been a devout "Mormon" throughout his life. He was born and raised in the small southeastern Idaho town of McCammon, which is not far from my hometown of Rockland.

Although our high schools competed against each other in athletics, I had not previously met him. Still, Dean and I had much in common and we frequently talked about "home" and the good people there. Dean's being drafted into the military service resulted in his being separated for the first time from his home and family. And, it was very much evident that he was suffering the terrible pangs of homesickness.

Dean bunked in the same tent as the fellow from Washington. Thus, he was subjected to much more chiding by this man than was I. In fact, Dean was almost continuously subjected to barbs such as, "Why don't you let yourself go a bit?" Or, "How will you know what life's about, if you never live on the other side of the fence?" In short, this fellow "Mormon" tried to convince Dean he should be like him and most of the other men in the 588th and at Camp Darby. This meant he should at least socially drink, use what commonly was called "GI English", and spend off-duty hours with a "regular" Italian girlfriend. Dean, however, steadfastly refused to listen to him.

Despite frequent verbal jabs from others about his "being different" or "not being one of the gang", Dean politely and resolutely refused to live different than he had been taught. It appeared that he began to take some pride in "being different" or not participating in activities he did not believe were right. As for me, seeing the results of the actions of others was sufficient to deter me from being like them. I did not want to experience "living on the other side of the fence". Neither did I want to experience the nausea and headaches associated with drinking or the humiliation, remorse and pain associated with VD. It appeared to be simpler and less painful to learn from the mistakes of others, rather than experiencing first-hand the remorse resulting from doing what one knew was not right.

The 588th was assigned the task of demobilizing the approximately ten-thousand-man Trieste Command immediately prior to Dean's arrival at Camp Darby. As a result, the entire Trieste Command, which included a "Mormon" Servicemen's Group of about thirty men, was temporarily stationed at Camp Darby. For the first time since my arrival in Italy I had the opportunity to attend regular "Mormon" Church services. It also meant Dean and I were not different from ALL of the men on Post and we enjoyed attending and participating in the group's meetings and activities. But, all too soon those in the Trieste Command were processed and shipped out. Although we had organized our own Camp Darby "Mormon" Servicemen's Group during the Trieste Group's presence, not more than a handful of men normally attended our Sunday meetings thereafter. In fact, Dean and I were the only ones present on a couple of occasions.

Dean had his nineteenth birthday. It was the first he'd ever spent away from his home and family. He also became more and more homesick and despondent with the approach of Christmas. He began to almost incessantly reminisce about the "good life" back home and how he missed his family. Based upon our conversations, I doubt Dean had ever done anything seriously wrong or contrary to what he had been taught at home or at Church. For example, he told about double dating with one of his friends for a school dance. His friend got permission to use the family car to take their dates to the dance. But, when he came to pick Dean up, he showed him a bottle of wine, which his father had left in the glove compartment. Dean refused to ride with him unless he threw the bottle away. He didn't want to be associated with alcohol in any way!

More and more problems seemed to confront Dean as Christmas drew nigh. His father became ill and had major back surgery. Then, soon after his release from the hospital, he returned to work – even though his doctor had ordered complete bed rest and warned that, if he returned to work too soon he might become an invalid for life. Dean pleaded with his father, both by letter and telephone, to follow the doctor's orders. But, his father claimed, "Someone has to support the family!" Although Dean had arranged for virtually all of his military pay to be sent to his family, for some reason they were not receiving his allocations. Dean was unsuccessful in trying to find out what happened to his allotment checks. This caused him to become even more perplexed and bewildered.

I could sense Dean's frustration and feeling of helplessness as he worried and struggled to help his family. The thousands of miles between Idaho and Italy, however, seemed to present an insurmountable barrier. To make his situation even more difficult, his buddies and especially his "Mormon" bunkmate seemed to take renewed delight in taunting him into being more like them.

One evening, while Dean and I were walking back to the Company area from the mess hall, he casually remarked, "You know, I'd like to get drunk just once to see what it's like. I wonder if getting drunk would help me to forget my troubles - at least for a little while?" I tried to tell him, "You shouldn't think that way." I had the foreboding, however, that I wasn't very convincing.

I was in the Orderly Room "In Charge of Quarters" or "CQ" one night just before Christmas. Most of the men in the 588th were "imbibing a bit of Christmas cheer" or having their not unusual evening "social" drinks in their tent or living quarters. One of them came to the Orderly Room and informed me, "Dean's finally one of the gang. He's not only taken his first drink with us, but he's now 'sousing' drunk!" Apparently, Dean had returned from the evening meal at the mess hall and his buddies had chided him for not joining them in a "friendly" drink. One fellow needled him with, "If you're such a good Christian, as you claim you are, why can't you at least drink a toast with us to celebrate Christ's birthday?" Dean refused. Then one of them hit him with, "What's wrong? Are you so good that you can't even drink a Coke with us?" Dean agreed to this. He then was given a Coke, which previously had been spiked with liquor. Whether or not he knew or detected it was spiked, I do not know. But, it was only a matter of a few more spiked Cokes and Dean's "friends" had him drinking straight whiskey.

I tried to talk to Dean the next day, but could not reason with him. He felt he had committed an unpardonable sin – one for which there was no forgiveness. Despite my pleadings, he insisted there was no return or repentance for what he had done. To make matters worse, his buddies now taunted him with remarks such as, "See, you're no better than us! Welcome to the gang!" Dean's mental anguish and depression quickly went from bad to worse. Some people claim alcoholism is a "chronic" disease, which normally takes years or at least a prolonged period of time for a person to succumb. This was not the case with Dean. Virtually overnight he went from a teetotaler to an alcoholic!

Dean's newly acquired drinking habit resulted in his skipping meals in the mess hall. Instead of going to meals, he started frequenting the next-door Servicemen's Club, "Just to have one drink with my friends before dinner." When I finally got Dean alone and tried to tell him what he was doing to himself, he broke down and cried. "How can I ever go home now?" he sobbed. "I'll never be able to face my family again. They trusted me. And, I've let them down. What's more, I just can't help myself!" Oddly, he claimed he didn't like the taste of liquor. "But," he said, "I just crave the stuff and can't wait to have another drink." Although he occasionally was able to control his craving for alcohol for one or two days, it was only a few weeks before Dean generally was recognized as "that drunk from the 588th".

It was a Saturday night and I again was in the Orderly Room on CQ. Except for me, the 588th Company area was deserted. The other men, including Dean, were "out celebrating" either at the Servicemen's Club or in nearby Livorno. Towards midnight, one of the fellows came into the Orderly Room and informed me, "Dean's drunk again. He's in pretty bad shape and is saying some pretty rash things. I've put him to bed, but maybe you'd better check on him from time to time." When I inquired as to "What kind of things has Dean been saying?" He said, "Things like, 'Why don't you leave me in the gutter where I belong – so I can die alone?' And, 'Why don't you kill me, so I won't have to do the job myself?'"

About a half hour later, I decided I'd better check on Dean. Members of the 588th lived in four permanent tents, each of which had a cement slab floor and a permanent wooden frame covered with heavy canvas. I walked the short distance from the Orderly Room to Dean's tent. I paused at the door to the tent and listened, to see if I could detect any sound from within. Hearing nothing, I quietly opened the door.

I'll never forget what I saw when I peered into the tent. Silhouetted by a dim light from a desk lamp at the far end of the tent was the limp form of a body, which was gently swaying back and forth, while hanging suspended in the air by a rope attached to a rafter. Dean apparently had taken a quarter-inch tent rope from a field pack on top of the wooden clothes closets, had formed a noose with a slipknot and placed it over his head and around his neck. Then, while standing on a chair, he had tied the end of the rope to a rafter, before kicking the chair out from under his feet.

I grabbed Dean's limp body and frantically tried to free the rope from around his neck. Although I was able to somewhat loosen the noose, try as I might I could not get it off. In desperation, I held Dean's limp form as high as I could and frantically shouted for help. In my mind, I also desperately prayed someone would hear my shouts and come quickly to help me. Although it seemed like hours, it probably was only minutes before a fellow ran into the tent – from where, I do not know. Quickly assessing the situation, he grabbed a bayonet off from one of the field packs on top of the clothes closets, pulled the blade out of the scabbard, and cut the rope from Dean's neck.

We lowered Dean's body onto a nearby cot. He was a gruesome sight. His eyes were bulged. His tongue protruded from his mouth almost to his chin. And, his face was a ghastly bluish-red. He didn't appear to be breathing, but we thought we could detect a weak pulse in his wrist. I applied artificial respiration and within minutes Dean began to gasp and eventually started to sob. When he regained consciousness and eventually could speak, though only in whispers, all he said was, "Why did you take me down? I felt so good! Why didn't you leave me alone?"

Fearing what action might be taken if the CO found out what Dean had done, I swore the other fellow to secrecy. We agreed neither of us would tell anyone what had happened. Still, the red welts and rope burns on Dean's neck were starkly evident above his shirt collar. I wondered how anyone could help but notice them. In fact, these marks persisted on Dean's neck for weeks and were still evident when I left Italy to return home. Insofar as I know, however, the other man and I were the only ones that knew what happened with Dean that night.

After I returned to the States and was discharged from the Army, I visited Dean's family several times. I, of course, never told them about that night or about Dean's problem with alcohol. I also corresponded quite frequently with Dean. One day I received a letter from him in which he stated, "You'll probably be happy to hear I'm back to drinking nothing stronger than pop." He even informed me he had made arrangements to attend the dedication of the new "Mormon" temple in Bern, Switzerland. It appeared Dean finally had gotten back "on the right side of the fence".

A few months later I received a call to serve as a "Mormon" missionary in South America for two and one-half years. As often is the case with busy missionaries, I then wrote only infrequently to Dean. His letters to me also stopped and I thought it odd he did not at least answer my Christmas card and letter. Then, months later, I finally received a letter from him. He informed me he had been discharged from the Army and was in Los Angeles, California. He thanked me for my Christmas card and letter, but stated, "You're probably wondering why I haven't written. To tell the truth, I'm ashamed to write. I'm afraid I've slipped again. This time, I don't know if I'll ever be able to get back on the straight and narrow." He went on to tell me how he had discredited his family and felt he could never face them again. Also, given his shame and guilt, he felt it was impossible for him to remain at home. "Just the same," he stated, "if you should return home by way of Los Angeles, I'd sure like to see you again. Please look me up."

I completed my two and one-half years of missionary service. Although I visited Los Angeles in route home, I forgot about Dean being there and didn't look him up. Thereafter, I enrolled at Brigham Young University. Also, although I passed through Dean's hometown several times, I never visited his family.

One Sunday, while attending Church services at the University, one of the speakers mentioned she was from McCammon, Dean's hometown. I sought her out after the meeting and asked if she knew Dean. An odd expression crossed her face and she asked, "Why? What do you know about Dean?" I explained how Dean and I had been in the military service together in Italy. But, I had lost track of him. Although she admitted she knew Dean "rather well", she acted strange and essentially refused to say anything about him. Eventually, however, I became better acquainted with her and she explained why she had acted so strangely when we first met. She not only knew Dean, she had been his girlfriend when he was drafted into the Army. "You know," she said, "Dean was one of the neatest guys I'd ever met. He was so clean-cut and so much fun to be with. But, that was BEFORE he went into the Army. What happened to him there?" She continued, "When he came home, he was completely changed. He was a different person." He had changed so drastically, she decided to have nothing more to do with him.

This girl later told me about some of Dean's problems after he returned home from the Army. He had been involved in one "scrape" after another. In order to finance his drinking habit, he had forged some checks. This resulted in his being arrested. Through the efforts of his family and because of their good name, the judge had placed him on probation, rather than putting him in jail. However, she claimed the judge had warned Dean, "If you don't straighten up, I'll send you to the State Penitentiary!"

One day, Dean's former girlfriend brought me the tragic news. Sobbing and with tears in her eyes, she cried, "Dean's dead!" He had been arrested – at night - in Idaho Falls for drunken driving. The arresting officer placed him in a cell "to sleep it off", prior to his having to appear before the judge for sentencing the next morning. Morning, however, never came for Dean. He twisted and knotted a bed sheet to form a "hangman's noose". When the jailer came to take Dean before the judge, he found only his lifeless body hanging from the cell bars. He had finished what he had attempted to do some four years before, when we were in Italy!

What had started with only "one drink" ended in tragedy. It was a tragedy not only for Dean, but also for his family and friends. Dean's story is one of the reasons why I firmly believe, "One drink is too many"!

"A MOTHER'S INTUITION"

"Only God can make a mother."

I think most people agree, "Mothers are special!" I know my mother is very special. It is our mothers who bring us into the world and give us life. More than anyone else, it is our mothers who love us, guide us, and do all in their power to help us overcome our aches, pains, illnesses, difficulties and the temptations that confront us during our lives.

Many mothers intuitively seem to know when their children need to be loved, held tightly, and protected from the obstacles they encounter in life. They also seem to know when their offspring need to be gently prodded or even pushed and made to stand on their feet – to meet the world on their own. Though it may be difficult for some mothers to do, they sometimes need to reprimand, correct or even punish their children for their wrong doings or mistakes. Then, afterwards, they may comfort and encourage them – so they can gain strength to again press forward. I don't know what I would have done during my life if it had not been for my mother. I always knew I could go to her for consolation and encouragement. Often, when it seemed the whole world was against me or I had lost faith in myself, it was my mother who encouraged and helped me to regain the strength I needed to again face the world.

Something very special about my mother was her seeming to know where I was, what I was doing, and when I needed her help – even though we might be miles apart. This knowing and caring may be innate or it may result from a mother's love for her children. I believe "a mother's intuition" is a special gift – one for which I am very thankful.

I feel fortunate for having been an only child for the first ten years of my life. This meant I did not have to share or compete with other siblings for my mother's attention and affection. I had her all to myself. She read to me, played with me, told me stories, and taught me many important lessons; how to pray, as well as to believe and trust in God; to be honest, to treat others with respect or as you would like them to treat you. She also taught me how to work. I learned how to make beds, do dishes, clean house, cook and even to sew. Knowing how to do the many things my mother taught me has been a boon in my life. Perhaps most important, she taught me primarily by example. As a result, before doing something I often ask myself, "If my mother was here, what would she do or would what I am doing please or displease her?"

Throughout my life, my mother somehow usually seemed to know my whereabouts, my activities, and when I needed her help. As a child, it invariably seemed whenever I had problems, got into fights with my playmates, or needed her help, she would almost magically appear. Everything then would be made right, even though it might mean I would be justifiably reprimanded or even punished – if it was me who had caused the problem. Still, it baffled me as to how she could know who was at fault, especially when she had not been present. As a small child I simply assumed all mothers had such intuitive abilities. However, during adolescence and adulthood, I've repeatedly been impressed that perhaps my mother's intuition with regards to my whereabouts, actions and needs was something extraordinary.

My mother is the eldest of my maternal grandparent's nine children. My Uncle Karl, who is six months younger than me, is the youngest. I also am the eldest of my grandparents numerous grandchildren and they essentially treated me as one of their own children, rather than as a grandson. Karl and I were raised almost like twins. Some family members claimed we were "spoiled rotten" and we could get away with "murder" without getting punished. Although we might have gotten into more than our share of mischief and were almost continually involved in or trying to think up new pranks we might play on others, I honestly believe we never did anything terribly wrong. This primarily was because of my mother's intuition. Furthermore, if we did something wrong we "knew" she would make certain we received our "just reward".

Shortly after beginning high school in the fall of 1947 and after attending Sunday evening Church services, Karl and I decided to walk a couple of girls to the old flour mill on the west side of Rockland. We thought our going through the interior labyrinth of corridors and machinery, in the dark, would present us with opportunities to scare the girls. However, while walking to the old mill, a couple of friends, Richard Kelly and LeRoy Baker, pulled alongside us in Richard's father's car. They invited us to "pile in". The next thing we knew, we were in American Falls, some fifteen miles from Rockland. This was despite Richard not having a driver's license. In fact, none of us were old enough to have a driver's license.

We "cruised" the streets of American Falls, looking for someone we knew or with whom we might visit. In short, we were just looking for something to do. Not encountering any acquaintances or anything of interest, we decided to visit Aberdeen, which is across the Snake River and an additional fifteen miles.

It was rather late at night when we arrived in Aberdeen. The streets were deserted. As we "tooled" down Main Street, Richard, "our chauffeur", suddenly accelerated, while exclaiming, "If there's a speed limit here, we're sure breaking it now!" As we speeded through town, we observed a solitary car stopped for a red light at the town's only traffic light. Honking loudly, Richard passed the car on the wrong side, ran the red light, and roared on through town. Too late, we realized the car we had passed was the local sheriff's!

The shriek of a siren and a flashing red light behind us indicated we were in trouble. Realizing he didn't have a driver's license, Richard accelerated to the maximum. In his efforts to "ditch" the pursuing sheriff, he skidded off from the main highway onto a rough, dirt and gravel country road. This was a mistake! We shortly came to a dead end and the sheriff had us cornered. With his drawn revolver in one hand and an illuminated flashlight in the other, the sheriff cautiously approached our car. He flashed the light inside the car. Upon seeing only the faces of six "scared" kids, his tense countenance seemed to relax. Then, in a gruff voice and, while indicating towards Aberdeen with his gun, he asked Richard, "Do you happen to know what the speed limit is back there?" Richard meekly answered, "No, sir." "Well," he replied, "it happens to be twenty-five miles per hour. I think you were slightly exceeding that!" He then asked Richard, "Do you have a driver's license?" Again, Richard's meek reply was, "No, sir." The sheriff then shined the bright beam of his flashlight onto our faces - one by one. While carefully scrutinizing each of us, he asked our names, our parents' names, where we were from, and what we thought we were doing. Following this inquiry, he again stared intently at each of us. Finally, he said, "If you'll promise not to pull any more stunts like you pulled back there. And, if you'll make sure you get a driver's license before you ever come back, I'll let you go this time. BUT, if I ever catch you acting off like this again, I'll throw the book at you! Understand?"

We timidly expressed our thanks to the sheriff and quietly breathed a sigh of relief. The sheriff holstered his revolver, turned off his flashlight, and returned to his vehicle. We waited till he slowly drove off. We could not believe he let us go with only a reprimand. We sat there in silent disbelief. After Richard regained his composure, he suggested, "Maybe we'd better go home." We heartily agreed. However, soon after starting our return home, the engine to the car started to cough and buck. It would sputter and almost quit, before suddenly coming to life and then again sputter and die. This continued throughout our return trip. We did well to average fifteen miles per hour. As a result, it was early morning when we arrived in Rockland.

I did not dare go home at such an hour. If I did, I knew I'd have to tell my parents where I'd been and what we'd been doing. My mother also would know whether or not I told the truth. My grandparents were away and Karl was staying at home alone. Thus, I decided it would be best if I spent the few hours before having to go to school with him at my grandparents' house.

When I returned home from school that afternoon, I meekly informed my mother, "I stayed with Karl last night." "Yes, I know," she replied. When I asked how she knew, she simply said, "I just know." Then, when I added, "We went to Aberdeen last night." She again said, "I know." "How do you know?" I asked. She then said, "You told me when I talked to you this morning." I didn't remember talking to my mother. I wondered if Karl had told her where we had gone and what we had done. But, when I confronted him about my mother knowing I had stayed with him and our having gone to

Aberdeen, he claimed he knew nothing about it. How did my mother know where we had gone and what we had done?

Basic training at Ft. Ord, California was a difficult period of my life. My having been involved in athletics and having spent days at hard labor on the farm prior to being drafted into the U.S. Army meant I was in much better physical condition than were most recruits. Nevertheless, getting only a few hours sleep at night and being subjected to constant stress, including both the verbal and physical abuses associated with preparing us for war, adversely affected me both physically and mentally. The cold, damp, foggy nights and mornings, followed by blistering hot, dry days on the gun ranges eventually "got to me". I finally realized I had what was commonly referred to as the "Ft. Ord Hack". The "Hack" supposedly resulted from fatigue coupled with extremes in daily weather patterns, i.e. damp and cold nights and mornings, followed by blistering hot and dry days. The "Hack" predisposed one to a severe case of pneumonia.

After struggling through several days of burning fevers, followed by chills, and having a throat so sore I could barely swallow and only talk in whispers, I decided to go on "sick call". This meant going without breakfast, while packing all of my possessions into my footlocker and duffel bag and checking them into the Supply Room. I then would have to "fall into formation" in front of the Orderly Room and be marched to the Post Infirmary, where a medical doctor would examine me. Then, I'd either be sent to the hospital or back to the training company. The latter meant you would be assigned a "detail", such as "KP", for the remainder of the day, as well as perhaps much of the night. Thereafter, you also had to retrieve your belongings from the Supply Room and prepare them for inspection the following morning. Even the thought of these tasks deterred one from going on "sick call" – unless you felt you might die if you didn't!

The doctor at the Post Infirmary examined me. He sprayed some medication into my throat, which stung "like the Dickens" and made it even more difficult for me to talk. He then ordered a nurse to give me an injection of antibiotics, while he scribbled and handed me orders, which stated I was to report back to him each morning for the next three days for additional treatment. I was to do this prior to going into the field. For now, however, I was to return to my basic training company.

I returned from "sick call" to "Item" Company of the 20th Regiment and was assigned the "detail" of scrubbing pots and pans and cleaning filthy grease pits beneath the sinks in the Mess Hall for the rest of the day and well into the night. It was past midnight before I retrieved my belongings from the Supply Room and returned to the barracks. I then had to unpack and put everything in order for morning inspection. I swore, "I'll never go on 'sick call' again. I'll die first!"

After less than two hours of sleep, I arose with a burning fever and a throat so sore I could not even whisper. In fact, I was spitting blood and was so weak I could hardly stand. Nevertheless, after choking down some milk for breakfast, I resolutely prepared to go to the field. I was NEVER going on "sick call" again. Still, I had orders from the doctor at the Post Infirmary to report to him before going into the field. Thus, I laid my rifle on my cot, where I could readily retrieve it upon my return, and was marched to the infirmary with the "poor souls" who were going on "sick call".

A nurse at the Post Infirmary gave me a second injection of antibiotics and stuck a thermometer in my mouth. The doctor looked at the thermometer and then at my throat. He then ordered me to the hospital. I tried to tell him, "I can't go to the hospital. I left my rifle on my cot." This meant I might be court-martialed for not taking better care of my weapon. My efforts, however, were in vain. Try as I might, only unintelligible gurgles issued from my raw throat.

The white-clad nurses at the hospital insisted I remove my field gear, which consisted of my ammo belt, bayonet, backpack, steel helmet and helmet liner. Then, I had to take off my clothes and exchange them for a flimsy gown, which only tied in the back. This would be my uniform while I was in the hospital. They then ordered me into a nice, clean, and oh so soft bed. Despite a nurse ordering me to "roll over" so she could give me yet another injection, I almost immediately went to sleep. Except for nurses periodically disturbing me - to administer more injections - I slept as if in a coma the remainder of that day, throughout the night, and most of the following day. Thereafter, I felt much better. And, within three or four days I felt like my former self. My only problem was my rear end was so sore from so many needle punctures that I could not bear to sit down or even to lay on my back.

The doctor informed me, "When you entered the hospital, one of your lungs was filled with fluid and the other appeared to be rapidly filling." This was why he had prescribed injections of antibiotics every two hours the first day and periodically thereafter. He claimed, "There's no way your lungs could clear and you could completely recover so quickly – especially from such a severe case of pneumonia!" Thus, he ordered me to remain in the hospital for at least another week. This, he claimed was, "To ensure you don't have a relapse." This was despite the fact I felt great and he no longer could find anything wrong with me.

I received a letter from my mother soon after I entered the hospital. She had written it about the time I went on "sick call". Although I had not written nor told her or anyone else at home about not feeling well, she somehow "knew" I was not well. She also said she was praying for my well-being and felt certain I soon would be better. How did she know?

I received almost daily letters from my mother throughout the time I spent in the U.S. Army. These gave me strength and determination to overcome the many obstacles and temptations I encountered. My mother seemed to know what I was doing and when I needed encouragement, as well as when I needed to be reprimanded. Her intuition perhaps can be further exemplified by my futile attempts to surprise my family with my early return home from Italy.

I had been stationed in Italy for almost fifteen months when I was informed that my application for early discharge had been accepted. I would be shipped back to the States and discharged almost three months earlier than originally scheduled. I thought, "Wouldn't it be great to surprise my family by walking into our house weeks before they expected me?" I wrote to them, stating, "It appears I might be home a few days earlier than expected." However, I then explained, "I won't disembark from Italy until May 20. The trip across the Atlantic (by ship) probably will take six or seven days. Then, I'll probably have to spend a week or more at Camp Kilmer, New Jersey, prior to being shipped across the States, which undoubtedly will be by train. Thus, I probably won't arrive at Camp Carson, Colorado before the third of June." I further explained, "Processing at Camp Carson will take perhaps a week. Thus, I'm planning on being discharged from the Army about June 10. I'll then catch a bus back to Idaho, so you can expect me around June 12."

My departure from Italy actually was May 17th, rather than the 20th. The trans-Atlantic crossing took only four days, rather than six or seven. After docking in New York, instead of being sent to Camp Kilmer, we immediately were placed on a plane at Newark and flown straight to Colorado Springs. We arrived at Ft. Carson on a weekend, so were given a three-day pass, after which we would be processed for discharge. Our processing took only three days, rather than the anticipated week. Thus, I calculated I should be home at least two weeks before my family could possibly expect me. I was looking forward to walking into our house and really surprising everyone, including my mother.

I spent my three-day pass with a friend (LeRoy Coombs) at his home in Alamosa, in southwestern Colorado. Thereafter, we returned to Camp Carson in his family's car. Just prior to noon the following Friday, LeRoy and I received our long-awaited discharge papers. He, I and a friend from Riggins, Idaho then decided to see some of the sights in and around Colorado Springs, before LeRoy took the two of us to Denver, where my friend and I would catch a bus to Idaho.

We drove to the top of Pike's Peak, visited the Cheyenne Mountain Zoo, the Garden of the Gods, and several other sites before heading towards Denver. In route to Denver, my Idaho buddy turned to me and asked, "Would you split the cost of gas with me, rather than buy a bus ticket – if I can find a car I can afford in Denver?" I agreed to do so. Thus, instead of going to the bus depot, LeRoy took us on a tour of used car lots on the outskirts of Denver. After carefully considering perhaps a dozen cars and haggling with the overly anxious and determined salesmen, my friend finally purchased a two-door Mercury. It was well past midnight by the time the required paperwork was completed and the car purchased. Although we were both worn out from the day's activities, we were anxious to return home. Thus, we decided to drive straight through from Denver to my family's home in Burley, Idaho. We would take turns driving; one would sleep on the back seat, while the other drove.

Dawn was breaking as I drove over Rabbit Ears Pass in the Colorado Rockies. Then, just outside of Craig, a rear tire blew out. I managed to keep the car on the highway, but when we attempted to change the tire, we found the jack from the trunk would not raise the rear end of the car high enough to get the wheel off the road. By using large, flat rocks from alongside the highway, we finally got the rear end of the car high enough so we could change the tire. We then discovered the spare tire was no good.

I caught a ride into Craig with a passing motorist. There, I got the flat tire fixed and bargained with the service station attendant, "If you'll take me back to the car, we'll buy a new tire from you to replace the worthless spare." Thus, we shortly resumed our journey towards home and we never stopped, except to purchase gas and to get an occasional bite to eat during our trip to Idaho.

It was late afternoon when we finally pulled up in front of my family's home in Burley. My father met us at the door. Instead of acting surprised, he questioned, "Where have you been? What took you so long? Your mother had a big meal prepared and waiting for you hours ago. Now, it's probably cold and ruined!" My efforts to surprise my family were for naught!

After I greeted my mother and two brothers, my father explained, "Despite what you wrote in your letter, your mother was certain you'd be in Camp Carson much sooner than you said you would. She wanted to call Camp Carson several days ago to see if she could locate you, but I told her she'd just be wasting time and money. Anyway, she persisted and yesterday about noon I told her to go ahead and call – if she thought it would do any good." My mother had called about the same time we had been discharged from the Army.

When she inquired as to how she could locate me, she was told, "He left just a few minutes ago with some of his buddies." She then figured I should be home by noon the next day, which I would have been - if we had not had tire problems. Instead of me surprising her, she planned to surprise me with a big meal upon my return.

Although both of my parents have now passed away and I lived away from them for many years, it seemed my mother continued to intuitively know where I was, what I was doing, and whether or not I needed her encouragement. Over the years, her frequent letters and occasional telephone calls were a source of strength to me. She also maintained her interest in my plans and goals and seemed to understand my periodic moods of both elation and depression. Then, more often than not, she was able to bolster my spirits and convince me I always should try to do my best.

I am truly thankful for my mother. I don't know what I would have done throughout my life without her love, patience, faith and encouragement. I thank her and wish I could emulate her good qualities, as well as have the intuition she had to help me better rear my children!

"MY PAL ELMER"

**Every boy needs someone special and Elmer Robinson was my
Brother Gary's special "pal".**

The Rockland Valley is nestled between two rows of mountains
in southeastern Idaho. The town of Rockland has approximately three
hundred inhabitants and is located in the northern portion of the
Valley. The gently rolling hills surrounding the town are a patchwork
of fields of waving grain and barren, plowed fields or "summer
fallow". The common practice in this dry land wheat farming area is
to raise a crop one year and then cultivate the soil the following year,
in order to conserve sufficient moisture to produce a crop every other
or on alternate years. The low mountains on either side of the Valley
serve as summer range for cattle and sheep, most of which are
wintered on the small irrigated farms that border two small streams,
the East and South Forks of Rock Creek, which generally flow
through the Valley from south to north.

Elmer Robinson was a local sheep man. He and his wife, Gwen,
who taught in the local school, lived in a modest, white frame house
located about a block from our home in Rockland. Though Elmer and
Gwen had a genuine love for children, they were not blessed with any
during their marriage of more than twenty years. Thus, Gwen
showered her love upon her pupils, both in the public school and in
the Sunday School class she taught each Sunday in the local
congregation or "ward" of the "Mormon" Church. Elmer also had a
close relationship with many of the neighborhood children and spent
many hours playing "horse" or "bear" with them, or telling about his
adventures while herding his sheep. Many of the stories he related
were about how he had killed predatory animals to protect his sheep.
Although many of the neighborhood children spent much time with
Elmer and were special to him, my brother Gary, who is ten years
younger than me, seemed to be "extra special" to him. Gary virtually
worshipped Elmer and always referred to him as "My Pal Elmer".

Gary was irresistibly drawn to Elmer. More and more frequently,
whenever he was missing from home, we could expect to find him at

"My Pal Elmer's." Elmer seemed to fill a void in Gary's life. He did not treat him as a little boy, but as an equal. In his quiet way, he would counsel or advise Gary, as well as set a proper example for him. Gary often would tell us about how "My Pal Elmer" would do this or that. One could easily discern how Gary not only revered Elmer as a friend, but considered him almost as a father.

As time passed, Gary and Elmer's friendship grew. Whereas Gary often was at Elmer's place, Elmer also began to appear more and more frequently at our house. He would ask if it was "Ok" if Gary had dinner with him and Gwen. Or, "Can Gary go to the sheep camp with me?" The latter particularly thrilled Gary and almost invariably he would return home with glowing accounts of what happened while he and "My Pal Elmer" were herding sheep or living in Elmer's sheep camp. Gary's lifetime ambition was to become a sheepherder – just like "My Pal Elmer".

Elmer presented Gary with a little orphaned lamb or "bummer" one spring. Gary immediately named his new pet "Woolly". He and the neighborhood kids took great delight in giving Woolly her frequent feedings of milk, which she drank through a nipple attached to a pop bottle. Gary and Woolly became almost inseparable. She followed him everywhere and loved to romp and play with him and his playmates. Woolly was a general nuisance for most of our family and our neighbors. She continually seemed to be under foot or where she shouldn't be. But, because Gary loved her so much, we tolerated her. In short, Woolly became the neighborhood pet and pest.

All too soon Woolly changed from a cute little lamb into a full-grown sheep. We now felt it would be impossible to keep her in town any longer. We debated as to whether we should sell Woolly, give her away, or possibly even butcher and eat her. We knew, however, that any of these alternatives would break Gary's heart. What were we to do? It was Elmer who graciously solved our dilemma. In a "man-to-man" transaction he purchased Woolly from Gary and "installed" Woolly as a lead sheep in his herd. Rather than let Gary think he was doing him a favor by purchasing Woolly, he impressed upon him that it was he who was doing him a favor. He claimed Woolly would be an asset to his sheep operation. As a lead sheep, Woolly would readily follow a herder and help to keep the herd together and near the sheep camp at night. This would lessen the chance of the flock being attacked by predators. As a lead sheep, Woolly also would have a bell around her neck and Gary could readily locate and recognize her during his frequent visits to the sheep camp. Thus, through Elmer's wisdom and kindness, Gary regularly renewed acquaintances with his beloved Woolly whenever he accompanied Elmer to his sheep camp.

The years passed and the bond between Gary and Elmer strengthened. Elmer came to my parents one day and asked if Gary could spend the summer with him herding his sheep in the mountains. When my parents consented, Gary was in "seventh heaven". Shortly, he and Elmer were off to the mountains for a summer full of adventures. I was serving in the U.S. Army in Italy when Gary joined Elmer to become a sheepherder. Although the letters I received from Gary were infrequent and short, they invariably gave glowing accounts of his adventures with "My Pal Elmer". Rather than write, he often would merely enclose snapshots in my mother's frequent letters. These usually depicted the lifeless form of a marauding bobcat or coyote he and/or Elmer had shot, as well as different poses of Gary and his faithful white horse "Poncho", which Elmer had given him.

With the approach of winter, Gary had to forsake his adventurous life as a sheepherder and return home to attend school. Our family also had moved from Rockland to Burley, a distance of some fifty miles. Thus, Gary and Elmer would be separated and Gary's visits with Elmer to his sheep camp would be greatly limited. I believe the only thing that kept Gary from rebelling was his remembering his adventures of the past summer and his dreaming about again herding sheep with "My Pal Elmer" the next summer.

Sunday, March 30, 1955, dawned as a bright and beautiful spring morning. However, by mid-morning a ferocious wind was lashing across much of southeastern Idaho. The wind had the icy tinge of winter in it and was even more vicious than had been many of the winds that had accompanied the blizzards of winter. Late in the afternoon the wind died down and a wet snow began to fall on the newly leafed trees and bushes. The branches soon were heavily laden with new snow and many broke under their new burden.

Gary attended Sunday School in Burley that morning. Afterwards, he went to visit a friend in the nearby countryside. About 5:00 o'clock that afternoon, my mother drove out to get Gary. They arrived home at about 5:30. Gary opened the car door and started to get out. He then stopped. The wind had suddenly quit blowing and there was a deathly silence. Although the sky was overcast with gray-white clouds and the sun was not shining, the whole world seemed to radiate with a celestial whiteness. Not even a breeze penetrated or broke the eerie silence. Gary slowly turned towards his mother and softly whispered, "Listen, Mom! It's just like being in a temple!" The presence of something heavenly or spiritual was deeply impressed upon their minds.

Sunday, March 30, also was "Stake Conference Day" for the Rockland Ward and members of the American Falls Stake of the "Mormon" Church. The Conference was to be held during much of the day in Aberdeen, which is about thirty miles from Rockland. Here, members of the Stake would receive counsel from a General Authority of The Church of Jesus Christ of Latter-day Saints from Salt Lake City as well as from local Church leaders. Elmer desired to attend the Conference. Although he was not a member of the Church, as of late he had been investigating or studying the doctrines of the Church and was contemplating being baptized. He had diligently searched for someone to look after his sheep, while he attended the meetings in Aberdeen. But, he could find no one who could do so for him. Reluctantly, he told Gwen she would have to attend the Conference without him.

Gwen did not return from Aberdeen to her home in Rockland until late that evening. The house was dark and empty when she arrived. This was unusual. Elmer usually came home from the sheep camp before dark. She had a feeling of foreboding. After nervously waiting for Elmer for some time, she called his nephew, Bob Robinson, and asked him to accompany her to the sheep camp to look for Elmer.

When Gwen and Bob arrived at the sheep camp, they saw Elmer's pickup. It was not parked where Elmer usually parked it.

Instead, it appeared to have been moved slightly, as if Elmer had backed it around, before heading down the road toward home. As they approached the vehicle, they noted the door on the driver's side was part way open. Then, they saw Elmer's lifeless body sprawled behind the steering wheel. He apparently had seen a coyote or bobcat while leaving the sheep camp. It appeared he had partially opened the pickup door, while retrieving a carbine rifle from behind the pickup seat. It further appeared, while attempting to remove the rifle from its scabbard, the weapon either had fallen from his grasp or the wind had blown the pickup door so it struck the hammer of the rifle. In some manner, the rifle had discharged, while still inside the scabbard, and the bullet had passed through the end of the leather scabbard and then hit Elmer in the head. Death appeared to have been instantaneous!

The time when the tragedy occurred initially was not evident. However, as the news about Elmer's death spread, a neighbor woman reported that, while driving along the road to the highway from her and her husband's ranch, at about 4:30 that afternoon, she had seen Elmer riding his horse back to the sheep camp. He had even waved to her. Later, it was determined that Elmer died between 5:30 and 6:00 p.m. – perhaps at the same time Gary and his mother had had what they considered to be a spiritual experience. Was Gary being bade farewell by Elmer?

There are many things about this life and the life hereafter we do not know or understand. Why were Gary and Elmer drawn so irresistibly together? Why did Elmer's death occur at the time and in the way it did? Also, why did the stormy weather so suddenly change that Sunday afternoon? And, why were both Gary and my mother so impressed with being in the presence of a spiritual being during those beautiful and peacefully quiet moments that briefly occurred during what otherwise was a stormy afternoon? I do not purport to know the answers to these questions. I do know, however, that Elmer filled a void in Gary's life and was a source of joy and a good influence for him. I further believe Gary also filled a void and was a source of joy for the man he called "My Pal Elmer".

"RUSSO" AND "NEGRO"

How can two brothers be so different and yet so much alike?

One of my most prized possessions lies on a shelf above my desk. This is an approximately five-inch-long wild boar's tusk. Whenever I see this relatively small object, it reminds me of "Russo" and "Negro", two young brothers with whom I associated during the early days of my "Mormon" missionary service in the town of Tacuarembo in Uruguay, South America.

I knew virtually no Spanish when I arrived in Uruguay in late February of 1956. This was despite the fact I had taken a Spanish class in high school. It was my most difficult subject. In fact, if it had not been for the assistance I received from the girl who sat behind me, I undoubtedly would have failed this class. My teacher (Mrs. Patricia Taylor) once told my mother, "I was in hopes Juan could learn Spanish, so he might go on a Spanish-speaking mission. But, I fear there is no hope for him. He just can't seem to learn Spanish, no matter how hard he tries!" Now, I was faced with the formidable task of somehow learning and becoming fluent in what was for me a most difficult language.

Soon after my arrival in the mission home in Montevideo, Uruguay, I was assigned to the interior town of Tacuarembo. My companion would be Elder David Peterson from Long Beach, California. Although He would be my first companion, I would be his last. He lacked less than three months to complete his two and one-half-year missionary calling. It seemed Elder Peterson had forgotten how difficult it was to learn a new language, as he offered little assistance to me and rather strongly indicated, "You should be able to learn Spanish on your own. You don't need help from me." Thus, early each morning and during the mid-day "siesta" break, I struggled to learn Spanish. But, my efforts seemed to be in vain. It even took me the better part of a week to learn how to correctly pronounce "Tacuarembo", the town to which I had been assigned. What was I to do?

Two young boys warmly greeted me when I arrived in Tacuarembo. They lived directly across the street from the Church's "Branch" building in which four of us missionaries lived and conducted Church services. One of these boys was thin and wiry, with a fair complexion and a tousled head of blond hair. In contrast, the other boy was somewhat larger, more stoutly built, and had a dark complexion, as well as black hair. I did not learn until later the larger and older-looking boy was a year and a half younger than his smaller, blond brother. The two boys carefully scrutinized me. Then, in faltering English, the blond-headed boy proudly proclaimed, "My name is Russo!" The dark-complexioned boy followed suit and stated, "My name is Negro!" When I told them, "My name is Elder Juan Spillett." They were not able to correctly pronounce my last name. From then on, they simply called me "Elder Juan".

When Elder Peterson told me Russo and Negro were brothers, I could not believe it. They were not at all alike, neither in appearance nor in behavior. Later, when I remarked to Elder Peterson, "Russo and Negro seem to be rather odd names for parents to give their children." He explained, "Russo and Negro are only nicknames." Nevertheless, they were the only names by which I heard these two boys called during the six months I spent in Tacuarembo. Elder Peterson further explained, "Most Uruguayans believe almost all Russians or "Russo's" have blond hair. Therefore, 'Russo' is a common nickname for boys with blond hair. Similarly, boys with a dark complexion and black hair frequently are called 'Negro'." I asked Russo and Negro what their "real" names were. They told me, but I can't remember what they were. And, I never heard anyone - not even their parents - call them by such.

I think Russo and Negro spent more time in the Tacuarembo "Branch" building and with us missionaries than they spent at home with their family. The first thing each morning, usually while we were eating breakfast, they would appear inside the kitchen with us. They did not even knock at the door, but simply walked in as if they lived with us, which they virtually did. One day, Elder Peterson told them they had to knock before entering. Thus, from then on they hurriedly knocked before entering on their own. When we Elders returned to the "Branch" at mid-day or in the evening, we could expect Russo and

Negro to quickly appear. They also insisted upon attending and being involved in ALL of our Church meetings. If someone was needed to offer an opening or closing prayer, or even give a talk, we could depend upon them.

Russo and Negro laughed and made fun of my attempts to learn Spanish. However, through my companion, they informed me they wanted to learn English and if I taught them English, they would teach me Spanish. Thus, we began to tutor each other. I would teach them a phrase in English, which they would quickly mimic. They then would teach me phrases in Spanish. These they would pronounce very carefully and slowly and I would painstakingly attempt to repeat them. This almost invariably would cause them to snicker or laugh, while pointing at me. I assumed their mirth was a result of my poor pronunciation, but soon learned this was not the case.

After a couple of weeks of intense study, I felt I had mastered a fair number of the phrases Russo and Negro had taught me. I decided it was time to try my newly acquired language skills on some of the members of our congregation. Following Sunday School services, while most members of our congregation were amiably visiting in the foyer of the "Branch", I approached an elderly sister and repeated one of the phrases Russo and Negro had taught me. A startled expression crossed her face and her mouth literally dropped open. "Maybe," I thought, "my pronunciation still needs some work". So, I repeated the phrase and continued with more of the phrases my mentors had taught me. The lady was aghast! She grabbed me by the arm and steered me towards my companion. Then, in an animated voice, she explained something to him. Instead of Russo and Negro teaching me what I thought they were, they had taught me as many vulgar words and expressions as they possibly could. I could have "murdered" the little brats!

I can still see and hear Russo and Negro giggling and laughing while I labored to learn and correctly pronounce what they were teaching me. They had played a real joke on me! Still, because of them, I probably learned some facets of Spanish most missionaries do not acquire!

My relationship with Russo and Negro was "cooled" for a number of days following this incident. They then came and put their arms around me and, with tears in their eyes, explained they were sorry for what they had done. They didn't mean any harm. And, it wasn't long before they were teaching me Spanish again, with me periodically checking with Elder Peterson to ensure they didn't play any more tricks.

The large, walled-in yard behind the Tacuarembo "Branch" building was a tangled mess of rubble and vegetation. It appeared this area had served as the neighborhood dump ground for many years. Perhaps because we repeatedly admonished Ruso and Negro not to throw or play ball inside the building, one day they enthusiastically approached me with the idea of cleaning up the back yard and making a volleyball and basketball court or "concha" out of it. I was skeptical. How could we get the rubble and trash out? The only entrance was through a narrow passageway alongside the building. Within a matter of hours, Russo and Negro returned with two wheelbarrows they had borrowed from neighbors. With some difficulty, one could maneuver these through the narrow passageway. I then asked, "What do we do with the trash when we get it to the street? We can't leave it there!" This deterred them only until the next morning. They then triumphantly proclaimed another neighbor would let us use his pickup truck to haul the trash to a dump outside of town.

Russo and Negro enlisted the aid of my new companion, Elder Marvin Spresser from Ohio, and the other two missionaries in the "Branch", Elders Larry Day from Idaho and Gaylord Hansen from Arizona. We then began in earnest to clean up the back yard. In no time they also spread the word and we soon were virtually over run with enthusiastic young men who wanted to help. Russo and Negro had extolled to other boys in the neighborhood the virtues of being able to play ball on a beautiful "concha". They even had begun to organize a club and were enthusiastically talking about competing with other clubs in the area. As we worked long hours together in the arduous task of clearing out the back yard and then developing a "concha" upon which we could play ball, young men who previously had ignored or even ridiculed us missionaries suddenly became our friends.

We finally cleared the back yard. It was unbelievable how many wheelbarrow and then pickup loads of trash we moved. But, we then found the remaining black, clay soil became a mire of mud whenever it rained. When wet, it also became so slick it was almost impossible to run or play on it. In addition, anyone entering the "Branch" from the "concha" tracked dirt or mud into the building. Russo and Negro again devised a solution. There was coarse sand, free for the taking, in a nearby riverbed. All we had to do was haul and spread it on our "concha". Pickups and wheelbarrows again were borrowed. And, with the assistance of the young men Russo and Negro enlisted, our "concha" soon had a beautiful, smooth, sand surface upon which we could play ball in almost any kind of weather.

Until we could raise sufficient funds to purchase a basketball hoop and standard, volleyball was the major activity on our "concha". Although the walls surrounding the court were a good eight feet high, they were not high enough to deter volleyballs from frequently being hit over them and into the neighbors' yards. When this happened, the young boys would nimbly scramble over the walls and into the neighbor's yards to retrieve the balls. These actions, however, resulted in complaints from the neighbors. What to do?

We finally decided the only practical solution was to purchase wire and build a fence an additional eight feet above the walls surrounding the "concha". This we did. Although it did not deter all of the hard-hit balls from going into the neighbors' yards, it deterred sufficient numbers to appease them.

Young men and then young women, who came to cheer on the boys in their athletic prowess, seemed to come out of the woodwork. Overnight, because of our "concha", we missionaries became friends of virtually all of the young people in the neighborhood. Most now would warmly greet us whenever we met in the street; whereas, it formerly was not "cool" for young people in the area to even admit they knew the "Mormon" missionaries. What a change!

Our "concha" became so popular there were not enough daylight hours to accommodate all who wanted to play on it. We needed lights, so ball games could continue after dark. Though most of the young people associated with our "concha" had very little money, we soon were able to raise sufficient funds to provide minimal lighting. We then could play even at night. The "concha" became so popular we had to establish rules, which included: There would be no playing on Sundays or while meetings were being conducted inside the "Branch" building. And, all play would stop and the lights would be turned off at 10:00 p.m. We had to get some sleep some time!

Older people also became interested in our "concha". They would come to watch and enjoy the activities of the young people, as well as to visit with each other. Some of the women indicated they would like to provide something to eat for those who came to participate in the activities. But, they didn't have anywhere to prepare hot food. With the help of our young friends, we constructed a fireplace and small barbecue pit in the back corner of the "concha". One thing led to another and before we knew it, our "concha" became the center of neighborhood activity. Without even realizing it, Russo's and Negro's ideas and enthusiasm for constructing a "concha" had become the best proselyting tool the "Mormon" missionaries in Tacuarembo had ever had. What's more, it was great fun!

I also had begun to learn Spanish. Although I still was not fluent, I could understand most of what others said, as well as communicate, in one way or another, what I wanted to say to them. Despite their initial misdirection, Russo and Negro had become true mentors for me.

As the rash of activities associated with the construction of our "concha" culminated and we faced primarily the task of organizing and supervising its use, I received a telegram from the Mission President in Montevideo. I was being transferred to Melo, a city in central Uruguay. When I told Russo and Negro and my many other friends in Tacuarembo about my pending departure, both they and I shed tears.

My dear friends organized a "farewell party", which, of course, was held on our "concha". Many kind and loving words were spoken, much food was eaten, and many tears of parting were shed. As I was leaving Tacuarembo, Russo and Negro lovingly wrapped their arms around me and tearfully told me how they had wanted to buy me a special present. But, they had spent all their money on our "concha". Therefore, if it was Ok with me, they wanted to give me one of their most prized possessions – a tusk their father had given them from a wild boar he had shot. I could not refuse their offer. This is why the boar's tusk on the shelf above my desk is one of my most prized possessions. It reminds me of the two young boys who helped me learn Spanish and taught me that working and playing together is a wonderful way to develop bonds of friendship. It also reminds me that some of the first Spanish I learned was vulgarisms taught to me by Russo and Negro – two of my young brothers in Tacuarembo, Uruguay!

MY MOST MEMORABLE CHRISTMAS

My first Christmas as a "Mormon" missionary was both the saddest and happiest I've experienced.

Christmas is a special time of year, one many of us await with anticipation. I have spent Christmas in a variety of lands and places, such as in Italy, Paraguay, Uruguay, Ecuador, India, Iran, Mexico and Australia. However, during my youth I spent almost every Christmas at the home of my maternal grandparents, whom I knew as "Daddy-pa" and "Mama". They lived in a large, brown, wooden-framed house on the "Bench", about a mile from the small town of Rockland in southeastern Idaho. Although my parents and I also lived in Rockland during the summer, we usually lived in Idaho Falls during the winter, where my father taught school. From Thanksgiving onwards, I could hardly wait to return to Rockland to spend Christmas with my grandparents, as well as with my uncles, aunts, other relatives and friends.

On Christmas Eve, the Primary children of the Rockland Ward of the "Mormon" Church invariably would present a Christmas program in the Church house, which many called the "brick hall" and was located across the street from the school. Virtually everyone in the Valley, whether they were members of the "Mormon" Church or not, came to watch the children perform. It was amazing how, by both their looks and actions, the adults identified the performing children with their parents. Following the program, the rows of wooden benches were moved to the sides of the hall and a children's dance was held. Some children would attempt to dance with each other or with their parents, most simply milled about the hall, talking, giggling and teasing each other. The adults, for the most part, huddled in small groups around the edge of the hall, while visiting with each other. All, however, awaited the grand finale or the arrival of Santa Claus.

There would be the stomping of feet at the door to the Church house. The dance music would stop and the children and parents would crowd around the entrance to the hall. Santa then would prance through the milling crowd, greeting some of the adults by name and shaking their extended hands. As he made his way through the center of the hall, he usually made remarks about his reindeer and the weather at the North Pole. Then, after mounting the steps to the stage, he would be seated on a chair in the center of the stage. The children would be instructed to form a line, so each could greet Santa and tell him what they wanted for Christmas and whether or not they had been good during the past year. Santa then presented each child with a brown paper bag filled with candy, nuts and perhaps an orange. As this was taking place, many of the parents and older children would ponder or debate among themselves as to "Who is Santa this year?"

Following the Primary program and activities at the Church, our family would retreat to my grandparents' home, to await a second or "personal" visit from Santa. In some manner, I don't know how, Daddy-pa always arranged for Santa to visit his family. We would assemble around the large Christmas tree in the living room at the front of the house. Shortly there would be a knock at the door and Santa would be ushered in. He would greet each of us by name and inquire of each of us - young and old alike - whether or not we had been good during the past year, what we wanted for Christmas, and what we planned to do during the coming year. We had to be truthful, because Santa seemed to know everything about us! After our "interviews" or "personal evaluations", Santa would let us select "JUST ONE" of our presents from beneath the tree. We could open this present during his visit. But, we had to wait until morning to open the rest of our presents.

After a sleepless night, because we wondered what our other presents might be, we boys would rush upstairs from the "boy's bedroom" in the basement. But, before we could open our presents, we first had to eat a "good" breakfast. Then, after hurriedly eating, we finally were allowed to open our presents. Thereafter we would assemble our prizes and try out each of our toys – before determining what each of the other family members had received. Past mid-day, we assembled at the long table in the dining room for Christmas dinner. As the family grew in numbers, additional tables were set in the kitchen for the smaller children.

The array of bounteous foods that Mama provided for us were a sight to behold. Wherein most families perhaps would have a turkey or a ham as a main course, we invariably had turkey and ham, as well as perhaps a large roast, a goose or some other meat dish. Of course, there would be the "trimmings", such as hot, homemade rolls, potatoes and gravy, a variety of vegetables, and on and on. For desert, we could count on pie, cake, fruit and possibly ice cream. When you felt you couldn't eat another bite, Daddy-pa would bring out the large boxes of chocolates, which he received from business associates and friends. These were in addition to the bowls of "hard-tack" and other types of candies scattered about the house.

Christmas at Daddy-pa's and Mama's home was truly a special occasion. But, despite the many memorable Christmases I experienced during my youth, my most memorable Christmas occurred during my first year as a "Mormon" missionary in South America. This also was both my saddest and happiest Christmas.

Seasons south of the Equator are the reverse of what they are in the northern hemisphere. Hence, Christmas in much of South America occurs during the warmest part of the year. December in Uruguay is similar to July in Idaho. Perhaps in keeping with the reversed seasons, many Latin Americans celebrate Christmas with fireworks, similar to how we celebrate the 4th of July in the United States!

The 1956 Christmas season was my first in the mission field. I was serving in the interior town of Melo, Uruguay. I and the other three missionaries in the Melo "Branch" had purchased a more than ample supply of fireworks. We were going to celebrate Christmas "like the locals"! We also had made plans with the young men of the "Branch" to go out into the countryside or "campo" on Christmas Eve. After cooking and eating an "asado" or big barbeque feast and playing games, we would set off our fireworks. Thereafter, we would sleep out under the stars, before holding a sunrise service on Christmas morning - to commemorate the birth of our Savior. However, a short while before this anticipated event, I received a telegram from the Mission President in Montevideo. I was being made a "Senior Companion" and being transferred to Asuncion, Paraguay!

Stepping off from the plane at the airport in Asuncion was like stepping into an oven. The humid heat was almost unbearable. There then were three "branches" of the "Mormon" Church in Paraguay and a total of twelve "Elders" or "Mormon" missionaries – four assigned to each "branch", all of which were in the capital city of Asuncion. Although a fair number of Paraguayans had joined the Church, most had immigrated to the United States, Uruguay or Argentina. The immigration of newly-baptized Paraguayans perhaps could be attributed as much to their desire to escape the tyrannies of a military dictatorship as to their wanting to join with larger or stronger bodies of Church members.

I was assigned to the recently established Sajonia "Branch", which was on the far side of the city from the other two "branches", namely Moroni and Amambay. Although I had been in the mission field only ten months and was still having difficulty with Spanish, I would be a "Senior Companion". In terms of missionary service, I was the youngest "Senior Companion" in the Uruguayan Mission. My "Junior Companion", Elder Kent Calvert from Reno, Nevada, had only recently arrived from the States and knew practically no Spanish. Thus, I would have to do most of the speaking for the two of us. I was overwhelmed with my new calling.

General Strossner's military government in Paraguay required us to obtain permission from the local authorities to hold our regular Sunday services, as well as for any meetings that might involve five or more people. Two soldiers then would be ordered to attend our meetings, apparently to ensure we did not plan any insurrections or say anything against the government. Because of government restrictions and possible reprisals, many Paraguayans were afraid to meet or even be seen with us. Besides these restrictions, which often made it difficult for us to teach the gospel, the intolerable heat and humidity also made life difficult.

The building in which we lived and held our Church meetings in Sajonia, was located on a main thoroughfare. An electric trolley passed immediately in front of the building. The rumbling of passing trolley cars and the associated clanging bells and sparks from the overhead wires and metal arms were enough to awaken even the most sound of sleepers. In addition, there was an open-air movie theater or "cinema" just down the street. High-volume movie sound tracks resounded from this "cinema" for much of every night. Less than a block down another street was a public park with "carnival" rides and an open-air dance pavilion, from which emanated the loudest imaginable music over loud speakers throughout most nights. If these were not enough, there was a small produce market across the street, in front of the "Branch", where market activities, including vociferous bargaining, commenced early each morning. In short, if you were lucky, you might get an hour or two, at most, of uninterrupted sleep between 2:00 and 4:00 a.m. during each night!

A District Missionary Conference was scheduled for Christmas Day. It would be held in the Moroni "Branch", on the far side of Asucion from Sajonia. Traveling from Sajonia to Moroni normally entailed catching a tram to the center of the city, then catching a bus, and finally walking the last few blocks to the Moroni "Branch" building that was located in a high-class residential area.

It was a typically hot, muggy day when we four missionaries in Sajonia arose on Christmas morning. There was no food in the "Branch" for breakfast. We normally bought bananas or other fresh fruits and bread each morning from the market in front of where we lived. Being Christmas day, however, the market wasn't open. "Oh well", we thought, "we can buy something to eat in the nearby shops". But, these also were closed. Likewise, neither the trolley nor the buses were operating. Christmas was truly a holiday in Paraguay! Furthermore, we would have to walk the approximately eight miles to the Moroni "Branch".

While complaining to each other about being hungry, we spent the morning writing letters and reminiscing about Christmas at home. Around 10:00 o'clock, we decided we'd better start our long trek to Moroni, in order to attend the District Meeting scheduled for late that afternoon. We surmised, "Surly we'll find a café or restaurant along the way, which will be open and where we can get something to eat." However, none were open.

The heat was untenable and, in addition to our hunger pangs, we soon were "dying" of thirst. This only caused us to complain more vociferously. Because of my recent transfer, I had not received any mail from home for several weeks, let alone any Christmas packages. Besides being hot, tired, hungry and thirsty, I was so homesick I could hardly stand it.

After walking for what seemed like hours, we finally chanced upon a filthy liitle bar that was open. This establishment consisted of a wooden frame, which supported rusty sheets of tin. These sheltered a greasy counter and a few rickety, wooden stools, which stood on a filthy, dirt floor. We entered the bar and eagerly asked the bartender if he had something we could drink and eat. He brought us each a bottle of orange soda and said he would cook us some meat and potatoes. The pop, which was warm and sickening sweet, did little to quench our thirst. Then, when the bartender eventually served each of us with a tin plate of fried meat and potatoes, they were so covered with flies that we could not stomach more than a few bites. Thus, we paid our bill and left our uneaten food and partially-filled bottles of pop, before continuing our trek to Moroni and our District Missionary Meeting.

As we trudged along the hot, sandy streets of Asuncion, I questioned, "Why am I here - especially when I could be home with my family and enjoying Christmas? Why am I wasting my time in a place like this - where the people don't want to listen to our gospel message anyway?" I literally had "had it!"

We arrived late for the meeting at the Moroni "Branch". The other missionaries wanted to know what took us so long. They had delayed starting the meeting, waiting for us. We then held what primarily was an instructional or training meeting. This was followed by a testimony meeting, during which each of us testified or bore witness to the truthfulness of the Gospel of Jesus Christ and its importance in our lives. During this testimony meeting, an indescribable warmth and joyful feeling came over me. Suddenly, I knew why I was in Paraguay and why it was so important for me to strive to teach the Gospel of Jesus Christ to the people of this country. This was the most important thing I could be doing – no matter how difficult it might be. I also began to realize how blessed I had been throughout my life. I also felt a strong desire to share my blessings with others.

What had been the saddest Christmas day of my life became my happiest. Suddenly, I was thrilled to be where I was and doing what I was trying to do. Perhaps for the first time, I began to partially realize the true meaning of Christmas and the importance of Christ's gift of salvation or eternal life for us. I was almost overwhelmed with a feeling of peace and happiness. It was an indescribable experience.

Following the testimony meeting, the missionaries from the Moroni and Amanbay "Branches" informed us, "We have a surprise for you!" They escorted us into the dining room. There, they presented us with a Christmas feast. Somehow they had acquired a turkey, with all the trimmings. Admittedly, it was not the same as my grandmother's cooking. Still, it was a fantastic meal and one I'll never forget.

Our late-night trek back to the Sajonia "Branch" was entirely different than our journey earlier that day to Moroni. We laughed and joked, rather than complained to each other. The distance seemed to be much shorter. The sky was clear and the stars seemed to be brighter and more numerous than I previously had witnessed. Our earlier dismal moods and misgivings about being in Paraguay had been replaced with joy and thanksgiving for the opportunity to try to serve the people in this country. The meaning of the Savior's words, "It is more blessed to give than receive" (Acts 20:35) held new meaning to me. I hope I always remember the lessons I learned that day and that I may again experience the warmth and happiness I felt during "My Most Memorable Christmas".

NANCY

"All we possess belongs to the Lord. We are only temporary guardians of our possessions."

Nancy was the prettiest and sweetest little girl imaginable. Her natural beauty immediately attracted attention. Her sweet and loving disposition also endeared her to everyone she met, young and old alike. It would be difficult to imagine a sweeter or more perfect child than five-year-old Nancy.

I met Nancy and her parents while serving as a "Mormon" missionary in Asuncion, Paraguay. I recently had been transferred from the Sajonia "Branch" to the Moroni "Branch", because I was suffering from severe infections of hepatitis and amoebic dysentery. The quiet neighborhood and better amenities in Moroni , hopefully, would help me to recuperate sooner from my maladies. While still trying to "get back on my feet", I was called to be the President of the Moroni "Branch". Elder Heber Dale Bartholomew from southern Utah would be my companion and we would serve with two other missionaries, one of which was the District President. Shortly thereafter, Mrs. Thomas, whose husband (a U.S. Marine sergeant) served with the nearby U.S. Embassy, inquired about the schedule for our religious services. Although her husband was not a member of the Church, she was a devout and active "Mormon". She also desired that her seven-year-old son participate in Church services and activities, to be prepared for baptism when he became eight years old or the "age of accountability". Although neither Mrs. Thomas nor her son spoke Spanish, they regularly attended Church services on Sunday and Primary activities on Saturday afternoons. Despite their inability to effectively communicate with the Paraguayans who attended these services, she and her son were welcomed members of our congregation. The Paraguayans delighted in practicing their limited English on them, as well trying to help them learn Spanish.

Several weeks after Mrs. Thomas and her son joined our congregation, they brought Nancy with them to Primary. Mrs. Thomas explained that, while attending a cocktail party presented by the U.S. Embassy to welcome Nancy's parents to Paraguay, Nancy's mother observed Mrs. Thomas neither drank nor smoked. She then commented, "You'd think you were a good 'Mormon', the way you don't drink or smoke like the rest of us." To this, Mrs. Thomas said, "Thank you! I am a 'Mormon' and I try to be a good one."

Sometime later, Nancy's mother confided to Mrs. Thomas, "My husband and I used to be 'good Mormons', but we found it was just too difficult, especially after we joined the State Department. Therefore, we've left such things as religion behind". Upon further discussion, Nancy's mother indicated both she and her husband wished their daughter could have the "good influence of the 'Mormon' Church in her life." Mrs. Thomas asked if Nancy might accompany her and her son to Primary and other Church services, which is how I became acquainted with Nancy and eventually with her parents.

Nancy's mother and father were refined and very good-looking people. They had lived in Denver, Colorado, before joining the State Department. Her father was an engineer and had attained considerable recognition in his profession. As a result, he had been offered a position with the U.S. State Department and had worked in several locations, the last of which was Washington, D.C. He also had received regular promotions. Paraguay, however, was his first foreign assignment and it was a new experience for him and his family.

I first met Nancy's parents several weeks after she started attending Church meetings with the Thomas's. I was impressed as to how friendly and outgoing they were. They were truly exceptional. I also quickly assessed that they adored their daughter Nancy. They later confided to me that Nancy would be their "only child". Her mother had had so much difficulty in giving birth to Nancy that – against her husband's wishes - she insisted upon having an operation so that she would not bear any more children. Given the joy Nancy had brought into their lives, I think she regretted having had such an operation. Both parents idolized their daughter. But, despite or perhaps because of the love and affection they showered upon her, Nancy was an amazingly kind and obedient child. It seemed she simply loved everyone she met. They, in turn, loved her.

Despite Nancy not being able to communicate in Spanish, the Paraguayans immediately loved her dearly and welcomed her into their lives and all of their activities. Whenever they played games, the Paraguayan children vied with each other to have Nancy on their side. The adults likewise adored this sweet little girl from "Norte America". In turn, Nancy loved and showed her affection for them. She even persisted in having her parents come to Sunday School and Primary with her, so they could meet her many "dear friends". I was impressed her parents would have liked to join our congregation and again become active "Mormons". But, when I approached them about doing so, with some embarrassment they answered, "No. I don't think we could."

One Sunday morning Nancy didn't come to Sunday School with the Thomas's. When I asked Mrs. Thomas, "Where is Nancy?" she explained, "The Embassy is holding a farewell party for the Ambassador at the country club." And, "Because the party will likely last all day and into the night, Nancy's parents thought it best she accompany them, rather than attend Church services with us."

There was a loud knock late that evening on the front door of the Moroni "Branch". It was a driver from the U.S. Embassy. He appeared to be upset and asked to see "Elder Spillett". When I told him, "I'm Elder Spillett." He insisted that my companion and I accompany him to the hospital. It was not until we were in the Embassy vehicle that he explained, "Little Nancy has drowned! Her parents asked me to get you."

Nancy's grief-stricken parents met us upon our arrival at the hospital. When they warmly embraced us, we could smell the strong odor of alcohol on their breath. Perhaps noting the expressions upon our faces, they quickly apologized for their "condition". They then tearfully pleaded, "Can't you please use 'your' priesthood authority to bring our dear Nancy back to us?"

We were led into a room where a large machine was pumping air into and out of the lifeless body of dear little Nancy. Her distraught mother kept insisting, "She can't die! You must bring her back!" My companion and I tried to explain, "It's not in our power to do other than what is the will of Our Father in Heaven." She wouldn't accept this for an answer. Instead, she kept insisting, "You've got to bring her back!" She became so distraught and so emotional the doctor gave her a sedative and had her taken out of the room. In contrast, her husband simply stood to one side, while silently weeping and sobbing.

Elder Bartholomew and I then asked everyone to "Please leave the room." The physician insisted he must remain with the little girl. We indicated we would accept his presence, but tried to gently move Nancy's father and others out of the room. We then closed the door and kneeled down together. In earnest prayer we pleaded with the Lord to let us know His will concerning dear little Nancy. Thereafter, we laid our hands on Nancy's head and gave her a blessing, asking that 'the Lord's will be done." I was impressed and think my companion likewise was impressed that the Lord wished to take Nancy "home". For some reason, over and over in my mind kept resounding the phrase, "The Lord giveth, and the Lord taketh away." I was impressed that Nancy was such a dear spirit the Lord would not entrust her upbringing to any but the most spiritual of parents.

We later pieced together some of the happenings of that fateful day during the farewell party for the American Ambassador. Apparently, from the start the party had been little more than a drinking social for the adults. The children essentially were left alone or to themselves. Early in the afternoon, a nearby property owner had accosted some of the children for throwing rocks at the ducks and geese on his pond. He then accompanied them back to their parents and reprimanded the parents for not taking better care of their children. Nevertheless, the parents quickly dismissed the incident and continued their drinking until dusk. They then began to look for their children. All but Nancy were soon located. A search was called and eventually Nancy's lifeless body was found floating, face down, on the pond where the landowner previously had castigated the children for disturbing the ducks and geese. Oddly, the water in the pond was no more than two feet deep in the deepest part. Even as small as Nancy was, if she had been standing, the water would have come up only to her waist. How could she have drowned in such shallow water? And, why had not any of the other children missed her presence?

Nancy's bereaved parents accompanied her body back to the States for burial. They did not return to Paraguay. I later was informed that Nancy's father had resigned his position with the State Department and I do not know what became of Nancy's parents thereafter. Still, I was strongly impressed that the Lord had entrusted to them one of His choice spirit children. But, they perhaps had not proven worthy of this trust. Thus, the Lord had taken sweet little Nancy back and her parents had lost their most precious possession. How often might not this be the case with us with regards to our most precious possessions or blessings? Are we so much taken up with the things of this world that we fail to realize "All we possess belongs to the Lord" and "We are only temporary guardians of our possessions"?

"I NEVER WANT TO BE RICH AGAIN!"

"There is that maketh himself rich, yet hath nothing. There is that maketh himself poor, yet hath great riches."   Prov. 13:7

"Seek not for riches but for wisdom and behold, the mysteries of God shall be unfolded unto you, then shall you be made rich."
Doctrine & Covenants 6:7

I was transferred to the Sajonia "Branch" in Asuncion, Paraguay after having served ten months as a "Mormon" missionary in Uruguay. Shortly thereafter I was stricken with infectious hepatitis and amoebic dysentery and was sent to the Moroni "Branch", on the other side of Asuncion, to recuperate from my maladies. I met and became well acquainted with Sister Violeta Daxzon and "her children" during the approximately seven months I served in Moroni.

Sister Daxzon did not favorably impress me when we first met. In fact, our first meeting was downright unpleasant. She stormed into the upstairs bedroom, where I was confined to bed, and gave me to understand, "You should return to the Sajonia 'Branch' where you belong!" And, "Elder Reynolds," the missionary sent from Moroni to Sajonia to take my place, "should be permitted to return to Moroni where he belongs!"

It was several weeks before I learned Sister Daxzon's harsh words were not because she disliked me, but because of her concern for Elder Reynolds. His first assignment as a missionary in the Uruguayan Mission was in the Moroni "Branch" and he was frustrated with trying to learn Spanish and adjusting to a new culture, as well as the fact he was suffering the pangs of homesickness. Sister Daxzon realized this and felt her and "her children" could help him. However, my taking his place had thwarted her plans to do so.

Despite our abrasive first meeting and my unfavorable initial opinion of Sister Daxzon, I eventually learned she was one of the most loving and caring women I have had the privilege to meet. Gradually, I developed a great admiration and then a genuine love for this dear sister. Little by little I also learned the remarkable story of her life, which is one of numerous trials and triumphs.

Sister Daxzon proudly proclaimed, "I am Paraguayan!" In reality, she was a citizen of the United States of America. Perhaps she also could be classified as an Argentinean. Her father was an American diplomat in Argentina when he met and fell in love with and married her mother. Her mother belonged to a wealthy, aristocratic Argentinean family. Soon after her parents were married they returned to the States. Thereafter, both her brother and she were born in the States and she spent her childhood and early school years here. Her mother then died and she was sent to live with her maternal grandmother in Argentina. Her brother, however, remained with their father in the States. Some years later her father also died.

Sister Daxzon led an indulgent and sheltered life, as if often the case with well-to-do or aristocratic Latin Americans. However, when she was in young adulthood, her grandmother died. Her brother, who was a few years older than her, came to Argentina to help settle their grandmother's estate. He planned to take his sister back to the States. But, before he could do so, he suddenly died. The shock of losing one loved one after another was more than Sister Daxzon could bear. The wealth to which she had always been accustomed and which should have been her inheritance also disappeared. She became so despondent she attempted to take her own life. Somehow her life was saved and she eventually regained her composure and completed nurse's training and became employed as a nurse. Eventually, she fell in love and married. Life again seemed to hold promise, but the premature deaths of her first two children, followed by the tragic death of her husband, left her bereaved and again despondent. She turned to alcohol, suffered a mental breakdown, and was committed to a mental institution - where she remained for several years.

Sister Daxzon explained, "Those I loved most always seemed to die prematurely." Also, "Money," which she had an abundance of during her early life, "seemed to bring me only misery, instead of happiness." She repeatedly told me, "I never want to be rich again - because I never was truly happy when I was rich!"

Following her release from a mental institution, Sister Daxzon resumed her career as a nurse and eventually remarried. She and her husband moved from Argentina to Paraguay, where she had a baby daughter, Hilda. She was extremely happy with her baby girl, but her husband started to drink and soon became an alcoholic. He then deserted them and Sister Daxzon was left to face the world alone with her small daughter. She once confided to me, "If it had not been for my love and concern for Hilda, I would have committed suicide. But, I couldn't imagine leaving her alone in the world." Nevertheless, her husband had left her destitute and she could rely only upon her training as a nurse to support herself and Hilda. Although she managed to eke out a living for the two of them, being a nurse meant she had to spend long hours away from her daughter. Thus, she began to search for a means whereby she could earn a living and still remain at home with little Hilda. It was during this trying period she first met the "Mormon" missionaries, who taught her the Gospel of Jesus Christ. This completely changed her life. For the first time she learned how to pray and to have faith in her Father in Heaven. She shortly was impressed she perhaps could earn a living by cooking meals at home and then distributing them, while still hot, to others. This she could do by placing the food in "viandas" or small, metal containers, which were stacked one on top of each other. She, thus, could earn a living, while still remaining at home with her daughter.

Sister Daxzon then began to encounter first one orphan or deserted child after another on the streets of Asuncion. She was moved to take these poor little waifs home and to raise them as her own. As a result, her life began to take on more and more meaning and purpose. When I met her, her "family" consisted of six children, including her daughter Hilda. She and "her children" also committed to purchasing a modest home in which they could live. Though this cause united their efforts, it often was difficult for them to earn enough just to live, let alone make a monthly house payment. Their lot was one of constant struggle and their faith and perseverance were frequently tested.

Sister Daxzon spent long hours cooking and preparing meals, while the children's task was to promptly deliver the hot "vianda" meals to their customers. The children also attempted to earn additional money with jobs such as shining shoes and delivering papers. Life was not easy for them.

Despite Sister Daxzon's and "her children's" constant struggle to make ends meet, they comprised one of the happiest and closest knit "families" imaginable. During my companion's and my frequent visits with them, I never failed to marvel at their unity and faith. Visiting them gave me added strength and courage to face my seemingly minor difficulties. Not infrequently during our visits, Sister Daxzon would state, "I never want to be rich again!" She also would explain how she feared worldly wealth might cause her to forget or quit trying to fully live the Gospel of Jesus Christ; thereby, losing the happiness she finally had realized after so many years of sorrow and despair.

I slowly came to realize, although Sister Daxzon and "her children" were extremely poor with respect to worldly wealth, they were among the richest people I have known with respect to "storing up treasures in heaven." Rarely does one encounter someone as rich in faith and love as were she and "her children". Also, rarely does one encounter a "family" as united, happy and willing to share and as concerned about the welfare of others as were they.

Sister Daxzon and "her children" religiously attended and participated in all of our Church meetings except Sunday School. Although some of "her children" attended Sunday School each week, they took turns staying home to help her prepare and deliver the Sunday mid-day meals for their customers. During one of our visits in their home, Sister Daxzon pensively asked my companion and me, "Are we doing wrong by preparing meals for others on Sunday and not attending Sunday School?" I didn't know how to answer her question. Cooking and delivering "vianda" meals to their customers probably was the only way they could earn a living. Their customers also had to eat on Sundays, the same as during other days of the week. Would this justify their working on Sundays? But, rather than give a direct answer, I was moved upon to open the Bible to the Ten Commandments, in the Book of Deuteronomy. Together we then read aloud the second Commandment (Deut. 5:12-15), wherein the Lord tells us we should, "Keep the Sabbath Day holy."

"That settles it!" exclaimed Sister Daxzon. "Our customers will just have to eat their meals elsewhere on Sunday or go without! From now on, we're all going to Sunday School! We're not going to work any more on Sundays!"

The next Sunday and each Sunday thereafter Sister Daxzon and "her children" faithfully attended Sunday School services. When I inquired as to how their clients reacted to not receiving meals on Sundays, she calmly explained, "We lost most of our clients. But," she added, "we'll make out – some way. The Lord never gives a commandment unless he opens the way for us to obey it!" Still, the number of their clients continued to dwindle and it became increasingly difficult for them to make ends meet. They also fell behind in their monthly house payments and were faced with the possibility of losing their home. In an effort to meet their financial obligations, they began to go without meals. Nevertheless, they remained undaunted. They were certain – IF they kept the Lord's commandments, He, in turn, would help them and everything would be all right.

After a trying period of many weeks, their situation slowly began to change. They began to find new customers that did not insist upon receiving meals on Sundays. Many of their former customers also returned. Some stated that they could not find better meals nor better delivery service elsewhere. They preferred her meals – even if they had to forego service on Sundays. I remember well the day Sister Daxzon triumphantly told me, "It was difficult for a while, but we now have more clients than we ever had!" Their faith and perseverance had paid off. They proved, if we keep the Lord's commandments, He will bless us!

Sometimes when I become engrossed in worldly things, in striving to make more money or to accumulate more material possessions, I think about Sister Daxzon and "her children". Then, I can almost hear her say, "I never want to be rich again!" This helps me realize worldly possessions are not riches. But, faith, love, family, good deeds and charity towards others provide real and eternal riches.

FAITH

"...If ye have faith as a grain of mustard seed, ye shall say unto this mountain, remove hence to yonder place, and it shall remove, and nothing shall be impossible to you."   **Matthew 17:20**

The scriptures repeatedly emphasize the importance and power of faith. But, how often do we see the power of faith manifested in our lives or in the lives of those with whom we associate? Sister Violeta Daxzon and "her children" repeatedly demonstrated to me the power of faith and how they were the epitome of true Christianity in action. During the approximately seven months I was associated with them as a "Mormon" missionary in the Moroni Branch in Asuncion, Paraguay, I almost continually was amazed by the results of Sister Daxzon's and "her children's" simple, unwavering trust and faith in God.

Sister Daxzon had six children in her "family" when I arrived in Paraguay. Except for her daughter Hilda, all essentially had been gleaned or picked up from off the streets of Asuncion. The eldest was Pablo, a boy of about twelve years of age. The youngest were little Pablo or "Pablito" and his sister Juanita.

Pablito and Juanita never knew their father. They did not even know his name. Their mother, after struggling to support them for a number of years, literally dumped them upon Sister Daxzon and then disappeared. The small, frail bodies of Pablito and Juanita bore mute testimony of malnutrition and perhaps near death from starvation. When Sister Daxzon took them into her home, they resembled small, frightened creatures, rather than children with a sense of worth or being. Under Sister Daxzon's tender, loving care, it wasn't long before their pinched faces began to fill out and their demeanor to change. Rather than being timid and acting as if they were lost and afraid of everyone, they became outgoing, loving and more like normal children.

Similar to all of Sister Daxzon's children, Pablito and Juanita attended Church services in the Moroni Branch. Gradually they learned how to interact with others and to participate in meetings and activities. Pablito particularly demonstrated a desire to become a scholar and to learn as much as he could about the gospel of Jesus Christ. He continually questioned the Branch members and missionaries concerning the scriptures and doctrines of The Church of Jesus Christ of Latter-day Saints. After many questions and much study and pondering, he expressed a desire to be baptized and become a member of the Church. He felt he was prepared for baptism. Thus, he came to me and asked if I would baptize him.

I tried to explain to Pablito that, in addition to understanding the Gospel of Jesus Christ and being committed to keeping the sacred covenants we make with Our Father in Heaven through the ordinance of baptism, one also must be at least eight years old or what is considered to be the "age of accountability". He assured me he understood this. Despite his miniscule size, he was certain he was eight years old.

I further explained to Pablito, "There is a matter of parental permission. We cannot baptize minors or those under nineteen years of age without parental permission." Although Sister Daxzon had taken him and his sister into her home and was rearing them as her own, she had not legally adopted them nor any of the other children she had taken in from off the streets of Asuncion. Furthermore, he and his sister had not seen their mother since she had left them with Sister Daxzon the previous year. They didn't even know where she was! Regretfully, I explained to Pablito, "Your mother, wherever she is, technically is still your legal guardian and we cannot baptize and confirm you a member of the Church unless you somehow obtain her permission. Otherwise, I'm afraid you'll just have to wait until you are of legal age or no longer a minor." Pablito was crest-fallen. What was he to do?

Time passed. Then, one day Sister Daxzon, Pablito and Juanita came to see me. They explained how Pablito had been heartbroken after his discussion with me. He knew the Gospel was true and he wanted "with all his heart" to be baptized. They had discussed what they might do. They then prayed for guidance. As a result, they were inspired to fast and pray - so they might locate Pablito's and Juanita's mother. Late in the afternoon of the third day of their fasting and praying, Pablito's and Juanita's mother appeared at their home. She said, "I don't know why, but for the past few days I've wanted to see my children." Thus, she had walked more than twenty miles from the countryside where she now lived into Asuncion. Still, she was at a loss as to why she had come. She claimed she had not even thought about her two children for some time.

Pablito's and Juanita's mother briefly visited with them. During this visit, both Pablito and Juanita asked for permission to be baptized, which their mother readily granted them. Then, almost as an afterthought, Pablito asked his mother if she remembered their birth dates. Ironically, he learned he was only seven years old - not eight! - and Juanita only six – not seven, as she thought she was.. Thus, Pablito had to patiently wait almost another year before being baptized. Thus, I never had the privilege of baptizing him.

The "Mormon" Church was relatively new in Paraguay when I arrived there in December of 1956. Only a few Paraguayans had accepted the gospel and been baptized members of the Church. Many of these also had emigrated from the Paraguay and there was a dearth of male members, particularly those who held the priesthood. In fact, Brother Davalos was the only local member who held the Melchizedek or "higher" Priesthood.

Brother Davalos and his family were among the first Paraguayans to be baptized into the "Mormon" Church. He was a lawyer of some note and a man who prided himself in being both an intellectual and a philosopher. In contrast, approximately three-fourths of the Paraguayan populace could neither read nor write. Furthermore, Brother Davalos took pride in eloquently expounding his beliefs; though he sometimes had difficulty practicing what he preached. It seemed, to me, he also was prone to being lazy, as well as proud. In contrast, Sister Davalos was a simple and pleasant woman. Her life seemed to evolve around her husband and their three children; namely, their two sons, one of whom was twelve and the other nine, and an infant daughter. The children appeared to be exemplary and paid strict obedience to their father, as did also their mother.

Prior to my being called to be the President of the Moroni Branch, my predecessor had strongly called Brother Davalos to repentance, apparently in an effort to goad him into better living the principles of the gospel of Jesus Christ. Brother Davalos took offense and then went to great lengths to malign the missionary who had called him to repentance. He even wrote to the Mission President, demanding he excommunicate this missionary from the Church. The Mission President, during his next visit to Paraguay, met with Brother Davalos and the missionary in an attempt to "iron out" the difficulty. After he ascertained the missionary had committed no wrong, other than perhaps not being very tactful in his calling Brother Davelos to repentance. And he likewise challenged Brother Davalos to try to live a more Christ-like life. This infuriated Brother Davalos and he became even more antagonistic towards the Church and particularly towards those in positions of authority. He then even wrote to the President or Prophet of the Church in Salt Lake City, demanding he excommunicate both the missionary and the Mission President, whom he felt had wronged him.

My companion and I went to visit the Davalos family soon after I was called to be the President of the Moroni Branch. We did not know what had previously transpired between Brother Davalos and my predecessor nor the Mission President. Based upon the attendance records for the Branch, we only knew the Davalos family previously had been very active, but for some reason had not participated in any Church meetings or activities for a number of months.

Sister Davalos and her children warmly welcomed us into their home. They anxiously inquired as to the well being of other members of the Branch and indicated they sorely missed not attending and participating in Church activities. They also expressed a strong desire to again associate with members of the Church. Brother Davalos returned home while we were visiting with his family. We immediately felt his coldness towards us and wondered why he felt this way. Then, within minutes he launched into a detailed and bitter account of how he had been grossly wronged by my predecessor and the Mission President. Still, he claimed he knew the gospel and the Church were true. Still, he resolutely refused to attend Church services or to let members of his family participate in Church meetings or activities.

Thereafter, my companion and I frequently visited Brother Davalos and his family in an effort to soften his heart. Though he eventually treated us more cordially and on one occasion even took us fishing in the nearby Rio Paraguay, he persisted in his refusal to attend Church services. He also denied our requests that he permit members of his family to participate in Church activities.

One Sunday morning, just before time to begin the Sunday School service, Sister Daxzon and "her children" approached me. They anxiously inquired, "Has the Davaloz family arrived yet?" I replied, "No." Then I quizzically inquired, "Why? Did you see or talk to them?" Their reply was, "No. We haven't seen the Davalos family in some time. But, we have been fasting and praying for them to come back to Church today." Then, with a knowing glance at "her children", Sister Daxzon said, "They'll be here! Just you wait and see!"

I don't think Sister Daxzon and "her children" knew anything about the confrontations between Brother Davalos and my predecessor or the Mission President. Furthermore, I doubt they knew about Brother Davalos repeatedly telling my companion and me that neither he nor any members of his family would "ever attend services in the Moroni Branch again." Both my companion and I were convinced nothing less than a miracle would change Brother Davalos' attitude and bring him and his family back into Church activity.

I then pondered, "What will it do to the faith of Sister Daxzon and 'her children' when the Davalos family doesn't come to Church today?" Also, "How can Sister Daxzon and 'her children' be so positive about the Davalos family coming, when they haven't seen them for weeks?" What to do? I delayed starting the Sunday School services for as long as I thought I could. Finally, when it was well past the scheduled time for the meeting to begin, I took my seat in front of the congregation. As usual, Sister Daxzon and "her children" were seated on the front row. I was conducting the opening exercises and as I listened to the strains of the musical prelude, I nervously watched the entrance to the small chapel and silently prayed the Davalos family would come. I fear I prayed primarily because of my concern for Sister Daxzon and "her children", rather than for my concern about the Davalos family. Admittedly, I also felt these prayers probably would be in vain. Then, just as the prelude music ended and I stood to welcome the congregation, the Davalos family quietly entered the chapel and sat on a bench near the door. Sister Daxzon and "her children" turned and smiled towards them. Then, looking intently up into my eyes, Sister Daxzon smiled warmly, as if to say, "See, I told you! Where is your faith?"

After the services, Sister Daxzon, "her children", and other members of the congregation joined around the Davalos family, warmly embraced them, and welcomed them back. Gradually, the Davalos family again became active members of "our" small Branch of the Church. Little by little Brother Davalos lost his bitterness towards my predecessor and the Mission President and demonstrated signs of repentance. This, I felt, was a miracle, which resulted primarily through the faith of Sister Daxzon and "her children".

Regretfully, I have forgotten many of the details and even some of Sister Daxzon's and "her children's" many acts of faith, which frequently occurred during the few months I was associated with them. Nevertheless, their acts of faith repeatedly amazed me and demonstrated that faith CAN move mountains. Faith is important in our everyday activities, as well as in the more monumental tasks or difficulties we might encounter.

Despite the many manifestations of the power of faith I have witnessed, my faith often seems to falter. This sometimes reminds me of the Savior's words to his apostles, "...O thou of little faith, wherefore didst thou doubt?" and, "Therefore take no thought, saying, What shall we eat? Or, What shall we drink? Or, Wherewithal shall we be clothed?... for your Heavenly Father knoweth that ye have need of all these things. But seek ye first the kingdom of God, and his righteousness; and all these things shall be added unto you. Take therefore, no thought for the morrow; for the morrow shall take thought for the things of itself."

I wish I could have faith such as I repeatedly saw exemplified by Sister Daxzon and "her children".

IN PRISON

"...We hold these truths to be self-evident, that all men are created equal, that they are endowed by their Creator with certain unalienable rights, that among these are Life, Liberty, and the pursuit of Happiness." And, no law shall be established "...prohibiting the free exercise thereof, or abridging the freedom of speech, or the press; or the right of the people to assemble, and to petition the Government for a redress of grievances."

The Declaration of Independence

The Bill of Rights and Constitution of the United States of America boldly proclaim to the world that we Americans believe ALL men are created equal, should be free, and have the right to pursue their own destiny. But, how many Americans realize the import these God-inspired words have upon our lives? I did not begin to realize how blessed I was nor how important these documents were in my life until I had the unpleasant experience of being forcibly thrown into prison in the dictator-dominated country of Paraguay.

I arrived in Asuncion, the capital of the Republic of Paraguay and then a city of about 350,000 inhabitants, in late December of 1956. I was serving as a missionary for two and one-half years in the Uruguayan Mission of the "Mormon" Church. Paraguay and Peru then were included in the Uruguayan Mission; whereas, today there are two missions in Uruguay, two in Paraguay and nine in Peru.

In addition to being one of the few remaining dictatorships in South America, Paraguay then was one of the poorest and most backward countries in the southern hemisphere. Even the more elite sections of Asuncion had neither culinary water nor a sewage system. In fact, there were fewer than twenty miles of paved road in the entire country. Traveling into the interior of Paraguay was like traveling back in time, into the 19th or even 18th centuries. Most men in the interior of the country carried guns and large knives in their belts. Few people wore shoes and most wore ragged, threadbare clothes. Generally speaking, most Paraguayans were a sorry-looking lot. The majority of the country's approximately one and a half million inhabitants had no more than a thatched roof or a mud hut with a dirt floor to call home. Malnutrition was common. The effects of dire poverty were present everywhere. One aspect of the country, however, presented an aura of prosperity. This was the Paraguayan Army. The military forces were the pride and glory of Alfredo Stroessner, the "President" or dictator.

I was assigned to the Sajonia Branch as a proselyting missionary. Sajonia was one of three branches of the "Mormon" Church in Paraguay, all of which were in Asuncion. Although "Mormon" missionaries had been proselyting in Paraguay for approximately eight years, there were only a few Paraguayan members in Asuncion. In part, this was because many who joined the Church emigrated to Uruguay, Argentina or the United States. Also, relatively few Paraguayans would listen to or even be associated with we predominately "Norte Americano" missionaries. This was because they were afraid to speak or be seen with foreigners and feared that by so doing they and/or their families might reap dire repercussions from the government. Many also refused to speak or associate with North Americans, because they believed it was U.S. aid, particularly in the form of military weapons, equipment and training, which kept Stroessner and his military regime in power. They probably were right!

Most of the freedoms we take for granted in the United States were not known, let alone enjoyed, by the people of Paraguay. There was no freedom of speech, of the press, or to peaceably assemble. In fact, whenever five or more people met, even in religious or worship services, a permit first had to be obtained from the government authorities. Military personnel then were ordered to attend and monitor the meetings. This was to ensure no insurrections were plotted or nothing derogatory was said about "President" Stroessner or the Republic of Paraguay.

The military personnel assigned to monitor our religious services in the Sajonia Branch initially stood quietly in the rear of our small chapel. However, when they soon realized we were not concerned about politics, let alone the overthrow of the government, they began standing outside the building. Here, they could talk to each other and even smoke, which we had requested they not do inside. The soldiers stationed themselves at the entrance to our building for a number of weeks and carefully scrutinized each person who entered or left the chapel. They also would periodically poke their heads inside and listen to what was being said during our church services. As time went on, however, their military bearing became more and more lax. This particularly was the case when services were conducted during the heat of the day. Nonetheless, whenever other military personnel approached or passed by our building, they quickly stiffened and acted as if they were intently listening to what was being said inside.

After several months of such surveillance, the soldiers assigned to monitor us began to lounge about on the street, outside of the building compound. Then, first one, then another, and finally both soldiers periodically would be absent from their duty stations. The government authorities eventually notified us we no longer needed to obtain permits or even permission to hold our "regularly scheduled" Church services. However, we still needed to obtain permits for special or unscheduled meetings. Those who attended Church services or meetings were much more relaxed and friendly after the military surveillance ended. They began to participate more freely and others, who previously had refused or had been hesitant to accept our invitations to attend services, began to attend and participate. This increased measure of freedom afforded to us by the government authorities resulted little by little in the growth of the "Mormon" congregations in Paraguay.

Although the Paraguayan authorities gradually afforded the "Mormon" Church some measure of religious freedom, such was not the case for the Paraguayan populace with respect to many activities. My companion and I often walked past a small military compound a few blocks from the Sajonia Branch. The young soldiers billeted here appeared to have little, if any, freedom. Young Paraguayan men, except for those from a few politically favored or wealthy families, commonly were drafted into military service at a very young age. Some recruits were not more than twelve years of age and many were in their mid-teens. Usually when we passed the military compound, young recruits inside would be scurrying hither and yon, trying to meet the demands of those barking orders at them. Those in command usually would be strutting back and forth, brandishing swagger sticks and thumping the heels of their short, black boots upon the ground. Not infrequently we observed men using their swagger sticks as clubs to enforce their orders or to punish the recruits for not meeting their demands.

Common exercises for the young recruits included running around the compound, while shouting in unison, or doing push-ups and other physical activities until they were totally exhausted. Daytime temperatures in Asuncion often exceed a hundred degrees Fahrenheit and the humidity normally was in the ninety percent range, which causes the heat to be even more oppressive. A disciplinary measure we frequently observed with recruits was their having to carry an empty fifty-gallon drum on their backs, while running a rectangular course and shouting at the top of their lungs. Guards on the street outside the compound refused to let us stop to closely observe such punishment. Sometimes we noted, however, that the same young boys carrying barrels on their backs when we passed, either early in the morning or afternoon, still would be struggling - with the barrels on their backs - when we passed hours later. Some apparently were forced to shout until only gurgles issued from their parched mouths. It was sickening to see young boys suffer such punishment.

Most recruits went barefooted. This caused my companion and I to wince. The hot sand and cobblestone streets of Asuncion often blistered our feet inside our shoes. We wondered, "How can these poor boys stand running on the rocky surface of the compound in their bare feet?" The plight of the young recruits we observed almost daily perhaps illustrated the lack of freedom experienced by many Paraguayans while I was there in 1956 and 1957.

The first of May or "May Day" is a national holiday in Paraguay. The businesses are closed. Not even the trams or buses operate in Asuncion during this holiday. None-the-less, on the first day of May in 1957 a political rally was being held in one of Asuncion's central plazas. Although Paraguay had only one political party, elections and political rallies periodically were held. However, "President" Stroessner's name was the only one on the ballot and the rallies - with their associated banners, speeches and so forth – apparently were held primarily to demonstrate to other nations how the Paraguayans supported their "President".

We missionaries had a mailbox in the post office in the center of Asuncion. As May Day was a holiday and no buses or trams were operating, my companion and I were walking to the post office to collect our hoped for mail from home. As we approached the plaza where the political rally was being held, we momentarily stopped to listen to the speaker. He stood on a raised, banner-covered platform and loudly extolled over a speaker system the virtues and achievements of "President" Stroessner. Suddenly, a number of young men, who we later learned were university students, began to shout, "Bajo Stroessner! Bajo Stroessner!" Their shouts were quickly followed with the shrill scream of sirens. Jeeps and bright red Chevrolet "paddy" wagons roared up to the plaza, screeched to a halt, and soldiers – who brandished large "billy" clubs - swarmed out of the vehicles and into the crowd. Shouts of "Bajo Stroessner!" then changed to cries of pain or agony, as the soldiers effectively used their clubs on the students.

My companion and I normally did not carry our cameras. But, for some reason, this day we had them with us. We mounted a small wall on the edge of the plaza, to better see what was taking place. Soldiers were bashing the now cowering students with their clubs and then dragging them to the nearby vehicles and literally throwing them inside. My companion raised his camera and snapped a photo. I did likewise. Suddenly, we were seized from behind by two soldiers. Our cameras were wrenched from our hands. And, we and some badly beaten students were forcefully dragged and shoved into some "paddy" wagons.

With sirens screaming, we were driven through the streets of Asuncion to a large prison complex near the edge of the city. The vehicles stopped inside the prison walls and we were herded by men armed with submachine guns into a barbed-wire enclosure inside a walled courtyard. The vehicles departed and the prison gates were closed. There were armed guards at either end of the enclosure and, looking up, we stared into the barrels of machine guns, which were aimed down at us from a parapet running along the top of the stonewall that surrounded the courtyard. We and the students in the barbed-wire enclosure huddled together, much like a band of frightened sheep.

In muffled tones, we began to discuss our dilemma. The students quickly ascertained my companion and I were "Norte Americanos". They couldn't believe it. "What are you doing here?" they queried. "Don't you realize it is aid from North America that keeps Stroessner in power? If it wasn't for the United States, we wouldn't be here!"

The Chevrolet "paddy" wagon that brought us to prison bore a sign in English, which stated it had been given to Paraguay by the United States. The students in our compound informed us our captor's uniforms and weapons also were from the United States. In addition, almost ALL of the military equipment, uniforms and arms used in Stroessner's Army were given to Paraguay primarily through the "Point Four Program" – "for the strengthening of a FREE WORLD and, to improve relations between Paraguay and the U.S." Our fellow prisoners further claimed "Most of Stroessner's military officers are trained in the United States." They could not understand, nor could we, how a nation that proclaims ALL men should be free could support a dictatorial government.

Two army officers, accompanied by several armed guards, approached the compound in which we were incarcerated. One by one they began to remove members of our group. These were escorted into the confines of a large building, apparently for interrogation. Shortly it was learned my companion and I were North Americans. We then were hurriedly escorted into an office inside the large prison building. Though still under armed guard, we were seated and an officer seated behind a large wooden desk began to question us. He claimed, "The Government of Paraguay is having much difficulty from Communist insurgents, who use every means possible to incite the Paraguayan people, particularly the poor and uneducated, to revolt." He failed to mention most of the Paraguayans were poor and uneducated and less than thirty percent of the populace was literate. The officer further explained, "My men had no way of knowing you were North Americans and not Communists intent upon using the photographs you took in false propaganda against the Government of Paraguay."

My companion and I were anxious and fearful because of our situation. No one knew where we were. How were we going to get out of this predicament? As the minutes lengthened into hours, our initial fear gradually turned into anger. I insisted we be permitted to telephone the American Embassy. I thought, "The Embassy surely will take action to get us out of prison." The officer in charge eventually relented to my demands and took us into an office where there was a telephone. When I finally contacted the American Embassy, the man who answered the phone explained, "All of the Embassy staff is on holiday." He further claimed, "There is no one available who could help you." However, he politely suggested, "Why don't you call back in the morning? I'm sure there then will be someone here who can help you!"

I then demanded we be permitted to see the commanding officer of the prison. The officer in charge of us explained, "The 'Comandante' is taking advantage of the holiday. He won't be back till tomorrow morning." When I insisted we be told why we were being held and asked, "What are the charges against us?" The officer shrugged and said, "I don't know." Nevertheless, he claimed we had to wait until the officer who brought us in returned. This officer then would state the charges or reason why we had been brought to prison. It then was mid-day, which meant we had been in prison about four hours. The officers and soldiers who had brought us in would not go off duty until evening. Thus, we were informed, "You'll just have to wait until then."

We had some interesting conversations with our captors as we waited for evening and the return of our "arresting officer". Although we discussed many topics, such as why my companion and I were in Paraguay and what it was like to live in North America, our captors repeatedly tried to impress us as to how there were strong ties between Paraguay and the United States and how the U.S. had helped their country establish a "strong and efficient" army. We also spent time reading posters and bulletins displayed on the walls of the office in which we were being held. Almost all of these extolled the glories of the Republic of Paraguay, the merits and qualifications of "President" Stroessner and how, because of his impeccable record, he was certain to win the forthcoming presidential election.

Soldiers periodically entered the office and reported to the officer in charge before going on or off duty. Each of those going off duty would unload their weapons, take off their ammunition belts, and place all of these on the desk in front of the officer. Both then would carefully check each item and count every round of ammunition and check their tally against an inventory held by the officer. Those going on duty went through a similar process before they were issued weapons and ammunition. I asked the officer, "Why does each item have to be so carefully inspected and accounted for?" His reply was, "We can't let such things get into the hands of the wrong people, can we?"

Towards evening, officers began to filter into the office prior to going off duty. They carefully scrutinized my companion and me. In lowered voices, they inquired of the officer in charge, "Why are they here?" None, however, accepted responsibility for having brought us to prison that morning. Thus, no charges were filed against my companion and me. Finally, the officer in charge said, "If you promise to return promptly at 8:00 o'clock in the morning to meet with the 'Commandante', I'll let you go home for the night." This was the best news we'd heard all day. We committed to do so. The officer even agreed to return our cameras, "If you'll be sure to bring them back with you in the morning." This we also agreed to do.

I'll never forget how good it felt to walk out of that prison and onto the street. The relatively cool night air seemed to denote freedom. It had been a long, trying day. We wondered what had happened to the students who had been arrested with us. We were certain they had not been released, as we had been.

We returned to the prison the next morning just prior to 8:00 o'clock. An armed guard escorted us into the office where we had spent most of the previous day. The officer in charge, with whom we had become well acquainted, arose from behind his big, wooden desk and cheerfully greeted us. He appeared both surprised and nervous about our having returned as we had promised to do. He hastened to inform us, "I've taken care of everything. There's no need for you to meet with the 'Comandante'." We insisted, "We're here and we'd like to meet him." This noticeably disturbed the officer. "Why do you want to see him?" he asked. "Don't you understand? I've straightened out everything for you. There's no need for you to see him!"

When we persisted in our demands to see the 'Comandante', the officer almost pleaded with us to, "Be sure and request permission from the 'Comandante' to take photographs in Paraguay." This we promised to do. He also repeatedly begged us to "Tell the 'Comandante' how well we treated you!" This we likewise assured him we would do. He then meekly and nervously escorted us to the "Comandante's" office.

We entered a large, relatively well-furnished office. A good-looking man with a drooping black mustache arose from behind a large desk and greeted us in English. He immediately made apologies, "...for any inconvenience you might have suffered because of the actions of my men." He then proceeded to tell us how much he liked Americans and admired the United States. He had spent time in the States, while receiving military training. We told him why we were in Paraguay and, for the better part of an hour, we discussed a variety of subjects. He was a very personable man and we could not help but like him. It was hard to imagine why he was in charge of one of Paraguay's largest and most maligned prisons. He even invited us to his home to meet his family, which we eventually did.

We remembered our promises to the officer under whose custody we had spent the previous day. We requested permission from the "Comandante" to take photographs. He stiffened and his friendly countenance vanished. In detail, he explained, "Photographs, particularly of the poverty in Paraguay, could be misused. If such photographs fell into the hands of the wrong people, it would not look good for Paraguay or for the United States." He finally agreed, however, to let us take photographs – IF, prior to doing so, we first would contact him – "So I can have one of my men accompany and assist you and make sure you don't have any problems." He further asked us to promise we would carefully guard any photographs we might take, "So they won't fall into the hands of those who might wrongfully use them!" Though we could not understand so much concern about photographs, we agreed to his requests.

Several months passed and my companion and I had almost forgotten how frightened we had been when we were dragged off to prison. Then, late one night, there was a knock on the back door of the Branch where we were living. It was one of the students with whom we had been taken to prison. He asked permission to come inside and tell us what had happened to him. After a couple of "horrible" months in prison, he had managed to escape and determine our whereabouts. He claimed he and others who had been with us had been sent to a concentration camp in the "Chaco", a primitive jungle area between Paraguay and Bolivia, some distance up river from Asuncion. He described some of the tortures and hardships they endured. We were acquainted with some of these, as we had met two other men who claimed they had escaped from the "Chaco". One had mutilated fingers, which he explained, were the result of his captors extracting his fingernails – an excruciatingly painful form of torture. The other showed us massive scars on the backs of his legs and back. These almost solid masses of scar tissue, he claimed, were the result of repeated whip lashings inflicted upon him · while he was in the "Chaco".

We asked our nighttime informant, "What happened to the other students who were imprisoned with us?" He didn't know. However, he was certain at least some would remain in the "Chaco" until death freed them from the tyrannies of his country's present government. "Death", he claimed, "will be their reward for having spoken out against 'President' Stroessner!" He then begged, "When you return to the United States, tell others about our bad government and how it is a terrible thing for your government to support a dictator like Stroessner." We promised him we would.

It was more than a year before I returned to the United States. I then attempted to tell some Government officials, "The United States shouldn't support dictatorial countries." But, my words seemed to fall on deaf ears. I was told, "The United States assists those countries which have the most stable and progressive governments, which does not necessarily mean they have to be democracies. Paraguay is such a country." Also, "The United States attempts to help those countries which will further the best interests of the United States." It was not explained what such "interests" might be or who determined what they were. None would fathom to guess as to what or how U.S. interests would be furthered by our supporting Stroessner's dictatorial military regime in the poor, backward and land-locked country of Paraguay.

Since my prison stint in Paraguay, I often have wondered, "What would it be like to live without the freedoms we Americans take for granted?" I since also have visited other countries that afford their citizens little freedom and have wondered, "What should be the role of the United States, which stands as an ensign of freedom to the world, with regard to governments that suppress their people's freedom?" Should we not strive to help those who are less fortunate than we to obtain this most precious gift? It still perplexes me – how can we, as a nation espousing freedom, support oppressive forms of government?

"WON'T YOU HAVE A CUP OF TEA?"

"And again, hot drinks are not for the body or belly."
Doctrine & Covenants 89:9

The Rodo Branch was the largest congregation in the Uruguayan Mission of the "Mormon" Church when I served as the "Presiding Elder" there in 1957 and 1958. The chapel, a beautiful, modern, brick building was the newest in the Mission. Six Elders or male missionaries, including myself, and four lady missionaries were assigned to Rodo as proselyting missionaries. The Branch Presidency was one of the few in the Mission then comprised of local members, rather than of missionaries. We six Elders lived in the old Rodo Branch, which was a dilapidated building about ten blocks distant from the new chapel. Still, this old building continued to be used for Boy Scout meetings and activities, weekly Primary or children's meetings and as a warehouse or storage facility for missionaries serving throughout the Uruguayan Mission, which then included Uruguay, Paraguay and Peru. Trunks or excess luggage belonging to missionaries were stored in a large room, which previously served as a chapel. Missionaries newly arriving from the States, as well as those in transit to or from Paraguay and Peru or recuperating from severe illnesses also were often quartered here. In short, the old Rodo Branch building usually was buzzing with activity and with the comings and goings of missionaries, Boy Scouts, children and others. In contrast, the lady missionaries lived in an immaculate, modern and quiet apartment on the second floor of the new Rodo Branch. Our contact with them was primarily during the Sunday meetings held there. I then would review their proselyting activities for the previous week and pick up their weekly activity reports.

I also taught an "Investigators' Class", which was part of the Sunday School services held each week in the new Rodo Branch. Basic principles of the gospel of Jesus Christ were taught to those investigating the "Mormon" Church. The size of the class varied from half a dozen to more than thirty, depending primarily upon how many of the Elders' and lady missionaries' contacts were genuinely interested in learning more about the gospel and doctrines of The

Church of Jesus Christ of Latter-day Saints. Classes were informal and those attending were encouraged to ask questions about gospel principles and doctrines. This often resulted in lively discussions. Class membership continually changed. After those attending became better versed in the gospel, they usually were baptized and moved into regular Sunday School classes with other members. Having new class members almost weekly was interesting, exciting and challenging for me.

The Elders and lady missionaries usually introduced their new investigators to me before the beginning of the class each Sunday. However, one Sunday, near the beginning of the New Year, there was a tall, thin, elderly woman who wore thick, plastic-rimmed glasses in the class whom I had not met. Her glasses remained perched high up on her long, thin nose and accented her kindly face, which usually reflected a shy smile. Her enthusiasm about what was being taught was striking. Though she appeared to be shy in nature, it seemed she could not refrain from taking part in the gospel discussions. She was indeed impressive. I determined I'd become acquainted with her, but she disappeared immediately following the dismissal of the class. I described her to the Elders and asked if they knew her. They did not, but suggested, "She might be one of the lady missionaries' investigators."

The mysterious woman again was in the class the next Sunday and participated in class discussions with even more enthusiasm than she had during the previous week. Although I again attempted to meet her after the class, she again had disappeared. I described her to the lady missionaries and asked if she was one of their investigators. Their reply was, "No. We thought she was one of yours!" They then added, "She really knows the scriptures, doesn't she?" Thus, this woman's identity remained a mystery.

The following Sunday, the "mystery woman" sat on the front row of the class. Again, she enthusiastically participated in the class discussions. This time, however, I stationed myself by the classroom door - prior to class dismissal. Then, as she attempted to quietly leave, I introduced myself and asked her name. She rather shyly told me, "I am Elida Winns Otero". When I inquired as to whether or not the missionaries had visited her, she said, "No. They have not. But, my sister told me a little about the 'Mormon' Church. And, what she told me interested me. So, I decided to try to find out more." She continued with, "I've been impressed by what I've learned in your class. And, if possible, I'd like to learn more about the 'Mormon' Church." She further explained how she felt her asking me or the other missionaries to teach her might be "a bit too forward." Thus, she had reasoned, "If I attend classes long enough, perhaps someone will tell me how I can learn more." As to her sudden disappearances following the previous classes, she explained, "I have to rush home to prepare the noon-day meal for my son and my two small grandsons."

I told Mrs. Otero my companion and I would be happy to visit with her at her home to further discuss the gospel, if she so desired. "Would you?" she exclaimed, "I would be so happy if you would!" She then wanted to know, "When would it be most convenient for you to come to my house?" We scheduled an appointment for the coming Tuesday. But, when I asked for directions to her home, I was not acquainted with the street or even the general location she described. I thought I knew virtually every street in our proselyting area and was somewhat perplexed by the address she gave me. When I asked how far she lived from the chapel, she claimed, "It's not far! If you walk the six or eight blocks from here to such and such a bus stop, then take bus number so-and-so, it will take you to a corner near my home." She then described in detail the corner and area surrounding her home.

I wrote down the detailed directions Mrs. Otero gave me and the following Tuesday my companion and I caught the indicated bus at the designated stop. We then rode for almost an hour, while continually looking for the landmarks indicating where we should get off. We finally spied them and got off from the bus. It certainly was not the "short" bus ride Mrs. Otero had described. In fact, my companion and I had come to the realization Mrs. Otero's house was only a few blocks from the Las Piedras Branch building, where she could easily attend "Mormon" Church services. Thus, while walking from the bus stop to her home, we determined we'd teach her only one lesson - before requesting she be taught by the missionaries in the Las Piedras Branch. We were certain the Elders in Las Piedras would be more than pleased to teach a "golden" investigator such as Mrs. Otero.

Because our bus ride took longer than we had anticipated, when we finally knocked on Mrs. Oter's door it was much later than the time we had scheduled to meet her. When she opened the door, she greeted us warmly and invited us into her humble, but very neat and tidy home.. She then explained, "I was afraid you had forgotten to come. I can't wait to learn more about the 'Mormon' Church." She also explained how her husband had died some years previous. Their only son, who now was a man, had married and she had two grandsons, who were one and three years old. However, her son's wife had left him and their two children and they had moved in with her. She cared for her grandchildren, while her son worked. This was the reason she had left immediately following the "Investigators' Classes" the previous Sundays.

We presented our first lesson or gospel discussion to Mrs. Otero. She enthusiastically listened and eagerly accepted what we taught. When we questioned her, to ensure she understood what we taught, she invariably answered correctly. Then, when we attempted to end the discussion, she begged us to "stay a little longer" and "teach me some more". We presented a second discussion and gave her several pamphlets or "tracts", which explain gospel principles. We suggested she read these and, if she had questions or did not understand nor believe everything presented in them, we would discuss such during a future visit.

As we again prepared to leave, Mrs. Otero again begged us to stay longer. "You've already done so much for me, " she explained, "Isn't there something I can do for you in return?" She then tried to pay us for our having taught her. We explained, "We do not accept money for teaching the gospel of Jesus Christ." Taken aback, she said, "I should have known that. But, can't I at least offer you something? Won't you have a cup of tea?"

We thanked Mrs. Otero for her thoughtfulness and gracious hospitality, and said, "We really must be going." Still, she persisted with, "I forgot. You are North Americans. You don't drink tea. You'd probably prefer coffee. Couldn't you wait just a minute while I fix you a cup of coffee?" We did not wish to offend her by telling her we drank neither tea nor coffee. So, we again thanked her for her hospitality and insisted, "We really must be going!" This was true, as we were late for other scheduled appointments.

Prior to our leaving, Mrs. Otero assured us she would see us in Church on Sunday and would look forward to our again coming to her home for another gospel discussion the following week. As my companion and I walked from her home to the nearby bus stop, we simultaneously turned and said to each other, "We're not going to give her to the Las Piedras Elders!" We agreed she was too good an investigator to let go. People like her were what made it worthwhile for us missionaries to leave our families and homes and come to a foreign land to teach the gospel of Jesus Christ in a foreign tongue for two and one-half years.

The following Sunday, just prior to commencement of the "Investigators' Class", Mrs. Otero meekly approached my companion and me. She ashamedly apologized for having offered us first a cup of tea and then a cup of coffee. She explained, "I didn't know you didn't believe in drinking tea or coffee or alcoholic beverages." She also stated, "Truthfully, I was upset when you wouldn't at least let me prepare something for you. I was afraid I'd somehow offended you. But, when I told my sister about it, she told me, 'Mormons' don't believe in drinking tea, coffee or alcohol. And, they also do not smoke. I didn't know! I'm so embarrassed! I hope I didn't offend you."

We assured her she had not offended us. She then said, "You know, I've never believed it was right to smoke or drink alcohol. But, I've drunk tea all my life. I also usually have a cup of coffee each morning for breakfast. However, I've thought about it. I believe you are right. Therefore, I've quit! I'm never going to drink another cup of coffee or tea!" We had not even mentioned, let alone explained to her what "Mormons" refer to as "The Word of Wisdom" or "The Lord's Law of Health." This is a revelation received by the Prophet Joseph Smith and recorded in the 89th Section of the Doctrine and Covenants.

This remarkable woman had accepted and already was living this law, without us even explaining it to her!

Mrs. Otero went on to explain, "I asked one of the members here this morning what I could offer you missionaries when you visit me in my home. They said, 'All missionaries like to eat food and drink milk.' Would it be all right if I offered you some cake and milk the next time you visit me?" We assured her, "Cake and milk would be great." Thus began the practice of Mrs. Otero baking a cake and serving us cake and milk whenever we visited her in her home.

Mrs. Otero's freshly baked cakes were delicious. This was despite the fact she had to bake them in a small, tin oven, which she placed on top of a "Primus" or small, one-burner kerosene stove. The large glasses of cold milk, which she provided with ample pieces of cake, also were most refreshing. She was a most gracious hostess and despite the long rides to her home, my companion and I looked forward to our weekly visits with her.

One time when we arrived at Mrs. Otero's, she was very much agitated and flustered. "My cake didn't turn out. And, I didn't have time to bake you another one." She explained. "Rather than eat my terrible cake, would you prefer some cookies instead – even though they're a day or two old?" We assured her, "The cake will be just fine." But, when my companion went to eat his piece of cake with his fork, the fork handle broke. Mrs. Otero was mortified. I feared she might literally die on the spot. I've never seen anyone so humiliated and apologetic as she was. Actually, the cake wasn't all that bad. I think the fork just had a weak handle.

An Elder other than my regular companion accompanied me on one of the visits to Mrs. Otero's home. He was a tall, redheaded fellow from Tooele, Utah that was noted for his voracious appetite. Following our gospel discussion, Mrs. Otero presented us with an unusually large cake. She asked, "Do you want to cut it or should I?" My companion insisted upon cutting it. Pointing to each of us with the knife Mrs. Otero provided him, he counted, "One. Two. Three!" He then cut the cake into three enormous pieces, placed each piece upon a plate, and placed them in front of us. Although Mrs. Otero said nothing, the look on her face indicated my companion's actions had shocked her. This Elder then also drank all of the milk she offered him, which was in excess of two liters and all the milk she had in her home. Still, Mrs. Otero said nothing. But, during a subsequent visit, she mustered sufficient courage to inquire of me, "Does that Elder always eat like that?"

I've never seen anyone so anxious or so quick to learn about the gospel as was Mrs. Otero, whom we now knew as "Sister" Otero. She practically memorized the tracts we left with her. She also almost always seemed to understand and accept what we taught. But, if she did not understand or did not fully believe something, she did not hesitate to question and discuss it with us – until it was clear and acceptable to her. She was a most remarkable scholar and an avid student of the scriptures.

Following our second visit, we left a "Book of Mormon" with Sister Otero. I explained, "This book contains the fullness of the gospel of Jesus Christ, as well as a history of people who inhabited the American continents before the time of Columbus. I suggest you read and study it." When we visited her the following week, she profusely apologized for not having been able to read and study ALL of the more than five-hundred-page book during the intervening week. She explained, "My two grandsons were ill and I had to care for them. I just didn't have time to read and study like I wanted to do". She had ONLY read and studied a little more than three hundred pages!

Visiting with and teaching Sister Otero was a joy. I've never known anyone who has so enthusiastically studied and then so readily accepted and lived gospel principles as did she. She explained, "The gospel principles you've taught me have miraculously brought joy and meaning into my life; whereas, I previously was sad much of the time and my life seemed to be without purpose." She claimed it was impossible for her to describe how happy "your gospel message has made me". She claimed she could never thank us enough for the wonderful change it had wrought in her life. This, in turn, brought joy to my companion and me.

All too quickly, it seemed, Sister Otero was ready for baptism. I would miss not having her in the "Investigators' Class" each Sunday. I'd also miss our weekly visits in her home. And, yes! I would miss her delicious cakes and the large glasses of cold milk she served us. My companion, Elder David Weight from Provo, Utah, baptized Sister Otero and I confirmed her a member of The Church of Jesus Christ of Latter-day Saints. When she came up out of the waters of baptism, I had never seen anyone's face radiate a light such as did hers. Neither have I known anyone to be happier and more at peace than she seemed to be.

Shortly after Sister Otero's baptism, I was transferred from the Rodo "Branch" in Montevideo to the town of Rocha, Uruguay. Thereafter, I periodically corresponded with Sister Otero. Without fail, whenever she wrote to me, she profusely thanked me for having taught her the gospel, which she claimed, "Has brought immeasurable joy into my life." Over the years, I have lost track of Sister Otero. The last I heard, however, she was a stalwart in the Church and even had transferred from the Rodo to the Las Piedras "Branch" near her home. Through her example, her son also joined the Church. And, her two grandsons were "being raised as 'Mormons'."

After becoming well acquainted with Sister Otero and much to her chagrin, whenever I visited or wrote to her, I chided her about her trying to tempt my companion and me, during our first visit to her home, with: "Won't You Have A Cup Of Tea?"

SISTER GONELLA

"Blessed be ye poor, for yours is the kingdom of God"
Luke 6:20

She was known by her non-member neighbors and friends, as well as by her fellow members of the "Mormon" Church, as "Hermana" or "Sister" Gonella. . She was in her eighties when I first met her while serving as a "Mormon" missionary in Rocha, Uruguay, in 1958. Her wrinkled and scared hands and face testified that she had had a difficult life. Nevertheless, she never complained. Instead, she dwelt upon her blessings and how fortunate she had been. One exception was her lamentation, "Oh, if I could have learned how to read earlier in life, think of how much I could have learned." And, "Think of all the time I wasted during those many years when I didn't know how to read." She had been illiterate until she was in her seventies. Then, virtually on her own and with the Bible as her text, she had learned how to read.

Little by little Sister Gonella divulged some of the difficulties she had confronted during her life. She was born on the frontier between Uruguay and Brazil in the 1800's. She remembered little about her parents and lived in abject poverty throughout her life. When she was just a few years old, she fell into an open fire and was badly burned over much of her body. No one expected her to live and her parents abandoned her. She did live, however, but throughout her life she carried grotesque scars on her hands, arms, face and apparently over much of her body. She essentially was a servant for the major portion of her life, working for one family and then another or anyone who would provide her with food and shelter in exchange for her labor. Thus, most of Sister Gonella's life had been one of toil.

She never had an opportunity to attend school, to belong to a family, or to marry. "Who would want to marry a woman with a face like mine?" she stated. It was true, the grotesque scars, which covered one side of her face, were not a pleasing sight. Still, she had a remarkable and beautiful countenance, especially after you became acquainted with her. Later in life, she obtained employment whereby she earned a bit of money. This apparently was because of her pleasant disposition, her willingness to work, and the fact she had an alert mind and learned quickly. She also learned how to sew and knit. With these abilities she eventually earned a meager living on her own. Although she frequently stated, "My eyes are not what they used to be." And, "With age, my fingers have all become thumbs." She still was noted for producing many beautiful handicrafts and in this she took great pride. Poor as she was and as difficult as it was for her to knit, she also persisted in knitting and presenting a beautiful blanket to each newborn child in the Rocha "Branch" of the "Mormon" Church.

Shortly after my arrival in Rocha, I evaluated the attendance records for the members in the "Branch". I noted that Sister Gonella only infrequently attended Church services. Thus, my companion and I decided to visit her and determine why she did not attend more regularly. A specific address was not recorded for her home, only the "barrio" or neighborhood in which she lived. Upon reaching this neighborhood, we inquired of those we met whether or not they knew Sister Gonella. To our surprise, they not only knew her, but they also loved and respected her and quickly led us to her humble abode.

She lived in a small, one-roomed hut in back of a house in a large compound. Her small and extremely humble quarters consisted of nothing more than some white-washed mud walls, a thatched roof, and a dirt floor. She had no electricity - not even a lamp. Candles served as her sole source of light. Neither did she have running water. An "out-house" served as her bathroom. A faucet on the street provided both her drinking and culinary water. Her furniture consisted solely of a wooden bed, a small nightstand – next to the bed and upon which rested her precious books - two wooden chairs, and a wooden closet, which apparently held her meager worldly possessions. A neighbor woman provided her cooking privileges in her small, lean-to kitchen. But, according to this neighbor, Sister Gonella often was not able to make it to her kitchen or lacked the stamina to cook regular meals. Much of the time she somehow survived primarily upon bread, raw vegetables and fruit.

We found Sister Gonella in bed. When we inquired as to whether or not she was ill, she claimed she was not. Only, "My back hurts so much, it's difficult for me to sit." Thus, she spent much of her time in bed. We later learned she was so poor she had no money or the means to heat her small room. Thus, during the winter months, she remained in bed in order to keep warm. She walked with difficulty and needed a cane for support and to keep her balance. This, she claimed, was why she did not attend Church services regularly. Nevertheless, she anxiously inquired as to the well being of virtually every member of the "Branch". And, prior to our leaving, she made us promise to convey her greetings to each of them.

We quickly learned Sister Gonella considered her copies of the scriptures to be her most priceless possessions. She told how, many years previous to her learning how to read, she used her meager savings to purchase a Bible from a traveling salesman. Others ridiculed her for wasting her money on such a purchase, especially when she could not read. But, she claimed, "I knew the Bible contained the word of God." And, "I wanted to have God's word – even if I could not read or perhaps understand it." Many years later, when she was "old and no longer had to work ALL the time", she determined she was somehow going to learn how to read. Through the help of fellow Church members, neighbors and friends, and with the Bible serving as her textbook, she eventually learned how to read. Also, although she handled her scriptures with care, during her long struggle to master the art of reading, she claimed she literally wore out two Bibles in so doing. Furthermore, her present Bible likewise was almost worn out from constant use.

Despite Sister Gonella's frequent lament about having wasted most of her life - because she could not read until she was in her seventies - it was amazing how much she had read and learned in a relatively few years. She knew the scriptures well and could quickly locate almost any scripture to which my companion and I might refer. Her depth of understanding also was impressive. Frequently she would ask, "Am I correct in understanding this scripture to mean ..." such and such. Almost invariably I came to realize she understood the true meaning of the scriptures better than either my companion or me. Reading and discussing the scriptures with her was truly a learning process. Without even realizing it, she was an inspirational teacher and my companion and I shortly began to save our gospel questions to discuss with her. Nevertheless, each time we visited her, she insisted we give her a reading assignment in the scriptures on a gospel subject. Then, during a subsequent visit, we HAD to discuss it with her – "to make sure I understand it correctly!"

Besides using Sister Gonella as a teacher to help us better understand various aspects of the gospel, visits with her bolstered us up and helped us not to become discouraged about others not accepting our gospel message. Nevertheless, we refrained from visiting her "too frequently", because following our visits she always gave us gifts. Despite her abject poverty and dire circumstances, she would insist upon giving us something "to partially repay you for your kindness to a poor old woman" or "for helping me to better understand the gospel of Jesus Christ." Her gifts usually consisted of an orange, a piece of bread and butter, or some small "goody" she'd saved for us - even though it often appeared she did not have adequate food even for herself. If we tried to politely refuse her gifts, it seemed to sorely offend her. Thus, we tried to limit our visits to her humble abode. Still, even as poor as she was, her giving seemed to make her happy. And, she would castigate us and tell us how much she missed us and our gospel discussions if she felt our visits were not frequent enough. What were we to do?

One cold, winter day my companion and I were feeling discouraged. We decided a visit with Sister Gonella might bolster our spirits. When we knocked on the door to her humble quarters, a pleasant voice invited us to, "Pasa!" She was propped up in bed, smothered in blankets, apparently in an effort to keep warm. By the light of a candle, she was reading her scriptures. "I'm so happy you came." She said. "I've been thinking about a scripture in the reading assignment you gave me. I want to make sure I understand it correctly." She then turned to and read the scripture, before telling us her interpretation of it. Although I used this scripture frequently in my teaching and even had memorized it, her interpretation gave it much more meaning and depth for me. She seemed to be the epitome of, "Seek and you shall find; knock and it shall be opened unto you."

(Matt. 7:7). Through faith, study and prayer, she had "knocked" and the scriptures had been "opened unto" her!

Prior to my companion and I leaving Sister Gonella's home that day, she asked me to retrieve her purse from her closet. She then rummaged through the large, well-worn bag and handed each of us a peso bill. We knew this was a considerable amount of money for her, but she insisted we accept it. She apologetically explained, "I don't have anything else I can give you." She hadn't even been able to go out for food for a day or two! We tried to graciously refuse her gift, but she persisted in our accepting it. As a result, I thereafter carried this peso bill in my wallet for many years - until it literally wore out. Thus, each time I opened my wallet and saw this bill, it reminded me of how Sister Gonella had learned to read and had become knowledgeable in the gospel of Jesus Christ - despite her abject poverty and the many difficulties she had encountered during her life. This, in turn, had brought her peace and happiness.

Sister Gonella is one of the most content, peaceful and happy persons I have known. To me, she exemplified "the true love of Christ". I hope I never forget the wonderful lessons she taught me.

BETTY

"Ask the Father in my name, in faith believing that you shall receive..."   **Doctrine & Covenants 18:18**

"...And verily I say unto you, whatsoever things ye shall ask the Father in my name shall be given unto you. Therefore, ask and ye shall receive, knock, and it shall be opened unto you, for he that asketh, receiveth...."   **III Nephi 27:28-29**

I had mixed emotions as the end of the two and one-half years I was called to serve as a "Mormon" missionary in the Uruguayan Mission rapidly approached. I was anxious to return home to my family and friends, but I did not want to leave the many dear people I had come to love and cherish in the mission field.

My mission had at times been trying and difficult. For example: I struggled for many months to learn Spanish. Then, while serving in Melo, Uruguay, on a dare I dove off a high, steel bridge into the Tacuari River. I executed the dive successfully, but a steel rod penetrated my kneecap and entered the joint of my knee as I surfaced alongside a bridge pillar. Thereafter, I spent some excruciatingly painful days in bed with my swollen leg packed in ice, wondering if I might not be a cripple for the rest of my life. However, I was miraculously healed and today have only a small scar to remind me of this mishap. While serving in Paraguay, I was severely stricken with infectious hepatitis and amoebic dysentery. The medical doctor claimed I would have to spend a minimum of sixteen weeks in bed - flat on my back. However, after being bedridden only a couple of weeks, I returned to my missionary labors. Even today, I suffer somewhat from this debilitating illness. Nevertheless, my many memorable and joyful experiences during my missionary service far outweigh these difficulties.

Reminiscing about my missionary service and the six congregations or "branches" in which I served (Tacuarembo and Melo in Uruguay, then Sajonia and Moroni in Paraguay, and finally Rodo and Rocha in Uruguay) and the ten full-time companions with whom I served (Elders David Petersen, Marvin F. Spresser, Westlyn C. Riggs, John Edwin Belliston, Kent W. Calvert, Heber Dale Bartholemew, David G. Weight, Larry K. Macdonald, Alfred Wilbur Jensen, and Kenneth D. Peabody) brings back many choice memories. However, the nine months I spent in Paraguay undoubtedly were both the most trying and rewarding period of my mission. Trying, because I was ill much of the time I was there. Rewarding, primarily because I never have known people with such simple, undaunted faith as was repeatedly demonstrated by some of the Paraguayans with whom I associated.

As our missions drew to a close, Elder Wayne Crismon and I began to plan an extensive travel itinerary for our return journey home. We had entered missionary service together. We first spent almost a week in the Mission Home in Salt Lake City. Thereafter, we'd spent the better part of a month traveling to Uruguay, first by train from Salt Lake City to New York, via Chicago and Niagara Falls, and then by ship from New York to Montevideo, via Rio de Janeiro, Santos and Sao Paulo, Brazil. Although in different "branches", we served during the same time in Paraguay and returned to Uruguay together. We had become close friends and desired to see as much as possible of Latin America while returning to the United States. While returning home, we planned to visit Argentina, Paraguay, Bolivia, Peru, Ecuador, Panama, Costa Rica, Nicaragua, El Salvador, Guatemala, and Mexico, as well as a number of locations in the States. Most importantly, we looked forward to again visiting our dear friends in Paraguay.

As planned, we started our journey by taking the weekly seaplane flight from Montevideo across the Rio de la Plata to Buenos Aires. We then spent three days seeing the sights in Buenos Aires and renewing acquaintances with missionaries with whom we had traveled to South America two and one-half years previously. Following our three-day stay in Buenos Aires, flights to Asuncion, Paraguay were canceled because of inclement weather and we had to spend an additional three days in Argentina. In order to adhere to our planned travel itinerary, it appeared we'd have to forego the three-day visit we had scheduled for Paraguay. In fact, the flight we finally took from Buenos Aires was the one we had scheduled to take from

Asuncion to La Paz, Bolivia. We'd only be able to spend a few minutes in the airport at Asuncion. Also, there was no way we could contact our Paraguayan friends so they could meet us during our brief stop at the airport in Asuncion.

As we stepped off from the plane in the Asuncion Airport, there on the runway were more than thirty of our Paraguayan friends waiting for our arrival. I don't know and we did not ask how they knew we would be on this plane. But, here they were! We warmly greeted and embraced each other. Then, when we tried to explain, "We can't stay in Paraguay. We have to go on to Bolivia." They pleaded with us to "please stay!" Elder Crismon's and my eyes met. We said nothing, but we knew we were in agreement. Schedule or no schedule we were going to stay and visit our Paraguayan friends. We ran into the terminal and frantically requested our luggage be taken off the plane and our reservations for the onward flight to La Paz cancelled. With this accomplished, we again joined our friends.

Sister Violeta Daxzon, her daughter Hilda, and most of "her children", whom she had taken into her home from off the streets of Asuncion, were among those who greeted us. She informed me, "I now have eight children!" She had added two to her brood since I left Paraguay approximately a year previously. She also insisted that Elder Crismon and I "first" had to come to her home, "Before you visit anyone else." Her only explanation for her insisting we visit her first was, "There's someone there I want you to meet."

When we arrived at Sister Daxzon's home, the children who had not accompanied her to the airport affectionately greeted us. They then solemnly escorted us into their home and into a bedroom. There, lying upon a bed was a beautiful little, black-haired, dark-eyed girl – the most recent addition to Sister Daxzon's ever-growing family. "This," they exclaimed, is Betty!" It seemed no one else wanted this beautiful little girl. This was because she was a cripple. One of her legs was much smaller and shorter than the other. Also, the smaller leg was not growing. The Paraguayan doctors claimed this was because she had a "dry hip socket". And, "There is nothing we can do for her". However, Sister Daxzon informed us, "We've been fasting and praying. We believe, if you will bless Betty she will be made well." How could we deny such a request? But, how could we pronounce such a blessing?

Sister Daxzon requested that we kneel with her and "her children" around the bed upon which Betty lay. Each of us then offered a prayer to Our Father in Heaven in behalf of Betty. Sister Daxzon then insisted that, by the power of the priesthood that we held, Elder Crismon and I should anoint and bless little Betty. Elder Crismon anointed Betty's head with olive oil, which had been "consecrated and dedicated for the healing of the sick in the household of faith." Elder Crismon and I then laid our hands upon Betty's head and I pronounced a blessing. This I did with much trepidation. I don't know what words were uttered from my mouth. They were not mine! Sister Daxzon and "her children", however, were elated by what was said. "Now," they enthusiastically stated, "Betty will be made well!"

The few days we spent in Paraguay passed all too quickly. We rushed from the home of one dear friend to another, in an effort to visit all whom we had come to love during our period of missionary service there. Invariably, the topic of discussion was how the gospel of Jesus Christ had changed and given meaning to the lives of those with whom we had associated. Time and time again our friends expressed thanks for the "Mormon" missionaries and the gospel message they had brought. This gave them an understanding about the purpose of life and brought joy to them and the members of their families. Although virtually all with whom we met lived in what most North Americans would consider to be abject poverty and many of them still faced seemingly insurmountable trials and tribulations, they expressed gratitude for their many blessings. They also told how the gospel had brought peace and happiness into their lives.

With sadness, Elder Crismon and I returned to the Asuncion Airport with many of our friends. They begged us to stay longer, but we could not. We felt we must continue our homeward journey. Sister Daxzon presented me with a hand-woven "aopoi" or knitted white shirt, which she had trimmed in red and blue. "This," she said, "is to remind you of your friends in Paraguay." We tearfully said goodbye.

Because of our stop in Paraguay, thereafter we did not take a single flight as originally scheduled in our return journey home. Also, although we visited numerous beautiful and interesting places and had a memorable journey during the ensuing weeks, all were an anticlimax as compared to our return visit to Paraguay.

When I arrived home more than a month after having left Paraguay, there was a letter from Sister Daxzon waiting for me. She informed me, "All is well with me and my children." And, "Betty's leg is starting to grow!" Periodic letters during the following months continued to inform me of Betty's progress. Then, Sister Daxzon eventually wrote, "Betty can now walk. Her legs are the same size." Betty no longer was a cripple! She could run and play with the other children!

As the years passed, the frequency of letters to and from Sister Daxzon diminished. Eventually, our communications consisted primarily of an annual Christmas card and letter. Then, one of mine was returned unopened and stamped, "Address Unknown". Although never confirmed, I assumed Sister Daxzon had died. Nevertheless, my memories of her and "her family" and their unwavering faith in the goodness and mercy of Our Father in Heaven still persists. Because of their faith, Betty also was no longer a cripple!

"BE A GOOD BOY, SON!"

Funerals often are a family reunion, minus one.

Saturday, the 4th of July in 1959, dawned bright and warm. Although I had spent most of the night traveling from my employment in Yellowstone National Park to my parents' home in Burley, Idaho, I had a pleasant sensation of anticipation for the events of that day. In addition to being a holiday in which to commemorate the birth of the United States of America, it also was the day on which a reunion for my maternal grandparent's family had been scheduled.

My maternal grandparents, Raymond Madsen and Opal Hulet Whittier, their nine children, the eldest of which is my mother, their spouses and children were going to gather in the Burley City Park for a day of feasting, visiting, and, most importantly, renewing family ties and relationships. The City Park had been reserved for this special occasion. The women in the family had arranged among themselves as to what foods each would bring. The grandchildren, of which I am the eldest, anxiously awaited the opportunity to again visit and play, as well as to partake of the many delicious foods that ALWAYS were provided for such occasions.

In previous years, it was a common practice for our family to frequently gather at my grandparents' home to celebrate birthdays, holidays and other occasions. However, as the family became larger and more scattered, such gatherings had become less common. Nevertheless, ties remained strong and family members still anticipated get-togethers. This was evidenced by the fact that all but one of my grandparents' nine children and all but two of their then thirty-seven grandchildren attended this reunion. Burley, rather than Rockland - where my grandparents lived - had been selected as our gathering place. This was because it was considered to be the most convenient and centrally located for the now scattered family members.

As each family group arrived at the park, those present would surge forward to greet them, usually with a kiss, an embrace or a hearty handshake. They then would assist in carrying the many foods or supplies that had been brought in that family's car. These were placed upon a long row of wooden picnic tables, which had been placed end-to-end in the shade of some large weeping willow and cottonwood trees in the center of the park. The newly arrived children, my cousins, almost immediately would be absorbed into the ongoing games of tag, keep-away, or in trying to snatch and quickly gobble down a choice tidbit from the array of tantalizing foods displayed upon the tables. The latter took planning and stealth in order to ensure you were not observed or caught by any of the women hovering around the tables.

Finally, when it was determined all were present, the activities and games temporarily were halted. Everyone sat down at the long row of tables in more-or-less family groups. My grandfather, who I and most family members affectionately called "Daddy Pa", took his place at the head of the tables. Heads were bowed and Daddy Pa offered a prayer of thanksgiving. He gave thanks for the food, the bounties of life, the good weather, the crops, and numerous other blessings. Above all, he gave thanks for the family and the opportunity we had to again join together and enjoy each others' company. Because of Daddy Pa's generally lengthy prayers, it had become somewhat of a family joke to question, after he had finished praying, as to whether or not he may have forgotten to bless the "Ten Lost Tribes."

Following my grandfather's prayer and a unison of "Amens", plates were loaded to overflowing and everyone became engrossed in trying to eat and visit at the same time. There was a pleasant buzz of voices as we attempted to catch up on the latest happenings among the many family members. Eventually, however, the eating subsided to little more than taking "just one more bite" of this or that special dish. Virtually each woman present had a special recipe or dish for which she was noted. And, she usually was expected to bring ample servings of her specialty to such gatherings. Then, of course, those present had to sample her offering, as well as pass judgment on whether or not it was up to her standard culinary efforts.

The children gradually dispersed from the tables and resumed their activities, but not in as boisterous a manner as prior to the meal. The women gathered in a group near one end of the row of tables, where they exchanged recipes and discussed whatever it is women discuss. The men retired to the cool, green grass beneath the shade of nearby trees. Here, they simply relaxed from their everyday labors, talked crops and business or merely watched the activities of the younger family members.

I spent the better part of the afternoon playing with my younger cousins, throwing a ball, playing tag and so forth. Late in the afternoon, however, there was a lull in our activities. I sat down next to Daddy Pa to rest a minute. As I sat next to my beloved grandfather, we talked about many things. While we visited, I thought of how he always had been more like a father than a grandfather to me. My Uncle Karl and I essentially were raised as brothers or almost like twins for much of our lives. Until we were twelve years old, we even were dressed alike. Throughout much of my life, if Daddy Pa bought something for Karl, he bought the same or similar for me. For example, if Karl got a new shirt, so did I. If he got a new toy, I got one also. Especially during summer vacations from school, I often lived in my grandparents' home. When he took his family on an outing or their regular summer vacation or fishing trips, I almost invariably accompanied them. I did not begin to realize until I was in high school that the relationship I had with my grandfather and his family was unique. I simply thought the choice treatment I received from Daddy Pa and his family must be the way it was in most families. As I grew older, however, I realized more and more how special our relationships were.

I also recalled how Uncle Karl and I, perhaps because we received so much attention from Daddy Pa and the older members of the family, were more mischievous than most young boys. As a result, it quite frequently became Daddy Pa's lot to have to discipline us. But, I cannot recall him every spanking or striking one of us. In fact, I don't remember him ever raising his voice in anger towards us, although our actions on many occasions undoubtedly justified him doing so. Nevertheless, I feared a quiet "talking to" from Daddy Pa much more than I feared a spanking from my grandmother or my parents. In his quiet manner and in a calm voice, Daddy Pa could make me regret whatever wrong I had committed. He often made me feel so ashamed for my misdeeds that I felt a spanking would have been preferable to a "talking to". A "good licking" might have at least made partial retribution for the wrong I had committed.

Daddy Pa and I visited for some time. We casually discussed a variety of topics. Suddenly, his pleasant and cheerful demeanor changed. He became very serious and inquired, "There are a lot of temptations in Yellowstone Park where you are working, aren't there?" I replied, "Yes, there are. In fact, the environment in the Park often is worse than what I had to contend with in the Army." Daddy Pa then told me he was proud of me, how he trusted me, and how he hoped I would always choose the right. One of my cousins then threw me a football and invited me to play catch with him. Daddy Pa then concluded our visit with, "Be a good boy, Son!"

I wondered why my grandfather suddenly had become so serious and why he was counseling me to "be a good boy". Didn't he realize I was no longer a boy? I was twenty six years old and a man! Hadn't I withstood the temptations with which I was confronted almost daily during almost two years in the Army? And, hadn't I just recently returned from serving as a "Mormon" missionary for two and one-half years in South America? Why then was he so concerned about me? And, why did he call me a "boy"?

Pondering Daddy Pa's words, I realized on some occasions I had been tempted while working in Yellowstone Park. Also, I often struggled to do those things I knew I should do and knew to be right. I did not realize, however, that Daddy Pa's counsel to "Be a good boy, Son!" would be the last words he would speak to me in mortality.

The hours passed quickly and soon most of those attending our family reunion realized they must begin their return journeys home. One family group and then another reluctantly departed. Fond farewells were bid to each. A few, however, including my grandparents and my family, decided first to visit a short while at my

Aunt Melba's and Uncle Ezra Moore's home, which was located only a few blocks from the Burley City Park.

Daddy Pa often would lie down and rest for a few minutes before driving or traveling for an extended distance. Thus, shortly after we arrived at my Aunt Melba's, she asked him, "Wouldn't you like to go into the bedroom and rest for a few minutes before driving home?" His reply was, "No. I want to visit with the family just as long as I can. Then I'll go!"

It seemed like only a few minutes later, my grandparents announced they must start their journey home. My Aunt Carol and Uncle Logan Barnard plus their three young daughters, who lived in California, had accompanied my grandparents to the reunion. Rather than drive his car home, Daddy Pa asked Logan to drive for him. He also insisted my grandmother and Aunt Carol sit in the front seat with Uncle Logan, "So I can sit in the back and visit with the kids just as long as I can!" Rather than return to Rockland by the most direct route, he suggested they return via Declo, a small community about ten miles from Burley. He and his family had lived on a farm near Declo prior to moving to Rockland some thirty years previously. He also had served as a "Mormon" bishop while in Declo and knew the area and people well. He simply stated, "I'd like to see and show you the old home place."

On the outskirts of Declo, Daddy Pa suddenly complained, "I can't breathe! Stop the car!" Logan braked the vehicle to a halt. Daddy Pa immediately opened the back door, got out, and then stumbled and fell towards the back of the vehicle. Before Logan could get out of the driver's seat and reach him, Daddy Pa laid unconscious upon the highway.

Somehow a call for help was sent and shortly an ambulance was rushing my grandfather back to the small hospital in Burley. Frantic telephone calls were made, including a call to the Idaho State Highway Patrol to intercept family members returning to their homes. Within a few hours, my grandparents' family again was assembled together. This time, however, it was not a joyous occasion such as had been the case earlier in the day at the Burley City Park.

The attending physician permitted my grandmother and one or two family members at a time to remain in the room where they had placed my grandfather. He remained unconscious beneath an oxygen tent. Tubes had been inserted into his nose and these were attached to a machine, which kept him breathing.

Most members of the family were confined to a nearby waiting room, where they nervously awaited reports as to Daddy Pa's condition. Looks of shock and disbelief were on their faces. No one expected something like this to happen, especially to Daddy Pa. We talked in muffled tones. Over and over it was repeated, "How could this happen? Daddy Pa has always been so healthy and active." No one could recall him ever having spent a day in bed. Although he occasionally took a short nap during the day, he usually arose each morning by 5:00 o'clock, and rarely retired prior to 10:00 o'clock at night. He invariably was cheerful and never mentioned, let alone complained, about not feeling well. This was despite the fact he had long suffered acute attacks of hay fever or asthma, especially during harvest seasons. He also had occasional bouts of influenza and other minor ailments, but always had resolutely continued his normal activities, as if he were completely well.

In addition to being actively engaged in his profession as a farmer and rancher, Daddy Pa was a member of the Stake Presidency of the American Falls Stake of The Church of Jesus Christ of Latter-day Saints. He held important positions in the Idaho State Legislature, Farmers' Grain Growers Association, Rockland School Board, and many other organizations. As a result, he traveled extensively and always seemed to be going to one meeting or another. Nevertheless, he always had time for his family, as well as for those whom he met or who came to him for counsel or advice. It seemed he always was so busy helping others and so concerned about them that he paid little attention to himself and never thought about his health or well being. The only concern any of us could remember him voicing was, "I hope when my time comes, it will come quickly. I especially hope I will never be a burden to anyone or have to endure a long or lingering illness before I die."

Through the long hours and well into the night, more and more of Daddy Pa's many friends joined our family in the waiting room of the Burley Hospital. They, like we, were shocked by the news about Daddy Pa. All offered their assistance to the family. Many also told us about the service or kindnesses Daddy Pa had rendered to them and their families. For the most part, family members did not know about the many kind deeds he had done for others.

My grandmother, whom I always called "Mama", requested that my Uncle Logan and I administer a blessing to my grandfather, as commonly is practiced by members of the "Mormon" Church through the authority of the Melchizedek Priesthood. This we did. We did not, however, feel inspired to bless Daddy Pa "for the restoration of his health", but only that he might have "peace". Shortly after the administration of this blessing, my grandfather's heavy, irregular breathing ceased. He began to breathe normally and his drawn face assumed its naturally calm and pleasant countenance. He appeared to be in a restful sleep. Although he once mumbled a few incoherent words, he never opened his eyes nor did he regain consciousness.

We returned to the waiting room, where we sat in silence throughout the long night. As we waited, I pondered the events of the day. Over and over I could hear Daddy Pa saying, "Be a good boy, Son! Be a good boy, Son!" His words of counsel also were words of parting or farewell. And, they became more meaningful to me.

Sunday morning, July 5th, 1959, dawned bright and clear. A few minutes before sunrise, a nurse solemnly entered the silent waiting room and delivered the dreaded news. Daddy Pa no longer was with us. He had quietly departed from this life, apparently without pain. Many family members were overcome with grief. Although sorely saddened, I realized there was no need for me to grieve for my grandfather. Like Paul of old, he had "fought a good fight" and he had "finished his course and kept the faith." There is no doubt in my mind; he had "laid up a crown of righteousness," which the Lord will bestow upon him (II Tim. 4:7-9).

Daddy Pa lived an exemplary life. He had found joy in his family, in his work, and in serving others. His wishes concerning death also had been fulfilled. He had died quickly, without having to suffer a lingering illness and without having been a burden to anyone. He was at peace with the world and with man and God. What better way to go than to spend the day with one's family and then to quietly depart?

Could we, as a family, have paid any better tribute to Daddy Pa than by joyfully joining together for a day of feasting and strengthening family ties? Also, could we have paid better tribute to my grandfather if we had known or could have foreseen his pending departure? I think not. I feel we should not grieve his passing. Our grief should be for ourselves, as we no longer have this great man as a mentor during our lives here on earth. For this, I truly grieve!

A few days after Daddy Pa's passing, one of the largest funeral services ever held in the Rockland Valley was held in memory of Raymond Madsen Whittier. The Chapel was filled to overflowing. Although the family had requested no flowers be sent, there were numerous large and beautiful bouquets surrounding the casket, which contained the earthly remains of my grandfather. Wonderful eulogies and many kind words were spoken, but the sermon I heard most clearly was "Be a good boy, Son!"

Although many years since have passed, I still often think about and remember the wonderful times I had with my grandfather and his family. I wish I could be more like him and better emulate his example. I particularly hope I never forget Daddy Pa's final counsel to me of "Be a Good Boy, Son!"

FIRE!

Many things besides fire can burn us and damage our lives.

Saturday, July 4th 1959, is a day I shall never forget. More than fifty members of my maternal grandparents' family joined together in the Burley, Idaho City Park for a Whittier Family Reunion. We spent the day feasting, visiting, playing games, and renewing and strengthening family ties. We had a wonderful time. However, shortly after everyone had commenced their return journey home, we were notified my grandfather, who we affectionately called Daddy Pa, had suffered a heart attack. By ambulance, he had been rushed back to the Burley Hospital, where he now lay in a coma. And, during the evening of this warm and rather sultry day, we were assembled in the waiting room of the Hospital – awaiting the outcome of this tragedy.

I was sitting somewhat apart from the other family members, pondering the events of the day and my relationship with my beloved grandfather. I especially was thinking about the last words he spoke to me, which were "Be a good boy, Son!"

Suddenly, a door to the waiting room was flung open, and a man carrying a small boy in his arms burst into the room. He kept shouting, "Doctor! Doctor! Someone get a doctor!" The little boy he was carrying appeared to be five or six years old and was screaming at the top of his lungs. Except for the charred remains of what appeared to have been a T-shirt, he was bare from the waist up. His back and chest had the color and texture of a hot dog that had been roasted over an open fire. Large welts or the formative stages of huge blisters covered much of his upper body.

A white-smocked doctor, followed by a nurse, rushed into the room. They immediately took the small boy from the shouting man's arms and carried him into the interior of the hospital. The man who had carried the little boy into the room became silent. He stood motionless, as if he were lost. Then, he started to wander aimlessly among the assembled members of our family. Spying an unoccupied seat next to me, he sat down. Staring at the floor, he began to speak, but it seemed he was speaking to no one in particular. In a low voice, he explained what had happened.

He was driving into town when he noticed two small boys playing with sparklers on the front lawn of a house alongside the street. Suddenly, the shirt of one of the boys burst into flame. The boy started to scream and run along the sidewalk. The man claimed he slammed on his brakes, jumped out of the car, ran and caught the boy in his arms. He then rolled him in the grass of an adjacent lawn until the flames were extinguished. Thereafter, for a few desperate minutes, he tried to locate the little boy's parents. Although he shouted as loud as he could and banged on the doors of nearby houses, he did not arouse anyone, let alone find the poor boy's parents. Finally, he put the boy in his car and came as quickly as he could to the hospital. However, he had instructed the boy's frightened playmate to find his friend's parents as soon as possible and tell them a man had taken their son to the hospital.

As this man described what had happened, a nurse came into the room and began to question him. When she ascertained what had happened, where it occurred, and how the man had brought the boy to the hospital, she told him, "You might as well go. I'll get hold of the police and they'll help locate the child's parents." The still bewildered man then departed.

The little boy's mother and father entered the waiting room about an hour later. The nurse, who had questioned and dismissed the man who had brought their son to the hospital, told them, "Wait here! The doctor wants to see you as soon as he finishes with your son and is able to do so." Thus, the couple sat down next to me. Both obviously had been drinking and were very much under the influence of alcohol. They paid little attention to me or to the others in the waiting room. Instead, they immediately began to bicker back and forth, "You knew I wouldn't be home! Why weren't you watching him?" This resulted in, "You knew I didn't feel well! You should have been watching him!" So it went, on and on. Neither seemed concerned about the condition of their son, whom they still hadn't seen! Their major concern seemed to be that of placing the blame for what had happened on the other!

Upon re-entering the waiting room, the nurse interrupted the bickering between the little boy's mother and father. She told them, "The doctor would like to see you." She then ushered the now silent couple into the interior of the hospital. I never saw them or their little boy again. However, the nurse later informed me, "The poor little tyke has been so severely burned he'll probably carry large scars on his chest and back throughout his life." When I inquired as to the responsibility of the parents, her reply was, "That's up to the authorities to sort out."

As I continued to anxiously wait throughout the long hours of that night for word concerning my grandfather's condition, I relived over and over the events of the day. The family get-together had been great. We'd had a marvelous day. However, my grandfather's final words to me of, "Be a good boy, son!" intermingled with the tragedy of the severely burned young boy occupied my mind the most. I wondered, "How many of us, especially when we are away from our parents' vigil, play with fire?" And, "How many of us are burned, perhaps so severely that we may carry scars throughout our lives or perhaps even throughout eternity?" And, "How often do such things happen because of our carelessness?"

My grandfather's final words of counsel took on more and more meaning. No matter how tempting a flame might be, playing with fire is dangerous! Though we sometimes might escape from being burned, we never know whether or not nor how badly we might be burned – if we persist in playing with "FIRE!"

A FULBRIGHT SCHOLAR AND A REVOLUTION

"Life often is a dearer classroom than are the hallowed halls of institutions of learning!"

After ten days of orientation and sightseeing in Washington, D.C., Naomi Quinn, Robert Norris and I flew to Quito, Ecuador, via Miami, Panama City, and Cali, Columbia. We had been selected to be Fulbright Scholars for a year's graduate study in Ecuador. Naomi was from Boston, Massachusetts and a graduate of Rutgers University. She planned to study child development in a remote Indian village near the base of Mount Chimborazo, Ecuador's loftiest mountain peak. Robert was from Dallas, Texas and planned to study political science in the "Universidad Central" (Central University) in Quito, where I also planned to study natural history.

In route to Ecuador, we stopped briefly in Miami, but spent two days in Panama City, which we spent primarily sightseeing. It was here, while walking alone along a back street in the "barrios" or slums of the city, two young men approached Bob. One suddenly grasped his arms and pulled them behind him, while the other stripped his watch from off his wrist. Bob immediately wrenched free from the fellow's grasp and pursued the one with his watch. However, the guy had a good head start and Bob shortly lost him in a maze of narrow passageways and stairs. This experience, however, taught Bob a dear lesson. Thereafter, he rarely ventured into questionable areas alone.

We were scheduled to stop only briefly in Cali, but, due to a malfunction in the Panagra plane in which we were flying, we spent a "three-day vacation" in this city – courtesy of Panagra! Our plane was carrying a part needed to repair another Panagra plane stranded in Quito. Thus, both our plane and the one in Quito had to wait for the next scheduled flight from Miami, which was three days later.

We spent our three days in Cali seeing the sights, practicing our Spanish, and discussing what we planned to do or accomplish during our year in Ecuador. Naomi had spent the previous summer in

Ecuador in an undergraduate study program sponsored by Harvard University. Thus, she was fairly well acquainted with the country and had definite plans as to what she wanted to accomplish. Bob had never been further south than Mexico, but had spent a year at the University of Monterey. Thus, he had had experience in a Latin American university, as well as with the "Latin" people. As for myself, I had served two and one-half years as a "Mormon" missionary in Uruguay and Paraguay and had spent three days in the coastal city of Guayaquil, Ecuador while returning to the States. Guayaquil had not impressed me and I hoped Quito would contrast markedly with the squalor of Guayaquil. Fortunately, it did.

Quito is an ancient and beautiful city that is nestled in a high (ninety-five-hundred-feet) green valley surrounded by towering Andean peaks. Before the advent of the Spanish conquistadors, it served as the northern capital of the Inca Empire. It was in September of 1822 that General Antonio Jose de Sucre defeated the Spaniards in the "Battle of Pichincha", which was fought on the nearby slopes of Mount Pichincha and ended Spanish rule in Ecuador

Dr. Luis Andrade (Director of the Fulbright Program in Ecuador) and Senora Maria Alcon (his secretary) greeted us upon our arrival in Quito. Dr. Andrade was a noted lawyer and a former Ecuadorian naval commander. Senora Alcon was from an aristocratic and highly respected Ecuadorian family. They graciously showed us some of the sights in Quito, before depositing us at the "Pension Lutecia", a small hotel in one of the more exclusive parts of the city.

Senora Alcon insisted we stay at the "Pension Lutecia". She had convinced the owner he should give us a much lower than normal rate for our board and room. However, we quickly realized that even the lowered rate would leave us practically nothing for other expenditures. Our monthly stipends were about $160 and the lowered rate at the "Lutecia" approximated $140 per month. Thus, Robert and I began to search for cheaper quarters.

Naomi shortly departed for the remote Indian village of Pedro Juan Caballero on the slopes of Mount Chimborazo. Here, she would begin her studies on child development. Bob and I then moved into the recently constructed and ultra-modern, six-story men's dormitory on the campus of the "Universidad Central". We soon learned there were only four students other than us residing in the dormitory, which did not have a kitchen nor any eating facilities. In fact, there was no place on or near the campus where you could eat or purchase food. Thus, we had to seek our meals elsewhere.

Fall classes were slow in starting. Students seemed to be more interested in social gatherings and in espousing political views than in obtaining an education. The general consensus among our fellow students was that Bob and I represented the United States of America. Therefore, any opinions we might express or statements we might make were deemed to be the "official" position of the U.S. Government. We quickly learned to be cautious about whatever we said – especially if it had anything to do with politics.

When classes finally commenced, we learned that tardiness, absenteeism, and a general lack of interest in what the professors might be trying to teach were the norm. There were no textbooks. Professors also seemed to take pride in being able to lecture verbatim – without any notes – for an entire class period. No homework or outside reading was assigned. Quizzes or mid-term exams were unknown. Grades were determined solely by final exams, which were based upon information presented in the professors' lectures. Select students religiously copied virtually every word dictated by the professors. Copies of their notes then were distributed to other class members, most of whom never attended class. Then, about two weeks before final exams, there was a flurry of activity as students tried to virtually memorize these notes.

After spending two lecture periods in a zoology class recording the weights and measurements of the various organs of a blue whale – information the professor must have gleaned from an encyclopedia – I approached Dr. Andrade and asked if there might not be a better way for me to study natural history while in Ecuador. Dr. Andrade shortly informed me that Dr. Gustavo Orces V - the most eminent zoologist in Quito, if not in all of Ecuador - had agreed to personally tutor me. Dr. Orces taught a few zoology courses at the "Universidad Central", but his office and laboratory were in the "Escuela Polytecnica

Nacional", which was primarily an engineering institution. The "Polytecnica" was centrally located in Quito, near Dr. Andrade's office; whereas, the "Universidad Central" was located on the edge of the city, at the base of Mount Pichincha. Thus, began my close association with Dr. Orces, a truly remarkable man.

Dr. Orces was in his early seventies and a confirmed bachelor. He had devoted his entire life to studying zoology, particularly animal taxonomy. His first interest had been mammals. However, he had found it was difficult and expensive to collect mammal specimens. Nevertheless, he had amassed on the shelves and in the drawers in his laboratory a notable collection of Ecuadorian mammal skulls and skins. In fact, he had specimens of some mammal species represented in only a few museums in the world.

Dr. Orce's interest then shifted to neotropical birds. Through the services of three brothers - the Olayas, who were professional zoological specimen collectors – Dr. Orces assembled perhaps the most extensive collection of Ecuadorian bird skins in the world. Although Ecuador is a small country - only one-hundred and ten thousand square miles or about the size of the state of Colorado - it has one of the most abundant and diverse bird faunas of any country in the world. Whereas, the entire North American continent has only about eight hundred species of birds, Ecuador has in excess of two thousand!

Many bird species display sexual dimorphism in their plumage, i.e. the coloration of males and females of the same species may differ markedly. The same also may be true for young or immature birds as compared to adults. Thus, being able to readily identify virtually all of Ecuador's varied bird species, as could Dr. Orces, is truly a formidable feat. Not only could he readily identify almost any bird specimen to genus and species, he often also could tell almost the exact location from whence the specimen had come. For example, he might note, "See the white on the throat of this specimen? This is present only on birds from the south slope of Cotapaxi; whereas, those from elsewhere do not have it."

Dr. Orces had mastered the taxonomy of Ecuador's birds and it was no longer a challenge to him. Thus, he began to look for "new fields to conquer". He worked some on the taxonomy of toads and frogs. But, shortly before my arrival in Quito, he had become intrigued by the taxonomy of fish in Ecuador, which had been little studied. It amazed me how Dr. Orces could remain hunched over a dissecting microscope for literally hours, while counting the scales or determining identifying characteristics of a fish specimen he was studying. He oftentimes did not stop even long enough to eat his meals. Repeatedly, he would inquire of me, "What time is it?" Then, when I would inform him it was 3:00 or 4:00 p.m. or later, he'd simply remark, "Darn! I didn't realize it was so late. Guess I've missed lunch again!" Dr. Orces' interests apparently shifted to reptiles after my departure from Ecuador, as I recently noted in a travel brochure that a museum for reptiles, which bears his name, currently is one of the "must-see" places of interest in Quito.

Dr. Orces insisted he was "nothing more than a laboratory zoologist", in other words "ONLY a taxonomist". It was true, he rarely went into the field and he depended upon others to bring him specimens. Nevertheless, he was a most knowledgeable ecologist and probably knew more about the fauna of Ecuador than anyone. Besides the taxonomy or scientific names of animals, he also almost invariably knew their local or Indian names, as well as something about their natural history and behavior. He was remarkable! However, except for taxonomic papers, in which he presented information on new species for science, he published very little. This was despite his being a "walking encyclopedia" and his knowing more about Ecuador's fauna than was contained in all of the scientific literature. I thought, "What a pity it would be if Dr. Orces should die without at least some of his knowledge being recorded and published!" "How could this best be done?"

Dr. Orces decided to teach me the taxonomy of Ecuador's birds and mammals. I was overwhelmed. I also reasoned, "Even if I could learn the scientific names and could identify most of the birds and mammals in Ecuador, what good would that do?" I then discovered there were no books dealing solely with the taxonomy of Ecuadorian mammals. Thus, I approached Dr. Orces about the possibility of him helping me to write "A Guide to the Mammals of Ecuador." He pondered my request for several days before becoming enthusiastic about it. He then loaded me down with numerous scientific reports, which he had accumulated for many years and which were stacked in no particular order throughout his office and laboratory. He also began to sort through the many mammal skins and skulls, which were stored on the shelves and in the drawers lining the walls of his laboratory. I was to examine these and to record identifying characteristics; various measurements, color of pelage and variations occurring between specimens of the same species. Thus, I began the arduous task of developing "A Guide to the Mammals of Ecuador", which - without Dr. Orces' help and guidance - would have been a difficult task to accomplish even during a lifetime, let alone in a single year!

Bob and I continued to live in the student dormitory, although I now spent most of my time at the "Polytecnica". Bob continued to attended classes at the "Universidad Central", even though they were not much of a challenge to him and did not occupy much of his time. He also began to teach evening English classes at the U.S. Information Services' (USIS) Bi-national Center, which was near Dr. Andrade's office and the "Polytecnica". Although I was fully occupied with compiling a mammal guide, I also began to teach a few English classes at the Center, in order to supplement my meager Fulbright stipend.

Our student friends indicated there was considerable political unrest and opposition to the government in Ecuador. They particularly were opposed to President Velasco Ibarra. Although he had been elected by popular vote four times and was serving his fourth term as President, he had successfully completed only one term! Twice, he had been ousted from office by revolts and exiled from Ecuador. But, he then had run in absentia during subsequent elections and had won these by substantial margins and, thereafter, triumphantly returned to the country to again be President!

President Ibarra was a great orator. The Ecuadorian people loved to hear him speak. He could "sway" the masses with his orations. He would tell the people, "You may not need a bridge. But, if you want a bridge, I will give you a bridge!" Furthermore, he tried to keep his campaign promises – even though they could be ironical, foolish or might cause financial and/or political problems. He was a most interesting man.

Cuenca, a city in southern Ecuador, was celebrating its 300th anniversary. Cuenca's financial well being rested primarily upon the cottage industry of hand-woven "Panama" hats. As went the whims of fashion for Panama hats, so went Cuenca's economy. At the time of the scheduled tri-centennial celebration, there was little demand for Panama hats and many residents of Cuenca blamed President Ibarra for this. Nevertheless, during one of his many political speeches, President Ibarra had promised he'd personally come to Cuenca to help celebrate its 300th anniversary. Some of the city fathers wrote and told him not to come. But, the President's reply was, "When I make a promise, I keep my promise! Therefore, I will be in Cuenca for your celebration!" In short, President Ibarra attended the celebration. Some university students demonstrated. And, the President's military guards fired upon the student demonstrators and killed more than twenty of them.

President Ibarra also planned to attend a celebration in the coastal city of Guayaquil. Again, he was told he was not welcome. He went anyway. University students again demonstrated and some students again were shot and killed by the President's military guards. These events united the politically active university students throughout the country. Rallies and demonstrations demanding the President's resignation became common. Although the students appeared to be united against the President and vociferously advocated the overthrow of his government, they did not say neither whom they thought should replace President Ibarra nor how they felt the government should be changed.

Several students at the "Universidad Central" informed Bob and me that Vice President Arosamena was going to speak in downtown Quito. They invited us to accompany them, stating, "It should be very interesting!" Not realizing what they meant by "very interesting", we agreed to go with them to listen to the Vice President's speech.

When we arrived at the small plaza in front of the Teatro Sucre in downtown Quito, nothing seemed to be out of the ordinary. A large crowd - comprised mostly of students - had already assembled. There were a few policemen and military guards stationed in front of the theater and on the large balcony from which the Vice President was going to speak. This was to be expected. Across the plaza, directly in front of the balcony, a new building was under construction and the construction site was separated from the plaza by an approximately eight-foot-high wall. Unbeknown to us, some students had positioned themselves behind this wall. Shortly, some lesser government officials on the balcony made preliminary introductions over a noisy loudspeaker system. Vice President Arosamena then strode onto the balcony and began to address the crowd. Students in the plaza shortly began to shout protests and students on the other side of the wall began to toss bricks, rocks and other materials over the wall into the plaza. In turn, their colleagues in the plaza started to throw these at the Vice President. The Vice President immediately retreated from the balcony into the building. The curtains then opened and soldiers with machine guns on tripods rushed out of the building and took positions on the balcony. They then began to fire into the milling crowd in the plaza below. Canisters of tear gas also began to rain down upon those of us in the plaza. We were panic-stricken. To add to the confusion, mounted cavalry galloped into the midst of us from a side street. Both the mounted men and their horses were equipped with gas masks. These cavalrymen brandished large "billy" clubs, which they used to unmercifully strike those on either side of their charging mounts. All was bedlam!

The tear gas made it almost impossible for us to see or breathe. It also caused us to vomit until we thought we would throw up our insides. People were screaming and crying everywhere. Arms and legs of some who had been shot were flaying violently! Unbelievably, some students were trying to catch the blood from the wounded in their cupped hands and to use it to paint signs of protest on the wall. Others were trying to drag their fallen comrades out of the plaza by their arms and legs. It was complete chaos!

Bob and I did not know what to do. We surged one way and then another with the frightened mob. Finally, we spied an opening, which led to a side street. Screaming at each other, we ran as fast as we could out of the plaza and down the street. We feared the cavalry would pursue us. As we ran along the street, we tried first one door and then another – frantically searching for somewhere to hide. We found a door that was not locked. We opened it, rushed inside, hurriedly closed it behind us, and ran up a flight of stairs and into what looked like a living room. It did not appear anyone was home. Nevertheless, we dove over and behind a couch and laid huddled together on the floor beneath some large drapes.

Bob and I did not dare even to whisper for some time. Then, after what seemed to be an eternity, but probably was less than half an hour, we realized we no longer could hear any sounds from the street. We waited perhaps another fifteen minutes – just to make sure! We then cautiously crept out of the room and down the stairs. We carefully opened the door – just a crack – and peered out. The street appeared to be deserted. We scurried through the door, down the street, away from the plaza, and back to the student dormitory. Students at the University subsequently informed us that "at least twenty and perhaps more than thirty students were killed" and several times that number seriously injured during the melee in the plaza. This further incited and solidified their resolve to oust President Ibarra and overthrow his government. This was despite the fact the "incident" on the plaza in front of the Teatro Sucre had occurred in conjunction with a speech by Vice President Arosamena!

University students throughout Ecuador united in open defiance to the government. Vociferous cries were made for the President to resign and "get out of the country." Instead of fleeing, President Ibarra proclaimed, "I will meet force with force!" He called upon the military to "do whatever has to be done" to quell the student uprising.

An artillery battalion stationed on a hill on the outskirts of Quito, not far from the student dormitory where Bob and I resided, revolted against the President. The artillerymen claimed they would not shoot anymore "fellow countrymen" – no matter what the President ordered. President Ibarra then called upon the Air Force and other military units to attack and squelch the insurgent artillery battalion.

We had a ringside seat of the ensuing battle from our dormitory windows. Fighter planes streaked past and strafed the nearby artillery unit. In addition to the roar of fighter jets and the chatter of their machine guns, we could hear the boom of large guns and see white puffs of smoke rise from the hill where the artillery battalion was located. The out-manned and apparently out-gunned artillery battalion shortly surrendered. However, it appeared the conquerors then discussed matters with the vanquished artillerymen and agreed with their cause. As a result, they also claimed they no longer would fire upon their fellow countrymen. All then joined forces against the President.

President Ibarra apparently could see the "handwriting on the wall." On public radio, he announced, "I will resign - IF Vice President Arosamena also will resign and a provisional government comprised of a military junta will direct affairs of government until elections can be organized."

A military junta was quickly formed and supposedly took over the government. President Ibarra then publicly announced his resignation. But, Vice President Arosamena then announced, "Because President Ibarra has resigned, I now am automatically the President." To further complicate matters, President Ibarra was noted for his pro-U.S. stance, which had resulted in Ecuador receiving substantial aid from the U.S.; whereas, Vice President Arosamena was noted for his Communistic leanings and anti-American stance. Because of this, Ibarra and Arosamena often had been at odds while serving together as the heads of state. Now it would be anyone's guess as to what position the U.S. and other democratic nations would take in regards to Ecuador if Arosamena became President.

When Ibarra heard Arosamena's claim to the presidency, he came back on the air and claimed, "I am still President – BECAUSE my resignation was dependent upon the Vice President also resigning!" Meanwhile the military junta claimed it was now Ecuador's "governing body"! Thus, three parties – Ibarra, Arosamena and a military junta – simultaneously were claiming the leadership role for Ecuador!

Arosamena previously served as the commanding general of the Ecuadorian Air Force. Officers in the Air Force apparently still owed allegiance to him and they quickly announced their support for Arosamena, rather than for the military junta. Rather than face another military conflict, the military junta capitulated and also announced support for Arosamena. Thus, the balance of power was tilted against Velasco Ibarra and he again lost the Presidency and was exiled from Ecuador.

Fellow students frequently informed Bob and me about what was taking place with respect to the confusing game of political charades in Ecuador. Though they usually spoke authoritatively, sometimes their reports were contradictory. Therefore, Bob and I decided to venture across Quito to the American Embassy. Perhaps some of our friends there could set the record straight with respect to what had happened during the student-instigated revolution, as well as what was now happening with regards to the relationship between the U.S. and the "now" President Arosamena.

The streets were virtually deserted as we hurried across Quito to the American Embassy. We arrived without incident and asked to see Mr. Basine, who was Head of the USIS and in charge of the Fulbright Program in Ecuador. We knew Mr. Basine quite well and thought he might tell us "exactly" what was going on with regard to the Ecuadorian revolution and political circus. He met us at the front desk and pompously escorted us into his spacious office. When we explained why we wanted to see him, he carefully explained, "Much of what I am going to tell you is confidential or even secret. But, I know both of you well and I know I can trust you not to repeat anything I tell you." We agreed not to do so and Mr. Basine then methodically and authoritatively began to appraise us as to what had happened and what probably would still happen, as well as what would be the stance of the U.S. Government. Among other things, he claimed, "The U.S. WILL NOT recognize Arosamena as President, because of his Communistic leanings. However, the U.S. undoubtedly will support the military junta – until 'fair and impartial elections' can be held."

Much of what Mr. Basine told us was contradictory to what we had been told by students at the University, many of which had been leaders in the revolt. We felt, however, that Mr. Basine surely must know what he was talking about. Why, he's head of the USIS! However, only hours after our meeting with him, the U.S. officially announced its acceptance and support for Arosamena. Within a few weeks, we also determined much of what Mr. Basine had told us was erroneous.

Ecuador is one of the smallest countries in South America. What happens here usually is of little importance to the U.S. Major U.S. news networks were not even represented in Ecuador. The revolution and overthrow of the government happened so quickly that U.S. newsmen did not arrive in the country until after all hostilities had ceased. Bob and I, as well as many Ecuadorians, were shocked by what was presented in the U.S. news media about the 1961 Ecuadorian revolution. Reports in what we had considered to be reputable publications, i.e. the New York Times newspaper and Time Magazine, were grossly exaggerated and erroneous. Much of what was reported had no basis in fact! For example, it was claimed the Legislative Palace in Quito was strafed by Ecuadorian Air Force fighter planes. This was not true. The closest resemblance to such an occurrence was when some fighter pilots fired overhead salutes to celebrate the ousting of President Ibarra.

Bob and I were not prone to writing "Letters to the Editor." We strongly felt, however, someone should try to set the record straight with regards to what was erroneously reported in the U.S. news media about the revolution in Ecuador. Thus, we wrote a letter to the Editor of Time Magazine. We explained how there were twenty-one gross errors in the article Time Magazine had published about the Ecuadorian revolution. We then presented a factual version of what happened. Our letter was never published. However, we received a tart reply, which stated, "Anything published in Time Magazine is fact! Your claims are unfounded!" I previously had considered Time Magazine to be one of the best and most factual news sources available. I since have refused to purchase this magazine and now doubt the veracity of much of what is presented in the U.S. news media.

Students at the "Universidad Central" shortly informed Bob and me that university students from all of Ecuador were coming to Quito to celebrate "their victory" in ousting President Ibarra. Many would be staying in the dormitory where we resided. This six-story modern building was built by the U.S. government for a conference planned by the U.S. Embassy in Quito. The conference, however, was never held and the U.S. Government simply gave the building to the University. Although the dormitory was fully furnished and extravagant when compared to university dormitories in the U.S., only a few students resided in it. Nevertheless, the dormitory was provided with a rather large staff. Operators even were provided to run the automatic elevators! Although we did not ascertain whether or not it was true, we were told the U.S. Government paid the salaries for this staff.

Hoards of university students from throughout Ecuador soon descended upon the campus of the "Universidad Central". The dormitory was crowded to overflowing. There was such pandemonium that Bob announced, "I'm moving out, permanently!" I was expecting my wife Carol to arrive from the U.S. within a few weeks. Thus, I thought, "I'll stick it out here in the dormitory until I can locate a suitable apartment, which we can afford with my meager Fulbright stipend. Anyway, if I lay low or stay in my room most of the time, the celebrating students won't even know I am here."

The second night of the Ecuadorian students' victory celebration culminated in a major split between student factions. As a result, the non-Communist students returned to their homes and the pro-Communist students remained in Quito to debate what course they felt the new government should take. Thus, I was staying in the student dormitory with between three or four hundred "pro-Commies". Nevertheless, I reasoned, "If I remain inconspicuous and the students don't know I am here, there shouldn't be any problem. But, if they see me and recognize me as a 'Yankee', I might be in trouble!" Except for slipping out of the dormitory early in the morning and in the evening for meals, I remained in my room with the door locked. The second night, however, was disquieting. Many drunken students were noisily marching up and down the halls, shouting – to the accompaniment of drums and trumpets – "Cuba, Si! Yankee, No!"

It was well past midnight before the bedlam somewhat subsided and I finally went to sleep. Then, I was rudely awakened by a group of drunken students who had somehow entered my room. All I could think was, "I've had it!" I jumped out of bed and, with doubled-up fists, started swinging. I was certain I was fighting for my life. The students swarmed over me and pinned me helplessly to the floor. Then, to my surprise, they invited me to join them. They were so drunk they did not recognize me as a "Yankee". Somehow, I convinced them I was too tired to join them. And, I politely ushered the entourage out of my room.

I hurriedly locked the door. As I sat trembling on the edge of my bed, I resolved, "I'll pack my bags right now. Then, first thing in the morning, while they're sleeping off their drunken stupor, I'll get out of here!" After packing my bags, I laid upon my bed for sometime before again falling asleep. Then, I again was awakened by a group of students in my room that wanted me to join them. This time I feigned a terrible headache and prayed, under my breath, they wouldn't realize I was a "Yankee".

They shortly staggered out of my room and into the hall. As soon as I determined they were celebrating on another floor, I grabbed my bags, scurried to the rear entrance to the dormitory, and half-ran and half-walked all the way across Quito to the Hotel Alcron, where Bob had taken up residency. I then remained at the Hotel Alcron until I located an apartment for my wife and me.

It shortly was announced the "Universidad Central" was receiving a sizeable grant from the U.S. Government for the construction of new classrooms and the renovation of the student dormitory, which virtually had been demolished by the celebrating pro-Communist students. Bob and I could not believe it. Never more than half of the existing classrooms at the "Universidad Central" were ever in use at one time. The universities we had attended in the U.S. needed additional classroom space much more than did "Universidad Central". Also, why should American taxpayers pay to refurbish a dormitory that had been devastated by pro-Communist Ecuadorian students?

I encountered a former "Mormon" missionary friend ("Andy" Anderson) during the ten-day orientation period Naomi, Bob and I spent in Washington, D.C. Andy was from Utah, where his father was the Attorney General and a good friend of Utah's Senator Moss. Because of Senator Moss' relationship with Andy's father, he had hired Andy to work part time in his Washington office, while he was enrolled at George Washington University. Andy's employment consisted primarily of distributing the mail each morning onto the appropriate desks in Senator Moss' office complex.

Andy invited me to Senator Moss' office and introduced me to Senator Moss. The Senator seemed to take an interest in me and said, "If I can ever be of service to you, don't hesitate to let me know." I took him at his word. So, when Bob and I heard about the U.S. grant to the "Universidad Central", which we thought was ludicrous, I wrote a letter to Senator Moss. I explained the situation in Ecuador and how we thought the use of U.S. taxpayers' money for classrooms and the refurbishing of the dormitory were inappropriate. I also told the Senator how the Head of the USIS in Ecuador had wrongly appraised the political situation. And, after his having been in Ecuador more than two years, - during which he received daily Spanish lessons during work hours from a private tutor employed by the U.S. Embassy - he could not even pronounce "Buenos Dias" correctly. I also related how CARE packages, which were clearly marked in English "FOR FREE DISTRIBUTION, NOT FOR RESALE" were being sold through the Catholic Church and Ecuadorians were complaining about the high prices they thought were being charged by the U.S. Government. Further, I told how money provided through U.S. grants often was wasted or pocketed by already rich Ecuadorians, which was common knowledge throughout Ecuador. And, of course, I told him how the celebrating pro-Communist students had devastated the dormitory that had been built by the U.S. Government and donated to the "Universidad Central".

I had almost forgotten about my letter to Senator Moss when I was summoned to the U.S. Embassy in Quito. A Hispanic Embassy staff member (originally from New Mexico) began to interrogate me in Spanish. He wanted to know why and what I had written to Senator Moss. I told him. He then began to belittle me by saying, "Don't you realize you are a guest in Ecuador. As a guest, you should not find fault with or complain about what is going on here." When I tried to explain I was finding fault primarily with the actions of the U.S. Government, but still did not think it right for the Ecuadorians to destroy a building we had given them and then expect us to refurbish it. In turn, he claimed, "That's no different than in the U.S. Haven't you ever been to an American Legion Convention? They have a good time and sometimes destroy some property in the process." When I still insisted I didn't think it was right to "stick" the American taxpayer for inappropriate expenditures in Ecuador, he became even more agitated with me.

We then got into the subject of how many Ecuadorian students, who were avowed Communists and some of which received monthly stipends from the Communist Party, were sent on USIS fellowships to study in the U.S. My interrogator could not understand why I thought this was improper. He claimed, "If a student is qualified for a USIS fellowship, we cannot deny them such a fellowship – just because they are a Communist or have political views contrary to those of the U.S." He further assured me the U.S. Embassy knew which students were Communists and which were not. He also proudly proclaimed, "We have files on all the activities of such students – both before and after they go to the U.S." When I explained how such students, upon their return from the U.S., could better sway other students towards their Communistic views – primarily because of lies they told about the U.S. - he had little comment

Our heated debate quickly reverted into English. As I became more and more the interrogator, he became more and more agitated. This appeared to be because he could not adequately answer my questions. Finally, he ordered me out of his office and ordered others to escort me out of the Embassy. I was furious. Why couldn't he at least try to truthfully answer my questions?

Numerous incidents that occurred during my year in Ecuador greatly eroded my faith in the U.S. State Department. For example, while Bob and I were living in the Hotel Alcron, we became well acquainted with an American pilot and his Ecuadorian wife. He was a spray pilot for some banana plantations and had lived and worked in Ecuador for many years. He and his wife and another couple decided to explore some Incan ruins in the mountains of southern Ecuador. His wife was expecting a baby. Thus, they decided to buy some powdered milk for her in the city of Cuenca, before going into the mountains. The only powdered milk they could find was in a store owned and operated by the Catholic Church. Besides being shocked by the exorbitant price asked for the powdered milk, they noted it was clearly labeled, "A GIFT FROM THE PEOPLE OF THE UNITED STATES OF AMERICA, FOR FREE DISTRIBUTION, NOT FOR RESALE." This upset them and their friends. They decided to investigate. They found, for some unexplainable reason, CARE packages from the U.S. Government were being delivered directly to the Catholic Church, which then was selling these commodities. Flour was being sold to local bakeries and the CARE sacks in which it was received were being sold in the local market. Corn meal, which was intended for human consumption, also was being used to fatten pigs on a Church farm.

As the two couples delved more and more into how CARE packages and other products sent by the U.S. Government to Ecuador for free distribution were being used or sold by the Catholic Church, they were joined by a local priest and some nuns. The priest and nuns shouted accusations at them and attempted to incite the local people against them. As a result, they were thrown into jail and remained there for two days – until they got word to the American Consulate in Guayaquil and arrangements were made for their release.

On another occasion, the U.S. gave eleven million dollars to the city of Quito to start a new housing project. Ironically, a previously U.S.-financed housing project in Quito still sat unfinished. Almost three hundred previously constructed houses, which essentially lacked only doors and windows, sat unoccupied - while the new project was initiated. Rarely, it seemed, did the U.S. Government aid to Ecuador accomplish what it was supposed to do. As a result, Ecuadorians thought we North Americans were both rich and stupid. They also thought our politicians were even more dishonest than theirs!

Upon my return to the U.S. and graduate school at Utah State University, I related some of my experiences in Ecuador to fellow graduate students. One of these insisted I tell the press what I told them, "So the American people can know what is going on in Ecuador." The next thing I knew, a reporter from the *Salt Lake Tribune* (a major newspaper in Utah) was standing next to my desk. She wanted to interview me about what I had told the other students about my experiences in Ecuador.

I related some of these incidents and emphasized how I felt it was wrong for U.S. taxpayers' dollars to be misappropriated or wrongly spent in foreign countries. The reporter repeatedly questioned me as to the veracity of what I was telling her. I assured her I was telling the truth. Furthermore, if she so desired, I could prove everything I had told her. If nothing else, we could contact Bob Norris, who was enrolled in graduate school at the University of New Mexico. He could verify everything I had told her. I thought this would suffice.

I brought back with me a pet "kinkajou" from Ecuador. A kinkajou is a small, brown-furred member of the raccoon family. It looks much like a "Teddy Bear", except for its long, prehensile tail. I kept my pet in a cage in the behavior lab at the University and it had become well known to many of the students and staff. When mention was made of my pet, the reporter from the *Salt Lake Tribune* wanted to see it. She then took photographs of my kinkajou and me, while it dangled by its prehensile tail from my extended arm. Then, after reviewing with me the voluminous notes she had taken during the interview, she stated, "I'm sure this will be published in the Tribune."

The following Sunday – on the front page of the *Salt Lake Tribune* – there was a picture of my kinkajou and me. The accompanying article, however, said nothing about the misappropriation of taxpayers' dollars or of the politics in Ecuador. Instead, the article simply told how I had spent a year study natural history as a Fulbright Scholar in that country and had compiled "A Guide to the Mammals of Ecuador."

Why does the so-called "free press" in the U.S. so often fail to tell the truth? Truth is truth and there should be no fear in a free nation of reporting it. Likewise, there is a responsibility to ensure that what is reported is true, and that falsehoods – such as were presented in the U.S. media regarding the revolution in Ecuador – are NOT reported. As citizens of the United States of America, is it not our responsibility to try and ensure that what is reported by the news media in our country is "the truth and nothing but the truth?"

CLIMBING A MOUNTAIN

Just because you are near the Equator does not mean you can't almost literally freeze to death!

Immediately prior to going to Ecuador as a Fulbright scholar, I spent the summer as a seasonal park naturalist in Rocky Mountain National Park in Colorado. My new bride, the former Carol Taylor of Farr West, Utah, and I had a wonderful summer. I conducted numerous hikes and other outdoor activities. Carol usually accompanied me. We hiked to the tops of a number of peaks, including the more than fourteen-thousand-foot-high Long's Peak. But, I do not consider myself to be a mountain climber. To tell the truth, heights frighten me.

A few months after my arrival in Ecuador and while living at the Hotel Alcron, I became acquainted with Harold Kramer. He worked for the U.S. Department of Agriculture out of Beltsville, Maryland and was an expert in the storage of food grains and the construction of food storage facilities. Because of his expertise, he had traveled to many countries as a consultant for food storage programs and had come to Ecuador for this purpose.

Harold was born and raised in the flatlands of Iowa. However, he somehow had become a mountain-climbing fanatic. He had scaled a good number of notable peaks and had accompanied a number of mountain climbing expeditions. When at home in Maryland, he usually spent weekends with other climbing enthusiasts practicing the art of rock climbing on the shear, rocky ledges along the nearby Potomac River. One of his climbing "buddies" was Barry Bishop – the first American to summit Mount Everest. Barry worked at National Geographic and he and I also subsequently became friends, as a result of my helping with a 1976 National Geographic feature article ("India Strives to Save Her Wildlife"). Regretfully, Barry was killed in a car accident a few years ago near Montpelier, Idaho, which is not too far from where we live. Anyway, Ecuador and its numerous rugged, snow-capped mountain peaks enchanted Harold.

Ecuador's capital city of Quito lies in a beautiful green valley at an elevation of ninety-five-hundred feet. It is flanked on either side by Andean peaks, many of which exceed sixteen thousand feet. Harold had long been intrigued by the Andean "cordillera". Even before coming to Ecuador he had become familiar with the history of this country's lofty and sometimes formidable mountains. He not only knew the names and heights of major peaks but also whether or not they had been climbed and, if so, by whom, when and how.

Soon after I became acquainted with Harold, he invited me to climb Mount Pichincha with him. The student dormitory on the campus of the "Universidad Central", where I previously resided, was located at the base of this mountain. Although Pichincha exceeds fifteen-thousand-nine-hundred feet in height, it is not an impressive mountain. In fact, it looks more like a large, green hill. When compared to some of the other jagged and snow-capped mountains surrounding Quito, Pichincha does not appear to present much of a challenge. I heartily accepted Harold's invitation.

We began our ascent of Mount Pichincha early one Saturday morning. We each had a light lunch, a small plastic bottle of water, and a stout walking stick. Our sticks were used more to ward off vociferous dogs, which attempted to attack us whenever we passed an Indian "choza" or hut, than to help us walk. It was amazing how far up on Pichincha the Indians attempted to eke out a living by farming the precipitous slopes. Their dogs were their protection from robbers, which are common throughout much of Ecuador.

As we walked and then struggled up increasingly steep slopes, Harold recounted to me how "The Battle of Pichincha", which ended Spanish rule in the northwestern part of South America, was fought in September of 1822 on the slopes we were traversing. I wondered how the combatants had the stamina to fight at such a lofty elevation. Although we were not encumbered with weapons or field gear typically carried by soldiers, I had to frequently stop and gasp for air. How did those who fought on these mountain slopes do it?

Soon after our hike to the top of Pichincha, Harold informed me he had joined a local climbing club called *Nuevos Horizontes* (New

Horizons). The club had about four-dozen members, most of whom were enthusiastic and adventuresome young men and women. They met each week and usually planned at least one outing or climbing activity each month. They then were planning to climb "Las Ilanizas" - two peaks that are located a short distance north of Quito. This would be a three-day excursion and Harold wanted me to join them. "It should be fun!" he exclaimed. I accepted the invitation.

"Ilaniza" is the Quichua Indian word meaning twins. "Las Ilanizas" are two spectacular pinnacles that rise abruptly out of the "altoplano" north of Quito. The northern-most peak or "Ilaniza Del Norte" is slightly higher than the southern peak or "Ilaniza Del Sur". Both peaks exceed seventeen thousand feet in height! The members of *Nuevos Horizontes* had decided they would divide into two groups and climb both peaks simultaneously. Because "Ilaniza Del Norte" was slightly higher and more difficult to climb than "Ilaniza Del Sur", Harold insisted we join those climbing it.

Neither Harold nor I had any equipment. We did not even have a sleeping bag, let alone a tent, backpacks, a cooking stove, cooking utensils or any climbing gear. Our lack of such items did not bother Harold. He simply assured me, "We can make out fine!" We borrowed a few blankets from the Hotel Alcron and packed a change of clothes, including our warmest shirts and heaviest socks, in a plastic bag. We also purchased what we thought would be enough canned food to last the two of us for three days. Too late, we realized we did not have a can opener or any eating utensils. Thus, we had to open our canned food with a pocketknife and eat the cold contents with our fingers. Anyway, according to Harold, "We're ready!" And, "Everything is great!"

We joined members of *Nuevos Horizontes* early in the morning to travel from Quito to the base of 'Las Ilanizas". The young men and women we accompanied varied markedly in their mountaineering experience Some appeared to have done considerable climbing and were well-equipped with ropes, pitons and other climbing gear; whereas, others appeared to be novices – like me! – and not much better equipped than Harold and I. It was going to be interesting!

Much of the morning was spent loading first our gear and supplies and then ourselves, into what seemed to be far too little space in the small vehicles that would transport us from Quito to the base of "Las Ilanizas". While crammed into the vehicles, we bounced for what seemed like hours over rough mountainous roads. We were packed so tightly together we were unable to move, let alone get into a comfortable position. We simply had to endure the ride until we arrived at the "jumping off" place at the base of the "Las Ilanizas".

Upon our arrival, we unloaded, ate a hurried but late lunch, and then packed our gear well upon the mountain slope and made camp. The plan was to camp high enough up the slopes of the mountain so that – with an early morning start the next day – we could climb to the tops of the peaks and then get back down to camp before dark. We'd then spend the second night at camp, before returning to the vehicles and then back to Quito the following day.

The climb to where we made our base camp was rigorous. The closer we got to the mountain peaks the more formidable they appeared. Jagged rocks and sheer cliffs led upwards to two sharp, snow-clad pinnacles. Could we make it to the crests? I began to wonder!

I slept little that night. Besides my concern about the next day's climb, my feet and other parts of my body kept protruding out of the blankets I was rolled up in. Thus, I spent much of the night shivering because of the cold. Although some club members had lent Harold and me a small pup tent and we were camped essentially on the Equator during the middle of the summer, it was unbelievably cold. I thought I was going to freeze to death! Furthermore, how cold would it be on top of the mountain?

Our climbing group, the one "attacking" the northern peak, was pretty much a "mixed bag". There were eight men, including Harold and me, and three young women. A couple of the men appeared to have had some climbing experience. They had some climbing gear, including long nylon ropes. It appeared, however, the other men and the three women were novice climbers. In fact, two of the women admitted they'd never climbed before. Most, however, at least had backpacks in which to carry their food and gear. In contrast, Harold and I simply carried a few cans of food in plastic bags. I both appreciated and needed frequent rest stops. Our excuse for these was to rearrange our cans of food in the plastic bags and our wanting to enjoy the beautiful scenery below.

It was a beautiful, clear day the morning of our ascent. Only a few misty clouds enshrouded the peak of "Ilaniza Del Norte". There were some cloudbanks in the valleys below, but these shortly dissipated and we had a fantastic day in which to climb. It was as if we were sitting on the top of the world.

Our climb consisted primarily of hiking and scrambling over jagged rocks. However, there were places where we had to cross narrow ledges and vertical cliffs or climb straight up shear rock faces and steep, rugged chutes. These made my heart flutter and my knees shake. One such crossing was too much for one of the girls and she began to cry hysterically. Despite encouragement from the rest of us, her boyfriend finally had to escort her down the face of the mountain and back to our base camp.

We were crossing a sheer rock face, with a drop of more than one hundred and fifty feet and nothing more than a few cracks in which to place our toes and to hold onto with our fingers, when the fellow in front of me accidentally dropped his ice ax. It clattered down over the rocks for what seemed like minutes, before it finally came to rest hundreds of feet below. This unnerved me. I froze and thought, "What if that had been one of us?" Worse yet, "What if it had been me?" My knees suddenly became weak and I started to tremble. Try as I might, I could not continue forward. I had been all right before the fellow dropped his ax and I saw what was below us. One of the experienced climbers finally threw me a rope. Grasping it gave me somewhat a feeling of security and I then was able to make it across the sheer rock face to safety.

It was late afternoon when we finally scrambled to the crest of "Ilaniza Del Norte". I was too tired and too concerned about how we were going to get down off from that steep pinnacle before dark to be able to appreciate the magnificent vista that lay below us on every side. As we sat on what seemed to be the top of the world, we tried to catch our breath and munched on candy bars, hoping they would give us the strength we needed for our descent. We discussed whether we should return down the mountain the same way we had made our assent or should attempt to find an easier route. Thinking about the shear face, where I had become unnerved, I voted for the latter. Fortunately, this was what we chose to do. And, it proved to be the better choice, although at the time we did not know whether or not we might be choosing an even more difficult route.

As Harold and I stood up and started our descent, one of the fellows motioned for us to stop. He then started to take off his shirt. "What is the crazy guy doing?" I thought. "He'll freeze to death up here, especially with this wind!" As for me, I was shivering almost unbearably from the cold. Then, from beneath his shirt, he carefully withdrew a folded Ecuadorian flag, which had been wrapped around his body. He unfurled it into the wind and our group stood stiffly at attention, while the Ecuadorian National Anthem was sung. Thereafter, the fellow ceremoniously re-folded the flag and again wrapped it around his torso. He then put his shirt back on and signaled for us to begin our descent. Thus, we departed from the top of "Ilaniza Del Norte".

Fortunately, we found a rock chute, which offered a much easier descent than the route we had used to climb the mountain. As a result, it was not quite dark when we finally stumbled into our base camp. I was so tired I did not even eat before "sacking out" on the hard ground. Nevertheless, we were elated. We had had a fantastic and very memorable day. We also had "conquered" the mountain!

We shortly learned the group climbing "Ilaniza Del Sur" had not been as fortunate as we. One of their members had severely injured a leg during the early part of their climb. As a result, they had spent almost the entire day getting the injured person off from the mountain, down to a vehicle and back to Quito for medical aid. Thus, "Ilaniza Del Sur" had not been climbed. It was left for another time!

A few weeks after our excursion to "Las Ilanizas", Harold joined an English expedition in the ascent of Mount Chimborazo, which exceeds twenty-one-thousand feet and is the highest peak in Ecuador. In fact, some claim Chimborazo is the highest peak in the world. This is because the earth is not a perfect sphere and its greatest circumference is at the Equator. Therefore, the crest of Chimborazo is the point furthest from the earth's center and closest to the sun. This is why some claim it is the world's highest peak. At this time Mount Chimborazo had never been climbed. Thus, Harold became one of the first to stand on the top of this formidable peak. Fortunately, my wife and I were in the Galapagos Islands while Harold and the English expedition were climbing Mount Chimborazo. Otherwise, he might have asked me to accompany them. And, I just might have been foolish enough to have accepted the offer.

Harold returned to the States shortly after his triumphant climb of Chimborazo. He continued his enthusiasm for climbing and we kept in touch for many years. He also became noted for his testing of mountaineering equipment, much of which he did in the USDA's environmental chambers at Beltsville, Maryland.

Harold and some members of his family visited my family and me quite frequently while I was attending graduate school at The Johns Hopkins University in Baltimore, Maryland. He particularly liked to visit us when we lived on Ivy Neck, where we were the custodians of the Smithsonian Institution's research farm on the Chesapeake Bay. We spent time there hiking around the beautiful countryside, but we never climbed any mountains together again.

After I joined the staff at Utah State University, Harold and his son spent a few days with us at our home in North Logan during the summer of 1970. They were traveling throughout the States and Canada in a Volkswagen "bug", which they had modified so they could remove the bucket seats and sleep inside during inclement weather. Thereafter, our association eventually consisted of little more than Christmas cards and letters. Finally, in reply to one of my Christmas letters, Harold's wife informed me, "Harold often told me and the members of our family about you and your family, as well as about your special friendship. However, Harold recently suffered a severe stroke and died shortly thereafter."

Upon reading this letter, my thoughts were, "I hope Harold now can climb even higher mountains and ascend to heights not even he anticipated attaining in this life!" He was truly a remarkable man and a special friend. I will never forget him and our "Climbing a Mountain".

AN UNEXPECTED ARRIVAL

The premature birth of our daughter Cris Tina onboard the "Cristobal Carrier" in the Galapagos Islands was indeed "An Unexpected Arrival", but also a blessed event.

It had been a marvelous adventure for my wife Carol and me. Day after day was filled with fun and the excitement of visiting new places, meeting interesting people, and seeing some of nature's most unique and beautiful creatures. It was almost overwhelming.

We had planned to spend only two weeks visiting the Galapagos Islands onboard the "Tacuari", an Ecuadorian Navy LST. But, Dr. Robert I. Bowman from the University of California in Berkley had invited us to accompany him and one of his graduate students (Steve Billeb) while they conducted research on a number of the islands. Thus, we ended up spending six weeks in this unique and beautiful part of the world. We planned to return to Guayaquil on the "Cristobal Carrier", a cargo ship that brought supplies to the Galapagos Islands and took products, such as dried fish, cattle, coffee beans, etc. back to the mainland at about monthly intervals. Eventually we were informed the "Cristobal Carrier" had arrived at the Island of Santa Cruz. To ensure we would have accommodations onboard the "Carrier" for our return to the mainland, we booked passage for its scheduled tour of the Islands. This meant, in addition to visiting a few new islands, we re-visited many of the islands and people with whom we'd previously become acquainted. Repeat visits to these islands and with our friends were most enjoyable.

Onboard the "Carrier" we also had the good fortune of accompanying Dr. and Mrs. Robert Dawson. Dr. Dawson was a noted botanist, specializing in cacti and algae. He had come to the Galapagos to spend a few weeks at the Charles Darwin Research Station and to study the flora of the Islands. Despite being an eminent and one of the most efficient scientists I have ever met, he was "down to earth" and most enjoyable to work with. In short, both he and his wife were delightful people.

As soon as the "Carrier" dropped anchor near an island, Dr. Dawson would appear on deck with his collecting equipment. This consisted of a plastic bucket, in which he carried a kitchen knife, some plastic bags and a camera. I served as his assistant on these expeditions. If the tide was out, we first collected algae from along the shore. But, if the tide was in, we first concentrated upon collecting cacti. Dr. Dawson usually would have the specimens he desired within a relatively short time. We then would join others from the "Carrier" and become "common tourists". Upon re-boarding the "Carrier", Dr. Dawson would disappear into his cabin. An hour or two later he would emerge and announce whether or not we had collected a new plant species for science or if our specimens had previously been described by others. He systematically filed his taxonomic keys in a shoebox, which he claimed could be used by almost anyone to readily identify virtually any algae or cactus specimen in the world. The shoebox represented his "traveling library". Years later, while visiting the Smithsonian Institute in Washington, D.C., I learned about Dr. Dawson's untimely death. He accidentally drowned, while diving for algae specimens in the Red Sea. The world then lost a most remarkable scientist, as well as a warm and genuine person.

Friedel and Forest Nelson, who were building facilities for the Darwin Research Station and the first hotel in the Galapagos, insisted the Dawsons, Dr. Bowman and Steve Billeb, Raymond Leveque (Director of the Station) and others join us for dinner at their place the evening of our departure from Santa Cruz onboard the "Carrier". I do not remember what we had for dinner, whether it was fish or lobster or if the village hunter had been successful and we ate beef. Nevertheless, we had a most enjoyable time with our recently acquired friends. It saddened us to realize we might never again see these wonderful people and the enchanting Galapagos Islands.

While we were engaged in animated after-dinner conversation, Mrs. Dawson inquired, "Where is Carol?" I had been so engrossed in visiting I had not noticed her absence. I searched and found her outside, bent over in apparent pain. When I asked, "What's wrong?" she insisted, "It's nothing." After I persisted in knowing "What's the matter?" She explained, "I'm having cramps and some pain. And,

I've passed some water!" Still, this didn't mean much to me. The baby was not due for at least another six weeks.

The time for our departure from Santa Cruz came all too soon. About 10:00 p.m. we bid farewell to Friedel, Forest and our other friends and returned to the "Carrier", which was scheduled to sail before midnight. Carol no longer had cramps and didn't feel pain. Thus, upon boarding we simply tumbled into our bunks and I quickly fell asleep. A couple of hours later, Carol gently awakened and quietly informed me, "The pains are back." And, "They're stronger!" I couldn't believe it. It was weeks too soon! As Carol's pains increased both in intensity and regularity, I suddenly realized, "We're going to become parents NOW!"

I rushed about the now slumbering ship, hoping to find someone who could help. In desperation, I banged on the captain's door until he sleepily answered. When I explained, "My wife's having a baby." And queried, "Can you help me?" he turned and went back into his cabin. He soon returned and handed me two bottles. One was a bottle of rubbing alcohol and the other "paregoric". These were the only medicines onboard the "Carrier".

The captain then awoke the cook. After pulling on his pants, the cook started a fire in the ship's wood-burning cook stove. I guess he figured, "Hot water always is needed for the birth of a baby." With the bottle of alcohol in one hand and the paregoric in the other, I rushed back to the cabin. I poured some paregoric into a glass of water and gave it to Carol to drink. Not knowing what to do with the alcohol, I poured some on a cloth and scrubbed the bunk bed frames and surrounding dirty walls of the cabin. "This," I thought, "should kill any germs which might be on them."

I regained my composure, following the anxiety of realizing the potential premature birth of our first child. I then placed my hands upon Carol's head and fervently prayed to Our Father in Heaven for help. Shortly thereafter, Carol cried, "Here it comes!"

A small head first appeared and then, in a rush, came the rest of the body of a small baby. I recalled having read somewhere newborn babies should be held by their feet, head downward, and sharply spanked on the bottom – to help them start breathing. I tried to grasp the baby's feet, but they slipped out of my hand and the baby started to cry – before I could administer the supposedly required spanking. However, I eventually grasped the small ankles in one hand and, holding the baby aloft, I excitedly shouted, "He's all right! He's all right!" Carol, however, calmly looked up and announced, "It's not a he. It's a she!" How was I to notice small details at such a time?

As I stood holding the baby by the feet and wondering what to do next, the cook appeared at the door with two buckets full of hot water. I handed the baby to Carol and took the buckets from him. I then pondered, "What do we do with these?" Debating the issue with Carol, we decided I should use some of the water to wash my hands, before again holding the baby. We also decided Carol could use some of the water to bathe. This she did. However, one bucket full of hot water still remained. Not knowing what to do with it and not wishing to offend the cook - after his efforts to heat it - we simply dumped it out the cabin's porthole into the ocean.

Shortly, a short, heavy-set woman with dark hair and almost equally dark features appeared at the door of our cabin. She proudly announced, "My name is America." And "I've assisted in the delivery of several babies". Searching through her over-sized purse, she extracted a spool of thread and proceeded to show me how to twist the strands together. "These," she explained, "will be used to tie the baby's umbilical cord, before we cut it." Although she thought it unnecessary, I insisted we soak the twisted threads in alcohol before we used them to tie the umbilical cord. Then, when she ensured I had tied the twisted threads as tightly as possible in two places along the baby's umbilical cord, she again searched in her large purse until she found a pair of scissors. I again insisted we use alcohol to sterilize the scissors, before using them to cut the cord. Again, she thought this was unnecessary. Apparently, to get me out of the way, she ordered me to "Go, find some clothes for the baby." The baby now was wrapped in a bath towel and quietly sleeping upon Carol's chest. Where was I to find any baby clothes onboard the "Carrier"?

I reluctantly retreated from the cabin, which held Carol AND our new baby daughter. As I wandered about the ship, I wondered, "Where could I possibly find any baby clothes here?" I awakened a few passengers, who were sleeping on bags of coffee beans and boxes of dried fish, which were intermingled with chickens and other animals. I explained our need for some baby clothes and they awakened others and explained my plight. Shortly, I was directed to a man sleeping in the hold of the ship. He had been selling cloth at the settlements in the Galapagos Islands during the cruise. Perhaps he would have some suitable material for making baby clothes. When I awakened this man and explained our needs, he informed me his stock was almost depleted. There were only a few remnants left. I inspected these and determined a piece of cloth with small, black polka dots was both the softest and cleanest material he had. I bargained as to the purchase price, paid him and rushed back to our cabin with the cloth.

America deftly tore some of the black and white polka dot material into small diapers. One of these she placed upon our soundly sleeping baby. She pinned the diaper in the middle, directly over the navel, with a single, large safety pin, which she found in her trusty, large-sized purse. Then, with her scissors and a needle and thread, she cut and sewed a small gown from the remaining material. Although our diminutive-sized baby girl was not dressed in normally expected baby colors, she was at least dressed.

The "Carrier" pulled into Wreck Bay on the Island of San Cristobal late that afternoon. This was our last port of call before the three-day voyage to Guayaquil. I was informed there was a naval doctor in the village. After a few inquiries, I located the doctor and insisted he come onboard the "Carrier" to examine my wife and our new baby. He was reluctant to do so and acted as if women and babies were not within the line of duty of an Ecuadorian Navy doctor. Nevertheless, with further insistence from me, he finally consented to accompany me and examine Carol and our new baby daughter.

The doctor looked at our baby's face and stated, "She appears to be all right." He then added, "She's very small, isn't she?" He then looked at Carol's face and again stated, "She appears to be all right."

He did suggest, however, "She should rest during the voyage to the mainland – where she should be examined by a doctor." Wasn't he a doctor?

Despite the naval doctor's cursory examination of our new baby and Carol, he graciously offered to help me find some "more suitable baby clothes" in Wreck Bay. He then led me to a small shop in the village, where I found a pair of knit booties, a bright yellow knit sweater and cap, and some white material, which we thought would be appropriate for diapers. As I purchased these items, I thought, "Now our baby girl will be dressed in style when we dock in Guayaquil!"

I rushed back to "our" cabin onboard the "Carrier". When I arrived, I found a pile of baggage in front of the cabin door and a man facing a now defiant America. When I asked what was going on, the man explained, "I purchased a ticket for Guayaquil onboard the "Carrier". This ticket means I am going to share your cabin with you!" I informed him, "You are not going to share 'our' cabin with us. You are not even going to be permitted to enter 'our' cabin!" Leaving America in charge, I went in search of the captain. Upon finding him, I explained the situation. He claimed the man had a "right" to a cabin. I told him this did not mean it had to be "our" cabin. After some debate, he finally agreed to find other accommodations for the irate man in front of "our" cabin.

Our voyage from Guayaquil to the Galapagos onboard the "Tacuari" had been rough. Waves continually rocked us too and fro and many onboard were sea sick much of the time. In contrast, our three-day voyage from Wreck Bay to Guayaquil onboard the "Carrier" went very smoothly. The sea was like glass and the still air was hot and humid. The doctor in Quito later claimed the environment we encountered on the open sea probably was the same as what would have been provided by an incubator for our premature baby daughter.

Word spread quickly among the "Carrier's" passengers about the birth of our daughter. Many came to see her, but I resolutely guarded the cabin door. Except for the comings and goings of America, I would not let anyone enter. Those who came to see the baby had to be content to see her from a distance. The baby, in turn, paid no heed to the commotion caused by her unexpected arrival and most of the time she just calmly slept next to her mother.

Carol was not buxom. In fact, she was on the skinny side. I began to worry about what or how we were going to feed our infant daughter during the voyage to Guayaquil. Miraculously, nature provided! Literally overnight Carol became more shapely in the appropriate places! She not only was able to provide ample milk for the baby, she even complained of the discomfort caused by the little one not consuming more.

It was mid-day or "siesta time" when we docked in Guayaquil. The captain of the "Cristobal Carrier" presented us with a document upon which were recorded the location and date of birth of our daughter. We bade farewell to him, the cook, to America and others who had assisted us. Somehow, we managed to locate and check in to a modest, but clean and comfortable "pension" owned and operated by an elderly and pleasant German couple. Almost as soon as we had deposited our luggage in our assigned room the German couple insisted we have lunch. We quickly ascertained the food in the "pension" was much better fare than that on the "Carrier". We ate heartily.

We had open tickets on Ecuatoriana Airlines for our return to Quito. I thought, "Before we return to our home in Quito, Carol and the baby should first be examined by a competent doctor." But, how could I find a "good" doctor? I called an American I previously had met who worked for the U.S. Information Services (USIS) at the American Consulate in Guayaquil. When I told him about the birth of our daughter onboard the "Carrier" and explained how I felt Carol and the baby should be examined by a "good" doctor before we returned to Quito, He claimed, "I'm a bachelor and don't know any good baby doctors. But, some of my American friends should know where we can locate one. I'll contact them and call you right back." He also suggested, "You should go promptly to the nearby Ecuadorian Government offices and register the birth of your baby. "This," he explained, "is a legal requirement and should be taken care of as soon as possible."

The office where births were registered was only a few blocks from the "pension" where we were staying. When I arrived at the office, I noted there were two long lines of people standing in front of a door upon which a sign stated births were to be registered here. I stood in the shorter line and patiently waited. When it finally was my turn, the girl behind a battered, wooden desk informed me she registered deaths. The other line was for the registration of births. So, I went to the end of the other line and again patiently waited.

After waiting more than an hour, it again was my turn. The girl behind another battered, wooden desk placed some forms in front of me and asked, "What is the baby's name?" "I don't know." I explained. We hadn't even discussed what we were going to name our new daughter. The girl then informed me, "We can't fill out the forms unless we know the baby's name."

I hurried back to the "pension". Carol and I then pondered as to what we should call our new daughter. Being somewhat scientifically minded, I proposed we call her "Cris" – after the "Cristobal Carrier" upon which she was born, and "Tina" – because she was so small. To my surprise, Carol agreed. Thus, we named our daughter "Cris Tina".

I rushed back to the government office. This time I made sure I stood in the right line, but before it again was my turn to be waited upon, the door to the office was closed. I was informed that I would have to return the next day.

I returned to the "pension" and Carol told me the bachelor with the USIS had called. He had located a "good" baby doctor and had made arrangements for him to come to the "pension" to examine Carol and the baby – as soon as he finished his rounds at the hospital that afternoon. It then dawned upon Carol and me, "Our baby probably should have such things as baby powder, lotion, bottles and nipples, as well as some real diapers and more clothes." I was not acquainted with Guayaquil but surmised, "Perhaps a Fulbright professor and his wife, whom I had met at a Fulbright Commission meeting in Quito, might help me. He taught English at the University of Guayaquil and they lived here. Although I knew this elderly couple had never had children, I still thought they should know which stores in Guayaquil sold baby supplies. Thus, I telephoned them, explained our situation, and asked where they thought I should shop. Rather than simply telling me where to shop, they insisted I come to their apartment and that they should accompany me in "our making purchases for the new baby."

The couple lived in a large, multi-storied building not far from the "pension" where we were staying. I apparently arrived at their apartment sooner than they expected, as they were not fully dressed. It appeared they had adopted the Latin American custom of taking a mid-day nap or "siesta". Nevertheless, they invited me in. Between multitudes of questions about the arrival of our daughter, they tried to hurriedly dress. They wanted to make the purchases as quickly as possible – so they could see the new baby. They were in such a hurry that we were in the elevator, going down to the ground floor, before the professor realized he had forgotten to put on his trousers. He had on a shirt and tie and even a jacket, but no pants! Thus, we had to return to their apartment so the "absent-minded professor" could finish dressing.

The couple took me to a large department store, where we readily located the section where baby supplies were sold. They rushed here and there, trying to decide what or how much of this or that should be purchased. It was evident they knew little about babies. They frequently argued about what or how many things the baby needed. For example, the professor thought a dozen baby bottles should be sufficient; whereas, his wife insisted it should be at least two dozen. She emphatically stated, "They get dirty, you know! You can't drop everything every few minutes to wash bottles when you have a baby in the house!"

We eventually finished buying what we deemed necessary for the baby. I greatly reduced the quantity of most items the couple thought we should purchase. This I did by explaining, "We can't carry much on the plane to Quito." And, "Upon our arrival in Quito, we can obtain whatever additional items we need." Nevertheless, we left the department store with a very large box filled with baby supplies. As I struggled to carry the box, the professor and his wife kept asking me to "Please hurry!" They were anxious to see the baby.

When we arrived at the "pension" and entered the room where I had left Carol and the baby, we met a contingency of American women. In his efforts to locate a baby doctor, my friend with the USIS had spread the news about the "destitute" Fulbright student and his "poor" wife, who had had the "horrible experience" of delivering a baby onboard a "filthy tramp steamer in the Galapagos Islands." As a result, "hoards" of well meaning, but also inquisitive American women had descended upon the "pension".

Since my departure to obtain baby supplies, Carol had been inundated with calls and visits from concerned and curious American women. In fact, the bed upon which our daughter lay sleeping peacefully was completely surrounded by women. Many were insisting, "Please let me hold the precious thing!" It also seemed each woman had to remark about how "tiny" our daughter was and how "dreadful" it must have been for Carol to give birth to a baby on such a "filthy" ship. All sympathized with Carol about the "terrible ordeal" she had gone through. They repeatedly asked, "How did you ever stand it?" One lady even asked, "Weren't you afraid of getting septic poisoning or some kind of infection from being on such a dirty ship?" Another remarked, "Why the baby even has fingernails! Most premature babies born this small usually lack something." Then, turning to me, she inquired in a low voice, but loud enough so that Carol could hear, "Do you think she's all right mentally?"

The medical doctor finally arrived. He walked into the room smoking a cigarette. He then shook hands and introduced himself to each of those present. In turn, each of the many assembled women introduced themselves to him. Some even asked his professional opinion as to maladies suffered either by them or their children. Shortly, however, the doctor politely asked the women to wait in another room, while he examined Carol and the baby. I was impressed by the fact the doctor had asked the women to leave. But, when he walked over to the bed and picked up our baby without first washing his hands, I was shocked. While onboard the "Carrier", except for

Carol and America, I had not allowed anyone to even come near the baby, let alone hold her. I thought, "What kind of doctor is this?" I was about to tell him what I thought, when he turned and announced, "Although she's premature and very small, your daughter appears to be healthy and normal in every respect." He also indicated he wanted to examine Carol, but "This can best be done in my office." He then instructed us to be in his office "in about an hour", and gave me the directions to get there.

A Mrs. Johnson and two of her three children arrived at the "pension" while the doctor was examining the baby. She immediately enlisted the aid of the other women to help her carry the things she had brought for the baby in her station wagon. Thus, when the doctor opened the door of our bedroom to leave, he encountered a stack of baby and children's clothing, as well as a large crib. For some reason, Mrs. Johnson felt she should take charge. She wanted to know if we had done this and that. She also gave me strict orders as to what I "must" or "must not" do with regard to Carol and the baby.

After almost an hour of trying to answer Mrs. Johnson's probing questions and agreeing I would follow her many instructions, I realized it was time for us to visit the doctor's office. When I informed Mrs. Johnson, "I have to take Carol to the doctor's office for an examination," she insisted on taking us there in her station wagon. She further insisted I carry Carol down the stairs of the "pension", rather than merely assisting her. She also felt it was her duty to repeatedly remind me of my wife's "delicate" condition. "You must realize Carol is not now capable of such exertions as walking."

We shortly arrived at the doctor's office. Mrs. Johnson insisted she and her children be permitted in the examination room, while the doctor examined Carol. I thought the children should not be there, but did not dare state such to the domineering Mrs. Johnson. The doctor placed Carol on a table and proceeded with the examination, while Mrs. Johnson peered intently over his shoulder. The doctor soon announced, "Except for a few stitches being needed, everything seems to be all right. The stitches," he explained, "will require only a local anesthesia and can easily be done in a matter of minutes here in my office tomorrow morning." He then told me what time to bring Carol back to his office, wrote a couple of prescriptions, and told me where I could get them filled. We were ready to leave, but Mrs. Johnson insisted the doctor examine one of her children.

While we waited for the doctor to examine Mrs. Johnson's child, Carol and I discussed making arrangements for our return flight to Quito. We both were anxious to return home as soon as possible after our visit with the doctor the next morning. We also discussed what we might do to discourage or avoid the intrusions of the many well meaning, but bothersome, women we had left at the "pension". We did not have a ready solution.

Mrs. Johnson and her children emerged from the office. She immediately stated, "I would not consider letting you take Carol back to that dirty and dreadful 'pension'. I insist Carol and the baby must come home with me." I tried to politely explain, "We appreciate your concern. But, we'll be just fine in the 'pension'". She, in turn, gave me to understand, "The 'pension' might be all right for you. But, after all, you must consider the welfare of your wife and child!" I relented and said, "If Carol wants to go with you, its okay with me." Carol likewise tried to politely refuse but Mrs. Johnson persisted until we gave in to her demands.

Carol and I had been concerned about the early and unexpected arrival of our daughter, but we had not voiced these concerns to each other. We felt we had been richly blessed with what appeared to be a healthy and "perfect" baby girl. We also were looking forward to returning to and being together as a family in our home in Quito.

Prior to our arrival in Guayaquil and then hearing the voiced concerns of "what might have happened" by the American women who visited us, Carol had neither cried nor expressed fears regarding what could have happened during or following the birth of our daughter. Now, however, such possibilities had been so forcefully thrust upon her mind that she was reduced to tears and had a foreboding for what still might happen.

Mrs. Johnson instructed me, "Get the prescriptions the doctor wrote. Then, return to the 'pension' and pack your things. I'll first take Carol and the baby to my place. Then, I'll come right back and pick you and your things up. All of you can stay at my house." She then deposited me at the "pension" and departed.

I hurried to a nearby pharmacy and got the prescriptions filled. I then rushed back to the "pension" and hurriedly packed our belongings. I carried our suitcases, the large box of recently purchased baby supplies, and the many things Mrs. Johnson had brought down the "pension" stairs. These I neatly stacked next to the ground-level door. Everything would be ready to load into Mrs. Johnson's station wagon as soon as she returned. I hoped there would be enough room in the vehicle for all that had accumulated so quickly.

I settled our account with the kindly German couple that owned the "pension". I tried to assure them, "We enjoyed the meal we ate with you." And, "No, we are not displeased with the quarters you assigned us." I then anxiously waited for Mrs. Johnson's return.

Mealtime came. The German couple invited me to eat with them. I refused, explaining, "Mrs. Johnson should arrive any minute." I did not want to keep her waiting. Then, as the minutes dragged into hours, I became more and more concerned. I did not know Mrs. Johnson's first name or that of her husband. Neither did I know where they lived. I asked the German couple if I could see their telephone directory. There were more than twenty Johnsons listed for Guayaquil. How could I locate my wife and child? I began to imagine all kinds of terrible happenings. Maybe they had an accident! Perhaps something was wrong with the baby and they had to rush her to the hospital! Where were they? What should I do?

The telephone in the "pension" finally rang. It was Mrs. Johnson. She crisply informed me, "I've been delayed. I still have a few errands to run. I hope you don't mind." When I asked about Carol and the baby, she assured me "They're fine. I'll come to pick you up as soon as I can."

I waited. Minutes again stretched into hours. What had happened? What should I do? A man finally entered the "pension" and spoke my name. When I answered, he introduced himself as Mr.

Johnson and explained, "My wife was so busy taking care of your wife and child she did not have time to come."

We somehow loaded our luggage and the accumulated baby paraphernalia into the Johnson's station wagon. It was almost midnight when we arrived at the Johnson's house. Mrs. Johnson met us at the door and escorted me into the bedroom where she had lodged Carol and our baby. She informed me, "I didn't give Carol anything to eat, because I knew the two of you would want to eat together." However, both Carol and the baby were now sleeping soundly. Mrs. Johnson insisted I awaken Carol, so she could have something to eat. After I made repeated attempts to quietly awaken Carol, without disturbing the baby, she drowsily mumbled, "I'm too tired to eat. Just let me sleep." Mrs. Johnson persisted, "Don't you realize you're now a nursing mother? You can't think only of yourself. You must also consider the baby." So, Carol wearily arose and joined me to eat a midnight dinner.

The meal Mrs. Johnson provided consisted of fried eggs and French-fried potatoes. I wondered, "Is this proper food for a 'nursing' mother?" And, "This isn't anywhere near as good as the food we were served in that 'terrible pension', from which Mrs. Johnson had rescued us."

I shortly learned the Johnson's house was just off the end of the main runway of the Guayaquil airport. The roar of planes frequently taking off and landing at the airport literally shook the entire house and also caused their huge Alsatian dog to bark on each occasion. In turn, the dogs barking caused their pet llama, which they kept in the yard outside our bedroom window, to bleat loudly. The llama's bleating seemed to further incite the dog and we spent the remainder of the night and the following morning listening to the roar of planes, the barking of a dog and the bleating of a llama.

Additional sounds greeted us shortly after the break of day. Hearty shouts, frequent bickering and the almost constant banging on the keys of a piano informed the world that the Johnson's three children were early risers. The children's activities also caused the dog to bark and the llama to bleat. What a nightmare!

Mrs. Johnson eventually knocked on the bedroom door, poked her head into the room and announced, "Breakfast is ready." But, she informed Carol, "You can't eat anything, because you're due to undergo surgery this morning." By now, Carol was famished. She pleaded with Mrs. Johnson for something to eat. I also tried to explain that the doctor said all Carol needed was a local anesthesia and a few stitches. With continued pleading from both of us, Mrs. Johnson finally relented. But, she firmly stated to Carol, "Just ONE glass of orange juice. Nothing more! You can't have solid food prior to surgery!"

The time for our appointment at the doctor's office drew nigh. Although Mrs. Johnson let us know we were interrupting her busy schedule, she insisted upon driving us, rather than letting us take a taxi. Thus, because I had booked our return to Quito on the Ecuatoriana Airlines' flight that afternoon, we loaded our suitcases, the baby paraphernalia and ourselves into the Johnson's station wagon. Cramped as we were, it seemed good to leave the noisy Johnson children, as well as their dog and llama, behind.

I shortly observed that Mrs. Johnson drove past the area where the doctor's office was located. When I pointed this out and asked, "Where are we going?" She proudly announced, "I've arranged for a private room for Carol in the hospital. There, she will be attended to properly."

Upon our arrival at the hospital, Mrs. Johnson insisted two attendants had to lift Carol into a wheelchair and wheel her to the room she had reserved. After inspecting the room, she decided it was not good enough. It did not have air conditioning. She then insisted that Carol and the baby had to be moved to a better room, one with air conditioning. This was despite the doctor having advised us NOT to keep the baby in an air-conditioned room. Nevertheless, the attendants wheeled Carol and the baby to an air-conditioned room and we turned off the air conditioner.

Mrs. Johnson then informed us, "You can not return to Quito on the Ecuatoriana Airlines' flight this afternoon. Ecuatoriana's planes are not pressurized. I'm certain changes in cabin pressure could cause permanent damage to your child's hearing. Panagra is the only airline flying between Guayaquil and Quito that has pressurized planes. But, Panagra has only one flight per week from Guayaquil to Quito. And, Panagra's flight for tomorrow is fully booked. Therefore, you'll have to remain in Guayaquil until next week's Panagra flight."

I refused to accept Mrs. Johnson's verdict. I thought, "There is no way we can remain in Guayaquill another day, let alone another week." What could we do?

The doctor shortly informed us, "It will be several hours before I can take Carol into the operating room." I left Carol and the baby and went to the Panagra office. It was true. The next day's Panagra flight to Quito was fully booked. However, the ticket agent informed me, "One or two seats usually are kept in reserve. If 'proper pressure' was brought to bear, perhaps you could use those seats." The agent also could not understand why it was so important our baby be flown in a pressurized plane to Quito. He explained, "Planes flying from Guayaquil to Quito rarely exceed an altitude of fifteen thousand feet."

The Government office where births were registered was not far from Panagra. Thus, I decided to try again to register the birth of our daughter. This time I made certain I was in the right line, which was much shorter than during my previous visits. When the girl behind the battered, wooden desk asked me the baby's name, I proudly stated, "Its Cris Tina Spillett." She then asked, "Where was the baby born?" I told her, "It was in the Galapagos Islands, off the Island of Barrington." She then said, "I'm sorry. Births in the Galapagos Islands must be registered at the Governor's Office at Wreck Bay." Although the captain of the "Cristobal Carrier" had provided me with a document, which gave the time and location of our daughter's birth, the Galapagos Islands were outside the jurisdiction of the Guayaquil office. What was I to do? I tried to explain, "There's no way for us to return to the Galapagos Islands." The girl then suggested, "I can register the baby as having been born in Guayaquil – if that's all right with you." This accounts for Cris Tina's birth certificate stating she was born in Guayaquil; whereas, she was in reality born in the Galapagos Islands.

After I was assured our baby's birth had been "properly" registered and a birth certificate would be sent to our Quito address, I returned to the hospital. There, I met Mr. and Mrs. Johnson in the corridor. Mr. Johnson remarked, "I'm sorry you're unable to return to Quito till next week. But, we'd be happy to help you in any way we can." His words hit me like a bombshell. I then brusquely informed the Johnsons, "If you and the other well-meaning Americans we've met in Guayaquil REALLY want to help us, you'll get us on tomorrow's Panagra flight to Quito! Other than that, we'd like nothing more than for you to leave us alone!"

My forceful words affronted Mrs. Johnson. She sputtered something about, "How ungrateful can one be!" And, "After all we've tried to do for you!" Still, my words had the desired effect. The Johnsons left us alone at the hospital. Mr. Johnson, however, later called to inform us, "Arrangements have been made. You are now booked on tomorrow's Panagra flight to Quito." He further stated, "My wife has contacted the U.S. Embassy in Quito and made arrangements for you to be met at the Quito airport by a doctor and an incubator." I thanked him, while silently praying that what he told me was true.

Cris Tina was now a week old and paid no heed to the commotion and problems she had caused by her early and unexpected arrival. She rarely fussed, but only periodically awoke from her peaceful slumbers. She then would nurse until satisfied, before usually going back to sleep. We were proud of our dainty, beautiful, pink-cheeked girl, who now weighed a strapping four pounds and eleven ounces.

It was mid-day when I accompanied Carol and the doctor into the operating room. I wanted to insure he did his job properly. Instead of a local anesthesia, Carol was given a general anesthesia. The doctor explained, "If you had known enough to have supported the baby's head during delivery, your wife probably would not have required any stitches." He then inserted a needle and started to make the required stitches. The sight of blood, coupled with the heat, humidity and a lack of sleep since our arrival in Guayaquil, caused me to suddenly grow faint. Seeing my wane condition the doctor ordered me to "Sit down!" He also bluntly stated, "I don't have time to attend to you. If you pass out, you'll have to remain on the floor until I'm finished with your wife!" Thus, he completed the stitches without my supervision.

Carol did not regain consciousness from the anesthesia until late in the evening. Her voice then sounded like that from a run-down record player. Eventually, however, she awakened sufficiently to eat her first full meal in more than twenty-four hours. Thereafter, we spent a peaceful night – as a family – in the Guayaquil Hospital.

Mr. Johnson came to the hospital the next morning. He explained, "My wife wanted to come, but was too busy." He then offered to drive us to the airport. I gratefully accepted his offer. Feeling somewhat amiss for my previous harsh words to him and his wife, I attempted to thank them for their concern and efforts in our behalf. I hope they accepted my apology. However, I also insisted he take back the many things his wife had brought for our baby.

Our flight was uneventful. However, when we arrived at the Quito airport, one would have thought we were visiting dignitaries. Our names were announced over the loudspeaker. Two U.S. Marines, in smart dress uniforms, came onboard the plane and ceremoniously escorted us off and into a van parked on the runway alongside the plane. The incubator, which Mrs. Johnson had arranged for, was inside the van. But, we were told the doctor, who was supposed to meet us, became ill at the last moment and was unable to come to the airport. However, he had given strict instructions for us NOT to use the incubator nor even place the baby in it – until he was able to come to our home and give us detailed instructions on its use. This he hoped to be able to do the next day.

The Marine guards chauffeured us to our apartment at 725 Valladolid in Quito. They then insisted upon carrying Carol into the house and setting up the incubator in our bedroom. They then smartly saluted, before driving off in the van. We couldn't believe it. We were home and alone. What a wonderful feeling.

The doctor came to our home the next day. He explained, "If not properly used, an incubator can harm a newborn baby." After examining our baby, he announced, "She appears to be normal in every way. Despite her small size, there's no need to place her in an incubator." The incubator subsequently was returned to the hospital.

A young Indian girl we employed as a part-time maid insisted there was something wrong with our baby. She claimed, "She doesn't cry enough to be healthy." When I paid little heed to her warnings, she brought her older sister, who had "many" children, to speak to me. She told me, "You should spank your daughter at least once each day." And, "You should also spank her hard - so she will cry loud enough to properly develop her lungs." She assured me, "It's good for a baby to cry." And, "A crying baby is a normal or healthy baby." Although I think our daughter's lungs developed properly, I've often wondered, "Maybe the Indian woman's recommended daily hard spankings might have other beneficial effects." Who knows?

Our Indian maid also repeatedly demonstrated to us how we should wrap our daughter tightly in a blanket. She claimed this was so her back would be straight and her legs would develop properly. Much to the poor girl's dismay, we usually ignored her advice.

Many stories could be related about the early life and rearing of our daughter Cris Tina. For example, when she was three months old and before she could return to the U.S. with her mother, she had to be immunized against smallpox. The first immunization didn't "take" and she had to be vaccinated a second time. The doctor would not sign her shot record until there was evidence the vaccination "had taken". Thus, on the morning Cris Tina and her mother were scheduled to fly to the U.S., I had to frantically search for the doctor – so he could sign and stamp the "all-important" shot record that would permit Cris Tina to leave Ecuador. I finally found him in the delivery room at the hospital. After he had signed and stamped the shot record, I rushed Cris Tina and her mother to the waiting plane at the Quito airport. Then, after I escorted them onboard the delayed flight, the Ecuadorian authorities insisted upon detaining Carol, because her visa had expired the previous day. Finally, instead of detaining Carol, they confiscated my passport and I then spent three hectic days battling Ecuadorian bureaucracy to retrieve it.

Additional accounts of Cris Tina's growing up will be left until another time. Suffice it to say, five years and a month after her early and "Unexpected Arrival" she was joined by a baby sister, Rose Ann. Two years later, our two daughters welcomed the arrival of their first brother, James Kreg. Then, after another three years, Sheri Elizabeth also arrived much earlier than expected – while I was in Pakistan. Sheri then was followed two years later by Jay Juan, the baby of our family.

Cris Tina traveled extensively during her childhood. She lived in Ogden and Logan, Utah, before spending time in a trailer house in the Red Desert of Wyoming, where I was studying pronghorn antelope for an M.S. degree in Wildlife Biology at Utah State University. She then lived two years in India and two years in Maryland, before returning to Logan. Thereafter, she accompanied her family to Iran, where she attended high school in the American School in Tehran, before staying with her maternal grandparents in Utah and attending Weber High School. She then lived in Mapleton, Utah, and graduated from Springville High School after her family moved to College Station, Texas. Thereafter, she enrolled in Texas A&M University, where she received a B.S. after her family moved to Idaho. With various fellowships and teaching assistantships she then completed Master's and Doctorate degrees in chemistry at the University of California in Santa Barbara.

We often promised Cris Tina, "Someday we'll take you back to the Galapagos Islands and show you your birthplace." She got tired of us telling her this and our never keeping our promise. Thus, early in the year 2000 and not long after the birth of her daughter Natalie, she informed us, "I've made arrangements for all of us to return to Ecuador and take a cruise through the Galapagos Islands." When I asked, "How can you take your baby on such a trip?" Her reply was, "I was born on a boat there. What is the difference? Besides, my daughter is almost nine months old!" In short, we all returned to Ecuador and the Galapagos Islands. Everywhere we went people were enchanted with little Natalie and we all had a wonderful time.

Needless to say, "An Unexpected Arrival", which occurred in the Galapagos Islands in 1962, continues to be one of my most memorable "Happenings."

SANGAY

The conical-shaped Sangay in the lowlands of the Amazon Basin is Ecuador's most active volcano.

An oil painting on the wall of our living room depicted a conical, snow-capped mountain. This is Sangay, Ecuador's most active volcano, which is located in the "Oriente" or the tropical lowlands of the Amazon Basin. This impressive mountain rises to an elevation of more than seventeen thousand feet and almost continuously emits smoke or steam, as well as periodically spews out molten lava and/or volcanic ash.

Whenever I look at the painting of Sangay, it reminds me of two brothers (John and Frank Rocco) and an adventurous photographer (James Thomas) with whom I became well acquainted while I was a Fulbright scholar in Ecuador during 1961-62. John was last seen on the slopes of Sangay and probably died there. I last saw Frank when he was going back into the jungles of the "Oriente" in search of gold. As for "Jim", I don't know what happened to him after he returned to his wife in France. The lives of these men affected my life and their story perhaps may be of interest to others.

A recent revolution, instigated by university students, had resulted in the overthrow of the Ecuadorian government and the ousting of President Velasco Ibarra. Because of continued student unrest, Robert Norris and I moved out of the student dormitory on the campus of the "Universidad Central" and into the Hotel Alcron in downtown Quito.

The Hotel Alcron is a modest building with about twenty rooms for guests. It was owned and operated by Senor Alonzo and his family. As is common in many Latin American hotels, meals were included in the tariff for the rooms. Guests at the Alcron usually ate together at a large dining room table. This presented a family-like atmosphere. As a result, guests at the Alcron usually became well acquainted with each other in a relatively short time.

Generally, after each evening meal, Bob and I and most of the other guests would sit at the large dining room table and visit. We would discuss news, politics, religion, everyday occurrences, our families "back home", our problems, activities, adventures, and our ambitions or dreams. Recent arrivals were expected to tell about themselves, as well as what had brought them to Ecuador. Some of their accounts were hard to believe. They ranged all the way from senior government diplomats, who had heard about the comfortable quarters and good food served at the Alcron, to those seeking adventure or were simply vagabonding around the world. They also had heard about the relatively low rates at the Alcron. Some even knew, IF you talked to Senor Alonso in the "proper manner", the already reasonable rates could be reduced even more.

I remember well the arrival of John and Frank Rocco. We were attracted to a vociferous argument on the street in front of the hotel. Part of the heated exchange was in Spanish and the rest in explicative English. An irate taxi driver was demanding additional payment for having transported a voluminous amount and assortment of baggage; whereas, the two equally irate passengers were claiming they owed ONLY the amount shown on the taxi's meter. It was apparent neither the driver nor the passengers could understand the other. Bob and I intervened and became translators. A compromise eventually was reached wherein John and Frank paid a portion of the additional charges being demanded by the taxi driver.

We helped the two men carry their voluminous baggage into the hotel. We learned they were brothers and John was older than Frank. They had come to Ecuador in search of gold and were certain they soon would be rich. Their first order of business, however, was to retrieve their firearms, ammunition and some supplies, which the Ecuadorian authorities at the airport had confiscated. Miraculously, even though they knew no Spanish, they managed to retrieve these items within a very few days.

John and Frank originally were from Pennsylvania but had lived in California for a number of years. They claimed to have been employed in construction. However, John was certain there was a quicker and easier way to get rich. He enrolled in a course that taught how to prospect for precious metals, particularly gold. When we became better acquainted he confided, "I took the prospecting course while I was in the California State Prison." Apparently he previously had tried other methods to get rich quick!

John's studies in prospecting convinced him he could readily find gold almost anywhere in the Andes Mountains in South America. He also convinced his brother Frank this was the case. They saved their money and planned to go to Venezuela. When they had saved what they believed was a sufficient amount to pay their passage and to undertake a gold-prospecting expedition in Venezuela, they obtained passports and went to the Venezuelan Consulate in San Francisco to obtain visas. Perhaps because of John's prison record, the Consulate refused to issue them visas. After leaving the Venezuelan Consulate, they happened to pass the Ecuadorian Consulate. They knew virtually nothing about Ecuador other than the Andes Mountains passed through this country. This was sufficient. They entered the Ecuadorian Consulate and obtained visas. They would search for gold in Ecuador!

The two brothers assembled the equipment and supplies they felt they needed to undertake a prospecting expedition on the eastern slopes of the Andes. Included were two 30:30 carbine rifles, two revolvers, and ample supplies of ammunition. They knew nothing about Latin American politics or the difficulties associated with importing firearms and ammunition. They also purchased one-way air tickets to Quito. When asked why they didn't buy round-trip tickets, John's reply was, "I decided I was either going to strike it rich or die in trying. Therefore, I didn't think I needed a return ticket."

Upon their arrival in Quito, their weapons and ammunition, as well as some of their equipment and supplies, were confiscated by the Ecuadorian customs officials. But, as previously mentioned, it took them only a few days to retrieve these items. I don't know how they did it. They then triumphantly returned to the Hotel Alcron with their revolvers strapped around their waists, brandishing their rifles, and carrying their equipment and supplies. We could not believe it. In little more than a week after their arrival they were ready for their gold-seeking expedition. They decided to embark into the jungles on the eastern slopes of the Andes from the city of Cuenca in southern Ecuador. How they determined to start there or even how they happened to come to the Hotel Alcron, I never determined.

Prior to the Rocco brothers' arrival at the Alcron, Bob and I had become well acquainted with James Thomas, an American adventurer and professional photographer. He had married a French woman, lived in Paris, and made his living primarily by photographing "adventure-type" 16mm movies and selling them to a TV series in the U.S. As a result, Jim had traveled extensively and had photographed many exotic areas around the world. He always was in search of situations or subjects to photograph that presented an aura of adventure and which could be marketed. He had read about the Jivaro Indians of Ecuador and their practice of shrinking human heads. He decided they might be suitable subjects.

The Jivaro Indians live in the Amazon Basin region of Ecuador. Although noted for their ancient practice of shrinking the heads of enemies they have killed in battle, for the most part they now are semi-civilized and no longer openly practice this ritual. In fact, Ecuadorian law bans the possession of a shrunken head or "tzantza". There is, however, some contraband trade in "tzantzas". For example, if a Jivaro needs money to purchase a new firearm, he might travel some distance from his village, kill someone in an area where he is not known, secretly shrink the head of his unfortunate victim, and sell the "tzantza". However, most of the "tzantzas" sold on the black market probably are not the work of Jivaro Indians but of enterprising entrepreneurs. I became acquainted with a few such men while living in Quito. They explained how they obtained the needed heads from derelicts who died on the streets of larger cities and whose bodies were not claimed by relatives or others. Nevertheless, while I was in the Amazon Basin with some herpetologists from the University of California, on three occasions Indians offered to sell me "tzantzas" for about $25 each. One was the head of a white man. This greatly intrigued me, but the Indian trying to sell it refused to tell me from whence it came or how he had obtained it.

To me, "tzantzas" are a work of art. The delicate features of the face and ears are retained in miniature; whereas, the hair protruding from the nostrils and the eyebrows, as well as the scalp, retain their size and abundance. These give the face of the "tzantza" a grotesque or eerie appearance. I was tempted to purchase one, but knew their possession was illegal. I did not want to get into trouble. Also, $25 was a lot of money for a student like me.

Jim did not know the situation regarding the Jivaro Indians and their "tzantzas" prior to his arrival in Ecuador. Nevertheless, after a brief stay at the Alcron, he departed for the Amazon Basin. He still planned to photograph the Jivaro Indians – even if they were partially civilized.

Jim returned to the Alcron just after the Rocco brothers had departed for Cuenca and their search for gold. His time with the Jivaros had not been too rewarding. By paying money, he'd obtained some footage of Indians decked out in their colorful costumes. They'd also performed some dances for him, but he thought he needed to photograph something more exciting to sell to his usual TV markets. Thus, he decided to wander about the country, looking for suitable subjects to photograph. When Bob and I told him about John and Frank, he admired their adventuresome attitude and stated, "I'd like to meet these guys and get acquainted with them – especially if they strike it rich!"

While Jim was wandering around Ecuador, John returned to Quito. He excitedly proclaimed, "We struck it rich!" He told how he and Frank had found a man in Cuenca who was well acquainted with the eastern slopes of the Andes in that region. He could speak English and had taken them to an uninhabited and inhospitable area. There, they began prospecting in dry riverbeds and had found gold.

John returned to Quito to file a claim on their gold find. As soon as he had accomplished this, he planned to return to the U.S. to purchase a portable dredge, which he claimed they could use to more effectively work their "claim". But, when he attempted to file a claim with the Ecuadorian Government, he learned the area where they had found gold already had been filed upon. A few years previous, in an attempt to raise revenue, the Ecuadorian Government opened vast areas to the filing of mineral rights. After filling out the required papers and paying a relatively small fee, speculators became the "legal owners" of any minerals that might be found upon "their" tracts of land. John considered returning to the jungles and extracting what gold they could without a legal claim. Officials warned him, however, that he could not sell nor take any gold out of the country – unless he could prove it came from a claim for which he had the mineral rights. He and his brother Frank were running low on money. He also knew he didn't want to go back to prison. How could he break the news to his brother and their guide, who they had taken into partnership with them? Over and over he stated, "I came here to get rich or to die in the process." And, "That is what I am going to do!"

Jim returned to the Alcron from his wanderings about Ecuador and quickly became acquainted with John and the problems he had encountered regarding his and his brother's gold strike. In fact, this became the primary topic of our after-dinner discussions. It seemed none of us could come up with a workable solution for the Rocco brothers' dilemma.

Jim had met a medicine man or "cacique" while among the Jivaro Indians. The "cacique" had given him a small bottle that contained a thick, brown liquid. He told Jim that, by drinking a small amount of this potion one could make divinations. For example, if a person was murdered by an unknown assailant, by drinking a small amount of this liquid one could have dreams in which would be revealed who the murderer was.

We debated during our after-dinner discussions whether or not what the "cacique" had told Jim might be true. We also surmised the potion must contain some kind of hallucinatory drug. Bob and I wanted nothing to do with taking or testing this liquid, but both Jim and John thought it might be "interesting" to try some and decided to do so. Bob and I suggested they should at least do so in a ""scientific manner", i.e. after taking some of the potion, they would tell us what they felt and saw or imagined. We then would record what they told us.

We went to John's room, which was in the basement of the Alcron. We would conduct the "experiment" here. Jim and John each took a small sip from the bottle. Both claimed it was bitter and tasted awful. Within minutes, Jim said, "I can't keep my eyes open." He then laid down on one of the two beds in the room and soon was in a deep slumber. For some time John claimed he felt nothing. Then, he exclaimed, "Look at all the pretty flowers! Look at the pretty colors! Isn't it beautiful?" When asked, "Where are the flowers? What do they look like?" he became agitated. "Can't you see them? They're right there!" He then became more and more excited and almost hysterical. Bob and I tried to calm him down, but he'd roughly push us aside and laugh like he was crazy. Then, he started to hit the cement walls of the room with his fists. He hit the walls so hard we feared he would break the bones in his hands. But, he'd just laugh and push us away when we tried to restrain him. He seemed to be endowed with an almost superhuman strength. We didn't know what to do. We thought maybe he'd damage or cripple his hands for life. Then, he suddenly collapsed upon the other bed and appeared to be in a deep sleep. We tried to awake him. But, even when we shook him violently, he continued as if in a deep slumber. It was scary!

Jim stirred and sat up about two hours later. It took some time for him to gain his senses. He then told us about the crazy dreams he had had. In contrast, when Frank awoke some hours later, he could remember nothing. He also could not understand why his hands and knuckles were bruised and hurt so bad. Admittedly, we learned little from the "experiment" with the "cacique's" potion. I determined, however, "I'll never knowingly take any drugs – as long as I live!"

Not long after the episode in John's basement bedroom, Jim began to discuss the possibility of climbing and photographing Sangay. Although the conical-shaped slopes of this volcano did not appear to present any major climbing difficulties, it apparently had never been climbed. Jim had some previous mountain climbing experience and had brought a backpack, a small mountain tent and a sleeping bag with him to Ecuador. He thought these and what supplies he could readily obtain in Quito would be sufficient for him to undertake an expedition to climb Sangay.

John expressed a desire to accompany Jim in his "Sangay adventure". He stated, "Like I've said, I came to Ecuador to either get rich or die trying. One place is as good as another." Unfortunately, none of us then could foresee the literal fulfillment of what he said.

My wife Carol thereafter arrived in Ecuador and I moved from the Hotel Alcron into an apartment. Although activities associated with the recent student-instigated revolution had subsided, classes still were not being held at the "Universidad Central." I, Bob and Naomi Quinn, the other Fulbright scholar in Ecuador, decided we would use this "lull" to travel and see as much as possible of Ecuador. Dr. Andrade, Director of the Fulbright program in Ecuador, used his influence from having been an Ecuadorian naval officer to make arrangements for us to accompany a two-week Navy patrol cruise to the Galapagos Islands. Thus, the four of us (Bob, Naomi, Carol and I) departed for the Galapagos, while Jim and John were planning their expedition to Sangay.

We joined the Ecuadorian Navy patrol cruise onboard the "Tacuari", a former U.S. Navy LST. Following this cruise, Bob and Naomi returned to the mainland with the cruise, while Carol and I remained an additional four weeks in the Galapagos. We then accompanied Dr. Robert I. Bowman and Steve Billeb, while they conducted evolutionary behavioral studies on mockingbirds on various islands. They had engaged Eddie Niles, the proud owner of the "Buzzo", a thirty-eight-foot, WW-I landing barge, to transport them to the islands upon which they were conducting their studies. Eddie originally was from Seattle, but had immigrated to the Islands on a now defunct land-settlement scheme. He had "inherited" the "Buzzo" and now was trying to make a living by fishing and transporting tourists around the Islands.

One evening, while Eddy was listening to "The Voice of America" upon his transistor radio, there was a report about two Americans "presumed" to be lost upon the volcanic mountain of Sangay in Ecuador. No names were given, but we speculated as to whether or not they might be Jim Thomas and John Rocco.

When Carol, Cris Tina - our recently-born daughter – and I returned to Quito some weeks later, Bob Norris told us what had happened on Sangay. He and Naomi had returned to Quito just in time for him to join the rescue party that was going to search for Jim and John on Sangay.

Shortly after we had departed for the Galapagos Islands, Jim and John had left Quito to photograph and climb Sangay. They had hired Indian porters to carry their food and supplies during the three-day trek through the jungle to the base of Sangay. The weather had been beautiful and they looked forward to climbing the mountain. Early the next morning, after having established a camp and spending the night at the foot of Sangay, Jim and John began their ascent of the volcano. They used Jim's backpack to carry a small mountain tent, a sleeping bag, some food, and an ample supply of film for Jim's photographic equipment, which consisted of a 35mm still camera and a 16mm movie camera. They left their Indian porters to "watch after" their camp.

Jim and John's ascent of Sangay was uneventful and much easier than Jim had anticipated. They reached the top or crater rim by late afternoon. Jim then spent time photographing the surrounding vistas and the active or molten interior of the volcano. They planned to camp on the snowfield near the summit and then take some more photographs before descending to their base camp the next morning. However, Sangay erupted during the night! Jim claimed, "The sulfur fumes were so dense that we almost suffocated!" Furthermore, "Molten masses – as large as houses – shot up out of the caldera, before falling back inside. Red hot cinders also kept falling on top of us and burned holes in our tent." They frantically kept throwing snow on the tent walls to quench the smoldering embers. "The tent", he claimed, "protected us from being severely burned." The eruption finally subsided and Jim said both he and John "felt fortunate to still be alive." They had "only a few blisters" on their arms and faces and they could hardly wait for morning to come – so they could get down and off from Sangay. In short, they spent "a horrible night" in the snowfield near the summit of the volcano.

The Indian porters at the base camp witnessed the violent nighttime eruption of Sangay. They were certain both Jim and John had been killed. They could not imagine how anyone on the mountain could have survived or not have been burned to death by the hot ashes and molten lava that spewed forth from the volcanic caldera. Thus, they loaded up all the remaining food and supplies and began their three-day trek back to the nearest road.

Upon their return to Quito, the porters reported to the Ecuadorian authorities that: "Jim Thomas and John Rocco were killed on the slopes of Sangay during a volcanic eruption." When questioned as to whether or not they had seen Jim's and John's bodies, they admitted they had not. Thus, official reports stated: "Two Americans are missing on Sangay."

The American Embassy in Quito assembled a search party. This consisted primarily of experienced climbers, most of whom were members of "Nuevo Horizontes" – a climbing club in Quito with which I was well acquainted. Only two Americans, Robert Norris and a representative from the American Embassy, were included. The search party believed their objective was to find and retrieve the bodies of Jim and John from the slopes of Sangay.

Following the nighttime eruption of Sangay, Jim and John crawled out of their tent at first light. Jim took some more photos. They ate breakfast and discussed their descent. However, soon after loading up their gear and starting down the slopes of the mountain, clouds from the jungles below rose up onto the mountain and they were soon enveloped in a dense fog. They could only see a few feet in front of them. They followed their previous tracks until they reached the edge of the snowfield. Then, they could not ascertain how to descend. Repeatedly, they would descend only to find themselves at the top of sheer cliffs, which appeared impossible to cross. They then would scramble back up the mountain, searching for another route of descent. This they continued to do for two days! There was never a break in the dense cloud cover that enveloped them and they began to think they were trapped on the slopes of this volcanic mountain. Try as they might, they could not find a way off!

By the third day, Jim and John's food supply had been reduced to a single can of sardines. They had abandoned the tent, sleeping bag, and even the precious, but bulky, 16mm movie camera. Both were nauseated, disoriented and apparently suffering the effects of altitude sickness. Nevertheless, they opened the can of sardines. But, both were too sick to eat. Thus, they simply left the opened can of fish on a flat rock and again attempted to find a way off from the mountain. Shortly thereafter, according to Jim, "The clouds briefly parted and we could see a river wending its way through the jungle below." John was elated and emphatically stated, "All we have to do is get to that river and follow it. Then, we'll find people!" Jim, in turn, tried to tell him he was wrong. The opposite was true. He claimed, "That river runs into the Amazon Basin. The only people we might encounter there would perhaps be a few primitive Indians. We need to go the other way in order to reach our base camp and get out of the jungle!"

Jim and John argued and the cloud cover again enveloped them. John insisted upon trying to cross some extremely precipitous terrain in order to reach the river they had briefly seen below, while Jim tried to convince him they had to go the opposite direction in order to find their way off from the mountain. Both were adamant! Thus, they parted company – going in opposite directions!

Late that afternoon Jim finally staggered out of the cloudy mist and made his way to base camp. He had been on the slopes of Sangay for almost four days. He was famished and could hardly wait to get to camp, where he could get both food and water. But, when he arrived at the campsite, there wasn't anything or anyone there. The Indian porters had taken everything. The fire pits were all that remained!

It was during Jim's second day on the trail, while he was struggling through the jungle towards the road where they had begun their trek to Sangay that he encountered the search party. After eating and drinking to regain his strength, he related details of what had happened during the time he and John had been on the slopes of Sangay. He told how they had abandoned the tent, sleeping, bag, and the 16mm movie camera. However, his 35mm camera still dangled from a cord around his neck and the last photo he remembered having taken was of John Rocco. He even told how he and John had been too sick to eat their last can of sardines and how they had left the opened tin on a flat rock. He also tried to explain how he was unable to convince John that they needed to go the opposite direction from the river, which they briefly had glimpsed in the jungle below.

Jim accompanied the search party back to the site of their camp at the foot of Sangay. He, Bob Norris and the American from the U.S. Embassy then remained at the campsite, while the experienced climbers searched the slopes of Sangay for John.

The experienced climbers returned to camp the following day. They told how they had found the opened can of sardines. It was laying on a flat rock, just like Jim had told them. They also found where Jim and John had parted company. Thereafter, they were able to follow John's tracks for some distance through the precipitous terrain. However, John's route of travel eventually entered such a hazardous area that they did not dare follow further. Although they did not find John, they were almost certain he could not have crossed the terrain into which his tracks led. They felt this area was too dangerous for them to enter, even with their experience and climbing gear.

Jim and the search party returned to Quito. After they had reported what had happened on Sangay, the U.S. Embassy sent an envoy to Cuenca to inform John's brother Frank about what had happened. At first, Frank would not believe what they told him. He claimed, "My brother's in the States, buying a portable dredge – so we can work our gold claim. Why would he be climbing a volcano? He's not a mountain climber!"

The envoy eventually convinced Frank he was telling the truth. Frank and he then returned to Quito. While in Quito, Frank again stayed at the Hotel Alcron for a few days. During this time, Jim gave him an enlarged black and white photo of his brother John. This was the last photo he had taken while he and John were together on the slopes of Sangay. Frank thereafter departed for the U.S. and Jim returned to France.

Some months later, after my wife Carol and our daughter Cris Tina had returned to the U.S., I moved back into the Hotel Alcron. One evening, while Bob and I waited for dinner to be served at the large dining room table, in walked Frank Rocco. We couldn't believe it! Frank shortly explained, "A 'ghost writer' wrote a story about my brother, John's, search for gold on Sangay." And, "He published it and the photo of John in 'Argosy' Magazine."

Frank gave Bob and I each a copy of this "adventure-type" magazine, which contained John's photo and the story about him. However, the story was almost pure fiction. It claimed John had learned about lost Inca gold on the slopes of Sangay from a chance acquaintance in a bar in Quito. He then had mounted an expedition to Sangay, which involved encounters with Jivaro Indians in the surrounding jungles and other nonsense. Nevertheless, the "ghost writer" had paid a substantial sum of money to Frank for John's photo and the rights to the story. Frank used this money to return to Ecuador and was going to join his and John's "old partner" in Cuenca to again search for gold. Like his brother John, Frank proclaimed, "I'm either going to strike it rich or die trying!" He was certain the riches of the Andes awaited him. What happened to Frank Rocco thereafter I do not know.

CALCUTTA now KOLKATA

Calcutta – "The City of Joy" – is NOT a joyful place.

I thought I was prepared for Calcutta. I was not! I had read much about India and had visited with many people who had lived and/or had traveled extensively in this country, which encompasses a million square miles and is about one-third the size of the United States. I listened attentively to their descriptions of the poverty, filth and crowded conditions that typify much of India and particularly Calcutta – a city of more than twenty-four million people. I also considered myself to be a seasoned traveler and believed conditions almost anywhere in the world would not startle, let alone shock me. I was wrong!

My first acquaintance with human poverty occurred while I was in the military service. The slums of Casablanca, Morocco, and of Naples, Italy, as well as the devastating effects of World War II, which still were starkly evident throughout much of Europe in the early 1950's, impressed upon me the trying and bleak conditions under which many people live. While serving as a "Mormon" missionary for two and one-half years in South America, I spent nine months in the "barrios" or slums of Asuncion, Paraguay. Paraguay then was considered to be one of the poorest nations in the southern hemisphere. There were fewer than twenty miles of paved road in the entire country. The capital city of Asuncion did not have either culinary water or a sewer system. Many Paraguayans went barefoot and lived in thatch-roofed shacks. I was certain people could not live in much poorer conditions than did they. Again, I was wrong. Between four and five million people in downtown Calcutta literally live in the streets – without even a roof over their head!

While returning to the U.S. from South America, I visited slums in La Paz, Bolivia; Lima, Peru; Guayaquil, Ecuador; Mexico City, and elsewhere. Thereafter, I returned to Ecuador for a year as a Fulbright scholar, during which time I visited many poverty-stricken towns and villages. Still, I'd never witnessed anything to equal the poverty, filth and squalor in which literally millions of people live in India and especially in Calcutta.

We (I, my wife Carol, and our two-and-one-half-year old daughter Cris Tina) arrived at the Dum Dum Airport outside of Calcutta in October 1964. I remembered Dum Dum's infamy for being the place where "Dum Dum bullets" were developed. These have wooden points or projectiles, which shatter upon impact and cause horrendous wounds. I later learned Dum Dum also was noted for "Dum Dum Fever". People living here commonly plaster the interior walls of their huts with cow dung. The dung provides harborage for insect vectors that transmit the dreaded "Dum Dum Fever" to humans.

After clearing Customs and Immigration at the airport, I hailed a taxi to take us into downtown Calcutta. We had reservations at the New Kenilworth Hotel, where most of the people associated with The Johns Hopkins University's Center for Medical Research and Training (CMRT) program resided. We loaded our luggage into the taxi and I told the driver, "New Kenilworth Hotel. Little Russell Street." The driver's eyes reflected what I took to be confusion. Thus, I repeated the address and asked, "Do you know Little Russell Street and the New Kenilworth Hotel?" His reply was, "Yes! Yes! Sahib." Thus, we crawled into the vehicle and the driver steered the taxi into a maze of human and vehicular traffic.

The ride from the airport into Calcutta was unbelievable. The humid stench was overpowering. Anywhere one looked there was a seething mass of humanity. How could people live under such crowded conditions? Most of the men wore only a small loin cloth or a pair of under-shorts; whereas, most of the women were modestly wrapped in "saris", which consist of a long piece of cloth that draped over the shoulder and tied at the waist. Most were barefoot or wore only thongs on their feet. Many young children were naked.

Literally hundreds of men – like beasts of burden – struggled to push or pull rickety, two-wheeled carts that were stacked unbelievably high with sacks of grain or other goods. Others pulled black, two-wheeled rickshaws, wherein fat men or women or young children placidly sat. Yet others carried poles across their shoulders, from either end of which dangled tins full of water or bundles of goods. Most seemed to be in a hurry and they appeared to be going in all directions. All also bore a grim countenance upon their face. No one smiled nor laughed. I could not imagine a more gruesome nor chaotic situation.

We observed people squatting at the side of the road or on a curb to relieve themselves. Even men squatted to urinate. Were they attempting to be somewhat modest? Numerous and usually skinny or mangy-looking tan or brown-colored dogs intermingled with the hoards of people and often fought over garbage. There also were hundreds of noisy birds. These included the raucous house crows, with their black bodies and gray heads, and the much smaller and more colorful mynas, which always seemed to be chattering. Hawk-like kites and bald-headed vultures circled overhead or gathered in large numbers around the carcasses of animals such as dogs and cows lying on the streets. Piles of garbage seemed to be everywhere. How could people retain their sanity amid such chaos? And, how could they survive under such filthy conditions?

We rode for what seemed like hours among never-ending streams of people, carts, rickshaws and an array of motor vehicles. The taxi driver almost continuously squeezed the rubber bulb of a noisy horn, while steering through the bedlam with his other hand. He also repeatedly shouted at people to get out of the way and frequently shook his upraised fist at them. He periodically stopped and jabbered with people. It appeared he was inquiring about directions. But, whenever I asked him whether or not he knew the way to the New Kenilworth Hotel, his reply was always, "Yes! Yes! Sahib."

After about a two and one-half-hour taxi ride, we finally arrived at the New Kenilworth Hotel. Little Russell Street and the hotel were just off from one of the main downtown streets in Calcutta and next to the U.S. Consulate. One would think these would be well known to almost any taxi driver.

I paid the fare indicated on the taxi's meter plus an additional fee for our luggage. It seemed like an exorbitant amount. I later learned it was! Thereafter, I flew out of and into Dum Dum Airport numerous times. Then, whenever I exited the airport, I would hail a taxi and simply tell the driver, "New Kenilworth Hotel". And they would drive me there in less than thirty minutes. How did the first driver know we were new to Calcutta? I soon learned, however, many astute Indians readily detect when people are not acquainted with local situations, fares or prices. And, almost invariably, they take advantage of such opportunities!

I told others about how a taxi driver had taken advantage of us when we first arrived in Calcutta. They, in turn, almost always related similar experiences they had had in India. For example, Dr. Kloona, a German M.D. conducting research on measles with the CMRT program, related: "Soon after I arrived in Calcutta, I was walking from the New Kenilworth to the nearby hospital where I was conducting my research (a distance of about five blocks), when a rickshaw 'walla' pulled up alongside me and kept saying, ''Rickshaw, Sahib? Rickshaw, Sahib?' It was a typically hot and humid day, so I climbed into the rickshaw and rode the two or three remaining blocks to the hospital. When we got there, I asked the 'walla', "How much?" He said, "Five rupee!" And, I paid him. While walking into the hospital, I thought, 'Five rupees is quite a bit for such a short ride.' So, I asked one of my Indian assistants, 'How much should one pay for a rickshaw ride from the New Kenilworth to the hospital?' His emphatic reply was, 'Not more than fifty paise' or half a rupee!"

When Dr. Kloona exited the gate from the New Kenilworth to walk to the hospital the next morning, another rickshaw "walla" was waiting for him. He also entreated the doctor to ride in his rickshaw. Thus, Dr. Kloona climbed into the rickshaw and rode to the hospital. He then handed the "walla" fifty paise and turned to enter the building. But, the rickshaw "walla" became livid and started to shout. "You pay five rupee to rickshaw boy yesterday! Why you no pay me five rupee? What you think I am?"

There are more than two thousand rickshaw "wallas" in Calcutta. How many of them had learned about a big German doctor staying at the New Kenilworth Hotel who paid five rupees or ten times the going rate for a ride to the nearby hospital? And, what arrangements had the second "walla" made with the first; whereby, he also could take advantage of a newcomer to Calcutta?

Most of the Johns Hopkins University CMRT personnel in Calcutta lived in the New Kenilworth Hotel. This was because it was much easier and cheaper to live in a hotel than to rent and furnish a house or an apartment. Living in a house or an apartment meant you had to employ a full entourage of servants; whereas, if you resided in a hotel you were expected to employ only a full-time "bearer", a part-time "sweeper" and a "dobie" or laundry man, as well as an "ayah" or baby-sitter – if you had children

A "Sahib" or anyone of any affluence whatsoever in India is expected to employ an array of servants. First, you need guards to protect your home and property. Then, you need a "bearer" to look after your personal needs, i.e. to serve your meals, make your beds, shine your shoes, and so forth. It also is the "bearer's" duty or privilege to give orders and "to lord it over" the other household servants. Then, of course, you need a "dobie" to beat the buttons off from your clothes, while he pounds them with rocks or on the pavement to get them clean. Likewise, you need a "sweeper" – the lowliest of servants – to keep your floors clean and to pay abeyance to all of the other servants. If you have small children, you MUST have an "ayah" or woman servant to tend them. Your "ayah" is expected to do both your bidding and that of your children. It is common for even very small children to shout orders to their "ayahs" and to administer punishment to them – if they fail to do their bidding. If you have a vehicle, you need a "driver". No "respectable" Sahib would drive his own car! Then, if you have any kind of a yard whatsoever, you definitely need a "gardener". On and on goes the list of domestic help a Sahib is expected to employ. Furthermore, one should not treat their servants or employees with any respect, whatsoever. You are their master and should act accordingly. Heaven forbid that you ever treat a servant or employee as an equal. If you do, both they and others will hold you in contempt. You must ALWAYS be the lord and master, as well as meet out punishment whenever your orders are not followed to the letter.

Having servants continually underfoot and never having any privacy was difficult for me. Treating our servants as inferiors was even more difficult. Throughout my life I was taught and firmly believe "all men are created equal" and we should treat everyone with courtesy and respect. Such is not the case in India!

The caste system has been "officially" outlawed in India. But, a very rigid hierarchy or "caste system" still persists. This is particularly evident among servants. The "bearer" is all-powerful among household servants. His word is "law". And, if the other servants do not quickly and strictly obey his commands, he will meet out harsh punishment. His rank or standing among other "bearers", however, is dependent primarily upon the status or rank of his employer, rather than upon how much he is paid or esteemed by his master. Although I paid our "bearer" more than most residents at the New Kenilworth paid theirs, the other "bearers" treated him with disdain and considered him to be inferior. This was because I did not "act" like a "true" Sahib. First, I wore khaki clothes, rather than a white shirt and white linen trousers, as did other Sahibs. Second, I went to work early each morning; whereas, "real" Sahibs remained at the hotel and ate a leisurely breakfast. What's more, I usually did not return from work until late in the evening; whereas, Sahibs rarely work early or late hours, but should be primarily "men of leisure"! Worst of all, I often worked with my hands while conducting research on rats. A Sahib should not engage in physical labor. Manual labor should be relegated to servants or common laborers!

The "sweeper" is the lowliest of household servants. His sole domain is the floor. Because of his low status, he would not dare stand erect in the presence of other servants, let alone when a Sahib is present. When spoken to, he never looks directly at or even towards those who are speaking to him. Instead, with bowed head, he must survey only his domain, which is the floor. In addition to sweeping and mopping the floors, his duties include cowering as close to the floor as possible, while slithering from room to room in his master's house. Whenever the "bearer" or others happen to drop something onto the floor or there is any kind of a mess there, it is his duty to retrieve it and/or to clean it up. It is unthinkable for a "bearer" or another servant to enter the "sweeper's" domain.

Shortly after we took up residency at the New Kenilworth, my wife Carol inadvertently committed what our "bearer" considered to be an almost unpardonable error. Some sugar accidentally was spilled upon the living room floor. While the "bearer" frantically searched for the "sweeper" – so he could clean it up – Carol simply cleaned up the mess. When the "bearer" returned with the "sweeper" in tow, he was aghast at what she had done. He could not imagine a "Memsahib" stooping so low or committing such a disgraceful act. For us, it often was difficult and frustrating to go through the "formality" of having the "proper" servants do "their" tasks, rather than simply doing them for ourselves.

Our cat appeared to be the only living creature to which our "sweeper" felt superior. Whenever he thought no one was around or they couldn't hear his shouts and foul language, he would vent his pent-up rage upon the hapless animal. While vociferously chasing it, he would shout obscenities and try to strike it with his short-handled broom. The cat usually sought refuge beneath our bed. But, even here, the "sweeper" would pursue the frightened animal. Then, when we would hear the commotion and enter the bedroom, he invariably would meekly crawl from beneath the bed and start sweeping the floor in his slinky manner – as if nothing had happened. Such was the life of servants in India!

It is impossible to describe the squalor of Calcutta. Half-naked men, "sari-draped" women and myriads of children, "pariah" or stray dogs, innumerable birds, and "sacred" cows or bulls mingle in what seems to be utter chaos. The seemingly omni-present cattle particularly intrigued me. Although they commonly are used as beasts of burden or draft animals throughout India, rarely do you see them used as such in Calcutta or other large Indian cities. I wondered why. An Indian friend then explained, "It's simple economics. If a bullock is injured or dies on the streets, the owner is responsible for the animal; whereas, if a 'coolie' (laborer) is killed or dies on the streets; the city picks up his body." In short, there is less risk and it is cheaper to use manpower or "coolie" labor than to use beasts of burden within the confines of a city!

It at first appeared to me the cattle wandering on the streets of Calcutta did not belong to anyone. Upon closer scrutiny, I observed young boys or girls accompanied most of the animals and they were tethered and tended by their owners at night. Also, these young caretakers usually carried bowls in which to collect the animals' droppings. Cow dung is considered as a precious commodity. Whenever a "sacred" cow or bull defecates, those accompanying the animal quickly rush in and, with their bare hands, collect the droppings. Thereafter, they pat and shape the odoriferous and gooey substance into neat "patties", which are plastered onto the trunk of a tree or a wall to dry. When dry, these cow-dung patties peel off and are collected and stored in neat stacks. They are later used for fuel - to cook food, to cremate dead bodies and to provide warmth during the winter months. While traveling throughout India, I noted the size and shape of cow-dung patties varies. In the north, they tend to be large and oblong; whereas, in the south, they tend to be small and round. None of those I asked could tell me the reason for the variations in size and shape. Could this be worthy of a scientific study?

We are much concerned in our modern world about air pollution. The burning of fossil fuels (i.e. coal and/or oil products) generally is blamed or considered to be the primary cause of our air pollution problems. However, if one wants to both see and smell air pollution at its zenith, they should visit Calcutta during the winter. The air in this city then is acrid with the smoke and smell emulating primarily from the burning of cow-dung patties.

Having cow's milk for your family is a sign of affluence in India. Owning a cow, even if you live in a city, is highly desirable. Although the average cow in Calcutta produces less than a liter of milk per day, this milk is highly prized. It surprises me that they produce any milk whatsoever. This is because cows in Calcutta rarely see, let alone get to eat, any green grass. Instead, they live almost entirely upon refuse, which includes banana peelings, coconut husks, rags and newspapers. It is not uncommon to see screaming women or children chasing after a cow that is trying to consume their laundry for forage. Carl Mitchell, a fellow graduate student with whom I conducted rodent research, and I often chided each other as to which of Calcutta's two daily newspapers would produce the most milk when consumed by a cow. Carl subscribed to the "Patrica" and was certain it would be the best milk producer; whereas, I took "The Statesman" and thought it would produce more. We never determined who was right.

A Dutch mechanic, who married an Indian woman during World War II and then took up residency in Calcutta, worked on the CMRT's vehicles. Similar to many of his Indian neighbors, he owned a cow – in order to have milk for his family. However, rather than simply turning his cow out onto the streets each day to scavenge for food, he fed it hay and grain. As a result, his cow produced many times over the amount of milk his neighbors' cows produced. When he milked his cow each morning and evening, his neighbors would watch and "Oh!" and "Awe! " as to how much milk his cow produced as compared to theirs. They repeatedly asked, "How come your cow gives so much more milk than ours?" His reply was, "It's because I feed my cow!" This simple explanation, however, never resulted in his neighbors feeding their cows and, thereby, obtaining more precious milk. Why?

The Ford Foundation conducted "A Study of Greater Calcutta" during the two years we lived in India. Much of the information gleaned about the megalopolis of Calcutta is almost unbelievable. For example, the mean human population density for downtown Calcutta is about sixty-nine thousand people per square mile; whereas, it is only thirty-five thousand in "greater" Tokyo and twenty-nine thousand for "greater" London. In contrast, my home state of Idaho has a mean population density of less than ten people per square mile! The total population for Greater Calcutta could not be accurately determined. It was ascertained to be well in excess of eleven million, and upwards of five million of these literally lived in the streets. They do not have any homes and most do nor even have a shack or roof to protect them from the elements. They simply exist on the crowded streets, alleys, sidewalks or anywhere they can find sufficient space to squat, sit or lie down. It was estimated that more than five thousand "squatters" lived in the Howrah Railroad Station, across the Hooghly River from Calcutta.

As for water, an average of twelve families share each of the water faucets scattered throughout much of Calcutta. These faucets, however, deliver only untreated water from the Hooghly River, which is little more than an open sewer. People, nevertheless, readily drink the water, as well as use it to wash their food, their ragged clothes and to bathe. As a result, dysentery and periodic outbreaks of cholera are common. As for sanitation, there are only one hundred and fifty thousand flush toilets to serve the city's burgeoning population. Sanitation, insofar as it is considered by most of the Western World, is almost completely lacking. Garbage simply is thrown into the streets or stacked at street corners, where it is scavenged by both people and animals. Refuse trucks attempt to collect and haul garbage to dumps along the city's perimeters. These trucks, however, operate primarily in the more affluent neighborhoods. Thus, literally hundreds of people vie with each other for the opportunity to be the first to scavenge the refuse hauled to the dumps. Virtually everything we Westerners throw away is considered to be of value to someone in India. Some people make a living by collecting tin cans, others collect old bottles and so on. I even encountered some men who made their living by scavenging bits of wire and other items from crows' nests. Not only do many Americans earn more in a single day than do many Indians during an entire year, but many of us also throw away more and better goods than many Indians ever could hope to own. What we consider to be dire poverty in the U.S. would be considered to be a life of luxury by many Indians!

Despite the filth in which the street people of Calcutta live, many religiously bathe every day. Many bathe beneath the faucets provided by the city, but most walk to and bathe at the "ghats" or bathing areas along the Hooghly River. Devout Hindus bathe only in running water. They consider it improper or unclean to bathe in "still" water, such as that in a bathtub. For me, it was truly amazing to watch literally thousands of people – both men and women – daily wade out into the river and bathe. They also were able to accomplish this in a modest manner, i.e. dropping out of their clothes and down into the water, and then coming back up into their clothes, without exposing themselves to onlookers. Rather than using toilet paper, as do Westerners, most Indians also wash themselves after defecating. They carry small vessels of water and, after relieving themselves, use the water and their left hand to wash their private parts. This is why the right hand – NEVER THE LEFT! – is used for eating. Small groves of bamboo commonly serve as latrines in rural areas or for villages. But, almost any curb, alley, refuse dump or open space may serve as a latrine in Calcutta!

Many common practices in India are repugnant to Westerners. In turn, Indians consider many of our habits as offensive or filthy. For example, they are appalled that we would bathe in a tub of "still" water. One should bathe ONLY in water that is flowing. Our sitting on a toilet to relieve ourselves and then using toilet paper likewise is repugnant to them. Many also shudder when they see Westerners use their left hand while eating. Rather than using utensils, Indians eat with their hands. However, they wash their hands both before and after eating. Upon finishing a meal, they also rinse out their mouth. Although some Indians will shake hands when greeting Westerners, they prefer their custom of greeting others by clasping their hands together, in front of their bodies, and bowing towards the person being greeted. Many are repulsed by bodily contact – even the shaking of hands.

Many of even the poorest people in Calcutta brush their teeth daily. They use "toothbrush sticks", which are small, green sticks that are cut and brought into the city in large bundles and sold for a few "paise" by vendors. The frayed ends of these sticks are rubbed up and down on the teeth, like a toothbrush. This action causes the sticks to emit foam or froth similar to what is produced by toothpaste. It amazed me how poor people, who often appeared to be starving, were so concerned about caring for their teeth. It also shocked me to observe how they frequently dipped water, in their cupped hand, from a gutter to rinse their mouths while brushing their teeth. It seemed ironical how, after being so fastidious about bathing and brushing their teeth, they paid no heed to the use of polluted water!

One can observe almost anything or everything on the streets of Calcutta. Millions of people literally are born, live and die here. It is next to impossible to clear an area to develop a park or to construct a new building. As soon as an open space appears, people swarm into it with cardboard boxes, sheets of rusted tin, woven mats, or anything they can obtain and use to erect a hovel in which they may live. It is amazing how quickly people occupy and territorialize almost any available space. It may be a concrete sewer pipe, which the city is trying to lay. Or, it may be a narrow passageway between two buildings, or even a large box that someone has discarded. There seems to be an innate need in people to possess or occupy an area they can consider as their own and to which they can retreat for refuge. To me, this need appears to be particularly evident among Calcutta's poor. Furthermore, once people here have established what they consider to be "their territorial rights", it is extremely difficult to dislodge them. Major strikes or "hartals" and demonstrations are common in Calcutta. Many of these also are accompanied by violence and result from attempts by the city or others to dislodge squatters from areas they have taken possession of.

I conducted studies on rats inhabiting the "godowns" or grain storage warehouses in and around Calcutta. I often set live-traps to catch rats in the evenings and then collected them the following mornings. To avoid heavy traffic, as well as daytime heat, I usually left the New Kenilworth about 5:30 a.m. To relieve the monotony, while being transported by a driver to my study sites, I often attempted to count the number of people sleeping on the sidewalks along the streets we traversed. The highest number of sleepers I counted in a block-long area was five hundred and forty! Not all of these necessarily lived on the street. Some had rooms or apartments, but slept on the sidewalk because it was cooler here than inside a closed or unventilated building. Nevertheless, most people sleeping on the streets lived on the streets – full time!

Many amenities taken for granted by Westerners are rarities in India. For example, during my extensive travels throughout this country, I did not encounter a single city or village in which one could safely drink the water from a tap. Drinking water ALWAYS has to be boiled! I also have been in cities with more than three hundred and fifty thousand inhabitants in which I could not locate a single refrigerator nor any form of refrigeration or air conditioning. Except in larger cities and better hotels and restaurants, one rarely can expect to be served a cool drink, let alone a cold one. For health's sake, you also quickly learn NEVER to eat foods or to drink beverages unless they are hot or you know they have been prepared with boiled water.

The mean life expectancy in India is less than fifty years; whereas, in the U.S. it exceeds seventy. Disease and sickness are common. Still, despite the terrible conditions in which many live in India, I was impressed by their efforts at cleanliness. A man might own but a single loincloth. But, while bathing each day, he usually will wash his meager clothing. Women's "saris" likewise usually appear to be clean. The floors and yards of humble mud huts in villages also are invariably swept and washed clean daily.

Western and Indian cultures contrast markedly. Indians prefer to sit, cross-legged on a mat or rug upon the floor, rather than in a chair. They also prefer to eat with their hands, rather than with utensils. This is despite most of their food being rice and liquid curries, which I found difficult to eat with my fingers. While eating, one also is expected to express enjoyment and/or gratitude for the food by belching both loudly and frequently. Upon entering a home, you are expected to remove your sandals or shoes. Men also are the masters of their homes and families. Women and children are subservient to them and must remain quiet or out of sight whenever men are together. Marks of distinction for a man include: a large stomach and a bald head (preferably with gray hair around the sides);whereas, these characteristics are considered undesirable by Westerners.

Dr. Warren Foote, a friend and colleague at Utah State University, visited India with me. His stomach is not unduly large, but the top of his head is bald and the hair on the sides of his head is gray. I chided him with, "You should have been born in India and you would have had it made! Here, you would be considered a real 'sadhu' or wise man!" I don't know why this upset, rather than pleased him.

Dr. George Schaller, a friend and noted wildlife ecologist with whom I worked in India, aptly described Calcutta as, "The greatest place in the world for people watching." Not only is Calcutta's human population one of the world's densest, but one also can literally see almost anything upon its streets. Furthermore, people here pay little heed to others around them. Somehow, they appear to mentally block out their surroundings and are able to do whatever they are doing as if they were completely alone. Thus, you usually can closely observe them without they're being offended or even paying any attention to you. I believe one perhaps may observe more human drama, chaos, and pathos upon Calcutta's streets than on the streets of any city in the world.

One day, while sitting in a vehicle awaiting the arrival of my assistant, I became engrossed in watching the hordes of people passing bye. One man in particular caught my attention. At first, I could not determine why he stood out so starkly from the other men around him. Like them, he wore only a pair of under shorts. Then, I suddenly realized what distinguished him from the others. It was because his shorts were clean and white; whereas, those of the others were dirty or dingy colored.

Carl Mitchell, a fellow graduate student, and I shared a laboratory in the Calcutta Science College. We also worked together in our research. He studied the ectoparasites of rodents, while I studied their reproductive physiology and ecology. We trapped rats together and, when traveling to and from our trapping sites, we usually tried to use the least congested streets. This meant we often passed through the "Maidan", a large, park-like area that formerly served as an open space around a British fort and in which stands the impressive Queen Victoria Memorial.

Early one morning, while passing through the "Maidan", Carl remarked, "Did you see that girl? The one lying in the center of the street! She didn't have any clothes on!" I had not noticed. Thus, we had the driver turn around and take us back for a second look. Carl was right! A shapely girl of perhaps eighteen or twenty years of age was lying flat on her back in the middle of the paved street. For some reason, she had a small cord threaded through her nostrils, the ends of which extended down past her thighs. She was grasping the ends of the cord with her hands and pulling it back and forth through her nose. While doing this, she also was moaning and writhing back and forth in apparent pain. We could not imagine why she would do such a thing. The driver drove our vehicle around her several times, while we gazed down upon her naked body. We assured each other, "She certainly is stark naked! Isn't she?" Not knowing what, if any action we should take, we decided to continue on to our study site to retrieve the traps we had set the previous evening.

About three hours later, while returning from our rat-trapping expedition, Carl suggested, "Let's see if that girl is still there." She was! She was still lying in the center of the street, pulling the cord back and forth through her nostrils, and writhing back and forth in apparent agony. Traffic, by this time, had markedly increased. However, a policeman now stood in front of the prostrate girl and was directing oncoming vehicles around her!

While I traversed the streets of Calcutta in the early morning, I often saw the prostrate forms of people who had died during the night. Occasionally, I also saw those who's task it was to gather up these bodies. They would simply grab them by the arms and legs and toss them – like cord wood – onto a flatbed truck. They then would take them to a government-operated incinerator for cremation. I was told most people who died on the streets were those who had come to the city looking for work or simply were "street people" that did not have any relatives or next-of-kin who could provide them with a "proper" cremation. In contrast, in family situations it is a matter of duty and honor to provide a "proper" cremation for departed family members. This particularly is true with respect to the eldest son providing for the cremation of his father. This often means the borrowing of money at exorbitant interest rates and family members going into financial bondage for the remainder of their lives – because they feel duty-bound to provide a "proper" cremation for a departed family member.

Most of those associated with the Johns Hopkins CMRT program resided in Calcutta, but the CMRT program also maintained a research station in Singur, a village of about twenty thousand inhabitants located some twenty miles northwest of Calcutta. Dr. Dwain Parrack established and operated this station, but other CMRT personnel also conducted studies there. While Dr. Parrack went on "home leave" to the States, my family and I lived at the station and oversaw its operation for approximately four months.

It usually is faster and easier to travel between Calcutta and Singur by train, rather than by vehicle. This is because of poor roads and unbelievably heavy traffic. However, in order to reach the Howrah Train Station, you first have to cross the bridge over the Hooghly River. The "Hooghly Bridge" is proudly proclaimed to be the largest cantilever bridge in the world, but the unbelievable traffic congestion on the bridge is not mentioned. By vehicle, it sometimes takes up to two hours to traverse this bridge! Thereafter, you purchase a ticket at the railroad station for any one of a number of open-door commuter trains that pass through Singur. It is claimed the Howrah Station is the busiest in the world, with more than a million passengers passing through it every day. This is in addition to several thousand people who have taken up residency on the station's floors.

I was traveling by train to Singur early one hot, muggy morning during the summer of 1965. As I traversed the station platform to reach my train, I observed the prostrate form of a man. He was lying face down, with his arms extended above his head. He was clothed only in a tattered loincloth and appeared to be dead. But, I was in a hurry to catch the train, so I simply stepped over his prostrate body and hurried on – as did hundreds of other scurrying passengers.

It was late afternoon when I returned to the Howrah Station from Singur. As I stepped off from the train, I again observed the prostrate form of the man on the platform. He was in the same position as he had been that morning. I approached him, stooped down and looked into his face. He was dead! Flies were crawling in and out of his mouth and nostrils and his body was beginning to bloat. None of the hundreds of people passing by paid any attention to either him or me. I debated as to what I should do. Finally, I rationalized, "It's too late for me to help this poor man." Thus, I simply arose, walked out of the station and hailed a taxi to take me to the New Kenilworth. I've since wondered, "How long did that poor man's body lay on the railroad platform?" And, "How many hundreds of people stepped over his body and, like me, did nothing?"

One early morning, while traveling to one of my rat trapping sites in the "godown area" of Howrah, I beheld a scene I'll never forget. A poor, starving man was staggering alongside the street. Only a ragged loincloth covered his nakedness and his body was little more than skin and bones. Suddenly, he fell into the gutter. With what appeared to be much effort, he managed to rise up onto his hands and knees. But, it appeared he did not have the strength to stand up. He then slowly collapsed into the gutter. Not ten feet away from this poor soul, a stoutly built and relatively well-dressed man was feeding a flock of pigeons from a large bucket full of grain. He was holding the bucket with one hand, while using the other to dip into and then strew the grain from the bucket onto the ground for the birds. He paid no heed whatsoever to the man in the gutter, but placidly continued to feed the pigeons assembled around him. Although seated in a vehicle some thirty or forty feet away, I could hear the starving man's groans, as well as the cooing of the pigeons. Still, the man scattering the grain paid no attention to the starving man in front of him. He simply continued to feed the pigeons!

We (my driver and I) left the two men, the one feeding the pigeons and the other lying in the gutter, and continued on to my rat-trapping site. It was several hours before we returned. The opulent man was gone, but a few pigeons remained. They appeared to be gleaning the last kernels of grain from off the street. The starving man still lay in the gutter. I got out of the vehicle and approached him. He was dead! My driver calmly explained, "The 'city' will pick up his body and cremate it." Thus, we left the scene and returned to the laboratory at the Science College where I processed my rat specimens.

Beggars are an integral part of Calcutta. They present a dilemma. If you listen to their pleading cries and give them something, you only encourage them to continue to beg. But, if you do not give them something, how do you soothe your conscience for not living the "Golden Rule", i.e. "Do unto others as you would have them do unto you"?

Given the number of beggars on Calcutta's streets, I doubt anyone would be able to give something to each of them. Thus, I decided, "I won't give anything to the beggars who approach me. But, if possible, I'll ask them to perform some small task, such as carry a package, and then pay them for their service." When I attempted to follow this policy, it was amazing how often the beggars refused my offers. Some even acted as if I had insulted them by asking them to do something for me. It was as if it was below their "professional" dignity.

I became well acquainted, not by name but by face, with many beggars in Calcutta. One young fellow, with a clubfoot and a deformed hand, would approach vehicles stopped at intersections in the center of the city. He would extend his deformed hand towards those in a vehicle and then mournfully beg for money. Perhaps because I wore khakis, whenever he saw me, he would stop begging, stand stiffly erect, and smartly salute me. Then, if there were other beggars nearby, he would direct them to me. If they followed his directions, he would laugh heartily. He knew I would not give them anything and acted as if he'd played a practical joke upon them. When we parted, following our frequent encounters in the congested traffic of downtown Calcutta, my beggar "friend" always would smile and wave goodbye to me and I would do likewise toward him.

One morning, while riding the train from Howrah to Singur, at one of the stops a young beggar of eighteen or twenty years of age entered the open-door carriage in which I was riding. He was led by a small boy of about eight years of age. By means of his hand resting upon the young boy's shoulder, he was led through the crowded carriage. The beggar held his other hand in front of him, in cupping shape, while tilting his head back and emitting one of the most pitiful cries I have ever heard. The pupils of his open eyes were an opaque white, apparently caused by cataracts. He most assuredly was blind. But, his startling cry was what was most impressionable.

Late that afternoon, while returning to Howrah, the train again stopped briefly at the station where the beggar had entered our carriage that morning. He and his small companion again entered the carriage. This time, however, the small boy was crying. Then, when they were standing directly in front of me, the little boy suddenly ducked down and out from under the beggar's hand and ran off the train. I thought, "What will this poor, blind beggar do now? How will he get off the train?" To my surprise, the beggar simply blinked his eyes, looked around, and calmly walked off the train. When I told some of my Indian friends what had happened, they told me, "It's a common practice for beggars to put fish scales on the pupils of their eyes. This makes them appear to be blind or to have cataracts." Similarly, I learned beggars used numerous other ploys to obtain the sympathy of the unsuspecting public.

It is not uncommon to observe mentally deranged people on Calcutta's streets. To me, it appeared many of these simply were unable to cope with the conditions in which they lived. Moreover, their irrational and sometimes violent behavior usually was ignored by others. For example, I repeatedly saw one crazy man stalking the streets in a particular section of Calcutta. Not only was he stark naked, but he always brandished a large stick. With this weapon, he would vociferously attack each passing streetcar. He reminded me of a modern-day Don Quixote, but without a horse and a Sancho Panza. Each time a streetcar entered his territory, he would scream, raise his club high over his head, and charge. He first would vainly attempt to "spear" the front of the streetcar. Then, as it passed, he would vociferously beat the sides, until it appeared he was physically exhausted. Equally amazing was the fact virtually no one, either within the streetcar nor on the street, seemed to pay any attention to the violent actions of this man.

I doubt most Americans could cope with the conditions in which most of the inhabitants of Calcutta live. Most that live here do not appear to be troubled by their lot. Perhaps this is because of their culture or faith, i.e. their belief that, if they endure well the adversities of this life, they will enjoy a higher realm hereafter. Or, perhaps it is because they have never known anything better. Nevertheless, they oftentimes become most violent. During our two years in India, rarely did a week go by without the occurrence of major acts of violence in Calcutta. Some inhabitants even seemed to take pride in the fact that at least one major incidence (i.e. one in which three or more people are killed) occurs in their city each month!

I could go on and on, attempting to describe what I experienced and observed during our two years in India. Sometimes I fear what I saw might be like a look into the future with regard to pending conditions in many of the world's large cities. I certainly hope not! Nevertheless, I wish every American could experience Calcutta. I believe they then would better realize and appreciate how blessed they are. I know I no longer take for granted even simple blessings, such as clean water, food and clothing. Sometimes when I am frustrated or feel life is difficult, I have to but think of India and Calcutta to realize how truly fortunate I am. I also often think, "But for the grace of God, I could be one of those poor people living in Calcutta."

MR. GEE

Too often we do not realize that "The truly important things in life are not things."

His friends and close associates called him "Mr. Gee", but most people called him "Mr. E. P. Gee". When I once asked Mr. Gee what names the initials "E. P." stood for, he told me. But, I have forgotten what they were. Others whom I asked also do not remember or never knew his given names. Although a prolific writer, he used only his initials and surname to denote authorship for his many articles, as well as for his notable book, "The Wild Life in India" – the forward for which was written by Prime Minister Jawaharlal Nehru.

Mr. Gee was a relatively short and stoutly built man. His metal-rimmed spectacles, which invariably were perched upon the bridge of his nose, distracted from his ruddy face and the bald center portion of his head. His most notable characteristic was not his looks, but his brusque, business-like demeanor, as well as his concern for the conservation of India's fast diminishing wildlife.

Similar to many adventurous young Englishmen of his day, at the age of twenty-three, Mr. Gee left his homeland in 1927 to become a tea planter in India. He signed a five-year contract to work on a plantation or tea estate in Assam, the eastern-most part of India. Here he was provided living quarters, a monthly stipend, and – upon the satisfactory completion of his contract – return passage to England plus a substantial bonus. The work was rigorous and conditions associated with living in India trying, not to mention the loneliness from being away from family and friends. Following a few months of "home leave", tea planters also were expected to sign another long-term contract and return to the Indian subcontinent.

A favorite pastime for English tea planters, during their "off-duty" hours, was "shooting" or the hunting of big game. Thus, according to Mr. Gee, he spent much time shooting India's then abundant wildlife. He even stated, "I probably shot more than my fair share of animals such as tiger, leopard, deer, antelope and even elephant."

As a young man, Mr. Gee also was an avid polo player. What time and money he did not spend on guns, ammunition and "shikari" or hunting expeditions, he claimed he spent on polo ponies. The training and care of a good polo pony required considerable time and no little expense. But, according to Mr. Gee, "It was jolly good sport!" During the cooler winter months, there were polo matches each Sunday in the tea estate areas of Assam. Then, when a young bachelor was not working nor engaged in "shooting" or polo, there was the enticement of the local "club". Here, while playing cards or billiards, having a drink or simply socializing with other tea planters, one momentarily could forget the monotony, loneliness and rigorous work associated with being a tea planter.

As good fortune perhaps would have it, Mr. Gee eventually became the manager of the Hathi Kuli Tea Estate. This plantation bordered Kaziranga, a one-hundred-and-fifty-square-mile riverine wilderness of dense "elephant grass", intermittent streams, and numerous small lakes or "bils". Kaziranga is formed by a large bow in the Bhramaputra River, which serves as its boundary on three sides. It also is noted for its abundant wildlife and especially for being one of the few remaining haunts of the great Indian one-horned rhinoceros. While managing the Hathi Kuli Estate, Mr. Gee became interested in aspects about wildlife other than "shooting". He began to observe animals other than through the sights of a rifle. He particularly became intrigued with the cantankerous, but usually elusive or perhaps even shy, prehistoric-looking Indian rhino. As his interests in "shooting", polo and frequenting the "club" waned, he became more and more interested in India's wildlife resources, including both plants and animals. He gradually changed from an ardent, if not downright bloodthirsty hunter, into one gravely concerned about India's disappearing wildlife. Furthermore, he determined he would do something about it.

According to Mr. Gee, "Although many people have written numerous books about India's wild animals, virtually all are about hunting. These also are usually exaggerated tales and do not accurately describe India's fabulous wild life." In contrast, he found a fair number of books that accurately described India's abundant and varied flora or plant life. Most Indian Forest Department personnel were well versed in plant taxonomy, but knew little about wild animals. Thus, Mr. Gee first became interested in plant taxonomy and then in the collecting and growing of many of India's beautiful wild flowers. He was partial to orchids and especially those growing in the Himalayan foothills bordering some of the tea estates in Assam. Although for the most part self-taught, he became a recognized authority on the flora of India. His gardens of wild flowers, which surrounded the bungalows in which he lived, also gained recognition.

Mr. Gee avidly collected wild flowers throughout India, but his specialization in Himalayan orchids also took him to Nepal and the Himalayan kingdom's of Bhutan and Sikkim. As a result, he assembled – in the four-acre garden surrounding his bungalow on the outskirts of the "hill city" of Shillong – the most notable collection of Himalayan orchids in the world. He took much pride in this garden. It indeed was spectacular and presented a beautiful array of color during much of the year. The size of his garden and his insistence upon its meticulous care required the employment of four full-time gardeners. His love for and interest in wild flowers continued throughout his life, but he also became interested in all wild things. His extensive travels in search of beautiful and/or rare flowers impressed upon him the fact that India's once abundant wildlife was rapidly disappearing. His attempts to capture the beauty of wild flowers upon film likewise resulted in his becoming interested in photographing wild animals. Thus, be shortly became a noted wildlife photographer, which led him to study and then write about India's unique wildlife.

Mr. Gee observed the demise of one wild animal species after another throughout India. Thus, he began to realize that if animals, such as the Asiatic lion, Bengal tiger, Indian one-horned rhino and others, were to be saved from extinction; definitive action must soon be taken. He then joined forces with Mr. P. D. Stracey, who then was the Conservator of Forests in Assam for the Forest Department of India.

Mr. Stracey, similar to Mr. Gee, initially had been an avid hunter. However, in an attempt to shoot an elephant, he "botched the job". Instead of killing the animal, he only wounded it. He then tracked the beast for several days, before finally being able to put the poor, suffering animal out of its misery. His witnessing the suffering of this animal resulted in him becoming a wildlife conservationist and especially of India's fast disappearing wild elephants. He thoroughly studied how marauding or "rogue" elephants could be killed as quickly and humanely as possible. After much study, including the dissection of elephant skulls, he determined a bullet can readily penetrate an Indian elephant's skull and enter its brain through three small areas. These are: in the center of the forehead, behind the ear and just behind the top of the head – where it joins the neck. However, these small target areas are difficult for many hunters to hit, especially if an elephant is charging or fleeing from a would-be shooter. As a result of his studies and interest in elephants, Mr. Stracey wrote the book "Elephant Gold".

Because of their mutual interest in wildlife conservation and especially in Kaziranga, Messrs. Gee and Stracey became united in their conservation efforts. First, they managed to get Kaziaranga, Manas, and other notable wildlife areas in Assam gazetted or established as "wild life sanctuaries" by the Government of India. Through their efforts, many people in India – including prominent politicians – also were made aware of the fact that their country's wildlife heritage was in jeopardy.

Mr. Stacey eventually became the Inspector General of Forests for India and was stationed in New Delhi. Thus, he and Mr. Gee became an even more effective team with regard to furthering the cause of wildlife conservation. However, perhaps because of his fervor and uncompromising stance for conservation, Mr. Stracey shortly lost political favor and was relieved of his position as "head" of the Indian Forest Department. Though he continued his conservation efforts, he lost much of his political clout and became less and less effective in his eschewed cause. Disheartened, he eventually accepted a wildlife staff position with the United Nation's Food and Agriculture Organization (FAO) in Africa. He died there some years later, shortly after fulfilling an FAO assignment in

Ethiopia. Both Messrs. Gee and Stracey were my dear friends and I consider Mr. Stracey's first leaving India and then dying in Africa as a personal loss to me and a tragic loss for wildlife conservation.

As Mr. Stracey's political influence lessened, Mr. Gee's increased. He became a close friend of Prime Minister Nehru, his daughter Indira Ghandi, (who became her father's successor), the King and Queen of Bhutan, many maharajas, and the governors and political leaders of almost every state in India. I think they were his friends because he always was "straight forward" and did not try to be a politician. In short, they trusted him. As a result, Mr. Gee perhaps became recognized as India's most influential and effective wildlife conservationist. Due in large measure to his efforts, the Indian Board for Wild Life was established and he became one of its most influential members. Wildlife staff positions were established in almost all State Forest Departments. State Departments then were charged with conserving and managing wild animals; whereas, they previously were concerned solely with the management of forests. Criteria for the establishment and management of wildlife sanctuaries and national parks also were developed and implemented in most of India's more than twenty states. And, Kaziranga became recognized as India's and perhaps southeastern Asia's most notable wildlife spectacle. However, it was not until after the deaths of both Messrs. Stracey and Gee that Kaziranga was established as a national park, rather than being merely a "wild life sanctuary".

One of my good friends, Mr. K. L. Lahiri (Superintendent of the Calcutta Zoo) was a good friend of Mr. Gee. He invited Mr. Gee to show some of his outstanding wildlife movies to the public in the Calcutta Zoo. Mr. Gee agreed to do so "ONLY if an entrance fee is charged and ALL of the proceeds are used for wildlife conservation in India." He later explained, "If someone gets something for nothing, they do not appreciate it. I want the people of India to appreciate their wild life heritage, which is something they have always taken for granted." Anyway, Mr. Lahiri agreed to Mr. Gee's terms and invited me to attend the showing. This was how I first met Mr. Gee.

Although Mr. Gee had published his notable book, "The Wild Life of India", only a few weeks prior to his showing of his wildlife movies in the Calcutta Zoo, I had read it and had been impressed with his knowledge of and experiences with many of India's remarkable wildlife species. I also had read some of the articles he had published in The Journal of the Bombay Natural History Society and had been impressed by his excellent wildlife photographs. The latter were widely distributed throughout India on calendars and in Government publications. In short, I was anxious to meet Mr. Gee, as well as to see his movies.

After Mr. Gee showed his movies at the Calcutta Zoo, Mr. Lahiri introduced me to him. I didn't know what to think about Mr. Gee's brusqueness and what I took to be his unfriendly manner. Nevertheless, our mutual interest in wildlife formed a bond between us. And, as I became better acquainted with him, I found his brusqueness merely camouflaged his warm personality that seemed to be reserved for close friends.

Thereafter, whenever Mr. Gee came to Calcutta, which was quite frequent, he usually would contact me. We then would discuss at length our views or philosophies concerning wildlife conservation. We also thoroughly discussed how we thought the many problems confronting India's wildlife could best be met and overcome. Almost invariably our major topic of discussion was, "How can we impress upon others – especially the people of India – the importance and value of wildlife?" I think our relationship was rather unique. Whereas, Mr. Gee was a notable and influential wildlife conservationist, both in India and internationally, I was a mere graduate student. However, I did have a B.S. degree in Wildlife Management and an M.S. degree in Wildlife Biology. Initially I planned to come to India to study black buck antelope under the supervision of Dr. George Schaller, but had been side-tracked and was studying "The Ecology of the Lesser Bandicoot Rat in Calcutta", which was a species in need of control, rather than protection or enhancement.

Dr. Fredrick D. Bang, Head of the Department of Pathobiology and Director of The Johns Hopkins Center for Medical Research and Training (CMRT) program in India – under whose auspices I was conducting my doctoral research – conceded: "IF you will first successfully conclude your rat studies. And, IF you can obtain funding elsewhere for travel and field expenses, the CMRT program will continue to provide you with a basic stipend while you conduct wildlife studies." Given this concession and through Mr. Gee's assistance and influence, I shortly obtained a grant from the World Wildlife Fund in Switzerland to conduct a survey of the Indian one-horned rhinoceros. The true status of this species was not known, but it was thought to be on the verge of extinction.

I had a fantastic time and many memorable experiences while determining the status of the Indian rhino throughout its range in northeastern India and central Nepal. For example, we used seventy-two riding elephants and approximately two hundred Forest Department personnel to conduct a rhino and other large animal census of the Kaziranga Wild Life Sanctuary. In short, we found there were more than eight hundred Indian rhino in India and Nepal and more than four hundred and fifty of these resided in Kaziranga. It previously had been thought that Kaziranga harbored fewer than three hundred! My rhino inventory, in turn, led to other short-term studies on species such as the Asiatic lion in the Gir Forest of northwestern India, the Indian wild ass in the Little Rann of Kutch, and the "chital" or spotted deer in a portion of Corbett National Park that was destined to be inundated by the construction of a dam on the Ramganga River. Thereafter, I also conducted a number of statewide wildlife surveys, such as for the states of Andhra Pradesh, Gujarat, Madras, and Mysore, as well as for some specific sanctuaries or parks in Rajasthan and elsewhere. These resulted in my having many interesting and exciting experiences.

Mr. Gee was in his early sixties when I first met him. In addition to being a tea planter for almost thirty years, he served as an officer in the Indian Army during World War II – from 1942 until 1946. He "saw service in different parts of the "Burma Front." Following his retirement in 1959, he essentially worked full-time in wildlife conservation. He also seemed to greatly enjoy accompanying and assisting me in the field, whenever his busy schedule would permit. I welcomed his company. Admittedly, his influence and political know-how opened many doors for me. His knowledge about India – both its people and its wildlife – also was invaluable.

I completed my rat studies in Calcutta during the fall of 1965. Thereafter, I spent six fabulous, adventure-filled months studying wildlife throughout much of India. What a marvelous country, endowed with so many spectacular wildlife species! All of North America has fewer than twenty wild animals which may be classified as "big game"; whereas, India has almost forty. Furthermore, North America has nothing to compare with species such as the elephant and rhino. I then returned to Baltimore, Maryland, to complete my doctoral coursework and thesis. However, even while attending the University, I intermittently returned to India to conduct additional short-term wildlife studies or to participate in conservation-oriented seminars and meetings. Many of these activities resulted from Mr. Gee's efforts in my behalf. I always will be grateful for his assistance and for him being my mentor.

Prior to completing my doctorate, I was offered a position at Utah State University (USU). I would serve as an Assistant Professor in the Department of Wildlife Science and as the Assistant Leader of the Utah Cooperative Wildlife Research Unit - under Dr. Jessop B. Low, the Unit Leader who served as my major professor during my M.S. program. Dr. Charles H. Southwick, my major professor at "Hopkins", made arrangements whereby I left my doctoral program prior to my completing the writing of my thesis, which I would do while working at USU. It was almost too good to be true! Still, my goal was to return to India. I reasoned, "After I become established at USU and with the help of Mr. Gee, I should be able to return to India to conduct some long-term wildlife studies." I particularly wanted to study the behavior and ecology of the Indian rhino in Kaziranga.

I shortly completed my doctorate and became involved in a good number of graduate-student wildlife research projects. I also worked with a number of notable scientists who helped me develop and submit a proposal for wildlife research in India to the Smithsonian Institution's Foreign Currency Program. We proposed a number of in-depth, long-term projects. These included a study of the Indian rhino in Kaziranga. The Smithsonian approved our proposal. But, just prior to our submitting it to the Government of India, I was informed Mr. Gee had suffered a severe stroke. He was almost completely paralyzed. He returned to England for medical treatment and died a few days later. India lost perhaps her greatest champion for wildlife conservation. I also lost a dear friend and my special mentor in India.

In an effort to steer our proposal through the government red tape in New Delhi, I made a number of trips to India. However, both my efforts and those of others from USU and the Smithsonian were in vain. Although the Smithsonian had agreed to finance our proposed program with funds from its Foreign Aid or U.S. Government's PL-480 Program, Government of India approval was needed in order for us to conduct our proposed research in India. Furthermore, even though verbal support was obtained from some notable government officials, our proposal somehow got lost in the Indian bureaucracy. As a result, we finally gave up. I don't think this would have happened IF we had had Mr. Gee's assistance.

I both admired and respected Mr. Gee and considered him as a dear friend. Still, I felt sorry for him. Except for an elderly sister in England, whom he only infrequently visited while on "home leave", he apparently had no immediate family. He never mentioned ever having dated or even being interested in the opposite sex. His life seemed to evolve around his beloved flowers, his numerous books, photography, and his efforts for wildlife conservation.

My wife Carol, our young daughter Cris Tina, and I stayed for ten days with Mr. Gee in his bungalow in Shillong, while I wrote reports on our wildlife surveys. I frequently noticed Mr. Gee's interest in our little girl. While watching her, he often had an expression upon his face that seemed to denote sadness or perhaps that he felt he had missed something important in life by not having had a family. I likewise feel this is true. No matter or to what extent we may become involved in a good cause, insofar as I am concerned, nothing can take the place of one's family.

The earthly possessions Mr. Gee left behind included: his notable collection of wild flowers (particularly Himalayan orchids); hundreds of books (many of which were personally signed by their authors and/or were collector's items); literally thousands of photographs depicting India's flora and fauna; his wildlife movies (many of which depict a splendor that no longer exists); and his beloved Hassleblad camera. Surprisingly, he did not own the bungalow in which he lived nor the land upon which he had his beloved flower garden. He previously had sold his collection of silver trophies and plaques, which he had garnered for many outstanding achievements. Once, while I was admiring his remarkable trophy collection, he claimed, "They're too much trouble to keep polished and they're a big a worry about being stolen. I think I'll just get rid of them." This he shortly did. He sold them merely for the value of the silver from which they were made.

In his will, Mr. Gee requested that his beloved flowers should go to the botanical section of the Indian Zoological Society and his photographs, movies and books to The Bombay Natural History Society. He also expressed a desire that these items "might continue to be used for wild life conservation in India."

I wonder if, on the "other side", Mr. Gee still is able to collect and nurture wild flowers, as he did so avidly in this life. I also wonder if he continues to eloquently extol the need for wildlife conservation. And, despite his having left behind his beloved Hassleblad camera, does he still continue to record the beauties of nature for the enjoyment of others. Most of all, I wonder if he still is known as "Mr. Gee" or whether his associates now know him by his given names, which were depicted during this life by the initials E. P.?

AN UNFINISHED JOURNEY

**"Our journey through life often does not go as we plan.
Sometimes this is indeed fortunate for us!"**

It was February, the season when the "hangul" or Kashmir stag congregates on its wintering grounds at Dachigam in the Vale of Kashmir near the city of Srinagar. Here, in the deep snows of winter and a Himalayan mountain setting, the regal stags engage in their annual mating rituals. These consist of the males whistling or "bugling" loudly on the still winter air and engaging in stiff-legged posturing to intimidate each other. These "carrying-ons" by the males culminate in their mating with the seemingly shy females, which are attracted by the males' activities.

Except when congregated on their wintering grounds, the "hangul" are scattered over the vast mountainous terrain of Kashmir and rarely are seen. It was reported that fewer and fewer stags were congregating each winter and there was concern this magnificent deer species might soon become extinct. Thus, Mr. Gee, an eminent conservationist in India, and I made plans to census the Kashmir stag population at Dachigam during its 1966 mating season.

Mr. Gee had contacted the "right" Government of India authorities and made the necessary arrangements for us to census the "hangul". The Kashmir Forest Department even assigned a couple of "qualified" Forest officers to assist us. Before going to Kashmir, however, both Mr. Gee and I had to return to Calcutta for a few days. He was to testify in a court case that concerned problems associated with the construction of an airstrip in Assam during World War II – some twenty years previous. As for me, I was scheduled to participate in an "All India Rodent Symposium", which resulted primarily because my rat studies had demonstrated there was substantial food loses to rodents in India. Symposium participants included both Indian and foreign experts.

While in Calcutta, Mr. Gee and I shared a room in the centrally located Grand Hotel. He thought his court case would be settled by late afternoon on Tuesday. My symposium was scheduled to end at noon on Wednesday. Therefore, we had purchased tickets for the India Airlines flight to New Delhi on Wednesday afternoon. We then planned to take the India Airlines early morning flight on Thursday from New Delhi to Srinagar.

Mr. Gee's court case did not terminate on Tuesday, but he was certain it would not last any longer than my symposium. My symposium concluded at noon on Wednesday and I returned to our hotel room. Mr. Gee was not there. I packed my bags, thinking, "He'll be here any minute." Still, he did not come. If he didn't soon come, we would not make it to the airport in time to catch our flight. I anxiously waited. Finally, the phone rang. It was Mr. Gee and he informed me, "The court case is taking longer than expected. But, I still think we will be finished in time for me to meet you at the airport." He then instructed me to, "Check out of the hotel. Take our luggage to the airport and check in for both of us. I'll try to meet you there as soon as I can." I tried to explain, "Our plane is scheduled to depart in less than two hours! Sometimes it takes an hour or more to get through the crowded streets of Calcutta to the airport!" He simply replied, "Yes, I know! But that flight's always late. With luck, I should be there on time. If not, you'll just have to retrieve our luggage and make arrangements to get us on tomorrow morning's flight!"

I carried our bags to the lobby, settled our hotel bill, and caught a taxi to the Dum Dum Airport. When I attempted to check in both Mr. Gee's and my luggage, their combined weight exceeded my allotted twenty kilos and the attendant claimed he could not check in Mr. Gee's luggage without his ticket – even though Mr. Gee's name was on the flight list. Thus, after I repeatedly explained our situation, the attendant finally accepted our luggage, checked off our names and gave me two boarding passes – as if both of us had checked in for the flight.

I again anxiously waited for Mr. Gee. The scheduled time for our plane's departure came and went. An apologetic voice then announced over a loud speaker, "Regretfully, the flight to New Delhi will be delayed. If the passengers will kindly proceed to the lounge, they will be issued a coupon, which will entitle them to free refreshment." This seemed to please most of the passengers. But, it did not please them near as much as it did me!

I went to the lounge, obtained a coupon, and with it obtained lemonade. As I slowly sipped my drink and as the minutes stretched into more than an hour, I wondered, "Where's Mr. Gee? How long will the flight be delayed?" A voice over the speaker then announced, "The flight for New Delhi is now ready for boarding. Will the passengers please proceed to the boarding gate?" What was I to do?

I hesitatingly approached the counter and the attendant with whom I previously had had the prolonged debate about checking in our luggage. Suddenly, I heard a roar. A red-faced and out-of-breath Mr. Gee miraculously appeared at my side. I handed him his boarding pass and we bustled into the line at the boarding gate. As we walked to the plane, Mr. Gee kept mumbling something about "Those bloody taxi drivers!" I didn't dare ask what had been the problem. I was greatly relieved that I didn't have to retrieve our luggage and try to make arrangements for the next morning's flight. As it was, our flight was almost three hours late and Mr. Gee had made it just in the nick of time!

Our flight to New Delhi was uneventful. Upon our arrival, we ensured our reservations were in order for the next morning's flight to Srinagar. The airline attendant happened to state, "The winter weather in Kashmir is more severe than usual this year." Mr. Gee and I thought this might be to our advantage. It might cause the Kashmir stags to be more concentrated than usual on their limited winter range; thereby, helping us to more readily and accurately determine their numbers. We then took a taxi into New Delhi, checked into a hotel and made arrangements for transportation back to the airport early the next morning.

New Delhi and the surrounding countryside were cloaked in a dense, low-lying fog the next morning. The ride to the airport was weird. The taxi driver would peer intently into the thick fog, as we slowly crept forward. Suddenly, there would be an opening and he would quickly accelerate. Then he would slam on the brakes, as we again entered the fog. Still, after what seemed to be an interminable and hectic ride, we finally arrived at the New Delhi Airport with plenty of time to spare before our flight to Kashmir.

We checked in for the Srinagar flight and questioned the India Airlines personnel as to whether or not the fog would affect the flight. We were assured it would not. It was further claimed, "The fog will disappear when the sun comes up." And, "The Kashmir flight never leaves unless there is visibility." Mr. Gee and I then commented as to, "Don't all modern airports have radar? And, don't they land the planes by instruments, rather than relying upon vision?"

We then went to the upper-level restaurant in the air terminal to have breakfast. While eating, we discussed our forthcoming flight and our plans to census the Kashmir stag. As we talked, we looked down upon the dense blanket of fog surrounding the terminal. We could not see the runway or the lights we knew were on it, let alone anything else on the ground. It was eerie. Then there was a sudden roar, as a low-flying jet passed directly over the terminal. The roar subsided, as the plane made a wide circle and dropped down towards the far end of the runway, which was hidden in the low-lying fog. This was the early morning flight from Calcutta - the one we would have been on - IF Mr. Gee had been only a few minutes later in his arrival at the Calcutta airport the previous afternoon!

We watched the approaching plane gently disappear into the fog in front of us. Then there was a muffled roar from the direction in which the plane had just disappeared. This was followed by what appeared to be a flickering of lights and some black smoke billowing up through the fog. The flickering was from flames, rather than lights! The plane, the one we came so close to being on, had crashed on the runway!

Fire wagons, followed by ambulances, rushed out from the terminal onto the runway and disappeared into the fog. The flicker of flames and the smoke shortly subsided. Word spread through the terminal, "No one onboard the flight from Calcutta had been killed!" We later learned, however, a number of passengers were severely burned and taken to the hospital. The plane and the luggage onboard were consumed by fire. Thereafter, a voice over the loud speaker requested, "Will those waiting to meet passengers from Calcutta please come to the ticket counter?" They would be informed where they might meet those for whom they were waiting. For some, this meant going to the hospital. Over and over I thought, "We could have been on that flight!"

The excitement subsided and the sun eventually dissipated the fog. The flight to Srinagar via Jammu was announced. Thereafter, Mr. Gee and I boarded the small, two-engine, propeller-driven "Folker Friendship" aircraft for our flight. This outmoded plane accommodates only about twenty passengers, but was the only one then being used for daily flights between New Delhi and Srinagar. I particularly enjoyed flying in the "Folker Friendships", because they usually fly low enough so you can observe everything on the ground below. Small, oval windows are located alongside each row of seats and below the wings of the aircraft. Thus, no matter where you sit, you have an unobstructed view of what is below.

We taxied down the now clearly visible runway and took off. We first flew over the open and rather bleak and desolate plains of northern India to Jammu, a city just inside the border of the State of Kashmir. After landing and disembarking from the plane, we found the small Jammu Airport was literally packed with people. Many were vociferously trying to get tickets at the counter for the onward flight to Srinagar. When we asked, "Why the commotion?" we were told the unusually heavy snows in Kashmir had resulted in avalanches. These had closed both the highway and railroad to Srinagar. Furthermore, "It might be days or even weeks before the road will be open!" The small "Folker Friendship", in which we had come to Jammu, presently was the only means of transportation to Srinagar. People were frantically trying to return to their homes and families there. Many had been stranded in Jammu for days. Some were sleeping on the floors of the air terminal, because there were no accommodations left in the city. The daily "Folker Friendship" flights offered their only hope to return to their homes. We were further informed, "Passengers from New Delhi to Srinagar have first priority. But, the weather report for Srinagar is not favorable!"

Following a prolonged wait in Jammu, we boarded the aircraft bound for Srinagar. When we took off, there was hardly a cloud in the sky. It was difficult to imagine there could be "bad" weather in Srinagar. Thus, we were confident we would make it over the mountains and to our destination. Then, within minutes, we flew from an almost cloudless sky into dense cloudbanks that had formed up against the Himalayas. Occasionally, there were small openings in the clouds and we were able to catch a glimpse of the rugged mountains and deep ravines below. As we approached our destination, the clouds suddenly parted and we looked down upon the snow-laden Vale of Kashmir. We could see the clustered buildings of Srinagar and the flat, snowy expanse of a nearby large lake. Our plane banked, to begin the approach into the valley. But, before we could descend through the opening, the clouds merged together and we could see nothing but white, puffy clouds around us. The aircraft's engines roared and we began to gain altitude. Shortly, the pilot announced over the intercom, "We will not be able to land in Srinagar because of bad weather. We will be returning to Jammu."

Upon again landing in Jammu, we were informed there were no overnight accommodations. They were all occupied. The Indian Airlines representative also informed us, "If you return to New Delhi onboard the plane, you will forfeit the New Delhi to Jammu and the Jammu to New Delhi portions of your tickets." This infuriated Mr. Gee. He was adamant in his claim, "We purchased Indian Airline tickets from New Delhi to Srinagar." And, "If the Indian Airlines can not deliver us to our destination, it is their obligation to return us to New Delhi or provide us accommodations in Jammu – until we can be flown to Srinagar!"

The intimidated Airlines representative apologetically explained, "There are no accommodations available in Jammu." Nevertheless, the hapless representative finally relented and said we could return to New Delhi without forfeiting any portions of our tickets. However, he explicitly stated, "If you again fly from New Delhi to Jammu, enroute to Srinagar, and if again – because of bad weather – you are unable to make your destination, you will have to forfeit the used portions of your tickets." Mr. Gee protested but eventually agreed to this ultimatum. Thus, we flew back to New Delhi and there made reservations for the next morning's flight to Srinagar.

Early the next morning we returned to the New Delhi Airport. We again checked in our luggage and went to the second floor restaurant to eat breakfast. After a long wait, it was announced, "We regret to inform you, because of bad weather, today's flight to Srinagar has been canceled." Upon inquiry, we were told the radio report from Srinagar indicated there was virtually no possibility of a plane being able to land there throughout the day. Thus, we made reservations for the next morning's flight, retrieved our luggage and returned to New Delhi to spend another night in a hotel there.

The following morning, we again checked in for the Srinagar flight and inquired as to the weather report from Srinagar. We were told the weather in Kashmir had improved. Thus, we optimistically boarded the little "Folker Friendship" and flew to Jammu. However, upon our arrival in Jammu, we were informed, "The weather above and beyond the mountains has deteriorated. The flight to Srinagar has been canceled!"

There still were no overnight accommodations available in Jammu. Rather than spend a sleepless night in the still crowded Jammu air terminal, Mr. Gee and I decided to return to New Delhi. We realized we'd have to forfeit the used portions of our tickets but rationalized, "If we begin our trip in New Delhi, we should get seats to Srinagar; whereas, if we remain in Jammu, we'll have to compete for seats with the people waiting there." Furthermore, "A hotel bed in New Delhi will be much more comfortable than a bench or the floor in the Jammu air terminal!"

Early the next morning we made the now familiar trip to the New Delhi Airport. This was the fourth consecutive day in which we had attempted to fly to Srinagar. But, similar to the second day, the weather report from Kashmir, which was not received until almost mid-day, indicated severe weather conditions persisted there. The flight again was cancelled. Nevertheless, Mr. Gee and I still were confident we would make it to Kashmir and be able to determine the status of the "hangul" on its winter breeding grounds. We wondered, however, "Have the Forest Department personnel assigned to assist us despaired of our coming?" Or, "Are they still coming to the airport each day to meet us?" As we had done previously, we made reservations for the next morning's flight to Srinagar prior to leaving the New Delhi Airport.

The next morning, for the fifth consecutive day, we returned to the New Delhi Airport. After checking in, we waited for the weather report from Srinagar. But, before it was received, a voice over the speaker announced, "Passengers for the Jammu and Srinagar flight should proceed immediately to the gate for boarding" We could not believe the plane would take off before the weather situation in Kashmir was known. Thus, Mr. Gee resolutely refused to board the plane until we knew about the weather in Srinagar.

Except for Mr. Gee and me, all of the passengers for the flight were onboard. We remained at the gate, while Mr. Gee gave the Indian Airline representative to understand, "We're not boarding that plane until we know the weather conditions in Srinagar!" The pilot shortly descended from the "Folker Friendship", approached the gate, and asked why two of the passengers had not boarded the aircraft. Mr. Gee emphatically informed him, "We're not boarding until we first know the weather conditions in Srinagar." He also explained how we'd previously forfeited portions of our tickets. And, "We're not going to do that again – if we can help it!"

Both the pilot and the Indian Airlines representative tried to explain, "Your luggage and all of the other passengers are onboard. We're waiting on you, so the plane can take off." In fact, the plane's engines were running. If it had not been for Mr. Gee, I probably would have relented and boarded the aircraft – so as not to inconvenience the other passengers nor delay the flight any longer. Mr. Gee, however, was not deterred. He was adamant and he emphatically stated, "We're not boarding the plane until we first hear the weather report from Srinagar!"

The pilot and other now-assembled Indian Airlines personnel escorted us back inside the terminal and to the radio room. Radio contact eventually was made with the operator in Srinagar. When asked about the weather conditions there, the operator hesitatingly stated, "They've improved somewhat from what they were yesterday." This was not adequate for Mr. Gee. He insisted he be allowed to speak to the operator in Srinagar. He then demanded that the operator state whether or not he thought today's flight would be able to land there. The operator apparently realized he was on the spot and he tried to hedge or be noncommittal. This convinced Mr. Gee the weather situation in Kashmir was not good. He brusquely announced, "We're not going! Let's get our luggage out of the plane!"

The pilot actually appeared to be relieved by our not being passengers on his plane. He even assisted us in untying the cargo net from around the luggage that was stacked in the tail section of the aircraft. We sorted through the jumble of baggage and eventually located and retrieved our bags. As soon as we disembarked, the plane door was shut behind us and within seconds the plane was roaring down the runway.

Disheartened, we returned to New Delhi, checked into the hotel, and then spent most of the day visiting Government of India officials, as well as discussing alternative plans. We still very much wanted to determine the status of the Kashmir stag. But, we already had wasted five precious days just attempting to get to Kashmir. If we still were able to get there, would we be similarly delayed in our return? If this should happen, other studies we had scheduled and made arrangements to conduct would be disrupted or perhaps have to be abandoned. What should we do?

The evening paper answered our question. Glaring headlines announced: The Delhi-Srinagar flight had crashed! All onboard had been killed!

Twice - in less than a week - Mr. Gee and I narrowly had missed being onboard planes that had crashed. Only Mr. Gee's insistence that he be allowed to talk to the radio operator in Srinagar had kept us from being onboard the flight in which everyone had perished. As a result, we did not make further attempts to travel to Kashmir. Fortunately, it was "An Unfinished Journey"!

Although I had a brief glimpse of Srinagar and the Vale of Kashmir in a winter setting and of the surrounding beautiful and rugged mountains, I've never set foot there. Mr. Gee also never returned to Kashmir. He suffered a stroke a few years thereafter and died shortly after returning to his homeland of England. Still, I have hopes of someday visiting Kashmir, which has been described by some as "a heaven on earth."

"BHABULLAL"

"Behold, to obey is better than sacrifice..."
I Samuel 15:22

His name was Boweji Jadav but everyone called him Bhabullal. He was a driver for The Johns Hopkins University Center for Medical Research and Training (CMRT) program in India and served as my chauffeur while I studied rats in Calcutta for my doctorate research.

My research involved the almost nightly trapping of rats in grain storage warehouses or "godowns" in and around Calcutta. Thus, Bhabullal picked me up at 5:30 a.m. almost every morning at the New Kenilworth Hotel, where I, my wife Carol and our young daughter Cris Tina resided He then would drive me to the sites where I had set traps the previous evening. After retrieving the traps and the captured rats, we would take them to the laboratory at the Science College. There I would necropsy and record data from the collected rat specimens. At noon, Bhabullal would return me to the Kenilworth for lunch. Thereafter, he would take me back to the laboratory, before taking me to another trapping site in the evening. Then, well after dark, we would return to the hotel. The hours were long, the weather almost invariably hot and humid, and the driving conditions difficult. Congestion and hazards associated with traffic in Calcutta are something one must experience first-hand in order to believe. They can be horrendous. Nevertheless, Bhabullal was always congenial and rarely complained about the long hours and the trying conditions he faced daily. He seemed to be content with his situation in life.

Although Bhabullal was congenial and could drive very well, he had three faults or shortcomings with respect to being an excellent chauffeur. First, he was an impetuous tinker. Although he lacked the ability to fix or even reassemble what he had taken apart, he could not resist taking things apart. He HAD to see what made them "tick". Second, he was adamant about having his way. Whenever he made up his mind or determined to do something, you could not deter him from doing it. No matter how unreasonable or ridiculous his actions might be, one could not reason with nor persuade him to do otherwise. In short, he was "hard-headed". And, third, Bhabullal often did not listen to or obey what he was instructed to do. Still, primarily because of his driving skills and congenial nature, I could not help but like him and I tried to overlook his rather frequent obstinate and erratic behavior. Furthermore, he usually was punctual and appeared to be completely devoted to me and my family. I honestly believe he would have given his life to protect us from danger.

Bhabullal's irresistible urge to take things apart was unbelievable. Most of the CMRT vehicles were Jeep station wagons. A basic set of tools was provided for each vehicle. These were to be used in case of emergencies or to make minor repairs or adjustments. However, rather than simply waiting while I was setting traps or working in the laboratory, Bhabullal insisted upon using these tools to disassemble various parts of our vehicle. This was despite the fact the CMRT vehicles invariably were in good condition and not in need of repair. He would remove the parking lights, the headlights, or attempt to dismantle almost anything he could figure out how to disassemble. However, when it came to putting things back together, rarely could he remember where all the parts went. We often had headlights directed heavenward or to one side and parking lights that did not function properly. I frequently found screws, nuts, bolts and other vehicle parts in the glove compartment. Furthermore, Bhabullal could not remember from whence he had taken them. This was despite my repeatedly admonishing him to "Leave things alone!" Over and over I tried to explain to him, "If something isn't broken, don't try to fix it!" And, I repeatedly threatened him with, "I'll fire you, if you EVER take anything apart again!" Still, he persisted in taking things apart.

Late one evening, I set some traps in an outlying grain-storage "godown". When I returned to the vehicle, Bhabullal was frantically trying to reassemble the vehicle's ignition system. He had disconnected all of the color-coded wires and completely disassembled the ignition. He did not know where any of the half dozen or more colored wires had been connected, let alone the original locations for an array of screws, nuts, and bolts. The area in which we were located was miles from a garage or service station. Even if there had been one nearby, it would have been closed because of the late hour. Fortunately, we had a flashlight that still worked, because Bhabullal apparently had not gotten around to taking it apart! Thus, while Bhabullal held the flashlight, I spent more than an hour trying one combination after another, until I finally found the proper location for each of the wires in the ignition. By this time, I was furious. I again emphatically warned Bhabullal, "If you EVER take anything apart on this vehicle, you'll be fired!"

It was only a few days, however, before Bhabullal again was disassembling our vehicle. My warnings were in vain! To keep him from dismantling our vehicle, I removed all of the tools from it and told him, "If I EVER see you with any tools again, irregardless of whether or not you have taken anything apart, I'll MURDER you! Do you understand?"

Shortly after my arrival in Calcutta, Bhabullal was driving me back to the hotel for lunch. We were traveling along one of the main thoroughfares in the center of the city. Policemen, who directed traffic or served as traffic signals in Calcutta dressed in stiffly starched uniforms. They stood on pedestals in the center of major intersections and would raise their arms, turn halfway, and then lower their arms to change the direction in which the traffic flowed. Vehicles on the front and rear sides of the policemen then had to stop. As we approached an intersection, the policeman on the pedestal suddenly raised his arms, turned towards us, and then lowered his extended arms. Bhabullal slammed on the brakes and our vehicle screeched to a halt – directly in front of the policeman. The vehicle behind us ran into our rear end. Fortunately, at least for us, our station wagon had a spare tire mounted on the rear. Thus, the grill and radiator of the other vehicle hit this tire, before hitting our rear bumper.

I quickly jumped out to assess the damage. Our Jeep essentially was unscathed, but the radiator of the other vehicle, an Indian-made Ambassador sedan, was spewing water onto the pavement. The lady riding on the rear seat of the Ambassador also had been thrown onto the floor of the vehicle. I opened the rear door, to determine whether or not she had been injured. After she assured me she was not hurt, I assisted her from the vehicle. Then, looking up, I saw Bhabullal handing some money to the policeman, who was still standing on the pedestal in the center of the intersection. When I demanded of

Bhabullal, "Why did you do that? It wasn't our fault!" He simply stated, "Now, the policeman knows it's not our fault. Now, we won't get into trouble!"

Dr. Charles H. Southwick, my major professor, also frequently used Bhabullal as his chauffeur. Once each year he conducted extensive field surveys of rhesus monkey populations in various parts of India. These surveys were conducted primarily along or just off from the "Grand Trunk Road", which is commonly called the "GT". The GT is an extensive road system that was built by the British in the 1800's to move troops and supplies between major population centers in India. Although much of the GT remained little improved in the 1960's, it still served as a major arterial road throughout much of the country. Thus, despite much of the GT consisting of only a one-lane, cobbled or "metalled" road, with dirt and usually very dusty and steep barrow pits on either side, it often carried unbelievably heavy volumes of traffic. Because there was not room for two vehicles to pass on the road's hard surface, there were frequent confrontations between drivers in vehicles going opposite directions as to who would give the right-of-way or who would drive off the road and enter into the deep and dusty barrow pits on either side.

Daytime traffic on the GT usually consisted of large numbers of large trucks or "lorries", cars, bicycles, bicycle rickshaws and "tongas" or two-wheeled, horse-drawn carts, as well as a myriad of people and animals, i.e. sheep, goats, burros, cattle, and in some areas camels and an occasional elephant. At night, however, traffic on the GT usually was sparse and would consist of only infrequent vehicles.

Drivers in India seem to have an aversion or innate fear of "night blindness", caused by the headlights of on-coming vehicles. Thus, while driving in the cities at night, they normally use only their parking lights. Although they turn on their headlights while driving on highways at night, they commonly turn them off before passing an oncoming vehicle. However, on narrow roads, such as the GT, before turning their headlights off, they invariably flash them off and on repeatedly – in order to warn the approaching driver of their presence and somehow determine which vehicle will remain on the narrow or hard surface of the road or which will drive into the barrow pit. This flashing of headlights often reminded me of a game we played when I was in high school. We called it "Chicken"!

One night, following a long day of surveying monkey populations and while returning to Calcutta along the GT, Bhabullal and Dr. Southwick had not encountered another vehicle for more than an hour. Then, in the distance, they observed the approaching headlights of a vehicle. Both Bhabullal and the other driver began to flash their headlights off and on. As the vehicles drew closer and closer, the light flashing became more frantic. Then, at the last moment, both vehicles screeched to a halt, with their bumpers only inches apart! Neither was willing to give the right-of-way to the other or to abandon the narrow "metalled" surface of the GT. The other vehicle was a large, fully loaded truck; whereas, Bhabullal was driving a much smaller Jeep station wagon.

Both Bhabullal and the truck driver first noisily honked their horns at each other. They then gestured and shouted at each other through their opened vehicle windows. Finally, they jumped out of their vehicles and met face-to-face in verbal confrontation. The truck driver was a big, burly man, with a turban on his head and a beard, which denoted him to be a Sikh. In contrast, Bhabullal was relatively short and thin, as well as a bareheaded and smooth-faced Hindu. Nevertheless, Bhabullal stood toe-to-toe with the large Sikh and even outdid him both in volume and vulgarity of epithets. While this was going on, Dr. Southwick repeatedly pleaded with Bhabullal to, "Please! Just drive around the other vehicle!" His pleas, however, were in vain. Bhabullal not only insisted that the truck driver must drive off the road and into the barrow pit but he also must back up his truck to do so. He was not going to budge – not even an inch! Thus, Dr. Southwick stood helplessly to one side while the heated confrontation went on and on. Finally, the truck driver climbed back into his truck, backed up, and drove down into the barrow pit and the triumphant Bhabullal continued on along the GT.

Despite frequent problems that arose from Bhabullal's tinkering and hardheadedness, his failure to listen to and then obey what others told him to do perhaps caused him the most grief.

I finished my rat studies in Calcutta the latter part of 1965. Thereafter, I conducted wildlife surveys throughout much of India for approximately six months, before returning to Baltimore, Maryland, to complete my doctorate program. I then accepted a position with the Utah Cooperative Wildlife Research Unit at Utah State University. But, for a number of years thereafter, I periodically returned to India for short periods of time. The Johns Hopkins CMRT program terminated. The years passed and I lost track of most of my former acquaintances in India. Then, in 1975, I returned to India to assist the National Geographic Society with putting together a feature article ("India Struggles to Save Her Wildlife"), which was published in the September 1976 issue of the National Geographic Magazine.

I was walking to the American Consulate in Calcutta, where I planned to exchange some U.S. dollars for Indian rupees, when a taxi suddenly swerved out of the congested street traffic, screeched – before hitting the curb - and then came to a halt directly in front of me. An Indian, with a turban on his head and a scraggly beard, then jumped from behind the steering wheel of the taxi, rushed towards me, and, with outstretched arms, strongly embraced me. While doing so, the taxi driver repeatedly cried, "Sahib! Sahib!" Thinking he was trying to mug me, I violently pushed him away. The man then dropped to his knees and continued to cry, "Sahib! Sahib!"

I finally realized the man kneeling in front of me was Bhabullal. It was difficult to recognize him. He now wore a turban, had grown a thin beard, and even wore a metal bracelet on his right wrist. These identified has as a Sikh, a religious sect from northern India. Many truck and taxi cab drivers, as well as military personnel in India are Sikhs. Bhabullal, however, was not a Sikh. He was a Hindu! What had happened?

When the sobbing Bhabullal had somewhat regained his composure, I stood him on his feet and asked, "How are you doing? How is your family?" He tearfully informed me, "Everything is bad since you and the CMRT left. I cannot earn any money. My wife and daughter are sick." He further explained he could not afford to buy medicine for his daughter, who they feared would soon die. It was all he could do to earn enough for food.

I was deeply touched by Bhabullal's plight and resolved to help him. I mentally calculated how much money I had brought with me to India and what would be the absolute minimum I would need while I was here. I then determined to change all I had into rupees and to give all I did not absolutely need to Bhabullal. This would provide medical aid for his daughter, as well meet his and his family's needs for an extended period of time. I hoped it would resolve their problems and get them back on their feet.

I listened as Bhabullal described in detail the many difficulties he and his family had faced since my family and I had left India. I also told him about my family and how, "I now have five children, rather than just one little girl." I then instructed him to, "Stay right here! Don't go away! I'll be back in just a few minutes. Then, I'll try to help you and your family. Do you understand?" He assured me he understood and that he would wait for me. Thus, I rushed to the American Consulate, which was less than a half a block away. I hurriedly changed my dollars into rupees and then returned to where I'd left Bhabullal. But, neither Bhabullal nor his taxi were there. I waited for a few minutes, thinking, "Maybe he will return." When he failed to do so, I walked throughout the surrounding area, searching for him and his taxi. It was to no avail. Bhabullal again had failed to listen or to obey what he had been told to do!

During my two remaining days in Calcutta, I walked the streets for hours – hoping to again encounter Bhabullal and, thereby, be able to help him and his family. However, I never saw him again. I've often wondered, "What happened to Bhabullal and his family? Why didn't he wait for me, as he said he would?" I've also thought, "How many of us are like Bhabullal with respect to listening to or obeying Our Father in Heaven's commandments? Do we continue to suffer or fail to receive assistance or blessings – because we are unwilling to listen and obey?"

"JUDGE NOT..."

"Judge not, and ye shall not be judged; condemn not, and ye shall not be condemned; forgive, and ye shall be forgiven." Luke 6:37

My wife Carol, our small daughter Cris Tina, Joel Cohen (a Harvard graduate on a year's traveling fellowship), and I were exhausted. We had had a most trying journey and had almost literally been running all day. We had arisen at 4:00 a.m., in order to catch the train from New Delhi to Ramnagar, which is at the end of the train line. Here, we somehow hoped to find a ride to Corbett National Park in the Kumaon Hills some thirty miles away.

We forewent eating breakfast, because of the early hour and our need to locate a taxi to take us to the railroad station. When we finally found a taxi, we loaded our cumbersome baggage inside and instructed the driver to take us to the railroad station. When traveling outside the major cities in India you quickly learn to carry bedding, food and particularly water with you. As is also customary in India, we had purchased our train tickets the previous day to travel from New Delhi to Ramnagar.

When we arrived at the railroad station, we unloaded our gear and paid the taxi driver, before carrying our bulky baggage into the station. A guard examined our tickets and directed us to a far platform that required our crossing up and over a number of train tracks. Upon reaching the designated platform, a conductor examined our tickets and then informed us, "The train for Ramnagar does not leave from here. It leaves from another station!" No one had told us there was ANOTHER railroad station in New Delhi. In fact, when we had asked at the tourist office about traveling to Corbett National Park, they simply had told us, "You take a train to Ramnagar. You should be able to hire a car or take a bus from there to Corbett National Park."

We grabbed our luggage and rushed back, up and over and down the walkway and out of the station. Again we searched for a taxi. When we finally located one, we hurriedly loaded our luggage into it and frantically instructed the driver, "Drive as fast as you can to the

OTHER railroad station!" Upon our arrival there, we gathered our luggage and scurried into the station. When we asked, "Where do we catch the train to Ramnagar?" The reply was, "The train is just leaving! You're probably too late!"

We dashed out onto the platform. I pushed my wife and daughter onto the moving train. Joel and I then ran alongside, while shoving our baggage through an open compartment window. At the last moment, we grabbed hold some bars and swung onboard. We sighed with relief and remarked to each other, "Well, we're FINALLY on our way to Ramnagar! I hope we don't have as much trouble getting from there to Corbett Park."

My family and I had been in India about a year and a half, during which we had lived in Calcutta and I had studied rats for my doctorate program with The Johns Hopkins University's Center for Medical Research and Training. Now, however, I was undertaking a number of wildlife surveys or short studies in various parts of India for the World Wildlife Fund in Morges, Switzerland. Joel Cohen had graduated, with high honors, from Harvard University a few months previous. He had received a prestigious fellowship, which provided for him to travel around the world for a year and to assist others in studies, as suited his fancy. Somehow, he had contacted and then joined me. We first spent time together in Calcutta, while I "wound up" my rat studies. We then had conducted a wildlife survey in the Keoladeo Ghana Wild Life Sanctuary near Bharatphur, about twenty miles west of Agra and the Taj Mahal. Now, we were going to study the "chital" or spotted deer in Corbett National Park.

Corbett is the largest and oldest of India's national parks. Although originally known as Hailey National Park, it was renamed in honor of Jim Corbett, who is renowned for his prowess in tracking down man-eating tigers and leopards. Jim Corbett also wrote a number of books about his exploits or hunting experiences, the most famous of which is "Maneaters of Kumaon". I had read his books and found he describes the people and wildlife very well in the areas where his adventures took place.

A dam was being constructed on the Ramganga River, near the boundary of Corbett Park. It was believed the backwaters from this dam eventually would inundate much of the spotted deer habitat within the Park; thereby, displacing most of the Park's "chital" population. We planned to survey deer numbers within the Park and assess potential impacts from the dam upon them and their habitat.

We arrived in New Delhi the previous day, after having inventoried the wild ungulates or deer and antelope in the seven-thousand-acre or eleven-square-mile Keoladeo Ghana Wild Life Sanctuary. Almost half of this small, but spectacular, sanctuary consists of marshland and is noted primarily for its bird life. Nevertheless, a good number of wild mammals also inhabit this unique area, which is completely surrounded by cultivated fields and human habitations. These animals include spotted deer, sambar, hog deer, "nilgai" or blue bull and black buck antelope, as well as wild boar, jackal, otter, mongoose, hyena, leopard, and a variety of smaller mammals such as rodents and rabbits.

We had contacted Government of India authorities and obtained permission to conduct our proposed studies in Corbett National Park, as well as elsewhere. Therefore, upon our arrival in New Delhi, we began to inquire as to how we best could travel to Corbett. Most of those with whom we met had heard of Corbett, but could not tell us how to get there. Even those in the Government of India's Tourist Office could not give us detailed travel information. Finally, by accident or good fortune, we ran into a man who actually had been to Corbett. He explained, "After taking the early morning train to Ramnagar, which is at the end of the line, you will have to hire a car to take you to Dikhala. Dikhala is about thirty miles from Ramnagar and is where the Park headquarters and 'rest house' for tourists are located." Thus, we purchased tickets for the next morning's train to Ramnagar. But, no one informed us there were two train stations in New Delhi and that the train for Ramnagar did not depart from the main station.

The narrow-gauge train to Ramnagar was crowded and dirty. The smoke and cinders from the coal-burning engine frequently blew into our compartment through the open windows. Food consisted of what you brought with you or could purchase from vendors on the platforms of the village stations in which the train frequently, but briefly, stopped. Safe drinking water, as usual, was restricted to what you carried with you.

We spent the better part of the day watching the green countryside "slide" past the train windows. The small, intensively cultivated fields gradually gave way to more and more extensive scrub and then forest. Still, almost anywhere one looked, there were people and, of course, lots of cattle.

It was late afternoon when we arrived in Ramnagar, which was a much larger village than we expected. Its major industry appeared to be the cutting and shipping of trees or lumber from the surrounding forests. Although there were numerous large trucks on the dirty and dusty streets, we were able to locate only two cars that were for hire. These were parked in a somewhat open area that served as a "bazaar" or marketplace. We asked the driver off each vehicle, "How much would you charge to take us to Corbett National Park?" Both quoted ridiculously high prices. They knew we were Americans and apparently thought, "ALL Americans are rich!" Therefore, "They will pay whatever we ask. They can afford it!" However, we were not rich. We were poor students. "No way" would we nor could we pay the prices they were asking, which exceeded more than a dollar per mile each way. We didn't have that much money among us!

We tried to bargain with the two men. They, however, refused to lower their originally quoted fares. Our pleas and explanations of, "We're not rich Americans nor tourists. We're only poor students and we need to get to Corbett Park to do a study," fell on deaf ears. Because it was late in the day, we decided to look for a place to eat and possibly stay for the night, until we could find some means whereby we could get to Corbett for a reasonable price. Within a short time we learned there were no restaurants or sleeping accommodations in Ramnagar. What were we to do?

We returned to the two drivers. This time they even refused to talk with us. Because of their adamant attitudes and apparent attempts to cheat us, not to mention the other difficulties we'd encountered in traveling to Ramnagar, we began to condemn not only these two men but ALL Indians. We made comments to each other, such as, "It appears ALL Indians are dishonest. Given the opportunity, they will try to make a 'quick buck' off from any unsuspecting tourist." And, "This is especially true if they are Americans!" In short, we harshly judged and condemned the Indian people in general.

In desperation, Joel and I decided to search for another vehicle. If we found one, we'd somehow try to convince the owner that they should take us to Corbett Park for a reasonable fare. I told Carol and Cris Tina, "Sit tight and be sure to carefully guard our luggage from these thieving Indians. We'll see if we can find a ride to Corbett."

Joel and I began to systematically walk the side and back streets of Ramnagar. We hoped to find a vehicle and then convince the owner to take us to Corbett for a reasonable fee. We shortly spotted a rather ancient, but well-kept Jeep station wagon. It was parked on a side street in front of a building with a faded sign that read, "Bhatnagar Clinic". Red crosses painted on the front and rear windows of the vehicle indicated it belonged to a medical doctor. Thus, we entered the clinic through an open door that led into a waiting room, with wooden benches on either side. Most of the benches were occupied by bare-footed villagers. It appeared they were waiting to see the doctor. Thus, we also sat down on one of the benches and waited.

We did not wait long before a man in a white lab coat and with a stethoscope hanging from his neck entered the room. Upon seeing us, he immediately asked, "May I help you?" We introduced ourselves. He, in turn, said, "I am Dr. Bhatnagar. May I be of service to you?" We explained our predicament and, indicating towards his jeep, asked if he would be willing to drive us to Corbett Park. He emphatically replied, "Yes! Yes! I'd be more than happy to do so!" Then, looking at the bare-footed villagers in the waiting room, he apologetically stated, "I hope you wouldn't mind if I first attended to these patients who have been waiting for me." We insisted that he do so and told him, "We can wait." Dr. Bhatnagar then offered us some tea, which we politely refused. He then insisted that we enter his living quarters, "Where you perhaps can make yourselves more comfortable."

While Dr. Bhatnagar attended to his patients, Joel and I quietly discussed, "What would be a reasonable amount to pay the doctor for taking us to Corbett? How much should we offer him?" And, "How can we then bargain with him?" Dikhala supposedly was about thirty miles from Ramnagar, which meant a round trip of sixty miles. This, supposedly, would be over rough dirt or gravel roads. While we debated about what we thought would be a reasonable amount, Dr. Bhatnagar appeared and announced he was ready for the journey. Then he also stated, "Couldn't I first offer you something to eat?" We thanked him and I explained, "My wife and daughter are waiting for us in the village. They'll probably worry if we don't return soon."

Dr. Bhatnagar motioned for us to get into his jeep with him and asked us to direct him to where we had left my wife and daughter. When we reached them and began to load our voluminous luggage into the jeep, he insisted we put it in the overhead rack on top of the vehicle, "So you can ride more comfortably."

We left Ramnagar by way of a rough dirt road that shortly entered into a forest. We caught occasional glimpses of the Ramganga River in a deep gorge below the road. Dr. Bhatnagar began to tell us about the surrounding countryside and insisted upon taking us on a few side-road excursions to see points of interest. One overlook provided a marvelous view of the Ramganga River and another presented a picturesque view of a small and very old Hindu temple. It was evident that Dr. Bhatnagar knew and loved the area in which he lived. Furthermore, he seemed to take delight in sharing it with others.

We eventually came to a large gate. A wooden sign indicated that it was the entrance to Corbett National Park. We passed through the gate and stopped at a small guard post. Before we realized what he was doing, Dr. Bhatnagar got out of the jeep and paid the guard our entrance fees for the Park. We attempted to repay him, but he refused our offer. He simply stated, "You are guests in my country. I'm sure you would do the same for me if I was a guest in America." However, we quietly contemplated, "Now he'll probably try to more than make up for the entrance fees when he asks us to pay him for bringing us to Corbett!"

It grew dark and the narrow road led through dense forests and small, open grassland areas or "maidans". Passing through the forest was almost like passing through a tunnel. The trees, for the most part, were, tall, slender-trunked and broad-leafed evergreens known as "sal", which formed a dense canopy over the road. We periodically saw the shining eyes of wild animals in the forest undergrowth and a few deer ran across or away from the road as we passed. Some of these barked, much like a dog. They were barking deer or "muntjac".

We finally arrived at Dikhala and checked in at the Park headquarters. We ensured we had lodging, for which we had made reservations by mail. Then, after depositing our luggage in our assigned quarters, we asked Dr.Bhatnagar if he cared to join us for dinner. We thought, "Perhaps if we feed him, he won't be so prone to overcharge us for bringing us to Corbett." Dr. Bhatnagar, however, politely refused our offer. He stated, "I really must return to Ramnagar. It is getting rather late." Thus, we broached the subject, "How much do we owe you?" Rather than request an exorbitant price, as we had expected, he first acted somewhat offended and then embarrassed by our offering to pay him. He resolutely insisted, "You owe me nothing! The pleasure was mine!" Instead of our being in the position we had expected, namely that of having to bargain for a reasonable fare, we now found ourselves trying to convince our host that we needed to pay for his services. Despite our pleas, Dr. Bhatnagar refused any payment whatsoever. He even expressed regret that time had not permitted him to show us more points of interest along the way. He also refused our second entreaty for him to join us for dinner. He claimed, "I really must be returning to my patients at the clinic."

We heartily shook hands with our newly found friend. Although Dr. Bhatnagar probably was a devout Hindu, in my book he was a "true Christian". He practiced the Christian ethic of "do unto others as you would have them do unto you." My previous condemnation and harsh judgments of Indians literally stung my conscience. Instead of taking advantage of or trying to cheat us, a stranger had taken us in and treated us with kindness. Furthermore, when we parted, Dr.

Bhatnagar kindly smiled and exclaimed, "I do hope I will have the pleasure of seeing all of you again soon!"

The next time I passed through Ramnagar on my way to Corbett Park, I took a copy of Mr. E. P. Gee's book, "The Wild Life of India", for Dr. Bhatnagar. When I entered his clinic, he greeted me warmly, as if we were old friends. He wanted to know where and how were my wife and daughter, as well as my friend Joel Cohen. He further entreated, "I do hope they also can visit me soon." When I presented him with the book, he said, "I'd very much like to read it. But, how can I return it to you?" I tried to explain the book was a gift. He then insisted, "It is too much!" Only after I showed him that I had written his name and our thanks for his kindness in the front of the book and, therefore, could not take it back, was he willing to accept it as a gift.

Regretfully, this was the last time I saw Dr. Bhatnagar. Still, I will always remember him and his kind hospitality. I also hope I never forget the dear lesson he taught me, namely that we should not judge others. This simple experience, wherein a stranger in a remote Indian village treated my family, my friend and me with kindness and hospitality – after we had harshly judged him and his countrymen - often comes to mind when I am tempted to judge others. It is true that, especially during my many travels, quite frequently I have encountered people who have taken advantage of or cheated me. But, similar to Dr. Bhatnagar, more often than not I have encountered those who have extended friendship and have been of service to me. It is not our prerogative to judge others. In short, "Judge not, and ye shall not be judged."

BEAUTY

True beauty is not just "skin deep". It is something that "comes from within"! True beauty also is felt, as well as seen.

I was dusting and straightening the books on the shelves in my study when I came upon my high school yearbooks. As I randomly thumbed through one of these now rather ancient "annuals", I encountered photographs that reminded me of experiences with former classmates and friends. I began to reminisce about the good times we had had and realized I had lost track of many of my school-day "chums". I pondered as to: "Where are they now? What are they doing?" And, "How much have they changed during the years since we were together in school?"

I chanced upon a photo of a girl I remembered very well. I remembered her as being one of the prettiest girls in our school. Also, not only was she pretty, but she almost always seemed to be happy and had a most pleasant disposition. As a result, I and many other boys in our school vied with each other for her attention. She never lacked for friends nor for invitations or dates for dances and other activities. However, as I studied her photograph, I was startled by the fact that it depicted her as being a rather plain and not very attractive girl. This could not be! She was one of the prettiest girls in our school! I hurriedly searched through the yearbooks, looking for other photographs of her. Each depicted the same. Based upon her photos, she actually was rather homely. I could not believe it. I distinctly remembered her as being VERY pretty. Yes, there were other girls who had a prettier face or perhaps a better figure than she, but they never were as attractive nor as popular. "Why?"

As I pondered this question, it dawned upon me that perhaps it was not this girl's "looks" or outward appearances that made her so attractive. Instead, it probably was her actions and how she treated others. These somehow masked her plain appearance and caused others to think and even see her as being beautiful. I fondly remembered how she always warmly greeted others and often extended words of encouragement to those who appeared to be disheartened or sad. She never gossiped or spoke ill of anyone. Although she was neither the smartest nor brightest in our classes, it seemed she always strived to do her best. Once, during an exam, I remember how another student offered to help her with some of the answers and she politely refused their assistance. Later, she informed us that honesty was more important to her than getting a better grade. She was trusted by students and teachers alike! Perhaps most important was her positive attitude and her pleasant and cheerful demeanor. This, however, did not mean she could not be stubborn or that she did not have a temper. I remember well how on a few occasions she strongly voiced her opinions and refused to "go along with the crowd". She always let you know where she stood and whether or not your actions met with her approval.

One of the boys in our high school class had a leg amputated during our senior year. Ironically, his nickname was "Stub" and most of us always called him either "Stub" or "Stubby". As a result, during his lengthy stay in the hospital, many of us hesitated to visit him. We feared we might call him by his nickname; thereby, reminding him of the loss of his leg. It just wasn't natural for us to call him by his given name. This, however, did not deter the "prettiest" girl in our class from visiting him and her taking us to task for not doing likewise.

The more I thought about what made this girl so attractive the more I realized it was because she showed genuine concern for others. It seemed she cared more about making others feel good about themselves than about what they might think of her. It appeared she treated others as she would like to have them treat her. She treated all of us with respect and seemed to enjoy trying to help us be happy. As a result, we respected her and enjoyed being around her. Further, I remembered seeing this girl at a class reunion commemorating the tenth anniversary of our graduation from high school. She then was happily married and the mother of five children. Several of my friends and I remarked to each other as to how she then was even prettier than she was when we were in school. We also chided each other as to, "How come one of us was not fortunate enough to marry her?" She truly was a beautiful woman. I honestly believe that through the years her "inner beauty" somehow had replaced the homeliness depicted by the photographs of her in our high school yearbooks.

Thinking about the "pretty girl" I knew in high school reminded me of another "beautiful girl" I met while serving as a "Mormon" missionary in South America.

I arrived in Uruguay in February of 1956. My first assignment was in the interior town of Tacuarembo. David Peterson, from Longbeach, California, was my first companion. He was a thin, six-foot-six-inch tall basketball player, who prided himself in being the fasted walker in the Uruguayan Mission. In contrast, I was short-legged and a stocky five-foot-ten. This meant I had to maintain an almost constant jog or dogtrot to keep up with my companion. We must have presented somewhat of a comical sight, because it wasn't long before the young people whom we met on the streets of Tacuarembo began to greet us with, "Ola, Flaco y Gordo!" Or, "Hello, Skinny and Fat!" "Flaco y Gordo" also were the nicknames for Laurel and Hardy, two popular comedians in the movies. After so greeting us, they also often would cheer me on in my efforts to keep up with Elder Peterson.

Prior to my arrival in Tacuarembo, other missionaries had "tracted" or visited, door-by-door, almost every house in the city. They had not, however, "tracted" the houses or huts in the surrounding "barrios" or poor districts. Thus, although the "barrios" were somewhat distant from where we lived, we resolved to visit the people living there – so they too might have the opportunity to hear our gospel message about Jesus Christ and His restored Church.

As Elder Peterson strode at his accelerated pace and I dogtrotted alongside or behind him, I asked him to translate English words or phrases into Spanish, so I might increase my limited Spanish vocabulary. Although I had studied Spanish for a year in high school, I could not – for the life of me – understand, let alone speak, Spanish. Whenever we met with anyone, Elder Peterson did all of the talking, while I simply smiled, listened and desperately tried to understand what was being said.

Most of those we visited in the "barrios" were extremely poor. Their humble homes, for the most part, consisted of a two or three-room mud hut with a thatch roof. Most were set back from the roadways and surrounded with a fence and small yard. Upon approaching the front gate or entrance to the yards for these humble abodes, the common practice was to clap loudly, until the house occupants heard you. The head of the house usually then would come to the gate to inquire what was wanted. Elder Peterson would explain, "We would like to meet with you and your family for a few minutes and give you a message about Jesus Christ." If they cared to listen, they'd usually invite us into their home. If not, they'd usually make some kind of an excuse and Elder Peterson would thank them and extend an invitation for them to attend our Church services.

Most of the "barrio" homes into which we were invited consisted of little more than whitewashed mud walls, plastered over a stick frame, a thatched roof and a dirt floor. Nevertheless, they almost invariably were tidy and the floors were swept clean and uncluttered. The yards also were usually neat and well kept. Many contained beautiful flower gardens. Although most of the people with whom we met were poor, they seemed to take pride in keeping themselves, their homes and their surroundings neat and clean. To me, it was remarkable how poverty did not deter these people from doing the best they could with what little they had.

There was little furniture in most of the "barrio" homes we entered. At best, furnishings usually consisted of one or two wooden-framed beds, a table, and perhaps a few chairs. Nevertheless, those with whom we visited were most hospitable. They would insist my companion and I should sit on the available chairs, while family members patiently stood and listened to our message. They also frequently insisted upon serving us food and beverages, even though it often appeared they did not have sufficient for themselves. I frequently thought of, "Blessed be ye poor: for yours is the kingdom of God." (Luke 6:20).

Elder Peterson and I eventually clapped at the gate of very humble, but exceptionally neat and well-kept "barrio" home. A tall, thin girl of perhaps twenty years of age greeted us at the gate. Elder

Peterson explained our purpose for being there. She bid us to enter and meet her family, which consisted of her mother, two younger sisters and a younger brother of perhaps ten years of age. We later learned the father had died a few years previous and this young girl had taken it upon herself to provide for her family. She insisted my companion and I should sit on two of their three chairs, while her ailing mother sat on the remaining one.

As Elder Peterson presented our gospel message to this girl and her family, I intently studied the face of each family member. My eyes, however, were irresistibly drawn back to this girl. Both her face and body were thin. It was evident she had not had an easy life. Her hands and fingers were callused. They indicated she was well acquainted with hard, physical work. Her clothing was neat and clean, but also plain and in some areas worn or threadbare. In a worldly sense, one probably would not call her pretty, but she had an almost indescribable and beautiful smile. Likewise, her pleasant manner and her long, black hair made her most attractive. To me, she was a VERY pretty young woman.

We visited with this girl and her family for approximately half an hour. My companion then made an appointment for us to return and teach them more about the gospel of Jesus Christ the following week. We then shook hands with each of them and departed.

As we walked down the road, away from this family's humble home, I remarked to Elder Peterson, "Isn't it remarkable that someone, like the girl we just met, can be so happy and content when living in such humble circumstances – especially when she has to work so hard to support her family." He nodded in agreement and added, "I thought the same, especially when she's a cripple." "What do you mean a cripple?" I asked. To this, he answered, "Didn't you notice her right arm? It was deformed. She must have had polio when she was a child."

I couldn't believe it. I had closely observed this girl during much of the time we visited with her and her family. I did notice, however, and had thought it odd when we departed from their home that she had shook hands with us with her left hand. Nevertheless, I did not notice her right arm was deformed. I thought, "Wouldn't I have noticed something like that? My companion surely must be mistaken!"

Elder Peterson was playing in a basketball tournament in Montevideo the following week. Thus, Elder Lind, who was serving in Rivera (a city on the Brazilian border), came to assist me during my companion's absence. Soon after Elder Lind's arrival in Tacuarembo, we returned to the young girl's home in the "barrios". We clapped at the gate and she came to greet and bid us to enter. She and her family again welcomed us into their humble home. This time I took special note of the girl's right arm. It was true! Her right arm was deformed. It was only about half the size of her left arm and she apparently had only limited use of this limb. How could I have missed noting such a gross deformity during our previous visit?

The girl and her family enthusiastically accepted the gospel message Elder Lind presented. As I listened and tried to understand what was being said, I pondered, "How could I have missed seeing this girl's deformed arm when we were here last week?" I pondered even more so than before. "How can she be so happy, despite being a cripple and having to struggle to provide for her family? Wouldn't just living under such poor conditions make one despondent and sad?" Still, she seemed to radiate a joy for living and an inner peace. She truly was a beautiful person!

When Elder Lind concluded the presentation of his gospel message, the girl and her family entreated us to share some refreshments with them. This we did. We then shook hands with each family member and departed. As Elder Lind and I walked along the road, away from this family's home, I remarked, "Isn't it something how that young girl can be so happy - especially when she's a cripple?" "What do you mean a cripple?" he queried. My reply was, "Didn't you notice her right arm and how it's deformed?" Elder Lind said, "No. I didn't." Then after thinking a minute he asked, "Was that why she shook hands with her left hand when we left?"

These and other experiences have led me to believe true beauty is not just "skin deep". It comes from within. This inner beauty also can hide a homely countenance and even make others unaware of our physical deformities. I likewise believe that through our living the beautiful Gospel of Jesus Christ we can erase our spiritual deformities or sins and shortcomings. Why are we so concerned about outward appearances or a "beauty" that is ONLY skin deep. And, why do we spend so much time, effort and money trying to improve our outward appearance, rather than diligently striving to develop our inner beauty?

THE CROCODILE

"Beware of the wily serpent!"

I was conducting a survey of the Indian one-horned rhinoceros in Assam, the eastern-most state in India, when Mr. Gohain, the Chief Wild Life Warden for Assam, accompanied me to The State of Assam Zoological Gardens in Gauhati. Gauhati is a bustling, dirty port city on the Brahmaputra River. Here, Mr. Ghohain introduced me to Mr. Kumar, the Superintendent of the "Gauhati Zoo". Mr. Kumar then insisted upon personally conducting me on a tour of "his zoo".

The Gauhati Zoo is not large when compared to many of the world's zoos or even many of those in India. It contains, however, a good number of animal species that are threatened with extinction and some of which are not represented in any other of the world's zoos. For example, it is the only zoo that has white-winged wood ducks, golden langurs, and the long thought to be extinct pygmy hog. Other rare and/or unique species in the Gauhati Zoo include: the Indian one-horned rhino, Manipur brow-antlered deer, and the "mugger" crocodile.

Mr. Kumar took great pride in showing these animals to me. As he did so, I imposed upon his hospitality and position of authority by requesting permission to enter some of the cages of these rare animals – so I could obtain better photographs of them. This, he graciously permitted me to do.

The pens or cages housing the animals at the Gauhati Zoo are scattered over a large, wooded hill, which affords a panoramic view of the Brahmaputra River and the city of Gauhati. While walking from cage to cage, we passed an oval-shaped moat, which was sixty or seventy feet long and thirty or forty feet wide. It was enclosed with an approximately four-foot-high concrete wall. Inside the moat, there was a small, grass-covered island. The water within the moat was covered with a dense, green mat of delicate-leafed "duckweed". I could not discern any form of animal life either on the small island or within the moat. Thus, I asked Mr. Kumar, "What's in there?" He proudly informed me that the moat contained a very large, man-eating "mugger" or Indian crocodile. "How large is it?" I inquired. He stated, "It's more than thirteen feet long." I facetiously retorted, "I don't believe it! If there's a crocodile that large in there, we'd certainly be able to see at least part of it!"

We walked completely around the outside wall of the moat, carefully searching with our eyes to detect the crocodile. We could see nothing resembling a crocodile. However, there was what appeared to be some large claw and drag marks along the edge of the island in the center of the moat. Nevertheless, I continued to chide Mr. Kumar with remarks such as, "There's no way this moat could contain a 'mugger' anywhere near as big as you claim it is! Are you sure it's still here?" These remarks seemed to affront my host and he repeatedly assured me the moat contained a large "mugger". Furthermore, "It is every bit as big as I told you it was." To this, I further needled him by stating, "I don't believe it! Are you sure it's still here?"

Mr. Kumar evidently did not realize I was merely heckling him and he became noticeably agitated. He tersely explained, "We feed the crocodile a generous ration of fresh meat every three or four days. It's been a couple of days since we fed him. Therefore, I'll have the keepers bring some meat – so you can see him." He also queried, "Would you like to photograph the crocodile? You'll have to be quick! Despite his size, he takes his meat very quickly." I assured him, "I'd very much like to photograph 'your mugger'!" But, I also thought, "Mr. Kumar now is trying to needle me. There's no way a big crocodile could move too fast for me to photograph it."

Mr. Kumar sent two keepers to get some meat for the crocodile. They shortly returned with a huge chunk of meat that weighed perhaps twenty pounds. They carried it between them on two long, metal hooks. As they approached the moat, one keeper withdrew his hook from the meat. He then began clanking his metal hook upon the cement wall surrounding the moat, while hoarsely calling, "Ahh! Ahh! Ahh!" The other keeper slowly lowered the meat on his hook over the wall, until it was about two feet above the weed-covered water surface. Mr. Kumar stationed me a few feet to one side of this keeper and again cautioned me, "You'll have to be very quick!" I assured him, "I will be!"

I readied my camera, while intently watching the large meat bait and the nearby surface of the moat. There was a slight rippling of the duckweed. But, it was such a slight movement that I would not have noticed it had I not been watching so intently. Suddenly, huge, gaping jaws surged up out of the water and the meat was gone. I could not believe it. It happened so fast that I did not have time even to release the shutter on my camera. It was unbelievable!

"Did you get a photograph?" inquired Mr. Kumar. I sheepishly replied, "No, I did not. It all happened too fast!" Shaking his head, he again sent the keepers to get some more meat. Upon their return, I again made ready to photograph the crocodile. This time I intently concentrated upon the bait and only that portion of the moat immediately below it. As a result, when the gaping jaws again suddenly thrust up out of the water, I hurriedly released the shutter. Still, it was unbelievable. I could not imagine an animal of such size moving with such stealth and quickness. It was frightening! Unfortunately, I later found that my photograph shows only a blur of gaping jaws.

I've read accounts of how hundreds of people in Southeast Asia are killed each year by crocodiles. Many of these lose their lives while washing their clothes or bathing in rivers such as the Brahmaputra. In the Zoological Museum in Calcutta, the contents of the gizzard of a large crocodile taken from the Hooghly River are on display. Included in the display are numerous bracelets, anklets, rings and bangles, which apparently were worn by its many human victims. I previously, had surmised that most victims of crocodile attacks probably were the result of carelessness or of people not closely watching the water around them. However, what I witnessed in the Gauhati Zoo impressed upon me that the crocodile is indeed a wily and formidable adversary.

Since this incident in the Gauhati Zoo, I've often pondered about the similarity of this experience with those we might encounter in life. The Bible frequently likens Satan or the devil to a wily serpent. Could not this serpent be a crocodile? In fact, I'm inclined to believe that the serpent that "beguiled" Eve in the Garden of Eden perhaps was more like a crocodile than a snake. Does not Satan use stealth, similar to a crocodile, to entrap or overcome his unsuspecting victims? Also, are his victims often not even aware of his presence – before it is too late? And, similar to a crocodile, does not Satan attack the unwary with lightning speed and viciousness, before quickly dragging them down into the abyss or moat?

Similar to my doubting Mr. Kumar's warning as to the quickness of the "mugger" in "his zoo", how many of us pay little heed to the warnings of others about Satan? Too often, we think we are safe or too smart or too fast to fall victim. We need moat walls or Our Father in Heaven's warnings – given to us through his servants the prophets – to protect us from the "wily serpent"!

"MAMA"

Upon the request of our family, I presented the following at my maternal grandmother's funeral in the Rockland Ward of The Church of Jesus Christ of Latter-day Saints on January 6, 1979.

OPEL HULET WHITTIER – who I never knew as grandmother, but instead as "Mama", was born July 16, 1891 at Summit, Utah. She is the daughter of Sylvanus Cyrus and Mary Ida Hulet and the fifth of twelve children (three sons and nine daughters). Her surviving brother and five sisters are: Howard Hulet, Hope Gardiner, Verda Rogers, Eleanor Adair, Belva Jensen, and Thora Johnson.

"Mama" married Raymond Madsen Whittier, who I always knew as "Daddy Pa", on September 4, 1912, in the Salt Lake Temple. They lived in the Peterson and Roy, Utah, areas before moving to Declo, Idaho, where they lived for twelve years and "Daddy Pa" served as the Bishop of the Declo Ward. They then moved to Rockland, Idaho, in December 1928, and lived here until "Daddy Pa" died on July 5, 1959, which was nineteen and one-half years ago yesterday. "Mama" then lived in Pocatello, Idaho; Logan, Utah; and then Idaho Falls, Idaho, where she died on January 3, 1979.

"Mama" and "Daddy Pa" had nine children, four daughters and five sons. All nine are here today, and for much of my life I have considered them as brothers and sisters, rather than as aunts and uncles. These nine children are: Ramona Ida Woirhaye (my mother), LaRee Peterson, James Chester or "Bud" Whittier, LaMar Hulet Whittier, Raymond Max Whittier, Melba Moore, Homer D. Whittier, Carol Barnard, and Karl Golden Whittier. Karl is six months younger than me and for much of our lives we essentially were raised as brothers or even as twins.

At the time of her death, "Mama" had forty-five grandchildren, of which I am the eldest, forty-four great-grandchildren, and one great-great-grandchild.

"Mama" always was active in The Church of Jesus Christ of Latter-day Saints and held numerous positions in the Church. During her later life she spent much of her time working in the temples of our Lord. "Mama' also was a charter member of the Rockland Chapter of the Daughters of the Utah Pioneers. She often told how, during her early life in southern Utah, she spent the summers in the high mountains caring for her father's cows and sheep, and how she especially loved to ride horses. She loved the out-of-doors and even requested a snowmobile suit and a pair of snow boots for her eighty-fourth birthday – because, "I sometimes get cold while riding a snowmobile!"

"Mama" loved the fine arts, such as music and art, and seemed always to be engaged in making another blanket for a new grandchild or crocheting something special for someone. I can never remember her ever being idle. She always was busy doing something, which almost invariably was for someone other than herself. I believe, however, "Mama's" most notable attribute was the fact she diligently strived throughout her life to be a good mother and homemaker. I also believe that for a woman to be a good mother and homemaker – such as was "Mama" – is a woman's greatest achievement.

"Mama" was not often in the limelight. Instead, she almost always was in the background, supporting "Daddy Pa" and the many members of her family. She graciously hosted literally hundreds of people in her home. Many of these were notable dignitaries, particularly many of the General Authorities of the Church, such as Hugh B. Brown, LeGrande Richards, Gordon B. Hinckley, Marion G. Romeny, Oscar A. Kirkam, Mark E. Peterson, and Ezra Taft Benson.

Anyone who has eaten "Mama's" cooking, I am sure will attest to the fact she was an excellent cook. This was despite the fact she never seemed to measure any ingredients, but intuitively seemed to know just how much of this or that to put in. It is told how Mark E. Peterson made it a special point to look "Mama" up, just to be able to have another piece of her delicious apple pie!

I know I will never forget the many happy hours and days I spent in "Mama's" home. Nor will I forget the many wonderful family dinners and get-to-gathers we had, which "Mama" always hosted. Further, I won't forget how I could drop in on "Mama" at any hour of the day or night or how I could stay for days or even weeks and still know she would continue to go out of her way to fix me something special to eat, as well as insist upon washing and pressing my clothes and doing everything she possibly could to make me feel at home.

Rather than our mourning "Mama's" passing and the fact we will be temporarily parted from her, I think we should rejoice for having been associated with her during her eighty-seven-year sojourn upon this earth. I especially feel we should rejoice with her in the fact that after nineteen and one-half years, which oftentimes must have been long and lonely years for her, "Mama" and "Daddy Pa" are together again.

Finally, in paying tribute to "Mama", I hope we can rededicate ourselves to living in such a manner that, at some future time, we again may be reunited with her in an eternal family.

This, I pray, in the name of Jesus Christ. Amen.

AUNT JESSE

My Great Aunt (Jesse Bell Blackburn Lasley) died on May 25, 1987 (Memorial Day). Upon request of the family, I presented the following at Aunt Jesse's funeral on May 28, 1987 in the Rockland Ward of The Church of Jesus Christ of Latter-day Saints.

We are assembled today as family and friends to pay tribute to Jesse Bell Blackburn Lasley. Although Aunt Jesse was born in Kansas, she spent seventy-one of her eighty-three years in Idaho. When she was twelve, she and her family moved from Kansas to Soda Springs, Idaho. The Blackburn farm was just north of the town of Soda Springs and is the present-day site of the Monsanto Chemical Company plant.

While working in Soda Springs, Charles Lasley met and then married Aunt Jesse. Thereafter, they lived in a number of homes, all of which are in southeastern Idaho and most in the Rockland Valley.

Aunt Jesse never traveled much, but preferred to stay at home. Although she probably didn't visit more than half a dozen states during her life, her influence for good has been felt literally throughout the world.

It is difficult for me to talk about Aunt Jesse without also talking about Uncle Charley. They rarely were apart. Throughout my life, we rarely mentioned one without mentioning the other. It always was simply, "Charley and Jesse".

Charley and Jesse reared a family of nine children, five boys and four girls. Gail, their third son and sixth child, is only a few months older than me. We went to school together and have been close friends throughout our lives. In fact, many members of the Lasley family were more like brothers and sisters to me than cousins. We had many good times together.

Regretfully, I do not even know many of Charley and Jesse's forty-one grandchildren and sixty-four great-grandchildren. Jesse, however, not only knew each of them by name, but she also could tell you their age and even their birth dates. Up until the past few years, she also knew virtually every student, as well as many of their birth dates, that graduated from the Rockland High School. How she did it, I do not know.

In addition to Charley and Jesse's one hundred and fourteen direct descendents, they had an even more extensive family. Their many sons and daughter-in-laws were family and they considered them as their own children. Charley and Jesse also essentially adopted my father, as well as his two brothers, Ray and Frank, when their mother, who was Uncle Charley's sister Rose, died. In addition, rarely could you go to Charley and Jesse's that there weren't other children there. They loved children, no matter who's they were. And, they welcomed them into their home and treated them like their family. Charley's and Jesse's home and their hearts were always open for others.

How many here have spent one or more nights in Charley and Jesse's home? Also, how many here have eaten one or more meals prepared by Aunt Jesse? I think this illustrates the hospitality and the love and concern they had for others.

We learn much more from example than we do from a preached sermon. I also think we'd all rather see a good example than to hear a sermon. Charley and Jesse were almost perfect examples of what parents should be. Their lives were their sermons. In fact, they were living textbooks in how to be successful parents, as well as loving neighbors and friends. Their formula perhaps was something like this: First, was their profound sense of the importance of family. Their children and grandchildren learned at an early age they belonged to something special and important. This was a family that looked back to its roots with reverence and gratitude and forward to future generations with love and concern.

Charley and Jesse never seemed to doubt the goodness in their children and in others. Although someone might wrong them or one of their own might go somewhat astray, this did not diminish their love and concern for that individual. They had faith in that person and firmly believed they eventually would do right. And, usually they did!

Unlike the biblical parent who was capable of welcoming back the prodigal son, they did not even recognize the concept of prodigal. A son simply was a son and that was that. Too bad every child cannot have parents such as Charley and Jesse. Better yet, it's too bad each of us cannot be parents such as were Charley and Jesse. The Savior once said, "No greater love hath any man, than that he give his life for a friend." Charley and Jesse exemplified this great love. They literally gave their lives for their family and for their many, many friends. Again, their lives, rather than their words, were their sermons.

As a child, I remember frequently staying at Charley and Jesse's. Often their beds were so full of children that, in addition to three or four at the top, there also were three or four tucked in at the bottom of the bed. No matter how many of us there were or how much noise we might make or even how much mischief we might get into, we always were welcome in Charley and Jesse's home. And, we knew it!

I remember when Gail and I gathered the eggs from the hen house and then broke them to use in making mud pies. Rather than scolding or spanking us, as we probably deserved, Charley and Jesse simply laughed. But, when we were older and supposedly knew better, they often kidded us about our actions when we were younger.

When Gail and I were in high school, we and our friends often would gather at Charley and Jesse's to play games at night. We would laugh and holler at each other – often into the wee hours of the morning. Instead of getting after us, Jesse would make batches of candy for us. And, we'd eat candy till we were almost sick. Then, she'd invite us to spend the night. Or, when we finally left, she'd invite us to, "Come back anytime!"

I remember the eating contests we kids used to have at Aunt Jesse's. She'd fill a big double boiler with ears of freshly picked corn and boil it on the old wood-burning stove. We kids then would vie with each other as to who could eat the most corn. If I remember correctly, Gail still holds the record at eighteen ears!

When Charley and Jesse lived up East Fork, I remember Jesse jumping into their Ford pickup and going to town to get a bag of potato chips and some pop – so we could have a picnic down by the creek. I also remember Jesse buying a billy goat, which they kept for years, because she thought the kids would enjoy having it.

In terms of worldly good, Charley and Jesse had relatively little. In the eyes of many, they were considered to be poor. But, in terms of those things that really count, such as family and friends, Charley and Jesse were some of the richest people I have known. Worldly goods seemed to be of little importance to them. Instead, people seemed to be of primary importance as far as they were concerned.

Charley and Jesse's home always was open to others. In the more than thirty years I lived away from Rockland, a visit to Rockland was not complete UNLESS it included a visit to Charley and Jesse's. I am sure many here felt the same way.

Sundays and holidays were especially important to Charley and Jesse. This was a time for family and friends to gather at their place, to eat and to visit. Also, insofar as Charley and Jesse were concerned, the more the better! There always was enough room and enough food for everyone! I once asked Aunt Jesse how many they had had for Thanksgiving dinner. Her reply was, "Only seventy-six!" She had hoped for more. How many of us would welcome seventy-six people into our home for dinner? How many would wish more had come?

Uncle Charley was the best Home Teaching companion I ever had. It then was called "Ward Teaching" and our beat consisted of almost all of the families up East Fork. It was true, we usually would procrastinate till the end of the month before making our visits. But, we then would spend a whole day or even two making them. Many we visited would ask us to hurry through our message – so we could visit. We also would often pitch in and help those we visited with whatever task they were doing. The kids usually would climb upon

Charley's lap. And, some would cry because their parents wouldn't let them go home with "Uncle Charley".

Charley and I visited Marty and Josie Peck, who lived just below Charley and Jesse's place. Almost invariably when Charley and I would go Home Teaching, we would start at the head of the canyon, at the Reed's home. Josie then would phone almost every home we visited. She would inform us, "I saw you go up the canyon. You can't get past our place without visiting Marty and me!" Then, when we'd eventually get to the Peck's, Marty and Josie would usher us into their home, as if we were visiting royalty. And, after we had given our message, Josie almost invariably would treat us to fresh baked bread, a piece of cake or something she had prepared especially for us.

Jesse's mother Grandma Blackburn, lived with Charley and Jesse for a number of years before she died. Although Grandma Blackburn became quite aged and feeble, Charley and Jesse and their family always treated her with love and respect. Grandma Blackburn, in turn, always tried to help around the house. But, when her eyes got bad, she couldn't see well enough to do many things well. This, however, didn't bother Jesse. She would let her mother try to do what she could and to feel useful and needed. I remember when Grandma Blackburn couldn't see to wash the dishes properly, Jesse simply would wait till she was taking a nap and then she or other family members would do the dishes over again. They would not think of saying or doing anything that might hurt Grandma Blackburn's feelings. Why cannot all of us show such respect for our parents and to others?

When my parents were in England and I was alone and struggling to run the family farm, Jesse frequently would invite me to come and stay with them. Whenever she would go to town, she would call and ask if I needed anything. At first, I'd give her a list of parts or whatever I felt I needed. But, when she delivered what I had ordered, more often than not she would refuse to let me pay for it. Instead, she'd simply say, "Maybe we'll want a favor from you someday!" It was the same at Christmas time. If you gave Jesse or her family a present, she'd insist upon giving a present to you in return. Jesse always was giving people presents or doing something for them. It's hard to imagine how many hours she spent crocheting or making presents for others.

I don't have to tell Charley and Jesse's family that they had very, very special parents – BECAUSE, for as long as I can remember, through their actions they have demonstrated their love for their parents and for each other.

Just prior to Gail and I being inducted into the military service, we did quite a bit of chasing around together. Quite often I would stay at Charley and Jesse's with Gail. No matter what time of night, actually more often than not it was early morning when we came home, Gail always would go into his parents' bedroom, wake up his mother, and tell her we were home, as well as where we had been and what we had done. Then he would kiss her goodnight. This was despite our being twenty years old and Gail no longer was a "little boy". In fact, Gail was a big man and a terror on the football field. Members of opposing football teams we played in high school all feared him.

I often have wished we'd all have the rapport with our parents and our children that Charley and Jesse had in their family. Wouldn't it be great if we could express or show the love we have for members of our own families like the Lasley family showed in theirs?

The last time I saw Aunt Jesse was at the family get-to-gather held at Paul and Kay Bammert's last March. It was to commemorate Jesse's 83rd birthday. All of Jesse's nine children, as well as a good many of her grand and great-grandchildren were there. It indeed was a marvelous occasion. What a demonstration of love and respect and of unity within a family!

Because of Aunt Jesse's passing, many of us may consider this a time of mourning. It is, however, also a time of rejoicing. Think of how happy many on the other side must be to again have Aunt Jesse with them. Especially, think of how happy Uncle Charley must be to again have his dear Jesse with him!

I often have wondered just how Uncle Charley has gotten along without Aunt Jesse during the years since his passing. He depended upon her so much in this life it is hard to imagine what he would do without her. There just seemed to be a quiet expression of love and respect between them. I cannot remember ever hearing a cross word spoken between them.

I personally believe Aunt Jesse was permitted to linger awhile longer with us than Uncle Charley just so she could further guide and strengthen their ever-expanding family. We should rejoice in that Charley and Jesse are again united! And, if we truly want to pay respect to them, we should try to emulate their good example. We should strive harder to love others, as they did, and to be kind and thoughtful to each other. Specifically, we should strive to prepare ourselves so we eventually can be with Charley and Jesse again – as part of an eternal family!

May we so live that we may be happy in this life, as well as gain eternal life and; thereby, have joy in the life to come. Thus, we may dwell with God and with our families and friends forever. This is my sincere prayer, in the name of Jesus Christ. Amen.

UNCLE MAX AND GOSPEL PRINCIPLES AND ORDINANCES

Upon request of the family, I presented the following at Uncle Max's funeral at the Pocatello, Idaho, 3rd Ward of The Church of Jesus Christ of Latter-day Saints on March 29, 2002.

RAYMOND MAX WHITTIER was the fifth child and third son born to Raymond Madsen Whittier, who I always called "Daddy Pa", and Opal Hulet Whittier, who I knew as "Mama". His four older brothers and sisters were: Ramona Ida (my mother), LaRee, James Chester (who we knew as "Bud"), and LaMar Hulet. All four have passed on and I am sure they have been anxiously waiting for Max to join them on the other side.

Max's four younger brothers and sisters are: Melba, Homer Dee, Carol, and Karl Golden. His four children are: Tonia Jean, Cheryl Christine, Charlene, and Monte Ray. He and Lucille also adopted Lucille's youngest sister Joyce and she lived with them for a number of years. At the time of his death, Max had ten grandchildren, nine great-grandchildren, and four great-great-grandchildren. He has a remarkable posterity.

Although Max is my uncle and twelve years older than me, he seemed more like a big brother. He had a real love for life. When he was around you were always doing something enjoyable. He loved to play baseball, basketball and to golf. He also loved to hunt and to fish. He was an excellent baseball pitcher and played for many years on American Legion teams. Baseball games were played on Sundays, which was a bone of contention between him and his father who was in the Ward Bishopric. A compromise finally was made between them, wherein Max would first attend Sunday-morning Church services BEFORE playing baseball on Sunday afternoons.

Max also played M-Men basketball. He was an avid sports fan throughout his life. When he was teaching school in Ammon and my family was living in Idaho Falls, he often would take me to athletic events. He sold candy bars and other goodies at high school basketball games. I remember how he and I often ate all of his profits. We once ate so many candy bars we were both sick all night.

Max often took Karl and me hunting and fishing. Although Karl is my uncle, he is six months younger than me. When we were small, my parents and grandparents often would admonish Max with, "Don't let those kids get near the guns." But, almost as soon as we were in the field, he'd hand us a gun and let us hunt along with him. I think both Karl and I were shooting rifles by the time we were five years old.

Max raised prized Spotted-Poland-China pigs. When he, "Bud" and LaMar were gone, working on the dry farm, Karl and I often would practice roping his pigs. He had a huge boar, which we were scared of. But, one day I bet Karl he couldn't rope this boar. Well, he did. Then we couldn't get the rope off of him. So, we simply tied the rope to a post and the boar almost died from being in the sun all day. Max was really upset when he came home that evening. When he saw what we had done to his prize boar, he was ready to skin the two of us alive. If it had not been for "Daddy Pa" protecting us, Karl and I might not be here today!

Max went into the U.S. Army during World War II. At about the same time his brother LaMar was shot down over Germany and missing in action, he was injured in an explosion in the Pacific. He lost his hearing and spent much time in hospitals because of his injuries. However, this didn't slow him down. He learned to read lips and shortly was as social as ever.

Following the War, Max worked for the Veteran's Administration. He had a car and his job with the VA took him all over southeastern Idaho. He often took Karl and me with him. We had a great time, fishing in the early morning and in the evenings, as well as visiting with disabled veterans with him during the day. During this time, Max met and married Marjorie Lucille Pea on May 10, 1947 in Pocatello, Idaho. Their marriage was later solemnized in the Idaho Falls Temple. At the time of his death, they had been married almost fifty-five years.

Although Max had a very good job with the VA and a family (Cheryl was born in 1948), he decided he wanted to become a lawyer. Many people tried to tell him he was crazy. He had a good job. He also had a family to support. Besides, how could he go to college when he couldn't hear? Nevertheless, Max persisted. As a result, he quit his job with the VA and returned to school. First he attended Idaho State and then the University of Utah. Lucille supported him by continuing her career as a nurse. I remember how she would tend Cheryl during the day and then work nights, while Max attended school during the day and studied and tended Cheryl nights. Through much sacrifice and hard work, Max eventually had a very successful career as a lawyer. However, even while going to school, I remember going to basketball and football games with him, as well as attending memorable boxing events and going golfing. Max even participated in the Intercollegiate Knights and other activities. He led a very full life!

Max was a very social person. Family members and family ties were especially important to him. More often than not, it was he who organized or arranged for our Whittier Family Reunions or get-togathers. Also, it usually was he who quietly paid for the facilities in which we met. Since Max has been unable to organize family get-togathers, Whittier Family Reunions have come to naught. It's a sorry state when we wait for occasions such as this to come together as a family – instead of emulating Max's example.

When Carol and I got married, I planned to spend our wedding night at my parents' home in Logan. I didn't have any money to pay for a hotel. It was Max who made arrangements and paid for us a room in the Hotel Ben Lomond in Ogden. It also was Max who paid for my air tickets to Pocatello, so I could show slides for firesides. In short, Max did many, many things to strengthen family ties and relationships. I don't think many people are even aware of the many things he did. He really was a neat guy!

These past few years have been difficult for Max, for Lucille and for their family. It hurt to see Max not be able to do those things he had always done and wanted to continue to do. It also hurt to see how difficult it was for Lucille and the rest of the family. We admire and commend them for their stamina, patience and endurance. I believe there was a reason for these difficulties and through these trials many important lessons were learned.

THE PRINCIPLES AND ORDINANCES OF THE GOSPEL OF JESUS CHRIST

At times like these, we should ponder: What is the purpose of life? Why are we here? And, what should we be doing?

First, we are here to receive a mortal body. For some reason, our spirit needs a body of flesh and bone in order to attain its full potential or celestial state. Our bodies are sacred. Thus, we should protect and take good care of them.

Second, we are here to be tried or tested. In other words, mortality provides us the opportunity to choose – on our own – between right and wrong or good and evil. Our state, following this probationary period called life or mortality depends largely upon how wisely we choose and how we act upon our choices.

In the early 1800's, a newspaperman asked the Prophet Joseph Smith, "What are the beliefs of the 'Mormon Church'?" Through inspiration, Joseph Smith then wrote what we know as the Thirteen Articles of Faith. These Thirteen Articles briefly state the basic beliefs or doctrines of The Church of Jesus Christ of Latter-day Saints, which is the only true Church and represents the Kingdom of God upon the earth today.

The Fourth Article of Faith states, **"We believe the first principles and ordinances of the Gospel are: first, Faith in the Lord Jesus Christ; second, Repentance; third, Baptism by immersion for the remission of sins; fourth, Laying on of hands for the gift of the Holy Ghost."**

Thus, in choosing the right, we must comply with these principles and ordinances of the Gospel. We must have Faith in Christ. We need to Repent of our sins. We also need to be baptized by immersion and by those having the authority or priesthood to administer this ordinance. Then, by the authority of the higher or Melchizadek

Priesthood, we need to be confirmed members of The Church and receive The Gift of the Holy Ghost.

However, Faith, Repentance, Baptism, and the Gift of the Holy Ghost are ONLY the FIRST principles and ordinances of the Gospel. There are more!

Men must receive the ordinance of being ordained to the Melchizadek Priesthood. Then, we must receive the ordinance of the "Endowment". The Endowment consists of washings and anointings and our making covenants with God to keep His commandments. Also, the Endowment can only be received in the Lord's House or His Holy Temples, which are built and dedicated solely to the Lord's work. Thereafter, the highest ordinance in which we can participate upon this earth is that of Eternal or Temple Marriage. Through the ordinance of Temple Marriage we are sealed – through the power of the priesthood – to our spouses and to our families for "All Time and Eternity". Similar to the Endowment, this ordinance also can be received ONLY in the Lord's House or His Holy Temples.

After receiving these sacred ordinances and after our having adhered to the principles of Faith and Repentance, there is yet another principle required of us – before we can receive Eternal Life or be privileged to live forever in the presence of Our Father in Heaven and His Son Jesus Christ. Even though this Gospel principle is iterated more than eighty times in The Book of Mormon, it is often overlooked. This principle is to "ENDURE TO THE END".

What does the principle of "endure to the end" mean? It means we will diligently strive – to the very end – to keep ALL of God's commandments and to ALWAYS try to do that which we know or believe to be right. This is why we do not believe in suicide or euthanasia – no matter how difficult life may become.

I believe this principle – to endure to the end – probably is the most difficult of all the Principles and Ordinances of the Gospel for many of us. Life can be difficult. And, as we get older, I think we usually face more and more difficulties. Some of these include: failing health, the loss of loved ones, the seeming injustices of life, the failings of our children or loved ones, loneliness, and feelings of depression and despair.

The Lord did not promise us that life would be easy. However, through the example of His life and through His prophets, as well as through revelation or the promptings of the Holy Ghost, we are continuously reminded that life is precious. Life is a gift we should strive to make the most of.

For those who have died without having had or not having taken the opportunity to receive the saving ordinances of the Gospel, these ordinances may be administered to others for them in the Lord's Temples. This is done vicariously; wherein, we – the living – take upon ourselves the names of those who have died and then receive – in the Temples – these ordinances for them. Then, it is up to them to accept or to reject the vicarious work that has been done for them. Thus, there is justice in ALL of the Lord's doings!

However, with respect to the Gospel principles of Faith, Repentance, and Enduring to the End, these are a different matter. Each of us is individually responsible with regards to our adherence to these principles. No one else can do it for us. Thus, again there is justice in ALL of the Lord's doings.

Raymond Max Whittier has received ALL of the ordinances required for him to receive exaltation in Our Father's Kingdom. He also has adhered to the Gospel Principles of Faith, Repentance, and Enduring to the End. May each of us do likewise, I pray, in the name of Jesus Christ. Amen.

TOM

Seemingly insignificant events may profoundly affect our lives.

I was not impressed with the quiet, sandy-haired fellow sitting alongside my desk. His name was Tom and his wife (Mary) sat on a chair on the far side of my office at Utah State University. Tom explained, "I'll soon graduate from Brigham Young University (BYU) with a degree in Biology. I then want to attend Utah State University to obtain a graduate degree in Wildlife Science." He also explained how his father-in-law, Dr. Homer Ellsworth - who was on the staff of the medical school at the University of Utah - had assured him Utah State and especially the Utah Cooperative Wildlife Research Unit had "the best wildlife program in the country." Dr. Ellsworth had further suggested Tom should try to study under the supervision of Dr. Jessop B. Low, Leader of the Cooperative Wildlife Research Unit, with whom I served as the Assistant Unit Leader.

Tom had made an appointment to meet with Dr. Low. Thus, he and his wife had driven from Provo to Logan, Utah. But, Dr. Low claimed, "I don't have time just now to meet with him. Could you spare a few minutes to assess this guy's qualifications as a prospective graduate student in the Unit?" I agreed to do so, which is why Tom and his wife Mary were now sitting in my office.

I asked Tom, "Let me look at your records." He handed me his application folder, which contained copies of his university transcripts, letters of recommendation, and a personal letter in which he stated his objectives or purpose for wanting to obtain an advanced degree in Wildlife Science. I glanced at the three letters of recommendation. Two were from staff members in BYU's Department of Biology and who I happened to know. Thus, I thought to myself, "If his other credentials look half-way promising, I can call my friends at the 'Y' and get the real 'skinny' on him. Otherwise, I'll somehow politely discourage him from attending Utah State or simply tell him he's not qualified." The third letter of recommendation was from Tom's Ward Bishop, who wrote in glowing terms of his "reliability and moral character." Though Tom and I had the same religious beliefs (i.e. we were "Mormons" or members of The Church of Jesus Christ of Latter-day Saints), I considered a letter from his Bishop as a negative factor. I felt one should endeavor to get favorable academic recommendations rather than those from clergy when applying for an academic program.

I then examined Tom's transcripts. All but a few of his credits were from BYU. His grades for upper division coursework were mostly A's. But, grades for his lower division coursework were poor. These, I determined, disqualified him for acceptance into the Unit program. I then read his personal letter of application and questioned him as to some statements he made in it. I surmised, "Here's another student who doesn't know what the wildlife field is really about. He probably just thinks it would be fun and glamorous to be a wildlife biologist." In short, I was not impressed with Tom and told him, "Perhaps you should consider a field other than wildlife for a career".

Tom was noticeably upset with what I told him. He explained, "One of my professors at BYU has offered me a graduate project in parasitology. He wants me to study coccidiosis. But, I want to study Wildlife Science." In turn, I told him, "A bird in the hand is worth two in the bush! If I had an offer for a funded M.S. program, I'd take it!" Further, "If you did well in a Master's program, even if it was in parasitology, you then could switch over to Wildlife Science for a Ph.D."

Tom appeared dejected as he left my office. He accepted the graduate project in parasitology at BYU. When I later questioned some of his professors at the 'Y' about him, they told me, "Tom's a solid student. He's no flash in the pan, but an exceptionally steady plodder – one you always can rely upon to get a job done."

About a year later, Tom again appeared at Utah State and applied for a Ph.D. program in Wildlife Science. Somehow, he had completed both his M.S. coursework and research in little more than a year; whereas, a Master's in Biological Sciences usually takes two or more years to complete. What's more, his research was commendable and all of his professors recommended him highly.

This time, Dr. Low accepted Tom as a Ph.D. candidate and assigned him a research project involving the determination of whether or not exposure to the pesticide "Dieldrin" caused genetical aberrations in mallard ducks. The Unit had maintained a captive flock of mallards on different levels of Dieldrin for a number of years and an array of graduate students had conducted behavioral and physiological studies on the effects of this pesticide on these birds. No one, however, had investigated whether or not long-term exposure and the possible "build-up" of Dieldrin in animal tissues caused genetic mutation or change. Use of karyotypes or "chromosome pictures" for "genetical mapping" is a tedious and highly technical procedure. It is more difficult with birds than with mammals. This is because, in addition to large or "macro" chromosomes common to mammals and birds, birds also have numerous small or "micro" chromosomes. In short, Tom was undertaking a formidable task!

Few professors at Utah State then were sufficiently knowledgeable in genetic techniques to supervise or even thoroughly evaluate much of Tom's research. Thus, qualified personnel to serve on his graduate committee were sought from other universities such as the University of Utah and BYU. Tom, however, appeared to be undaunted by the complexity of his project. He simply began to methodically review the literature and then systematically try one method after another in the laboratory, until he found what provided the desired results.

Tom enrolled in both of the wildlife courses I then taught and handily obtained the highest scores in both. This was despite more than seventy students being enrolled in each class. He did likewise in almost all of his other courses at Utah State. As a result, both students and staff shortly recognized him as a "brilliant student". I did not think Tom was exceptionally "bright", but believed he did exceptionally well because he was so methodical and persistent in all he undertook. In addition to a substantial number of classes, he also devoted considerable time and effort to his research. Although some members of his graduate committee thought definitive research results might take several years of concerted effort, if such could be obtained at all, Tom surprised everyone by successfully completing both his coursework and research in a little more than two years; whereas, a Ph.D. in Wildlife Science normally takes three or more years to complete. Furthermore, a research project as complex as his expectedly would take even longer. Tom indeed was remarkable!

Although Dr. Low was Tom's major professor, I frequently worked with Tom. As I became better acquainted with him, I gained more and more respect and admiration for him. Rarely did he get excited or upset, though it seemed he almost continually was confronted with formidable barriers in his research, coursework and personal life. Instead of becoming agitated or frustrated, it seemed he simply analyzed each situation and then methodically sought a solution. I could not believe his persistence. For example, when he could not detect any genetical aberrations in the thousands of chromosomes he studied from birds that had been maintained for several generations on extremely high levels of pesticides, he simply switched to "in vitro" cell cultures. He could subject these to pesticide levels so high they would kill experimental birds. Thus, he demonstrated that Dieldren can cause genetical aberrations, but only at levels which would be lethal to mallard ducks.

Results from Tom's studies opened many new venues for investigation in Wildlife Science and other fields. Such investigations, however, would require more technical expertise than most of us "old-time" biologists were used to using. Thus, I began to use Tom and his expertise more and more in some of the research projects I was conducting with graduate students.

Dr. Warren Foote, a notable reproductive physiologist in Utah State's Department of Animal Science, and I cooperatively studied reproduction in elk or "Wapati" for several years. During this time, I also was involved in a number of research projects involving bighorn sheep and Dr. Foote in research on domestic sheep. Although his interests were primarily in domestic animals; whereas, mine were in wild ones, we shortly realized there are many similarities between wild and domestic sheep and goats and their near relatives, We mutually concluded that ALL – both wild and domestic - have qualities which could contribute to the benefit of man. Thus, we established "The International Sheep and Goat Institute" (ISGI).

The genetical relationships of wild and domestic sheep and goats, as well as their near relatives, such as the tahr, serows and goat-antelopes, greatly intrigued Dr. Foote and I. Determining these relationships would require genetic studies. Thus, we turned to Tom for assistance. And, despite his then being committed to his Ph.D. research and coursework, he freely assisted us. Then, when he finished his doctorate, arrangements were made whereby we offered him a post-doctorate fellowship with the ISGI. This resulted in my being even more closely associated with Tom.

Under the ISGI program, one of the first major tasks we assigned Tom was to establish a genetical research laboratory and program in Iran. This would be a part of a five-year program we had negotiated with the Iranian Ministry of Agriculture and would require him and his family moving to and living in Iran for two years. Thereafter, under extremely difficult and trying conditions, Tom set up a laboratory and conducted some very notable research. I frequently worked with him during this time, even staying in his home with him and his family. We also collaborated in field expeditions to collect specimens from wild and domestic sheep in Iran, Afghanistan, Pakistan, India and Mexico. In short, our close association and our working together over a period of years resulted in my considering Tom to be a dear friend.

Little by little I learned about Tom's early life. He was adopted when but a small child and was sickly during much of his childhood. He was the only child of his foster parents, who apparently loved him dearly. His foster father was not well educated. He had only a fifth-grade education and earned a living by "tightening nuts and bolts" on an automobile assembly line near Detroit. Tom once stated, "I think the height of my father's ambition is to be able to watch baseball all day on TV, while drinking a six-pack of beer."

Tom did not find out about his natural parents and family until he was an adult. He then learned the reason they had put him up for adoption was because he was sickly and they did not have the financial means to provide proper medical attention for him. They loved him, but feared the only way his life could be saved was through adoption. He eventually contacted and then became well acquainted with his natural parents and numerous brothers and sisters. He also came to love them as much as he loved his foster parents and eventually made annual visits to Indiana to visit both his foster and natural parents and his siblings. As a geneticist, it was of major interest to him how similar he and his siblings were. Even though they did not know nor associate with each other until adulthood, they shared many likes and dislikes, as well as similar behaviors or habits. Tom repeatedly expressed amazement at these similarities, which led to consternation about the age-old question of, "Which is more important, heredity or environment?"

In addition to being frail and sickly during his youth, Tom apparently had little drive and did not excel in much of anything. However, during high school, he became proficient at working with his hands. He liked to work with wood and learned how to repair electrical apparatuses, such as pinball machines. Still, he was a below-average student in school. Soon after graduating from high school, he enlisted in the U.S. Army for four years. Because of his experience and interest in tinkering with electrical "gadgets", he trained in electronics and eventually was assigned to an isolated radar station on the Great Lakes. While stationed here, he happened to have a bunkmate who was a returned "Mormon" missionary. They became close friends, but this former missionary rarely, if ever, discussed religion with him. On a few occasions, however, he invited Tom to attend once-a-week evening meetings called "MIA". These were held in a church building not far from where they were stationed and, more often than not, consisted primarily of playing basketball. Tom enjoyed the activities, but was surprised the "Mormons" played basketball in the same hall where they held religious services. Tom's "Mormon" friend shortly was transferred and he no longer associated with any "Mormons".

Tom adjusted well to military service and began to think about making it a career. He further reasoned, "If I'm going to be a career soldier, I might just as well become an officer. There's no reason I should remain as just an enlisted man." Thus, he submitted an application to attend Officer's Candidate School or "OCS". He then was informed that OCS applicants no longer would be accepted unless they first had successfully completed some university-level coursework. However, he also was told this should not be a major problem, as he could attend evening courses while still in the military service. Thus, he enrolled in an evening course in philosophy.

Tom told me how shocked he was the first time he attended the philosophy class. Except for him, all in attendance were officers. A few were even colonels; whereas, he was a lowly corporal. Furthermore, the instructor stated, "Prior to our next class, each of you must select a specific church or religion, the philosophy of which you will study and present to the class. Then, following each presentation, the other class members are to evaluate and find flaws in the religious philosophy that has been presented. " Thereafter the instructor also stated, "How well each of you present and then defend the religion you have selected will, in large measure, determine your grade for the course."

Tom was flabbergasted. He had never been affiliated with any church and knew virtually nothing about religion. In fact, he claimed, "I'd never attended church services more than a few time during my entire life." Pondering as to which religion he should choose to study and then present its philosophy to the class, he thought about his former bunkmate, the returned "Mormon" missionary. Although this friend had been transferred and he did not even know his address, he thought he probably could find a "pastor" of a "Mormon" congregation who could tell him the beliefs of the "Mormon Church". He did not even know the real name of the "Mormon Church" is "The Church of Jesus Christ of Latter-day Saints".

Tom first searched in the military post's phone book for a "Mormon" pastor. In the Yellow Pages, beneath "Mormon", was listed a telephone number for a "Group Leader". He called the number and was surprised to hear a voice with an accent. It was a Spanish-American serviceman. He was an Army sergeant and informed Tom he served as the "Group Leader" for the "Mormon" servicemen in the area. When Tom explained what he wanted, the man made an appointment to meet with him. Tom explained, "When I met this guy, I couldn't believe the stack of 'Mormon' literature he gave me. It was at least a foot high!" Included were books, magazines, and missionary tracts or pamphlets explaining "Mormon" doctrine. When he started to go through the deluge of literature the sergeant had enthusiastically given him, he thought, "How will I ever read all of this, let alone prepare a presentation on the religious philosophy of the 'Mormons'?" However, while telling him about the Church, the sergeant had stated, "The Book of Mormon contains the fullness of the gospel of Jesus Christ and what members of the Church believe. It is because of this book, which was translated from ancient records by the prophet Joseph Smith, that members of the Church are called 'Mormons'." Thus, Tom reasoned, "If the Book of Mormon provides both the name and beliefs of the 'Mormon Church', I'll use it to prepare for my class presentation." Tom then began to read and study the Book of Mormon.

Regarding the philosophy class in which he enrolled, Tom claimed, "The presentations given by other class members were impressive. But, it startled me as to how difficult it was for them to defend the religious philosophies they presented." Other class members readily disputed or tore apart the philosophies presented. And, for some reason, this seemed to please the class instructor. As a result, Tom strove even harder to learn and understand the religious philosophies of the "Mormon Church" and the basis for the beliefs of its members.

The evening for Tom's presentation to the class arrived. He stood nervously before the group and began to present what he had gleaned from studying the philosophy of The Church of Jesus Christ of Latter-day Saints. Through diligent study and perhaps without even realizing it, he had come to accept the beliefs of the "Mormons" as his own. During the course of his presentation and to his amazement, rather than attacking or disputing what he presented, the class members began to ask questions. They wanted to know more about the beliefs of the "Mormons". Instead of a half-hour presentation, Tom expounded "Mormon" doctrine for more than two hours. Remarkably, interest by class members increased, rather than waned. Finally, the instructor chipped in with, "This is very interesting! But, we can't stay here all night." Tom not only had convinced himself as to the truthfulness of the doctrines of the "Mormon Church", he also had begun to expound these beliefs to others.

Somehow, after his successful completion of the philosophy class, a pair of "Mormon" missionaries contacted Tom. During his first discussion with these young men, he said, "I know the gospel of Jesus Christ and the 'Mormon Church' are true. I want to be baptized!" The missionaries were astonished. Their reply was, "You can't know it's true nor can you be baptized. That's because we haven't even had a chance to teach you!" Thus, they insisted upon presenting Tom a series of doctrinal discussions, before they would accept his request for baptism.

Tom shortly was baptized and confirmed a member of the Church. For the first time in his life, he began to attend church services. Everything was new to him and he had difficulty understanding many things about his newly accepted religion. However, he said, "I particularly was impressed with the friendliness of the other members and how important it seemed to them to answer my many questions and their desire to help me fully understand the gospel of Jesus Christ."

Studying the scriptures and becoming an active "Mormon" soon occupied much of Tom's free time. Still, he was determined to make a career of the military service and, in so doing, become an officer. This meant he must successfully complete a sufficient amount of university coursework to be accepted into OCS. Someone, he did not know who, gave him a subscription to the "Improvement Era", which was a monthly magazine published by the Church. Upon opening one of these magazines, he saw an advertisement for Brigham Young University (BYU) on the backside of the cover. The advertisement impressed him and he thought, "As soon as I finish my present enlistment, I should attend BYU and get a college education. Then, I can become an officer and continue my career in the U.S. Army." Thus, after completing his four-year enlistment in the U.S. Army, Tom enrolled at BYU.

Tom's first semester at BYU was literally a disaster. His academic background was poor. He'd never learned how to study. No matter how hard he tried, a "C" seemed to be about the best grade he could attain. He claimed, "I could not even understand what was presented in some of my classes, no matter how much I studied." What was particularly disheartening to him was the apparent ease with which others in his classes seemed to grasp subject material he could not understand. He further noted how returned missionaries almost invariably did well in coursework, while carrying on an active and enjoyable social life. They also could stand before a class and, with apparent ease, make excellent presentations. Some even seemed to enjoy making presentations. In contrast, standing before a class and giving a verbal presentation filled Tom with dread. As a result, the idea slowly fomented in Tom's mind, "I too should go on a mission!" He wanted to become like the returned missionaries he had come to know and admire in his classes. He didn't know what it was, but he was impressed that serving a mission did something special for a person.

Tom approached the Bishop of his student "ward" or congregation and expressed his desire to serve as a missionary. The Bishop was acquainted with Tom's circumstances. He knew he was a convert to the Church, had been adopted, and that his foster parents did not share his religious beliefs. Furthermore, Tom's parents probably did not have the financial means to support him – even if they approved of him serving a mission. When Tom persisted in wanting to serve a mission, in exasperation the Bishop exclaimed, "Tom! Don't you realize it takes money to go on a mission? Where would you ever get that kind of money? You certainly couldn't ask your parents for it!" Tom's reply was, "How much does it take? I saved most of my money during the four years I was in the service. Is $3,000 enough?"

The Bishop could not believe what he heard. Thus, after essentially a disastrous year at BYU, Tom received a call to serve a two-year mission in the Hawaiian Islands. Prior to his departure for the mission field, his Bishop called him into his office. He laid his hands upon his head and, by the power of the priesthood, he blessed and promised Tom, "If you will diligently strive to fulfill an honorable mission, you will be able to study and learn." In other words, if Tom would do all in his power to be a good missionary, it would no longer be difficult for him to study and to learn - as it had been in the past.

Tom desperately tried to be a good missionary. But, similar to the year he spent at BYU; his first six months in Hawaii were a disaster. He was sick much of the time. Although he believed the gospel with all his heart, he had had relatively little experience in living it. And, he had difficulty trying to teach it to others. He also had had only a short association with the Church and knew little about Church organizations such as the Primary, Relief Society, and Welfare Programs. How was he to teach others about things he did not know? He was ready to quit and return home. Then, very, very slowly he found he was beginning to understand what the gospel and the Church are all about. In short, primarily through perseverance and steadfast determination, he became one of the more knowledgeable and productive missionaries in the Hawaiian Mission. Eventually, he even was called to serve as a counselor to the Mission President. Perhaps his most important calling was to work with those missionaries who were having difficulties similar to what he had experienced during the first part of his mission.

Tom completed a very successful two-year mission in Hawaii and returned to BYU to continue his education. The "rest of the story" already has been related as to how Tom came to Utah State University, was an outstanding student, completed a Ph.D. in record time, and then undertook a post-doctorate position in the ISGI program in Iran for two years. He since has attained the rank of full professor in the Department of Animal, Dairy and Veterinary Sciences at Utah State, as well as considerable acclaim as a scientist and teacher. Likewise, he continues to be a devout "Mormon" and has served many important callings in the Church.

I now have known and cherished Tom as a friend for many years. We have had many interesting and enjoyable experiences together. Most important, he has taught me, "The race is neither to the swift nor to the strong, but to those that endure to the end!" I trust I never forget Tom's example and this lesson.

CHAD, AFRICA

The character of a nation is determined by the morals of its people.

I firmly believe the well-being of a nation is dependent upon the morality of its people, which is primarily how they treat each other and the environment in which they live. This premise has resulted from visits to many countries and was most indelibly impressed upon my mind during my 1990-91 sojourn in Chad.

Twenty of the twenty-five poorest nations in the world are in Africa and Chad is among the poorest of the African nations. A 1988 study reported: "The mean annual per capita income in Chad is $89." This might indicate or cause one to think food and living costs would be relatively inexpensive in this country. The opposite is true. Even basic food commodities – when or if they can be found – are very expensive. Eggs, for example, commonly sell for about thirty cents each in Chad; as compared to less than a dollar per dozen in the United States. This is despite the fact that eggs sold in Chadian markets almost invariably are of poor quality and often rotten. Vegetables, such as potatoes, carrots and onions, likewise are expensive and often sell for more than a dollar per pound. Fresh milk, canned goods, many fruits or most food items common in much of the western world are virtually unobtainable. When one finds such items in Chad, they are unbelievably expensive. A can of corn, for example, may sell for as much as seven dollars. Generally, food costs about four times more in Chad than in the United States!

Rent, for what would be considered sub-marginal housing in Europe or the U.S., usually exceeds $1,000 per month in the capital city of N'Djamena. Utilities likewise are very expensive. Electricity for a moderate-sized house in N'Djamena usually costs in excess of $1,000 per month. This is despite the fact that the electricity normally goes off at least three or four times each day and power surges are frequent. It is not uncommon for appliances to be burnt up or ruined and even for light bulbs to explode, because of violent voltage surges. The general practice is to install a back-up generator, because of frequent and sometimes long-term power failures. Water service likewise is erratic and of poor quality. Many city residents install a pressure pump, so there is enough water pressure for them to take a shower or for other purposes. The water also is not potable, which means it must be boiled or chemically treated before it is safe to drink. Bottled gas costs approximately $40 for a small container, which is why most Chadians cook with wood or charcoal. Except for individual septic systems, there is virtually no sanitation throughout Chad. Garbage simply is dumped into the streets, where it is scavenged by people and animals such as dogs, sheep, goats and pigs.

The mean human life expectancy for people in Chad is one of the lowest in the world. The average for Chadian women is forty-three years, and only thirty-eight years for men. Early mortality, however, is offset by one of the highest birthrates in the world. The mean birthrate for Chad is between five and six percent per annum; whereas, three percent is considered high for developed nations. There are children everywhere. Many do not wear clothes until they are six years of age or older. Between 1964 (when Chad gained independence from France) and 1991 (when my family and I departed from that country) Chad had experienced only six years of peace or stability. Thus, because of frequent conflicts or wars, Chad has many orphans and begging children are a common sight. These typically have small bowls and make their rounds of the villages each morning and evening, seeking something to eat. Nevertheless, Chadian children generally are happy. Almost invariably when you meet them they smile, wave and greet you with "Ce va?' or "How are you?" The bolder ones also often insist upon shaking hands with the strangers they meet.

Conditions under which most Chadians live would appall most Westerners. Housing generally consists of mud huts, with thatch or tin roofs. Very few have amenities such as electricity or running water. Water generally is lifted, by hand, from an open well in the center of the village or, at best, pumped by hand from "tube wells", that usually have been installed by the Peace Corps or other foreign assistance programs. There are no newspapers or trains in Chad. Except for a miniscule and poorly run national airline and a handful of dilapidated taxis and mini-buses in N'Djamena and a few other towns, there is little semblance of an organized transportation system. Chadians typically travel either by walking or riding on top of over-loaded "lorries" or trucks that transport goods throughout the country. Roads often consist of little more than sets of tracks leading from one village to another. These usually are impassable during the three to four-month rainy season (between July and October). There are frequent barriers along arterial roads, which are manned by military personnel. These guards stop traffic whenever there are rainy or muddy conditions and they commonly extract "tribute" from all but military or government-authorized vehicles. It is impossible to travel throughout Chad without government authorization. Then, even with such authorization, payment of bribes often is "the rule of the game"! Most Chadian roads are so poorly maintained that it usually is easier and faster to drive in the borrow pits than on the road surface. Four-wheel drive vehicles are virtually a necessity outside of downtown N'Djamena. When traveling, it likewise is necessary to carry fuel, equipment and parts, as there are no service stations or garages except in the cities. In short, living conditions are poor and travel is difficult in Chad.

Agriculture is Chad's basic industry and its major export item is cotton, which is grown in the south. Historically, Chad's three major export items were: ivory from elephants, slaves, and cotton. Elephants essentially have been exterminated. The slave trade has been outlawed. And, the international cotton market is extremely volatile, as well as monopolized by the government. Apart from cotton and foreign aid, the major source of revenue for the Government of Chad is from import duties or taxes on goods brought into the country. Thus, there is a flourishing black market. Most goods sold in Chadian markets have been brought into the country illegally, primarily across the Logone and Chari Rivers that constitute the country's western border.

Cereal grains (i.e. millet, sorghum, corn and to some extent rice) are staple food items for most Chadians. Fair amounts of meat (i.e. beef, mutton, goat and chicken) and vegetables (i.e. cassava or manioc, sweet potatoes, peanuts, onions, okra, tomatoes, and so forth) also are eaten. The average Chadian seems to care little as to how food tastes. Their major concern is getting enough to eat. Rarely does one see a fat person in Chad!

"Boule" ("bowl"), a thick paste made from millet flour, is the traditional or most common Chadian dish. It is made by pounding millet in a large wooden bowl with a wooden post, until the grain is reduced to fine flour. The flour then is mixed with water, boiled and shaped in a gourd bowl. A sauce, which usually is made with meat, fresh or dried okra and perhaps some other vegetables, is served with the millet paste or "boule". These are eaten with the fingers. You take some of the paste with your fingers and dip it into the sauce, before putting it into your mouth. You quickly learn to "tongue" your food before chewing, because there frequently are particles of sand or bone in the paste or sauce!

Central Chad, which lies between the Sahara Desert to the north and the relatively lush and semi-tropical south, is known as the "Sahel". Sahel is an Arabic word that means "shore". And, the Sahel essentially forms a "shore" or transitional zone between the dry Sahara and the more verdant areas to the south. Historically, the Sahel served as the "bread basket" for much of Africa. Today, however, it produces relatively little food and is fraught with many problems. Paramount among these is drought. Then, even when there is sufficient rain to produce dry-land crops of millet and sorghum, crops frequently are lost to insects, birds, rodents and plant diseases. These include devastating hoards of locusts; huge flocks of highly mobile birds (i.e. the "weaver finches" and the sparrow-like "quela"); plagues of rats, mice and gerbils; and numerous rusts, wilts and viruses. All of these frequently debilitate or destroy food-producing plants. Furthermore, political instability and dishonesty also thwart food production and prosperity in Chad. There is little incentive for one to produce more than is needed by them and their family when the fruits of their labor are stolen or forcefully taken from them. Since the 1980's, the result has been that most of sub-Saharan Africa has steadily become poorer and poorer. This is despite the efforts and large sums of money being provided by foreign countries to bolster the economy of this region.

Agricultural practices in Chad are among the most primitive in the world. Chadians use virtually no machinery or modern agricultural implements. Not even horses or bullocks are used to cultivate croplands in the Sahel. Bullocks, however, are used to some extent in the south. Most farm work is done by hand. A simple, short-handled hoe is used to till, plant and cultivate both grain and vegetable crops. Harvesting and threshing likewise are done by hand. Improving agriculture production in Chad means having to change traditional practices that have been used for hundreds of years. Poor people truly have poor ways!

In addition to primitive agricultural practices and a lack of moral values among its people, other major problems confronting Chad include overgrazing by domestic livestock and deforestation. Although many nations and private organizations have undertaken numerous projects and provided millions of dollars in aid, relatively very little has been accomplished with respect to improving the quality of life for people in this country. This, I believe, is because most have addressed the symptoms, rather than the underlying causes for Chad's problems.

A senior-level U.S. AID official told me, "In all my years in Africa, I have not seen a single successful grazing or livestock project. Therefore, I will not even consider such projects in my program." Too many foreign aid projects are similar to "putting a band aid on a person's sore toe, while ignoring their broken leg"!

Almost anywhere one looks in Chad – in the towns, villages and the countryside alike – they will see domestic livestock. Included are sheep, goats, cattle, burros and horses, as well as good numbers of camels in the drier, northern portions of the country. Historically and up until a few decades back, nomads owned and grazed most of the livestock in Chad. These nomads followed the rains or seasonal fluctuations in vegetation growth. However, because of severe droughts and the loss of their herds, many nomads have settled in villages. Here, wells developed through foreign assistance projects provide a year-round source of water, which previously was not available for the watering of livestock in many areas. Thus, ever-increasing numbers of livestock have become associated with villages. When one flies over Chad and looks down upon the countryside, the villages appear to be expanding cancerous sores. They are devoid of vegetation and barren trails extend ever further from them into the surrounding countryside. Because of expanding desertification, caused by uncontrolled livestock grazing, deforestation, and poor agricultural practices, both the countryside and the outlook for Chad are becoming increasingly bleak.

Oil resources have been discovered both in southern Chad and in the Lake Chad area. These, however, will be difficult to develop – primarily because of corruption and political instability. While we were in Chad, all petroleum products were imported and, as a result, were relatively expensive. The price for gasoline and diesel, for example, was more than four dollars per gallon, as compared to it then being little more than a dollar in the United States. Because of the high cost of petroleum products, wood and to some extent charcoal are used for cooking. However, rather than use stoves or methods which make more efficient use of these fuels, the traditional cooking method was to use an open flame and to place a cooking pot on top of three rocks or hardened mounds of dirt. As a result, most of the heat is lost. The harvesting of trees and even shrubs for fuel wood continues unabated. Formerly forested woodlands are rapidly becoming deserts. Construction of roads, primarily with foreign aid, means Chadians can more readily cut their rapidly dwindling forest resources. Although there are some token efforts for reforestation, the small trees and shrubs – provided primarily through foreign assistance programs – usually are destroyed by grazing animals. If not, they almost invariably fall prey to the axes of those gathering fuel.

In addition to the devastating effects of overgrazing and deforestation, poor agricultural practices result in low crop production and further devastation of Chad's land resources. Dry land cultivated areas, including the "dunes" of the Sahel region, are cropped and laid bare to the sun and wind, which results in both wind and water erosion. "Wadi" or oases areas, which are irrigated by shallow wells, from which water is raised by hand by means of pole frames called "shadoos", often are ruined by saltification as a result of poor water management. More and more of what were productive lands are becoming desolate wastes.

Chad has the lowest human population density of all African nations. Because of this, it still has an abundance of natural resources and much land still suitable for crop production. If these land resources were properly developed and utilized, Chad could produce much more food than is needed by its populace. In short, it could become a major food exporter, rather than an importing nation.

Lake Chad is the fifth largest fresh-water lake in the world. Although it is relatively shallow and rarely exceeds nine feet in depth, the potential for agricultural production on the vast "recessional" lands surrounding this lake or those lands from which the lake resides during annual water level fluctuations is virtually untapped. Some agriculture production already occurs on these "recessional" lands, but much could be done to make them much more productive. Similarly, the waters from the Chari and Logone Rivers are relatively little used for irrigated crop production. Land and water resources are available, but Chad presently seems to be unable to put these resources together, let alone properly manage them.

Communications is another major problem in Chad. Although the country's official language is French, less than ten percent of its populace is fluent in French. And, less than twenty percent are literate. Reportedly, about forty percent of the Chadians speak Arabic and the remaining sixty percent speak about one-hundred tribal languages or dialects. The people also are sharply divided into different ethnic, tribal and religious groups, between which there is little trust. Chad does not represent a homogeneous nation. Instead, it is a conglomerate of different peoples and ideologies, loosely held together by a boundary circumscribed by France at the time of Chad's independence.

Foreign aid is a major source of revenue in Chad. The U.S. AID program paid approximately eighty percent of the salaries for the Chadian Government officials during 1989. Then, in December 1990, this government was overthrown by a revolution. Former government officials largely were replaced. But, the United States continued to pay the bulk of their salaries. While we were in Chad, the U.S. AID program spent approximately $100 million per year in this country.

This equates to about $20 for each man, woman and child in this country of about five and a half million people. This also represents almost twenty-two percent of the reported mean gross annual income of $89 per person in Chad! Furthermore, there are numerous other foreign government and private assistance programs in Chad. These include: UNDP, FAO, UNICEF, VITA, Food for the Hungary, World Vision, SECADEV, ORT, numerous religious or missionary organizations, and on and on. Many of these assistance programs also rely heavily upon donations or tax dollars from the U.S. Where or how will it end?

I recorded the following quotations from a magazine article, which I happened to encounter. Regretfully, I failed to record the source. None-the-less, I feel it is apropos to Chad, as well as to other nations.

"Any nation is recognized by the character of its people. The character of a people is determined by how they conduct their daily lives. That's true today, it was true in the past, and it will be true in the future.

Poverty is not necessarily a virtue. Poverty can have a negative spiritual effect on a person's life. It can be dangerous to their ethics and values. Poverty can become fertile ground in which cheating and thievery flourish. Physical want also causes fear for self and alienates a person from society.

The poverty problem is compounded when nearly everyone cheats. People may get caught in a greed syndrome, feeling the need to get ahead or simply to survive.

Those in poverty can convince themselves that the end (financial security) justifies the means (cheating). When one is down-and-out it's easy to blame someone else for one's condition and feel that others 'owe you'.

Traditions of corruption and bribery have been ingrained in many societies over hundreds of years. They are seen as an indispensable part of life.

This is especially true in developing countries where economic and political skullduggery seem almost necessary for a person's survival.

As stated by Agur in the Bible, '...give me neither poverty nor riches; feed me with food convenient for me: Lest I be full, and deny thee, and say, who is the Lord? Or lest I be poor, and steal, and take the name of God in vain.'"

It is easy to become frustrated and depressed when considering conditions in countries such as Chad. If people do not nor will not practice moral laws, such as those espoused in the Ten Commandments, they have little chance for progress – no matter how much aid may be extended to them. Rather than simply providing economic aid to developing nations, such as Chad, should we not also try to teach moral principles? Otherwise, economic aid will do little, if any, good and will not be of lasting value. I have long believed in the adage, "God helps those who help themselves!" Should we not do likewise?

LIFE IN CHAD AND A REVOLUTION

I've always been intrigued with visiting new places and living under different conditions. Chad, however, was more than I bargained for!

I had been a Supervisory Wildlife Biologist for the Caribou National Forest in Pocatello, Idaho for more than eight years. It seemed I was spending more and more time in the office and on paperwork than in the field or on what I considered to be meaningful projects. More and more of my time and efforts were being spent in the writing of Environmental Assessments (EA's) or Environmental Impact Statements (EIS's) and management plans. The U.S. Forest Service seemed to be doing more and more planning, but never fully implementing these plans. In short, although I was happy to be living with my family on our farm in the Rockland Valley, I was becoming more and more frustrated. I wanted to be involved in more meaningful endeavors. If possible, I wanted to at least try to improve our world, before "hanging up my spurs" as a professional Wildlife Biologist.

I thought, "Maybe I could do more to help improve the world through another overseas assignment." Thus, I began to submit applications to various agencies or organizations that I thought might provide a meaningful overseas assignment for a biologist.

I tentatively was offered a number of foreign assignments. Most, however, appeared to be little more than "paperwork" positions. I was particularly interested in a ten-month lectureship position in Wildlife Ecology at the Tribhuvan University in Kathmandu, Nepal. This was under the auspices of the Fulbright Program, under which I had served in Ecuador. I wanted this position and felt it would afford meaningful opportunities for my family and me. We completed the required physical examinations and began to make preparations to travel to Nepal. However, virtually at the last minute and despite my having made prior arrangements for a leave of absence from the Forest Service, my Supervisory Staff Officer informed me, "We will not retain your position on the Caribou Forest for such an extended period of time. Although you will have a position with the Forest Service upon your return, it will NOT be on the Caribou National Forest!" We had recently built a new home on the family farm and I felt we could not financially afford to live elsewhere upon our return. Thus, I informed the Fulbright Commission, "Regretfully, I cannot accept the university lectureship position in Nepal."

The Denver Wildlife Research Center (DWRC) of the Animal and Plant Health Inspection Service of the U.S. Department of Agriculture eventually contacted me. They needed a biologist with overseas experience to conduct rodent research in Chad, Africa. I studied "The Ecology of the Lesser Bandicoot Rat in Calcutta" for my doctorate. My thesis was published in book form by the Rockefeller Foundation and the Bombay Natural History Society. Some DWRC biologists even had used my thesis as a basic reference for their rodent studies. This was why they thought I'd be a suitable candidate for the proposed research project in Chad. Fluency in French was a qualification for this position. I did not speak French, but was fluent in Spanish. The Chadian Project Assistant was fluent in English, as well as French. Therefore, my not knowing French did not appear to be a major problem. Thus, I began a long series of telephone conversations with Dr. Richard L. Bruggers, Chief of International Research Services with the DWRC, regarding my appointment as Project Leader for the Chad Rodent Control Research Project.

I was told, "The DWRC plans to fill the research biologist position in Chad during the early fall of 1989." However, because of "red tape" and the many requirements imposed upon an accepted candidate by "the people in Washington", the date for filling the position was repeatedly delayed. I and family members accompanying me to Africa each had to undergo thorough physical examinations, fill out numerous forms, and receive almost innumerable immunizations to protect us against diseases we might encounter in Africa. We also had to undergo extended security investigations, in order for us to be issued diplomatic passports. It appeared much time, effort and money was unnecessarily spent to determine our loyalty to the United States Government, even though we were going to a third-world country most Americans have never heard about and where I would study rodents.

We frantically tried to complete all we were requested to do, so we could travel to Chad in early January of 1990. Delayed security clearances and an apparent lack of communication between Denver and Washington, as well as between Washington offices, repeatedly delayed our departure. Finally, I was informed, "You and your family should depart for Chad no later than the first part of April." I informed the Forest Service of my pending departure. My associates on the Caribou Forest hosted a farewell luncheon for my wife and me. Speeches were made and gifts presented, but our departure again was delayed until early June. I think the Forest Service wondered if it would ever get rid of me. Finally, I was requested to travel to Denver in June, to receive a week's orientation at the DWRC. I then returned to Idaho, collected my family and we traveled to Washington, D.C. and received additional orientation and briefings, prior to traveling to N'Djamena, Chad via Paris, France.

Despite what we had read and heard about conditions in Chad, our arrival in N'Djamena early in the morning of July 3, 1990 was a shock. There was no one to meet us and no one at the airport spoke English. Our limited French was of no value as we were processed through various lines. Finally, it was indicated we could exit the air terminal. There was no place to exchange American dollars for local currency and the men who insisted upon carrying our luggage were upset when I tried to pay them in U.S. currency.

We loaded our luggage and ourselves into a ramshackle, yellow taxi. The vehicle did not appear to be in good enough shape to get us out of the parking lot, let alone take us anywhere. Nevertheless, we shortly were delivered to the "Novatel", where the desk clerk informed us "This is the ONLY good hotel in Chad!" The clerk also changed some money for me and I paid the taxi driver. Although I gave him the equivalent of $20 for an approximately eight-block ride, he was upset because I did not give him a tip. We asked for two hotel rooms, one for our daughter Sheri and our son Jay, and another for Carol and me. I then inquired what the rooms would cost and was told it would be in excess of $150 a day per room! This was despite the fact the "Novatel" would not even be comparable to a "Motel 6" in the U.S.! Never-the-less, we were so exhausted from almost ten days of travel that we simply followed the porter to our rooms and crawled into our beds for some much needed rest.

We arose about noon and went to the hotel dining room for lunch. When we converted the Chadian Franc or "CFA" prices on the menu into dollars, we could not believe it. A lunch, which would cost less than $5 in the U.S., was almost $40! Even a small serving of ice cream was almost $5. We later learned the "Novatel" was one of the few places in Chad that served ice cream. The only store which sold ice cream in N'Djamena sold it for $20 per liter!

The desk clerk at the hotel helped me contact the U.S. AID office. I eventually was connected with Namde, the assistant to Kurt Fuller, the AID Agricultural Development Officer under whom I would conduct my rodent research. Namde informed me, "Fuller is on home leave in the States. He should return to Chad in a few weeks." I had been informed both in Denver and in Washington, D.C., "As soon as you arrive in Chad, Kurt Fuller will meet you and get you started on the project." When I asked Namde about housing for my family and me, as well as, "What should I do until Fuller returns?" his reply was, "I don't know."

Namde arrived at the "Novatel" several hours later. He informed me arrangements had been made for us to temporarily occupy an apartment in the AID compound, until we could locate a permanent residence. We previously had been told, "A house will be provided for you in the AID compound upon your arrival." Further, "There's a good chance your house will have a swimming pool." The swimming pool had been the enticement we had used to convince Sheri and Jay they should accompany us to Chad!

An AID driver and vehicle transported our luggage and us from the "Novatel" to a fourth-story apartment in the AID compound the following morning. The apartment, which was located above the American School, was a mess and it took almost two days of scrubbing and mopping for us to clean and make it livable. We also had been told, "Upon your arrival in Chad, you will be provided a 'Welcome Kit', which will contain basic household items and enough food to tide you over – until you receive your air freight shipment from the States and become oriented to shopping in local markets." A few items were provided with the apartment, but they were not adequate for setting up housekeeping. Neither were we provided any food or instructions as to where and how we might make purchases in the local markets.

We were frustrated and dismayed. Fortunately, Paul and Betty Morris learned about our plight and came to our aid. Paul was an agricultural economist with AID and Betty a secretary. They were "Mormons" and perhaps the only members of The Church of Jesus Christ of Latter-day Saints then residing in Chad. They quickly assessed our situation and brought us an ample supply of basic household items and food. They also took us to the local markets and showed us where and how to shop in N'Djamena. They even provided games we could play as a family to help pass the long evening hours and perhaps somewhat overcome our culture shock. Without their help we would have been completely lost and overwhelmed.

We shipped two-hundred and fifty pounds of basic household effects and food by airfreight to Chad several weeks prior to our departure from the States. It did not arrive until several weeks after we did. We also shipped almost two-thousand pounds of food and other commodities by sea freight, as we had been informed these were either very expensive or not available in Chad. It took almost four months for this shipment to arrive. Despite my having traveled extensively throughout much of the world and having lived for more than ten years in foreign countries, I had never encountered such formidable language and cultural barriers.

The day following our arrival was the 4th of July. Paul and Betty Morris hosted us at the "holiday picnic" and celebration held at the American Embassy in N'Djamena. Thus, we met many of the approximately two-hundred and forty Americans then in Chad. Most were friendly and warmly welcomed us. It seemed visiting and private socials were major pastimes for most Americans in N'Djamena.

Shortly after we moved into the fourth-story apartment in the AID compound, we were informed, "You'll have to move out within two weeks. One of the new teachers for the American School will soon arrive and will need the apartment." Kurt Fuller still had not returned from "home leave". And, we were told, "He will have to make your housing arrangements." What were we to do? Again, Paul and Betty came to our rescue. They invited us to "house sit" or live in their house (one of the nicest in N'Djamena), while they returned to the U.S. for two months on "home leave" and for training. It was almost too good to be true. We moved into the Morris' completely furnished house and our airfreight shipment arrived just prior to their departure. Thus, we at least had nice quarters and would be able to eat for a few weeks. Hopefully, this also would provide sufficient time for Kurt Fuller to return and for him to make housing arrangements for us before Paul and Betty's return. However, virtually every promise made to us about Chad had failed to materialize. It appeared that the accomplishment of almost anything in Chad was extremely difficult.

Dr. John Wilson of Australia established the protocol for the rodent research I was to conduct during October of 1989. It was to be conducted in the "wadis" or oases and on "dune" or dry land agricultural sites in the N'Gouri area of the Sahel. Yacoub, a Chadian fluent in English and who was acquainted with people and programs both in U.S. AID and the Chadian Ministry of Agriculture, was to serve as the Project Assistant. However, prior to my arrival, AID sent Yacoub to the States to undertake an M.S. program at Michigan State University. He was replaced by Mornan, who had a doctorate in Botany from a French university. He had taught in Tunisia for two years, prior to undertaking a post-doctorate crop research project in Columbia. During his two and one-half years in South America, he married a Columbian woman and they had a baby daughter. However, both his wife and daughter remained in Columbia, while he returned to Chad to accept the Project Assistant position. Although born and reared in southern Chad, Mornan was not acquainted with the Sahel or with Arabic or other native dialects spoken in northern Chad. Furthermore, he did not speak English nor was he acquainted with U.S. AID or Chadian Ministry of Agriculture personnel and programs!

AID personnel assumed Mornan and I could communicate in Spanish. However, Mornan was not overly fluent in Spanish and I had not used Spanish extensively for several years. I would explain to

Mornan - in Spanish - what needed to be done with regard to our research program. He then would attempt to explain to our Chadian Ministry of Agriculture counterparts – in French - what I had said. They then would relay - in Arabic - our communications to villagers or others with whom we worked. It was confusing and sometimes chaotic. To further complicate the situation, Mornan was desperately trying to get his wife and daughter to come to Chad. His mind, efforts and much of his time were devoted to this cause. It often was difficult to get him to listen or to do what was needed with respect to our project. Sometimes he even stubbornly refused to do what I told him to do. As a result, I repeatedly warned him and eventually fired him. Still, his dismissal surprised him. He was certain I could not do without his services as an interpreter. I likewise was surprised to shortly learn we could accomplish much more without Mornan than we could with him. I also found I had much better rapport with my Chadian counterparts than I'd ever had with Mornan acting as my "go-between".

I spent my first few weeks in Chad getting acquainted with the complicated operating procedures required by AID, putting our project files in order and attempting to locate and organize a project office and laboratory, rather than merely working at a table in Kurt Fuller's office. I also attempted to meet and become acquainted with AID, U.S. Embassy, and Chadian Ministry of Agriculture personnel, as well as with people in other projects or programs that might be associated with or be of service to our project. No matter where I turned, it seemed I was confronted with formidable barriers with respect to our achieving our project goals.

Prior to his departure for the U.S., Paul Morris said I could use two rooms he had rented and was not using for an office and laboratory. These were adjacent to the AID office complex and well suited our needs. However, immediately following Paul's departure and after we had moved our files, equipment and furnishings into these rooms, an AID official informed me, "You'll have to move out!" This was despite the fact these rooms then remained vacant throughout our stay in Chad. Prior to my arrival and as a part of the cooperative agreement between the DWRC, AID and the Chadian Ministry of Agriculture, the Ministry had agreed to provide office and laboratory facilities for our project. However, upon my arrival in Chad, the Ministry insisted the project should completely renovate a dilapidated building adjacent to the Ministry's office complex; thereby, providing office and laboratory space both for the rodent project and for other projects. We eventually did this. But, while we renovated the building, AID refused to let us even use unoccupied space under its jurisdiction.

About a week after our arrival in Chad, my son Jay, Mornan, and my Chadian Ministry of Agriculture counterparts accompanied me on my first field trip to the N'Gouri area, which is about two-hundred and thirty kilometers northeast of N'Djamena. I was suffering with a severe case of diarrhea. The weather was extremely hot. Daytime temperatures frequently exceeded one hundred and twenty degrees Fahrenheit and nighttime temperatures rarely dropped below ninety degrees. To make life even more miserable, swarms of flies continually pestered us during the daytime. At night, hoards of mosquitoes replaced the flies and virtually ate you alive! Even a mosquito net did not fully protect us from their vicious attacks. I found it virtually impossible to sleep during either the day or night. As a result, I felt like I was ready to "cash it in"!

There were no roads to many of our "wadi" and "dune" study sites. We simply drove cross-country, through the sand, while dodging scattered shrubs and acacia trees. Although we had a four-wheel-drive vehicle, we occasionally became stuck. We then had to "dig out". This meant digging the sand away from the wheels and axles, "jacking-up" our vehicle, and then placing strips of metal airplane landing mat beneath the wheels of our vehicle then we hoped the mats would provide sufficient traction to get the vehicle moving again. We always would be sweaty, dirty and tired when we returned from the field to the mud huts in the compound where we resided in N'Gouri. I could not believe, "This is going to be my life for the next two years?"

I'd always considered myself to be an outdoorsman. Throughout my life I've enjoyed being in the out-of-doors, camping and doing fieldwork. However, fieldwork in Chad was different. Tolerating the heat, the insect pests, the lack of decent food, and the primitive living and working conditions during the ten to twelve days spent in the field each month was extremely difficult. In short, I often simply tried to survive!

Prior to our arrival in Chad, the rodent project rented two mud huts within a mud-walled compound on the edge of the village of N'Gouri. Staying in N'Gouri meant trying to tolerate the continuous noises of village life, i.e. the cries and shouting of children and people, the barking of dogs, the braying of donkeys, the crowing of roosters, and the sounds of drums and dancing virtually all night, every night! Village life also meant unbelievably filthy conditions. Refuse simply is dumped into the streets. Although most villagers use pit latrines, these usually are open and, like the refuse heaps in the streets, provide breeding areas for hordes of flies. These pesky beasts, however, disappear with the darkness of night. The flies then are replaced with swarms of mosquitoes. Repellants seemed to deter these pests for only a few minutes. Mosquito nets likewise did not fully protect you from their vicious onslaught. In an attempt to get some sleep, I would crawl under a mosquito net; liberally spray myself and the mosquito net with insecticide. I then would hope the "biting fiends" would leave me alone long enough for me to fall asleep. These procedures were frequently repeated throughout the night. I wanted to "camp out in the bush", but was told, "Camping in the bush is too dangerous. There are too many 'rebels' and thieves out there."

Our monthly visits to N'Gouri would have been almost intolerable for me if it had not been for David and Dawn Purkey. David was a young American hydrologist who worked for the Office for Rehabilitation through Training (ORT). He and his wife had met and married while they were Peace Corps volunteers in Africa. They later joined ORT and lived in an ORT compound a short distance from the village of N'Gouri. After trying to communicate all day with Mornan in Spanish or with my Chadian counterparts in my limited French, it was great to communicate in English with the Purkeys in the evenings. They also had running water and a kerosene refrigerator. It's truly amazing how good a cold glass of water tastes after a long, hot day in the Sahel. Likewise, being able to take a shower and rid oneself of the sweat and grime accumulated during a day in the desert is truly a blessing!

A typical day in the field at N'Gouri consisted of arising from a camp cot at daylight or shortly after 5:00 a.m. Then, with a small, one-burner camp stove, boiling water for breakfast. For me, this consisted of a cup of instant oatmeal and a cup of cocoa mix. The others usually had coffee and bread. By 6:00 a.m., we'd head for the field. Here, we would retrieve the rodent traps we'd set the previous evening and record data resulting from our trapping efforts. Recorded data included: The number of traps set off, lost or left untouched; and the species, sex, age, weight and body measurements for rodents captured. Study skins and skulls for museum specimens also were prepared.

We usually returned from the field to N'Gouri between 12:30 and 1:30 p.m. We'd then eat lunch and rest for an hour or two before returning to the field to set traps until about 6:00 p.m. We'd then return to N'Gouri and eat a "boule" or millet-paste supper, which was prepared by one of the wives of the man from whom we rented the compound. I then would usually visit David and Dawn Purkey.

Prior to each field trip I had to spend about three days completing the paperwork and obtaining the numerous signatures required by AID for all travel outside N'Djamena. I also had to assemble our camping gear, fuel, food, water and whatever else we might need while in the field. Likewise, upon our return to N'Djamena, it usually took almost three days to prepare and submit the required reports and to analyze the data we had collected.

Trapping results in the N'Gouri area were discouraging. We did well to catch twenty rodents with more than three-thousand "trap nights" or the overnight setting of three-thousand traps. In contrast, while studying rats in "godowns" or grain storage warehouses in Calcutta, India, I often caught almost one rat for every trap set. There is little suitable rodent habitat during much of the year in the "dune" areas of the Sahel. The green vegetation, which occurs primarily after the rainy season, is quickly grazed-off or devastated by livestock. Following crop harvest, the cultivated "wadi" or oasis areas likewise are left barren. Nevertheless, remnant rodent populations persist. And, when environmental conditions are right, rodent numbers sometimes virtually explode in a very short time.

Cultivated "wadi" or oasis areas in the Sahel are small and widely scattered. Many have less than ten acres of cultivated crops, which are watered by hand from shallow (ten to fifteen-foot-deep) wells. Typically, a pole frame or "shadoo" is erected above a shallow, hand-dug well. A pole with a counter-weight of mud on one end and a woven rope basket or water container on the other is placed across the pole frame. A farmer laboriously lowers the water container into the well and raises water in it to water his crops. It is about all a man can do to irrigate two acres of crops in this manner.

I soon learned there were only about five hundred "wadis" in the N'Gouri area. Furthermore, perhaps only half of these were being cultivated. This was primarily because of saltification resulting from poor water management. Thus, I surmised there probably were less than twenty-five-hundred acres of "wadi" cultivation in the entire N'Gouri area. Even if – through our research – we could predict when rodent eruptions would occur and then effectively control them, this would not significantly increase crop production for Chad. Essentially, even before I got a good start on rodent research in Chad, I was ready to quit. It wasn't worth the expenditures of time, effort and money!

I wrote a letter to Rick Bruegers in the DWRC about how I thought we were wasting time and money studying rodents in the N'Gouri area. However, before sending it, I showed it to Kurt Fuller and he convinced me I should not quit the project. He claimed there were other "meaningful" study sites in the Sahel – areas that had the potential for significant crop production. He suggested I look at "recessional cultivations" in the Karal area immediately south of Lake Chad. "Recessional agriculture" is the planting of crops on lands from which the waters of Lake Chad recede during the dry season. Thus, in early August we spent a week in the Karal area selecting additional rodent study sites. As Fuller had claimed, it appeared there was a great potential for crop production in this area. A paved road also was being built from N'Djamena almost to Karal. This road would provide the means whereby agriculture produce could be transported to market. Thus, I agreed to continue with the rodent research project.

We enlisted the assistance of SECADEV, an agricultural assistance program sponsored by the Catholic Church that had been working in the Karal area for a number of years. SECADEV even provided a compound we could occupy while working in the Karal area, and a mud building in which we could store equipment, i.e. rodent traps. Conditions in Karal, however, were even more primitive than in N'Gouri. We did not have a chair or even a bench upon which to sit or a table upon which we could work or eat our meals. Water for bathing and washing dishes was obtained by hand, with a bucket, from a deep, open well in the center of the village.

Most of my time in N'Djamena was spent preparing the unbelievable amount of paperwork required by AID, trying to complete the renovation of the old Chadian Ministry of Agriculture building – so we would have a project office and laboratory, and trying to obtain suitable housing for my family and me. Tasks that one could readily or quickly accomplish in the States often would take days or weeks and much effort in Chad. For example, although I readily found and purchased a battery for a UPS or backup power system for a computer, it took several days to find suitable cables and clamps to connect the battery. Similarly, between completing the required AID paperwork, obtaining the required number of bids, and then ordering and getting tires shipped to Chad for our project vehicle, it took more than six months to obtain a set of tires. In the meantime, because a Ministry driver drove our vehicle through a thorn fence and embedded the vehicle's tires with literally hundreds of thorns, we averaged two or three flats each field trip. Furthermore, we had to repair these flats with hand tools, because there were no service stations or garages outside of N'Djamena. It seemed I was confronted with at least one major crisis each day. It was difficult not to become discouraged and to think, "It's not worth it!" or, "Why even try!"

It took more than two months of concentrated effort to find and renovate a house for my family and me. Through frantic efforts, we moved into "our" house the day before Paul and Betty Morris returned to Chad. Renovating the Ministry building for a project office and laboratory took more than four months. We then scrounged furniture and equipment from previous projects and, thereafter, tried to be more effective in our research efforts.

Very slowly and with much effort somewhat a semblance of order began to evolve in our lives. We began to do more than simply exist. We became acquainted and began to associate with a fair number of Americans living in N'Djamena. Particularly Sheri and Jay established friendships. They played on volleyball and softball teams, went swimming, attended parties, and participated in numerous activities. Jay, however, returned to the States in mid-August. He was determined to play high school football. Sheri remained in Chad. She planned to complete her senior year of high school by taking correspondence courses through Utah State University.

We typically arose each morning before 6:00 a.m. I then would rush to take a shower. The gardener came at 6:30 and, when he turned the water on in the yard, there was no water in the house. Following breakfast, I'd drive Carol to the American School, where she worked as a secretary. I'd then arrive at work by 7:30. Sheri would get up somewhat later and, after breakfast, spend the morning working on here correspondence courses. At noon, she would walk to the American School, where she attended a class in French. After that, she'd usually spend the afternoon and evening with friends. I would return home at noon and eat lunch alone, before returning to work. Carol would return home in the mid-afternoon and I would return from work about 5:00 p.m. We usually spent our evenings reading or playing games. Occasionally, however, we would attend activities at the Embassy or AERAN Club, or visit with other Americans. Sometimes we even forgot about the frustrations associated with living and working in Chad. Our schedule, however, changed when I periodically went into the field.

An upsetting aspect associated with living in Chad was the unreliability of mail service. As Government employees, we were permitted to use the State Department's "pouch" service. Although our mail supposedly was sent directly from Washington, D.C. to the U.S. Embassy in N'Djamena, delivery often took six weeks or longer

– each way! Further, we had no assurance our mail would ever reach its destination. This made it extremely difficult to make mortgage payments or to conduct business transactions. For example, I received my bank statement for August in November, but did not receive my July statement until December. To further complicate matters, the State Department kept changing the "pouch" address for N'Djamena. Our official address changed five times during a six-month period!

We held church services each Sunday with Paul and Betty Morris, either in their home or ours. Following services, we would eat lunch together and visit. Sunday was the most welcomed day of the week. In addition to reading a good number of books and magazines, I began to read the scriptures daily. I also began to systematically compile experiences I have had during my life into book form. My primary purpose for doing this was to benefit members of my family.

I began to feel we were getting things somewhat under control and slowly accomplishing some meaningful goals. We also were looking forward to returning home for a couple of weeks of "R&R" (Rest and Recuperation) during the Holiday Season. However, "things" back home did not seem to be going too well. Jay lost his luggage while traveling back to the States. About three weeks after his departure, UTA Airlines asked me to come to the N'Djamena Airport to identify one of his bags. Although it was tagged for the "Final Destination" of Salt Lake City, It had been returned from Paris. Much of the bag's contents were missing and Jay ended up having to buy all new school clothes, new football shoes, and replacing other lost items. He then injured his knee playing football and had to have two operations. It took almost a dozen telephone calls – at a cost of more than $1,000 – for me to provide State-side medical personnel the parental consent they claimed was needed before they could perform the surgeries on Jay's knee. Each phone call from N'Djamena to the States cost a minimum of $30 for the first three minutes and $7.50 per minute thereafter. The septic system for our house in Rockland somehow became plugged and flooded the basement. The pump in our well, which services both our house and apple orchard, also burned out and had to be replaced. This cost us $3,500. Our "Chadian adventure" was fast becoming a financial disaster!

About a year prior to our arrival in N'Djamena, Chadian military forces had soundly defeated an invading Libyan army in northern Chad. The United States had provided assistance to the Chadian military and the American Ambassador had recommended the use of recoilless rifles and other large guns mounted on four-wheel drive Toyota pickups. As a result, these vehicles readily out-maneuvered the Libyan tanks, weapons carriers and large trucks. Thus, the Chadians soundly trounced a much larger and superior Libyan force. They also captured large amounts of equipment and supplies, as well as hundreds of Libyan soldiers. We eventually were informed the CIA attempted to indoctrinate or "train" about seven hundred of these Libyan prisoners at a camp in N'Djamena that was near where we lived. The CIA's objective was to prepare these prisoners to fight against their homeland and their former commander, Colonel Quadafi. In apparent retaliation for the United States' role and support of Chad in this conflict, a commercial UTA flight between N'Djamena and Paris was bombed by terrorists in September 1989. Everyone onboard was killed, including the U.S. Ambassador's wife, Peace Corps volunteers returning home after surviving two years in Chad, and some CIA agents. The culprits have never been brought to trial!

Frequent fighting along the Sudanese border seemed to be of little concern in N'Djamena. Periodic reports of skirmishes between "rebel" and Chadian government troops along the Sudanese border, likewise, did little to excite either the Chadians or U.S. Embassy personnel in N'Djamena. These skirmishes were more than four hundred miles or more than a two-day journey away on virtually impassable roads. Besides, fighting had become an accepted way of life in Chad since it received its independence from France in 1964. However, fighting by rebels in eastern Chad appeared to start in earnest on November 6, 1990. The rebels reportedly were under the command of Idriss Deby, the former Minister of Defense for President Hussain Habre. President Habre previously had accused Minister Deby of being involved in an attempted coup or overthrow of his government in 1989. Deby then fled to the Sudan and assembled an army of dissidents and Chadian Army deserters. Then, in November 1990, he and his army entered Chad and took a number of villages north of the city of Abeche.

The frequent night-time landings of aircraft at the N'Djamena Airport - a short distance from where we lived - were the first indication there was accelerated fighting on the Sudanese border. As I traveled to and from work and to the AID office, I observed increasing numbers of women assembled near the gates of the military compound and hospital located across from the central plaza – between the American School and the AID office building. It was rumored President Habre's forces had suffered two major defeats and the rebels controlled much of the Abeche area. Furthermore, two divisions of Habre's troops had deserted to the rebel forces. Still, no one seemed to know for certain just what was happening.

President Habre left N'Djamena reportedly, "to go to the front to bolster his troops". It shortly was reported that Habre had been killed by the rebels. However, he then made a public appearance in N'Djamena. It later was explained, "President Habre and his troops unexpectedly encountered a large force of rebels and were surrounded by them. Because they had good radio communications, a light plane managed to extract Habre from the ambush." And, "Many of Habre's loyal troops sacrificed their lives to save him."

Richard Bogosian, the American Ambassador, scheduled a briefing for State Department, AID direct-hires, and the "first class" American citizens in Chad on Friday, November 23. The remainder of us Americans were placated with, "You will be briefed in a couple of days." Finally, we were informed, "A briefing for ALL Americans in Chad will be held in the American Embassy compound at 5:00 p.m. on Friday, November 30, 1990. Everyone will be brought up-to-date as to what is happening in the Chadian conflict." In the meantime, it had been reported that the city of Abeche had fallen to the rebel forces and the Chadian Army had suffered additional setbacks. Additional numbers of women in front of the military compound and hospital likewise indicated heavy casualties.

More than a hundred of the approximately two hundred and forty Americans in Chad met in the AERAN Club in the American

Embassy compound at the appointed time. Ambassador Bogosian first presented Mark Caldwell, the U.S. State Department's Security Officer in Chad and one of our neighbors. He and his family lived in a house just through the block in front of our house. Mr. Caldwell briefed us as to the security situation for Americans in Chad. He essentially stated, "Although you should use caution, there presently is no reason for undue concern." Ambassador Bogosian then presented Colonel Foulds, the U.S. Military Attache in Chad. Colonel Foulds appraised us about the military situation between the Chadian government and the rebel forces. He presented a rather optimistic picture with regard to President Habre. Similar to Mr. Caldwell, he assured us, "There is nothing to worry about!"

Ambassador Bogosian then took the podium. He spoke at length as to his appraisal of the Chadian military situation. He then claimed, "Although President Habre's forces have been defeated by the rebels in three major battles, President Habre still is in control." And, "The American Government will continue to support him." In fact, the Chadian Army had not won a single engagement with the rebels! The French, who had large numbers of military personnel in Chad, had stated they were neutral with respect to the present conflict. Ambassador Bogosian said, "That is their choice." But, "The French are closely monitoring the conflict and are in almost constant communication with the American Embassy. We know about any changes in the current situation almost as soon as they occur." As to Abeche and the surrounding villages, which reportedly had fallen to the rebels, the Ambassador explained, "Many such towns are not strategic. They often may be taken by one side or the other without even a shot being fired." As to the defection of Chadian troops to the rebel forces, the Ambassador claimed, "These were almost entirely troops from southern Chad who feel the conflict is between Habre and Deby, both of whom are from ethnic groups in the north. They feel the war is a 'northern' conflict. And, they don't feel they should be involved." Ambassador Bogosian concluded with, "I feel certain – no matter what happens – there will be no fighting or shooting in N'Djamena, such as occurred during the 1987 revolution when Habre took over. Habre would not let this happen again!" When the Ambassador was asked to comment about the French authorities encouraging the evacuation of French dependents, Bogosian said he thought this was merely a financial ploy. Voluntary evacuations are at the expense of the evacuees, rather than their government. He further claimed, "In my communications with the French, they have demonstrated no undue concern regarding the present conflict. Neither do they indicate a possible peril to inhabitants in N'Djamena."

There were additional questions and discussion. Ambassador Bogosian, however, again assured everyone, "Everything is going to be fine in N'Djamena. Although, of course, I cannot guarantee it, I feel certain there will not be shooting in N'Djamena. After all, Abeche is six hundred and fifty kilometers away. It would take several days for the rebel forces to travel to N'Djamena from there – even if they had the vehicles, supplies and fuel to do so! However, if some Americans still are concerned about their safety, arrangements have been made whereby space on commercial airlines is reserved for their voluntary evacuation during the coming week."

Carol, Sheri and I returned home from the Ambassador's briefing. Carol insisted, "I don't like what I heard the Ambassador say!" A couple of days earlier she had seen soldiers storing food, medical supplies and even guns in a storeroom at the American School. As a result, she had started to pack – "In case there is an evacuation." She now began to pack in earnest for what she felt was our imminent evacuation. Although I too thought there would be an evacuation, I felt we probably had a day or two in which to prepare for it.

I had seen hundreds of evacuees from the Abeche area getting off from trucks on the outskirts of N'Djamena when we were going on our last field trip. We also had encountered large numbers of government troops, both to the north and south of N'Djamena, during recent excursions. There was evidence something big was going to happen, but we didn't fully recognize nor think it would happen quickly.

Following the Ambassador's briefing and while Carol packed her suitcases, I worked late into the night sorting through my papers and files. I tried to decide which papers I needed to take with me – should we be evacuated – and which I could leave behind. It was a perplexing situation.

It was about 3:30 a.m. on Saturday, December 1, when we were awakened by our two-way radio. The Security Office of the U.S. Embassy provided two-way radios to most American personnel in N'Djamena for use in case of emergencies. We had a radio check at 7:00 a.m. each Tuesday morning and each of us communicated with a code name. Loud and clear, we heard the words, "All Call! All Call! There is widespread shooting and looting activity in N'Djamena! Please report if there is any such activity in your area!"

We then realized there was considerable activity on the streets outside of our house, which was surrounded by seven-foot-high walls, topped with barbed wire. Normally, there was no nighttime traffic on the streets adjoining the walls on three sides of our compound. Now, however, we could hear the sounds of what appeared to be many people using them. Although our house was shielded from the streets by the surrounding walls and by closed metal shutters on most of the windows, we did not dare to turn on any lights. We feared lights might attract the attention of whoever was in the streets and possibly entice them to try to enter. All we could do was wait to see what would transpire.

We heard sporadic gunfire some distance away. Then, there was shooting nearby. We moved into our centrally-located living room and laid on the floor next to the davenport and over-stuffed chairs. As we huddled together on the floor, we tensely listened and waited to see what would happen next. In addition to activities on the streets outside our house, there were almost constant reports on the radio about shooting, looting, and movements of soldiers, vehicles and looters in sections of N'Djamena occupied by Americans. Those talking on the radio did so with their code or "call sign". We could not read our code list in the dark. Thus, we tried to identify callers by their voices and, thereby, know where the reported activities were occurring. It appeared much of the shooting and looting was taking place in the area where we lived! Then, there were bursts of gunfire immediately outside of our compound! It was mostly small arms fire and I could hear bullets hitting the roof and walls of our house! I said nothing to Carol and Sheri. I did not want to add to their fears.

If we had not been so concerned with our own situation, some of the communications on the two-way radio would have been amusing. For example, one man stated, "There are a dozen soldiers here! They're pointing guns at me and they want my car! What should I do?" The immediate reply was, "Give it to them!" Another man shrieked, "A missile or projectile of some kind has hit my house. It's cut off electricity and broke a water line. Water is running everywhere! What should I do?" The answer was, "Take cover! It doesn't look like you can do anything!"

There was enough light by about 6:00 a.m. to enable us to see inside our house. I again began to sort and then pack what I considered to be essential records and business papers. I was certain we soon were going to have to evacuate our house. While packing my papers, I pondered, "How much food and water should we try to take?" I thought, "It probably would be next to impossible to drive the length of N'Djamena, traverse the narrow bridge across the Chari River, and make it to Camaroon. Perhaps our best bet would be to try to make a dash to the AID compound. We could join the approximately half dozen families living there and, together, determine the best course of action."

Our night guard banged on the door at about 6:30 a.m. He wanted me to call the embassy on the radio and find out why the day guard had not come to relieve him. I tried to explain in my limited French, "I don't think the day guard will be coming. You should stay on duty!" I then accompanied him to the front gate and partially opened it. I could not believe what I saw in the streets in front of our house. Although we were several blocks from any major thoroughfares, there was a melee of people running everywhere. Many were carrying furniture or other pilfered goods on their heads or backs. Surprisingly, most were smiling and some were laughing. They apparently were happy to have an "opportunity" to loot. A dozen people or more were streaming out of a gate from a house just down the street. Based upon what they were carrying, they must have completely "sacked" the place. I quickly closed the gate and told the guard, "Keep the gate closed! Don't let ANYONE in!" And, "You stay inside – no matter what happens!" I hoped the milling mob would not try to loot our place. If they did, what would we do? We had nothing with which to defend ourselves. I surmised, "If needs be, we'll simply let them take everything – IF they will leave my family and me unharmed!"

I returned to the house and locked both the door to the enclosed porch and to the house. I then again tried frantically to pack my important papers. Carol had opened the three suitcases she had previously packed. She was mulling over what was most important for her to take. Sheri also was packing her suitcases. But, every few minutes she would come to our bedroom and ask, "Could you find room in your suitcases for this? I don't have room for it in mine!"

It was about 8:30 a.m. when we recognized the voice of Jean-Patrick Rene on the two-way radio. Jean-Patrick was a young Mauritian hired by AID to maintain their computer system. He informed the Marine guards monitoring radio traffic at the U.S. Embassy, "My French friends have informed me there is to be an evacuation of ALL dependents from the French School at 10:00 O'clock. What does the Embassy know about it?" And, "What should we do?" The Embassy spokesman hesitatingly replied, "We don't know anything about an evacuation. We'll let you know what we can find out!"

About 9:30 a.m. there was another "All Call." We were advised to, "Proceed immediately to the French School to be evacuated at 10:00 o'clock. Each person will be allowed ONLY one piece of hand luggage and no pets will be allowed!" It also was explained we should go to the "old gate" and not the "new gate" of the French School. I knew the location of the "new gate", but not of the "old gate". Therefore, I inquired over the radio, "Where is the 'old gate' to the French School located?" How do we find it?" The tart reply was, "It's just off Charles DeGaulle Avenue!" This added to my dilemma, as we previously had been advised to "Avoid Charles DeGaulle Avenue at all costs because there is rampant looting and shooting along this street!" Charles DeGaulle Avenue represented the business center of N'Djamena.

We hurriedly finished packing. Carol decided to pack the single suitcase she was allowed primarily with Christmas presents we had purchased for family members back home. She packed very few clothes and personnel items. In contrast, Sheri packed primarily clothes and personnel items. Her task was relatively easy because, following our "Holiday Season R & R", she planned to remain in the States to attend college. I had delivered almost two hundred and fifty pounds of her belongings to DMS (the service organization for AID) the previous Tuesday. We hoped DMS had shipped her things on the Friday afternoon flight, as they had promised to do. My bag was packed primarily with project and personal papers, as well as with Sheri's correspondence lessons and books. I also had included what I considered to be basic survival items, i.e. a flashlight, food, water, and basic clothing. At the last minute I decided to pack a flight bag full of clothes, including my suits and a warm coat.

I returned to the yard in front of our house. First, I drove the Rodent Research Project four-wheel drive Toyota crew-cab pickup behind a large, metal shipping container in which DMS had delivered furniture to the house. This would prevent people from seeing the vehicle, unless they entered our compound. I had filled a fifty-gallon drum in the back of the vehicle with diesel the previous day, in anticipation of our going on a field trip on Tuesday. I had debated as to whether to use the Project vehicle or our personal car to go to the French School. I decided the four-wheel drive vehicle probably would be more of an enticement to marauders than would be our 1983 Peugeot sedan. Next, I started and backed our sedan out of the garage and up to the entrance to our house. I then quickly loaded our suitcases into the trunk and told Carol and Sheri, "Get in!" They made fun of how nervous I acted and how my hands were shaking. They had not seen, as I had, what was going on in the streets outside. Neither did they realize the potential perils we faced if we were stopped at gunpoint. We could not speak the language. We wouldn't even be able to distinguish between the "rebels" and the government troops. Furthermore, I still did not know how to locate the "old gate" to the French School, where we were to meet for the 10:00 o'clock evacuation!

Our night guard approached us and explained, "They are selling rice at a good price outside. But I don't have any money." I gave him most of the Chadian francs or CFA in my pockets. I also tried to tell him, "You should remain on duty! Don't let anyone into the compound or into the house!" I then ordered him to, "Open the gate!" And, we roared out into the street.

People were scurrying everywhere. Most were carrying looted items on their heads or in their arms. Some of their burdens were unbelievably large, including items such as beds, tables, air conditioners, and over-stuffed chairs. Many carried sacks of what appeared to be rice or sugar. Most, fortunately, appeared to be in a festive mood and they readily moved out of our way when I honked the horn.

I determined we first should go to Kurt Fuller's house in the AID compound. I was certain he could tell us how to get to the 'old gate" at the French School. However, when we arrived at the gate to his house, the guard told us he and his family had gone. I again started to drive through the melee in the streets. We then saw a car we recognized. It was speeding towards the French School. I gave chase, figuring, "They should lead us to where we want to go!" We rounded a corner and directly in front of us were about a dozen armed soldiers. They aimed their rifles at us. What were we to do? I then realized, "They're white! That means they're French, not Chadian!" They motioned for me to park alongside the road, to unload our suitcases, and to move quickly through a nearby gate into the French School compound. It appeared we were safe!

We hurriedly retrieved our suitcases from the trunk of the car. I locked the car, thinking, "This should at least make it a little harder for someone to steal it." Inside the School compound, our names were added to a rapidly growing list of evacuees. We also stacked our bags onto a large pile of luggage situated alongside the gate we had entered.

I surveyed the mingling crowd and shortly spied the faces of Kurt Fuller, his wife and their three young sons. My family and I joined them and inquired about the well being of others from the AID compound. It soon was announced, "Women and children will be loaded first." onto a convoy of military trucks stationed in front of the compound. Kurt and I helped load the anxious women and excited children onto perhaps a half-dozen trucks. Then, he and his family and my family and I clamored onboard the last truck in the convoy. French soldiers with guns and full combat gear joined us on the back of the truck. With a roar, we were off!

We turned onto and traversed a portion of Charles DeGaulle Avenue. This was the only halfway fashionable shopping street in N'Djamena, but the shops on either side of the street were now in a shambles. People carrying an array of goods on their heads or in their arms were scurrying everywhere. Shop windows were broken and what looked like business papers were strewn all over the street. It appeared virtually all of the business establishments on Charles DeGaulle had been thoroughly ravaged.

Our convoy turned off from Charles DeGaulle onto a side street. There was a sudden burst of machinegun fire immediately to our left. The French soldiers quickly jumped off our truck and scurried in the direction where the gunfire had occurred. They tensely held their weapons and searched the nearby compounds, but did not find those responsible for the shooting. They apparently had fled. They clamored back onto the truck and we continued our journey to the French military compound that was located at the south end of the N'Djamena Airport. We passed a large warehouse, which formerly had housed a brewery, and joined the rest of the convoy that was parked in a large open area. We unloaded and were escorted into the warehouse, which we were informed would serve as "your temporary quarters – until you are evacuated."

There were large stacks of bottled water and soft drinks, as well as numerous cots and pads, inside the warehouse. The arrival of hundreds of evacuees apparently had been anticipated. In contrast to the American contingency in Chad, the French were well organized!

I strolled among the hundreds of evacuees, searching for familiar faces and trying to account for those people with whom we were well acquainted. The large number of pets I encountered surprised me.

These were mostly dogs, but included a fair number of cats. I thought pets were to have been left behind. Upon inquiry, I learned some people had resolutely refused to be evacuated – unless they could take their pets with them. Thus, the restriction against pets had been lifted.

We periodically observed French soldiers scurrying to the perimeters of the base. Antiaircraft guns were deployed around the warehouse in which we resided. There appeared to be a French soldier, perhaps a sharpshooter (?), in virtually every large tree on the base. There also was the almost constant noise of gunfire from the direction of N'Djamena, but very little in our immediate vicinity. Towards noon, the hottest part of the day, there was a noticeable lull in the gunfire. Shortly past mid-day, French soldiers loaded the women and children onto trucks and took them to a nearby military mess hall for lunch. We were the last to be escorted to the mess hall. I was genuinely surprised at the abundance and goodness of the food we were served. What a marked contrast to the normal fare served in Chad! It appeared the French imported everything.

We spent most of the afternoon standing in lines. First, our names and those of our dependents were recorded onto a lengthy roster, by hand and by a single person. Then, again by hand, our passport numbers and other information were recorded. It appeared they were using slow and tedious methods for recording data simply to keep us occupied.

Late in the evening, after having stood in lines for hours, providing information for the evacuation rosters, we were allowed to locate and retrieve our luggage. We then were again loaded onto trucks and taken to the mess hall for dinner. Thereafter, we were transported to the terminal building of the N'Djamena Airport. Here, we again stood in lines to check in our luggage and to be assigned aircraft boarding numbers. Women and children, of course, were to be boarded first. And, we were assembled into groups – so we would be ready to board as soon as the aircraft arrived from Paris.

Our group assembled on a portion of the steps leading from the terminal building to the runway. As we waited, we discussed over and over the happenings of the day. Suddenly, someone shouted, "Look!"

In the distance, on the far side of the landing strip, there was a column of tanks coming towards us. French soldiers piled into jeeps and other military vehicles and quickly drove towards the oncoming tanks. As the French vehicles approached the tanks, they stopped and their appeared to be a confrontation between them. However, no shots were fired and the tanks shortly retreated in the direction from which they had come. The French military vehicles then returned to our side of the runway. The rumor was, "The French and the rebel forces have an 'understanding': If you don't bother us, we won't bother you!"

Just after noon, while waiting at the warehouse, we observed an Ethiopian Airlines plane land and then very shortly depart from the N'Djamena Airport. We initially thought it might be an evacuation aircraft. But, following its quick departure, wondered what was going on. Then, while eating dinner at the French military mess hall, a young American girl in our group explained how she had arrived about noon in N'Djamena on the Ethiopian Airlines flight from Nairobi. She claimed, "Nothing was mentioned during the flight about a revolution in Chad. Our plane simply landed here in N'Djamena and about a half-dozen of us disembarked." She further explained, "We wondered why there were armed soldiers lying in the grass alongside the landing strip while we were landing." Upon getting off the plane, "We also wondered why there were only French soldiers in the terminal building." After retrieving her luggage and exiting the terminal, she found there were no taxis or transport into N'Djamena. French soldiers then approached her and said, "You'll have to come with us." They brought her and the other disembarking passengers to the warehouse, where we were located, and told them, "You'll be evacuated to Paris with the others."

Dr. Richard Bruggers, my supervisor with the DWRC, was scheduled to arrive in N'Djamena at 12:30 p.m. this same day on the Air Afrique flight from Paris. As we waited at the warehouse, I wondered whether or not his flight would come. At approximately 12:30 – only a few minutes after the Ethiopian Airlines flight had landed and quickly departed – another large plane approached the airport runway. Although it descended, it did not land. The plane merely dipped its wings and continued towards the south. Joe Hindman, Director of the Peace Corps program in Chad, was scheduled to return to N'Djamena on this flight. Thus, as the Air Afrique flight continued on its way, many in the warehouse who had awaited his arrival shouted, "There goes Joe!" I wondered, "Does there also go Rick Bruggers?"

Towards midnight, as many of us sat or sprawled on the steps leading from the air terminal to the runway, we spotted the lights of an approaching aircraft. A small, sleek jet landed and taxied onto the paraport in front of us. We wondered, "How could many people be evacuated in such a small aircraft?" It then became evident this was only a TV news team. A cameraman and several reporters methodically moved among us evacuees. They asked questions and periodically videotaped interviews with selected people. We strained to hear what was being said. But, after only a few interviews, the news team hurriedly boarded their trim craft and departed. The "world" now would be informed as to what was happening in N'Djamena, Chad!

Well past 1:00 a.m. on Sunday, December 2, a UTA 747 jet airliner landed at the N'Djamena Airport. A veterinarian arrived with the plane. It was announced, "ALL pets will have to be given a tranquilizer, before they can be evacuated with their owners." The veterinarian then began to administer injections to a hurriedly assembled group of dogs and cats. After that, about an hour and a half was spent loading the huge plane with evacuees with small children. The plane then departed. About an hour later, an Air France 747 jet airliner landed. It was "our plane"! We boarded much quicker than did the first group. And, in less than an hour – at about 3:30 a.m. – we were airborne.

What a relief! We were leaving the revolution in Chad behind us! As we watched the scattered lights of N'Djamena disappear below, I wondered, "Will we return? Are all of our friends remaining in Chad OK?" We did not know.

Our flight to Paris, except for the presence of a good number of sedated dogs and cats, was similar to almost any commercial airline flight. We were served an excellent meal. Many of us then tried to get some much-needed sleep. It had been more than twenty-four hours since any of us had been in bed. Nevertheless, I could not sleep. Miraculously, it appeared not even a single American had been killed or even injured during the revolt. Many had witnessed the killing of literally hundreds of Chadians. And, given the amount of shooting that took place, one would think at least someone among the approximately two hundred and forty Americans in N'Djamena should have been hit by a stray bullet. I silently prayed and gave thanks to my Father in Heaven for the protection provided for my family and me. It was difficult to believe we had escaped unharmed.

We landed at the Charles DeGaulle Airport in Paris at approximately 9:00 a.m. After disembarking the aircraft, we were herded through the air terminal. Immigration and other formalities normally associated with landing in a foreign country were foregone. We were directed into a waiting room already occupied by evacuees who were on the first flight from N'Djamna. Although they had departed several hours before us, they had arrived only minutes prior to us. For some reason, their plane had made a stop in Marseille. Thereafter, we were loaded into buses and transported to the Hotel Lutecia, a grand old hotel in downtown Paris. We would be quartered here, until the authorities decided what to do with us. We and our luggage were assembled in a large room. We were given rolls and juice for breakfast, prior to being given room assignments.

Finally, we and our luggage were deposited in our assigned rooms. We could not believe how good it felt to crawl into a nice soft bed. We had had but a few snatches of sleep during the previous two days. Nevertheless, each time the subway train passed through the tunnel beneath the hotel or there were other unexpected noises, we awoke with a start. At times, it seemed we still could hear gunfire.

We spent most of the next three days at the American Embassy in Paris. We filled out numerous forms, discussed over and over again what had happened in Chad, and wondered what would happen next. We were especially concerned about our friends who had not been evacuated from Chad. These included Paul and Betty Morris.

Soon after our arrival in Paris, many of the children with us insisted we take them to McDonalds "for a hamburger". Some had been evacuated with only the clothes they were wearing. Very few had any warm clothing and it was winter in Paris. While our entourage walked from the hotel to McDonalds, with many of the children wearing nothing but T-shirts, shorts and thongs - common dress throughout the year in Chad – it was amazing how much attention we received from the usually sedate Parisians. Perhaps as a result of this excursion, soon after our return to the hotel we were assembled in the lobby and warm clothing was distributed among us evacuees. Sheri was thrilled to have "a coat from Paris".

After almost a week in Paris, we eventually were transported back to the Charles DeGaulle Airport and placed on a plane to the U.S. We were being sent to Washington, D.C. Chad and the events of recent days almost seemed to be little more than a bad dream. There were, however, the nagging worries of, "What will we do now? Will we have to return to Chad? If so, when?" The uncertainty of our future sometimes seemed to be more frightening than the experiences associated with the revolt. It was difficult to "come down" from the "high" resulting from our experiences during the revolution and evacuation. Would our lives ever return to "normal"?

I previously had spent a day in a stockade, while serving as a "Mormon" missionary in Paraguay. I also had some harrowing experiences associated with a revolution, while I was a Fulbright scholar in Ecuador. And, Carol and I had experienced an air raid bombing in southern India during the first Indo-Pakistani War, while we were living in India. However, I think our experiences associated with the revolution in Chad more forcibly impressed upon my mind that life is both very tenuous and precious. What would I have done if I had lost my wife and/or our daughter? The possessions we left in Chad were nothing compared to our lives and well-being. I pondered, "What are the truly important things in life?" It certainly is not our material possessions. Neither is it prestige or the acclaim we might attain through work or our professional activities. Our lives and how we live them are important. Perhaps most important is how we treat each other. I trust I never forget these important lessons, which were so indelibly impressed upon my mind as a result of my "LIFE IN CHAD AND A REVOLUTION".

YET ANOTHER REVOLUTION

Revolutionists rarely make good rulers. Though often idealists and good fighters, they usually do not do well in establishing and maintaining peace.

Following the evacuation of my wife Carol, our daughter Sheri and me from N'Djamena by the French on December 2, 1990, we spent the better part of a week in Paris. The U.S. State Department then insisted I and other American evacuees should spend a week in Washington, D.C. for "debriefing". They wanted to record our observations concerning the revolt and overthrow of the Chadian government. I refused. I felt my going to Washington would be a waste of time and money. Besides, my family and I previously had scheduled R&R to spend the Holiday Season with our family at home.

The previous Friday, immediately before the Saturday morning hostilities, Brahim, AID's travel coordinator, insisted I give him our R&R air tickets. He claimed he needed the tickets "to confirm your flight reservations from N'Djamena to Paris". I did not want to give our tickets to him, but he insisted he needed them. Thus, Brahim still had our air tickets. When I mentioned this to Jean-Patrick Renee, he said, "Didn't you know, Brahim is an undercover agent for Hussain Habre (the deposed President of Chad)? He's probably taken your tickets and fled the country!" To further complicate matters, the State Department claimed, "Unless you have tickets or at least travel authorization from your agency, we cannot let you fly from Paris to Salt Lake City." There was no way I could obtain our air tickets from Brahim. Dr. Richard Bruggers, my immediate supervisor with the Denver Wildlife Research Center (DWRC) was supposed to arrive in N'Djamena the day we were evacuated. We didn't know what happened to him or how I could get travel authorization from him?

With assistance from U.S. Embassy personnel in Paris, we learned Rick Bruggers had been on the December 2nd Air Afrique flight from Paris to N'Djamena – the one which passed overhead, without landing - while we were awaiting evacuation at the

N'Djamena Airport. His flight had continued on to the Central African Republic. From there, he had flown to Rome.

Through telephone calls to Rome and Denver, we learned Dr. Bruggers was meeting with Mr. Clyde Elliot, who was with the FAO in Rome. I telephoned Mr. Elliot the next morning. He assured me, "I'll have Dr. Bruggers call you at the Embassy in Paris at 1:00 p.m. this afternoon." I waited at the Embassy until after 3:00 p.m. for Rick's call. It never came. Thereafter, I made additional calls to Denver and the USDA in Washington and obtained authorization for my family and me to fly from Paris to Salt Lake City, rather than my going to Washington, D.C.

I returned to my family at the Hotel Lutecia that evening. Carol then informed me, "While you were at the Embassy, Dr. Bruggers called. He told me to tell you that you should go to Washington, as the State Department wants you to." What a mess!

My family and I went to dinner that evening with Jean-Patrick Renee, AID's computer specialist in Chad, and Felix Lee, a Chinese fellow in charge of the "Famine Early Warning System" (FEWS) program in Chad. FEWS uses satellite imagery and local weather data to predict crop production in the Sahel region of Africa. Similar to me, Jean-Patrick and Felix were having problems with respect to travel. The U.S. State Department had requested they go to Washington for "debriefing". But, the State Department refused to pay their travel expenses, because they did not have U.S. passports. Although they both worked for the U.S. Government, they had Mauritian and British passports, respectively. Further, they were told they might have to pay back expenses incurred by the U.S. Government in bringing them to Paris and perhaps even for their return to Chad.

The following morning I told the State Department, "I'm ready to go to Washington, if you wish." I then was told, "We've already made arrangements for you and your family to fly to Salt Lake City. There's no need for you to go to Washington." Happy day!

We were given air tickets from Paris to Salt Lake City via New York City. Then, along with the American evacuees going to Washington, D.C., we were taken by bus to the Charles DeGaulle Airport. Thereafter, we had an uneventful flight from Paris to New York, where we went through immigration and customs – just like other American tourists. Family members met us at the airport in Salt Lake City and be began our R&R by visiting family and friends. Over and over again we were asked to relate our experiences associated with the revolution in Chad.

When we went to visit my mother in Cache Valley, Utah, she had both a reporter and photographer from the "Herald Journal" newspaper in Logan waiting to interview us. The woman reporter previously served as a Peace Corps volunteer in Liberia and had been evacuated from there the previous May. Thus, she was acquainted with Africa and the traumas we had experienced. On the front page of the following Sunday edition of the "Herald Journal" was a colored photograph of my family and me and a feature article entitled, "Spillett Family Slips Away From Violence in Chad". Thereafter, relatives and friends routinely relayed to us whatever news they encountered regarding happenings in Chad. It was amazing how so many of these reports were contradictory and some had little basis in fact.

We returned to the snows and cold winter weather in southeastern Idaho, which was a marked contrast to the hot weather to which we'd become accustomed in Chad. The people in our house moved out and we moved back in. I began to search for employment, so we wouldn't have to return to Chad. I preferred to return to the Forest Service, but there were no openings. I was offered a biologist position with the Bureau of Land Management, but I would have to accept a reduced grade and salary. Moreover, if I accepted this position, my retirement annuity in approximately two years would be greatly reduced. Thus, at least temporarily, I decided to "tough it out" with the DWRC, which probably meant I would have to return to Chad. In any case, we decided Carol would remain at home with Sheri and our son Jay until school was out in late May.

Following several weeks of R&R, I spent much of the following three months in Denver. There, I spent nights alone in a motel and days analyzing and writing up our Chad rodent data at the DWRC. The Gulf War or "Desert Storm" occurred during this period. As a result, there were relatively few reports about Chad. International news dealt almost entirely with events in Kuwait and Iraq. International travel also was severely restricted, primarily because of fears regarding terrorists. The Mid-East conflict, however, eventually subsided and communications with Chad again were established. Thus, it was decided I should return to Chad and continue the rodent research project.

I returned alone to N'Djamena on March 15, 1991. Except for the presence of many Libyans and of soldiers almost everywhere, N'Djamena appeared to be similar to when we left. Sounds of gunfire within the city were common, especially at night. There were numerous reports about crime and violence. These, however, were confined primarily to the Chadian and not the expatriate communities. It seemed the conquering forces felt they had a right to the spoils of war. They often simply took from others whatever they wanted. Surprisingly, except for a thick layer of dust, I found our house and belongings almost exactly as we had left them. More remarkable yet was the fact our Peugeot sedan, which we'd left on the street outside the French School, was unscathed. The DMS (the AID service organization) had towed it into their compound. I only had to charge the battery before starting and driving it home. Insofar as I could determine, only one American (Kevin Guild, the DMS Director) had their house ransacked. This was despite rampant looting throughout most of N'Djamena!

Life in N'Djamena returned only to a semblance of what it had been prior to the revolution. Many Americans, primarily dependents, did not return. Many who returned sought means whereby they could leave Chad as soon as possible. For security reasons, softball games no longer were played on the banks of the Chari River each Saturday afternoon. Evenings or nighttime activities likewise were strictly curtailed. Everyone seemed to be more cautious and social activities or gatherings were greatly diminished.

It was mid-April before AID would authorize me to again make field trips to collect rodent data. When we finally traveled to N'Gouri, we encountered soldiers almost everywhere. This was a matter of concern. While we were returning from N'Gouri to N'Djamena, some armed soldiers stopped us. Their Toyota four-wheel-drive pickup, on top of which was mounted a machine gun, had quit running. The temperature was in excess of one hundred and ten degrees Fahrenheit and we were in the middle of nowhere. The nearest village was about twenty miles away. Although I did not think the soldiers would shoot us, I feared they might commandeer our vehicle and leave us stranded in the desert. Without water, given the heat, we could die within a matter of hours.

The military driver, a young fellow in a white "boo-boo", approached our vehicle. He had his right hand on the butt of his low-slung pistol. But, when he saw and recognized me as an American, he simply asked if we had any tools. Our driver got out of our vehicle and retrieved some tools from beneath the seat. He then accompanied the white-clad driver back to his vehicle. A soldier in the back of the Toyota pickup nervously covered us with the mounted machine gun. More unnerving to me was a young boy who, although in uniform, could not have been more than ten years old. He stood alongside our vehicle and pointed an automatic weapon at us. As our driver worked on the soldiers' vehicle this boy kept moving his finger back and forth on the trigger of his weapon. I kept thinking, "I hope this kid doesn't accidentally shoot us." And, "What will we do if they take our vehicle and leave us stranded here?"

Our driver eventually got the soldiers' vehicle started. They then piled into their Toyota pickup and departed in a cloud of dust. I and those with me gave sighs of relief. We were all sweating profusely, perhaps as much from fear as from the heat. We then continued on our return journey to N'Djamena.

I missed my wife and family dearly. Nevertheless, the situation in Chad was so tenuous I did not dare have them return. Although my efforts to find other suitable Federal employment had been futile during the three months I spent in the States, I continued to seek such employment. It previously had been difficult living in Chad with my family. Without my family, it was almost unbearable.

Working conditions in Chad then became even more difficult. Kurt Fuller, my supervisor with AID, departed. He took an AID assignment in Rwanda. He and his wife claimed, "It will be great to have an assignment in a peaceful African nation!" The last I heard, Kurt and his wife had separated. He also lost all of his belongings during his third evacuation from Rwanda. So much for having an assignment in a **"peaceful"** African nation!

Namde, Fuller's Chadian AID assistant, resigned and moved to the States with his American wife. Other AID personnel, such as Bill Deese, the Program Officer, likewise resigned. Almost invariably when you met with another American the conversation eventually would include, "When do you leave?" Or, "How much longer do you have to serve in this God-forsaken place?" In a security briefing, Mark Caldwell, the State Department Security Officer – who did not bring his family back to Chad after the revolution – told me, "It's not a matter of IF, but WHEN the present regime in Chad will be overthrown!"

Dr. Tridib ("Trid") Mukerjee eventually replaced Kurt Fuller as AID's Agricultural Deveopment Officer in Chad. He then appointed two Chadian assistants to replace Namde. Although Dr. Mukerjee had obtained U.S. citizenship, he still adhered to the domineering behaviorisms inherent to the "aristocracy" in his native land of West Bengal, India. He was not a pleasant man to work with.

I had two brief reprieves during my lonely sojourn following my return to Chad. The DWRC first sent Joe Brooks and then Keith LaVoie to assist me with the rodent project. Each stayed with me for two weeks. Joe previously conducted long-term rodent research projects in Bangladesh and Pakistan, during which he used my doctoral thesis ("The Ecology of the Lesser Bandicoot Rat in Calcutta") as a guide. He was welcome company and did much to help with the research. Although Keith previously had spent time in Chad and helped establish the project, he was sick during much of his stay. He blamed his illness upon the malaria medication required in

Chad. It appeared to me, however, that his consumption of alcohol was his major problem.

During the almost six months I was alone and trying to maintain my sanity, I spent evenings and weekends writing or revising much of what is contained herein. Finally, I decided the situation in Chad was stable enough for my wife Carol to join me. Libyans no longer were evident upon the streets of N'Djamena. The presence of soldiers likewise had diminished in many parts of the city. Shooting, particularly during the night, was still fairly common, but was something to which we in N'Djamena had become accustomed. Jerry Penno, AID's Executive Officer, also had asked me if I would like to occupy a house in the AID compound. Such housing would provide more security and an opportunity to readily associate with other Americans living in the compound. I heartily accepted the offer. I also informed Carol about the "good news" and asked her to return to Chad "as quickly as possible!" I moved our household effects into the house in the AID compound on September 7, 1991, the day before Carol returned to Chad.

Carol's return made life much more tolerable. I again could look forward to returning home, following a day at the office or after my jaunts into the field. It truly seemed good to have someone with whom I could associate. We spent many hours playing chess or "Rummikub", watching videos, or simply enjoying each other's company.

Two Peace Corps volunteers, Bryn Randolph from California and Marie Bradshaw from Provo, Utah, stayed with us a few weeks. Bryn was recuperating from a severe illness and Marie was preparing for an English teaching assignment in southern Chad. We greatly enjoyed their company. We also made friends with others living in the AID compound and visits with them became more and more commonplace. I even began to think, "Maybe I should quit looking for other employment and stay with the DWRC until my retirement in October 1992 – especially since we'll be able to take almost a month's R&R at home during the Holiday Season". Forthcoming events, however, quickly changed my mind!

There was more "traffic" than normal on our two-way radio during the night of Saturday, October 12. Because of static, we could not decipher much of what was being said. But, what we could understand did not appear to be "out of the ordinary." Carol suggested I "Turn off the radio, so we can get some sleep." However, I failed to do so. Then, early Sunday morning, there was an "All Call! All Call!" This was followed by, "There are military personnel in the streets. Please report military activities in your area." And, "Everyone remain in your homes until further notice." My first thought was, "Here we go again!"

We anxiously waited and listened. Above the din of the air conditioner, we could hear more shooting than normal. Most of the shooting seemed to be some distance away. Then, tanks, trucks and soldiers began to pass on the street in front of our house. We watched these activities through our kitchen window, from which we could see over the eight-foot-high wall surrounding the compound. We couldn't understand what was going on. Military forces would rush past, going one direction. Very shortly, they would rush back, going the other direction. People were milling in the street and, whenever these military movements occurred, they would scream and frantically search for somewhere to hide. Many would cower next to the walls on either side of the street, while they waited for the soldiers to pass. Others banged upon our gate and begged to be let in. Those, which our guard permitted to enter, huddled against the wall in our driveway and fearfully sobbed until there was no further evidence of military personnel in the nearby street. We heard and saw soldiers firing upon some of the people in the street. Some soldiers literally dragged some poor screaming souls from a car at a nearby corner and then unmercifully beat them. Our guard later told us four or five people were shot and killed immediately in front of our house.

Gunfire during the December 1990 revolution was primarily from small arms. This time, in addition to small arms fire, many "big guns" also were fired. The boom or roar of these literally shook our house and caused us to instinctively clasp our hands over our ears and to seek cover. It was like being in an earthquake. It did not seem possible that the shaking and trembling would not cause the house windows to shatter. We saw a good number of mid-air explosions.

Some were in the vicinity of our previous house. We were thankful we no longer lived there. In addition to the roar of canons and recoilless rifles, as well as mortars and grenades, there was the almost constant chatter of machine guns and other small arms. We could hear shooting first from one direction and then from another. Although military action was widespread, much appeared to center in the area where we formerly lived. There was bedlam almost everywhere. "Where could we hide?" Or, "What should we do?"

There was considerable "traffic" throughout the day on our two-way radio. This consisted primarily of reports of troop movements or of houses and buildings being hit by gunfire. There also were bits or pieces of information about what was taking place. It appeared some dissident soldiers were attempting a "coup" or to overthrow the military regime of Idris Deby, who ten months pervious had overthrown the military regime of Husain Habre. The rebels first stormed an ammunition dump near the N'Djamena Airport. There were heavy casualties on both sides, but the troops loyal to President Deby repelled the rebels. The rebels, however, commandeered a good number of military vehicles, including weapons carriers and the ubiquitous and very effective four-wheel-drive Toyota pickups. With these, they tried to entice others to join their cause, as well as to wreak vengeance upon those they believed to be loyal to Deby or who were from southern rather than northern Chadian tribes. Basically, it was tribal warfare – the north against the south. Our guard was from the south. He was so frightened his normally black countenance was almost white or at least an ashen gray. Soldiers loyal to Idris Deby also were chasing around N'Djamena, trying to catch and punish the rebels. It was like a grandiose game of "cops and robbers". But, they were using real ammunition and killing hundreds of people!

Bernie Wilder, the Director for AID in Chad, and his wife Shirley, lived in the house next to ours in the AID compound. Bernie was suffering from a severe case of hepatitis. In fact, he was "medivaced" from Chad as soon as hostilities subsided. Around noon, a group of soldiers entered his compound and then left with his bulletproof sedan. The vehicle was returned the following day. We never learned who had taken it or for what purpose it was used.

Carole Palma, the Assistant Director for AID, lived "kitty-corner" from the house where we previously lived. Her husband worked for ESSO Oil Company and was on a business trip to France during the attempted "coup". Carole made a number of calls on the two-way radio. First, soldiers took her guards' two-way radios away from them. They later returned and took one of the guards into custody. Thereafter, she periodically reported shooting and other military activities in the streets near her house. Her final reports were, "There's overhead fire!" And then, "There's incoming fire! My house has been hit!"

We later learned Carole had taken refuge in a centrally located bathroom in her house. The "overhead fire" shattered the ceiling windows in the bathroom. Broken glass literally showered down upon her, as she lay on the bathroom floor. Soldiers also were chasing a man in the street behind her house. The man took refuge in a lean-to shed outside her compound. The pursuing soldiers fired an anti-tank missile into the shed. The missile went through the shed, through the compound wall, and then exploded – before penetrating the kitchen wall of the house and narrowly missing a propane gas tank next to the kitchen stove. Miraculously, Carole was not injured. In fact, she and her voice remained calm while these events occurred and she reported them on the radio. However, upon the return of her husband the following week, she broke down and became almost completely unnerved.

Richard Sands, the Superintendent of the American School in N'Djamena, and his family lived in the house immediately behind our former residence. Across the street from their house was a large lot. It contained residential ruins - "a reminder of the 1980 revolution". The 1980 revolution perhaps was the worst of the many conflicts occurring in Chad following its independence from France in 1964. During this revolt, much of N'Djamena was literally leveled. Although much renovation and rebuilding had since occurred, there still remained many stark reminders of Chad's tumultuous post-independence history. Following the December 1990 revolution, families of soldiers from southern Chad took up residency on vacant lots throughout much of N'Djamena. Hundreds of women and children lived in hovels or crudely constructed thatch huts. Such was the case in the lot across the street from the Sands' residence.

Rebel soldiers noisily stormed the area in which the Sands lived during the early morning of October 13, 1991. They entered the lot across the street from their house and assembled the men and boys. At gunpoint, they marched them away. They also bound the hands and feet of the remaining women and children, before leaving them lying on the ground. The soldiers, however, shortly returned. They then methodically shot each of the women and children in the head. The Sands did not know how many the soldiers killed, but surmised it was upwards of forty women and children. As to what happened to the men and boys, it was never determined. Such happenings apparently were commonplace throughout N'Djamena. The reason for these atrocities was that these people were from southern Chadian tribes; whereas, the rebels were from northern tribes!

A man, whose voice was unfamiliar to us, made frequent and oftentimes ridiculous inquiries over the two-way radio throughout the day. One of his inquiries was, "My guard says it's dangerous for him to remain outside of my compound in the street. He wants to come inside. What should I do?" The terse reply was, "For heaven's sake, let him in!" Later, the same voice inquired, "My guard says he's hungry. He doesn't have any food. What should I do?" The reply was, "Why don't you feed him?" During an apparent lull in the shooting, the voice inquired, "Do you think it would be OK for my family and me to come to the Embassy to use the swimming pool?" The emphatic reply was, "No! You were told to remain in your residence until further notice!" Then, later in the day, the same voice asked, "Will there be school tomorrow at the American School? Should I plan on taking my children there?" This apparently was the "last straw" for the Duty Officer monitoring the radio traffic at the U.S. Embassy. In no uncertain terms, he told the man to remain at home and not to make any more inquiries. We later learned the man making these repeated and ludicrous inquiries was the new Communications Officer for the U.S. State Department in Chad! This further eroded the little faith I have for U.S. State Department personnel.

Fighting in N'Djamena had subsided somewhat by the evening of the first day. There still were sporadic bursts of small arms fire. Thankfully, the roar of big guns had all but ceased. By "All Call" on our two-way radios, we repeatedly had been warned to "Remain in your houses until further notice!" We also had been informed, "The 'official' government is still in charge." We assumed this meant Idris Deby's troops had squelched the attempted "coup". Still, we wondered, "Why the sporadic small arms fire?" We were further informed, "A STRICT curfew will be in effect and STRONGLY ENFORCED from 6:00 p.m. until 6:00 a.m." It was implied that anyone on the streets during nighttime hours possibly would be shot.

Ten of us living in the AID compound assembled in Trid and Debi Mukerjee's house that evening, while eating pizza, we discussed the events of the day. Trid proudly proclaimed how he'd captured on videotape, from his bedroom window, the passing of the military vehicles on the street in front of their house. Bijan Yazdani, the Assistant Comptroller for AID, and his wife Mavash, listened intently to our discussions regarding the situation. They and their family had to flee from their native country of Iran in 1979. This was because of the Shah being ousted and replaced by Khomeni. The Yazdanis were Bahai and, similar to the situation in Chad (i.e. the northern tribes persecuting those from the south), many Muslims in Iran will not tolerate the presence of those with other religious beliefs. Although Bijan's father once was a senior government official in Iran, he now was in prison - because of his religious beliefs.

Mavash then began to tell about some of their experiences. During their approximately fourteen years in Chad they had experienced five revolutions and had been evacuated from the country three times. According to her, the 1980 revolt was the worst. They and their young family then spent three days "holed up" in their house without water, electricity or food. Chadian soldiers from the north went from house to house, searching for and then killing any southern Chadians they found – including women and small children. The bodies of the thousands of people killed were not even buried. They simply were dragged into the streets and stacked in piles as much as eight feet high. Here, they were left to be fed upon by stray dogs, vultures and other carnivores or to deteriorate until there was nothing left but bones. The stench was unbearable. The Yazdanis told how they tried to reach the French Embassy, to seek asylum from the atrocities surrounding them. But, the soldiers repeatedly turned them back. Finally, after three consecutive days of trying, they managed to traverse the approximately eight blocks between their house in the AID compound and the French Embassy. The French gave them asylum and eventually evacuated them into nearby Cameroon.

When the Yazdanis returned to N'Djamena from Cameroon, they found their house completely stripped. Besides all of the furniture and their belongings having been taken, even the windows, doors and roof were gone. According to Mavash, the present revolt, as well as that which occurred the previous December, was nothing compared to the 1980 revolt. We did not realize how fortunate we were!

That night was relatively quiet and we were able to get some much needed sleep. It's surprising how worrying and fretting makes one so tired. There wasn't even any "traffic" on our two-way radio during the night. At about 8:30 a.m. there was an "All Call" in which we were told, "Remain in your houses! Do not go out on the streets! There will be no school at the American School today, but there will be school tomorrow."

We called Paul and Betty Morris by telephone. They had planned to come to our house to hold Church services the previous morning, but neither we nor they had been able to contact the other throughout the day by telephone. They informed us how two Nigerians (Jefferson and Femi), who had planned to join us for Church services, had taken refuge in the Vogue Cinema to escape marauding soldiers. After remaining hidden there for more than four hours, they finally made it to the Morris' house. They also told us, "There is good news coverage on the 'attempted coup' in Chad on the BBC radio network." I was unable to locate BBC on my short-wave radio; however, other reports indicated conditions in the Sudan were worse than in Chad. It appeared most of Africa was in chaos!

There was sporadic shooting – some of it nearby – during the day, but it was reported that the rebels had fled from N'Djamena. Carol and I spent a relatively quiet day at home. We wrote letters, read and played games. Even Luc, our houseboy, and Ali, our gardener, came to work. Luc claimed food prices in the "marche" or market were "much higher" because of the revolt. He also claimed, "It's not over yet!"

It was quiet Monday night and Tuesday morning. For some reason, the Embassy did not have its regular Tuesday-morning radio check. However, there was an "All Call" and we were informed "There will be no school again today. However, the AID and Embassy offices will be open. Everyone should return to work!" I first went to the AID office. In the mailroom, I noted a letter I had left the previous week to be sent to Rick Bruggers in Denver had not been sent. Thus, I opened it and scribbled some lines about the attempted "coup", before re-sealing it and again leaving it to be posted. I and others also met with Bernie Wilder that afternoon, prior to his being "medivaced" to Washington, D.C. Bernie acted as if he thought we were trying to get rid of him and the AID program in Chad could not survive without his leadership. I wondered if his hepatitis infection had affected his brain.

I located the BBC news report on my short-wave radio that evening. It was reported that four and one-half million people were starving in Somalia because of warfare. There had been a riot in Nigeria. Muslims had attacked Christians, because they didn't want them to open a Christian mission. Ugandan troops were lined up on the border of Rwanda, ready to attack. We wondered how Kurt Fuller and his wife were faring in their assignment to a "peaceful African nation". There also were problems in Togo. Bill Stringfellow, who previously had directed the "Office for Rehabilitation through Training" (ORT) in Chad, had recently transferred to Togo. His wife and family still were in N'Djamena. No matter where one turned, there was no good news about Africa!

At 5:00 a.m. on Wednesday, October 16, we again awoke to the sound of gunfire. Following an extended burst of small weapons fire nearby, there was a single shot fired just outside our compound. As usual, we could not determine what had happened. Although some of our acquaintances remained somewhat in a state of shock for days or even weeks following the attempted "coup", most of us had become accustomed to the sounds of periodic gunfire and paid little heed to the military activities around us.

Carole Palma invited us and approximately fifteen other couples to her house for Thanksgiving dinner on Thursday, November 28. This day also was a Chadian holiday. My wife Carol prepared a turkey and others provided the "fixins" for a traditional Thanksgiving feast. Following our arrival at Carole's house, she showed us how the missile holes in the house and compound walls had been repaired. Thereafter, we were seated at tables in her yard. We were just beginning to partake of the feast when there was a burst of machine gun fire nearby. Someone queried, "What's that?" The reply was, "It's only some more shooting". We continued to eat. Then, a colored lady contemplatively stated, "You know, that shooting makes me homesick. It's just like being back home in Detroit!"

The attempted "coup" caused me to increase my efforts to find suitable employment back in the States. Eventually, Norman Huntsman, a Staff Officer on the Uinta National Forest in Provo, Utah, contacted me. He wanted to know if I was interested in a Forest biologist position on the Uinta. Was I! This was the same position in which I had served after my family and I returned from Iran in 1978 and which I left in 1980 to accept a position at Texas A&M University. Not infrequently, members of my family had indicated they wished we'd never left our home in Mapleton, which is where we lived while I worked on the Uinta Forest in nearby Provo.

I called Norm Huntsman and told him, "I'm definitely interested in your job offer. What do I have to do to get it?" Thereafter, I submitted the required forms. The next thing I knew, Rick Bruggers called me from Denver. He was furious. "What's going on?" The Forest Service had contacted the DWRC, requesting information about me. Further, they stated I was returning to the Forest Service. In short, Carol and I returned to the States in mid-December. After a trip to Cancun, Mexico, we spent Christmas at home with our family. I then moved to Provo and returned to my former position on the Uinta National Forest. It was good to be back! Perhaps of interest, after having survived two revolutions unscathed in Chad, I was robbed during my first day in Provo! That, however, is another story.

I've often been impressed that I should take every possible opportunity to travel and to see as many places and meet as many people as I can. For what purpose, I do not know. However, I know my travels have given me a much greater appreciation for my country and the freedoms afforded under the Constitution of the United States of America. My understanding of the purpose of life, which I have obtained through my "Mormon" heritage and studying the Gospel of Jesus Christ, likewise has been enhanced by my travel experiences. More and more I am convinced that true peace and happiness can be obtained only by our adherence to the great commandments, namely: "Thou shalt love the Lord thy God with all thy heart ..." And, "Thou shalt love they neighbor as thyself." (Matt. 22:37-38).

DEATH ON THE OKAVANGO

Chasing wild animals can be exciting and sometimes downright dangerous!

The mighty Okavango, the third largest river system in southern Africa, arises in the Angola highlands and flows for eight hundred and seventy-two miles (one thousand four-hundred and thirty km). However, instead of flowing into the ocean, it flows into the Kalahari Desert in northern Botswana. Here, it forms the six-thousand-square-mile (more than fifteen thousand square kilometers) Okavango Delta. This huge swamp or marshland, which is interspersed with numerous islands, is described by many as "one of the world's last great wildernesses." And, it includes the notable four thousand eight hundred and seventy-two-square-kilometer Moremi Game Reserve, which covers almost one-third of the Delta.

The vast web of lagoons and lush wetlands formed by the Okavango provide an almost unimaginable diversity of vegetation and wildlife. Furthermore, this immense area has largely escaped the ravages of man and his livestock This primarily is because of the presence of the tsetse fly and difficulties associated with settling or even moving through this swampy or marshland terrain. As a result, the Okavango Delta beckons to many as being one of the few remaining places in the world where one can have a "true wildlife experience". This, in turn, has resulted in the city of Maun becoming a thriving tourist center and the "jumping off" place for the Okavango. It is claimed that the Maun Airport is the second busiest (next to Johannesburg) in southern Africa during the May to October tourist season.

Through reading and watching TV documentaries on the Okavango, I became obsessed with a desire to visit the Okavango and to witness – first hand – its varied and abundant wildlife. Thus, I began to search for an affordable way whereby I could visit this area. Although there are approximately thirty camps with adjacent landing strips for small planes within the Okavango, most of these are what I consider to be in the "expensive" or "luxury" class, i.e. charging in excess of $200 per day. However, I eventually stumbled upon a brochure that advertised an all-inclusive, eighteen-day camping "South Africa Delta and Desert Expedition" that included a four-day stay within the Delta for less than $3,000.

I tried to entice my wife into accompanying me on this camping safari, but she felt she should not go. Our having survived two revolutions in Chad, while I was studying rodents in the Sahel region of that country, might have contributed to her foreboding about returning to Africa. However, our youngest son Jay was more than willing to accompany me. November, the end of the dry season in southern Africa, appeared to be the best time for our trip. But, we had other commitments during this time. Therefore, we decided to go in March, which is after the rainy season. On Saturday, March 4, 2000, we flew from Salt Lake City, Utah to Johannesburg, South Africa via New York City. Then, on Monday, March 6, we flew from Johannesburg to Victoria Falls in Zimbabwe. Here, we would join our eighteen-day camping tour.

We met our South African tour guides, Jacques – a young, energetic fellow - and Kim – an athletic, but very good-looking blond girl – in a campground outside Victoria Falls. For some reason it seemed everyone we met in southern Africa gave us only their first name and never their last. Shortly thereafter we were joined by two young couples that would be traveling with us through Botswana, Namibia and then to Cape Town, South Africa - from whence we would return to the States via Johannesburg and Cape Verde.

Ken and Nikki originally were from Eugene, Oregon, but now lived in Seattle, Washington. Ken had been a high-school exchange student to Johannesburg in 1990 and wanted his wife to see some of the areas he had visited ten years previous. Rob and Sagit or "Ziggy" were from Melbourne, Australia. They were newlyweds on a six-week honeymoon tour in Africa. Rob had spent time in India and had lived in Calcutta, where my wife and I also had lived while I was with the Johns Hopkins University Center for Medical Research and Training (CMRT) program. Thus, he and I had much to discuss about India. We even discovered we had some mutual acquaintances in

India, i.e. Mr. and Mrs. Smith who owned and operated the Fairlawn Hotel on Sudder Street in Calcutta. It is indeed a small world!

The next day, after viewing and taking numerous photos of the spectacular Victoria Falls, we boarded a truck/bus (i.e. a truck cab with bus and luggage compartments behind) and began our safari. Kim and Jacques informed us, "You are indeed fortunate. On most of our tours the twenty-one-seat bus is usually completely full." In contrast, we had more than ample room to stretch out and make ourselves comfortable.

From Victoria Falls we traveled over good roads and through endless miles of "bush" to Nata, which is on the Makgadikgadi Pan in Botswana. In route, we saw only a few elephant, kudu and other forms of wildlife. We were told, "Following the rainy season, the animals are scattered and difficult to see." However, while staying in a campground outside of Nata that night, we had some excitement.

Another group of about twenty Europeans staying in the campground insisted upon "raising Cain" throughout most of the night. Despite our being completely worn out from our long day of travel, we were unable to sleep because of the ruckus they were making. When Rob, who was a good-sized and muscular man, asked them to, "Please cool it!", their harsh and foul-language retort essentially was, "Bug off! Or, we'll clean you!" Then, when the noise finally subsided during the early morning hours, I was awakened by someone slowly unzipping the opening to our tent. I nudged Jay. Then, when a black arm was thrust into our tent, Jay clobbered it and chased off the would-be intruder. However, before going back to sleep, we placed our luggage between us – in the center of the tent – so that it would not be accessible to intruders.

Upon arising in the morning, we learned that Ken and Nikki, who slept in a tent next to ours, had been robbed. Rather than gaining entrance by unzipping their tent, the thief had slit open the side. Their cameras, video camcorder and money had been stolen. Fortunately, however, the thief had left their passports and other belongings. While we were reporting the theft to the authorities at the Nata Police Station later that morning, the "rowdy bunch" from the campground also came to report that some members of their group had been robbed. Most disconcerting, at least to me, was the attitude of those to whom the thefts were being reported. They essentially stated, "You should expect such to happen. This is Africa! Besides, you foreigners are ALL rich. It doesn't hurt you to lose a few things!"

We traveled through more "bush" between Nata and Maun, which would be our "springboard" into the Okavango Delta. After stocking up on bottled water and reducing our luggage to the bare-minimum we thought would be needed for our four-day stay in the Delta, we boarded an eight-passenger plane for a twenty-minute flight to Oddball's Camp on the Okavango River. Oddball's is across the river from the magnificent Chief's Island, which is in the Moremi Game Reserve. We would eat dinner and spend the night at Oddball's. Then, after breakfast the next morning, we'd take "mokoros" (small, wooden, dugout canoes) into the Delta and spend three-days in the "bush" on Chief's Island. Here, our native guides would take us on "game walks" to see hippo, elephants, buffalo, lion and other wild animals. This was to be our "true wildlife experience" in "pristine" Africa!

Upon our arrival at Oddball's, we were met by Vic, who was in charge of the Camp. Prior to dinner and our getting settled into our tents for the night, Vic gave us an orientation as to what we could expect in the Okavango. Primarily, he tried to impress upon us how "This is not a zoo! These animals are wild and can be dangerous!" However, "Your native guides were born and raised here. They know the animals and what to do. You do whatever they do. If they stand still – even if an animal is charging you – you stand still. If they climb a tree, you do the same." And, "If they run, you should try to run faster than they!" He assured us, "If you'll do this, you have nothing to worry about." He emphatically stated, "We've never lost a client. And, we don't intend to!" Nevertheless, following dinner, Vic related how – just the previous month – a twelve-foot crocodile had grabbed the arm of one of their clients and drug him from a mokoro. Although the crocodile was dragging this man into deeper water, somehow he was able to break free and was miraculously saved. He'd broken the bones in his hand, while striking the crocodile with his free arm. Reportedly, he also would regain about seventy percent use of the arm injured by the crocodile. Vic claimed, however, this was unprecedented. They could only surmise that the crocodile's "erratic" behavior resulted from it trying to defend its nest. He again assured us we had nothing to fear - "IF you follow the example and instructions of your native guides."

Our night at Oddball's was memorable. Wart hogs grunted almost continually around our tents. We could hear the sounds of Cape buffalo grazing in the nearby grass and hippos snorting in the river below. Most notable were the occasional roars of lions. Fortunately, these did not appear to be very close. In jest, the next morning I told our friends that, except for the wart hogs, these wildlife sounds probably were from recordings played by Vic.

While eating breakfast in the Camp's open, lean-to lodge, our three native guides appeared in the slough-like Okavango River. They silently poled their mokoros through the grass, reeds and water lilies up to the shore in front of us. I could not believe we, as well as our tents, sleeping bags, food and other gear could fit into such small dugout canoes.

Vic introduced us to our guides, "Mpula, Mox and Lucas". They then began to stack our gear into the aft portions of their three mokoros. Vic also informed us, "Your guides will stand on the stern, from which they will pole and guide the mokoro. Two of you will sit in front of each mokoro, where you'll be able to see everything around you." I wondered, "How can we even see over or through the grass and reeds, let alone 'see everything around us' when we're seated so far down into the water?"

Mpula was Mox's father. He was by far the eldest of our three guides. He stood a slender six feet tall and limped about on a clubfoot. He was to be Rob's and Ken's guide in the lead mokoro. Mox was nineteen years old, stocky and much shorter than his father. He would be Ziggy's and Nikki's guide. Lucas, who was twenty-six, as well as shorter and almost as slender as Mpula, proudly informed us, "I am not married." He was to be Jay's and my guide and we'd bring up the rear of our entourage.

We shakily boarded the small, rustic mokoros and, with their long, slender poles, our guides shoved us off into the marsh. Jay and I each weigh in excess of two hundred pounds and we quickly noted the sides of our craft were less than two inches above the water. Thus, Lucas poled us back to the shore and loaded our gear and then us into a somewhat larger and more modern fiberglass mokoro that belonged to Oddball's.

It was a titillating experience to be seated below water level, while being gracefully poled through a marshland habitat. I was tempted to pick a few of the beautiful blossoms from the myriad of water lilies we floated through. But, remembering how a crocodile had grabbed a man's hand and drug him into the water the previous month, I determined to keep my hands and arms well within the confines of our small craft!

About an hour out of Oddball's we passed Delta Camp, which also was operated by Oddball's. Delta Camp, however, was for "richer" clientele than we. We waved at the people sitting on the Camp's wooden deck above the river. They, in turn, waved to us as we continued on into the marsh.

About a half-hour later, we came upon a cow hippo with a calf. They were in the open water of the river; whereas, our guides were poling us through the reeds and grass closer to shore. Rob encouraged Mpula to take them closer to the hippos, so he could better photograph them with his camcorder. Nikki, however, kept repeating, "I'm afraid! I'm afraid! Let's not get any closer!" Thus, we continued on through the marsh, rather than approaching closer to the hippos.

Except for the cow hippo and calf, the only wildlife we'd seen thus far in the Okavango consisted of several species of birds. The most spectacular were the white-headed fish eagles, which circled overhead while making raucous calls. For me, the most intriguing were the jacanas. These bright-colored birds, with stilt-like legs and ungainly large feet, would run on the tops of the lily pads before taking flight. One jacana made an unusual twittering sound while encircling our mokoro. Lucas then pointed to a small, stick nest on the surface of a lily pad. I had him pole closer to the nest, so I could photograph it. I wondered, "How can a bird possibly incubate its eggs and raise its young in such a watery habitat?"

Our guides eventually informed us we were approaching the area where we were going to camp on Chief's Island. Then, while they were poling us through some dense grass, there suddenly was an unearthly roar and a huge hippo rose up out of the water and charged the lead mokoro. The beast grabbed Rob in its cavernous mouth and drug him into the water. Ken was simultaneously knocked out of the mokoro and into the water on the other side, while Mpula was vaulted into the air from off of the stern of the mokoro. Mpula, however, quickly stood up in the waist-deep water and began to shout and frantically wave his arms, in an attempt to frighten off the hippo. Meanwhile, Lucas frantically began to pole us forward. "What is he doing?" I questioned. "Is he trying to get us all killed?"

Coming alongside Rob and Ken's now sunken mokoro, Lucus jumped out and he and Mpula tried in vain to get Rob's limp body into our mokoro. Jay also jumped into the now blood-stained water and the three of them were able to lift Rob and place him in front of me in our mokoro. I grabbed Rob by his arms and chest and tried to position him between my legs. His eyes were closed and his face was ashen-white. Except for a few stifled moans, he made no sound.. While trying to lift Rob out of the water, Mpula wrapped and tied a sweatshirt around Rob's chest. I thought, "He's been bitten on the chest, as well as on the legs." I later learned he had not been bitten there. Instead, the whole upper groin area of his right leg was ripped away. There was no place where one could place a tourniquet. There also was a huge, open gash from the calf of his left leg all the way down to his heel. The bone and sinew were clearly exposed. What could one do?

Lucas grabbed his pole and jumped back upon the stern of our mokoro. He deftly turned our craft around and frantically began to pole us back towards Delta Camp. I cradled Rob's head next to my chest and tried to offer him words of encouragement. There was no reply. His eyes remained closed and, except for a few sporadic gasps, his body remained motionless. The gasping ceased after only a few minutes and I could not feel a pulse in Rob's wrist. I feared the worst had happened.

As Lucas continued to frantically pole our mokoro towards Delta Camp, I began to realize our efforts to help Rob probably were futile. I then began to worry about Jay and the others that we'd left behind with the marauding hippo. I was certain the hippo had completely demolished Rob's and Ken's mokoro. Thus, my son Jay, Ken and Mpula were stranded with the hippo! Furthermore, wouldn't the blood in the water attract crocodiles? Although Lucas continued to frantically pole our mokoro towards Delta Camp. What would I do if he became completely exhausted?" And, "How could we return to rescue Jay, Ken and Mpula?

It seemed like hours but probably was only about thirty minutes before Delta Camp appeared on the horizon. I began to shout, "Help! Help!", as loudly as I could. Shortly, the outlines of curious people appeared on the Camp's deck. As Lucas pushed us up onto the shore, alongside the lodge, Vic pushed his way through a small throng of assembled native staff. He inquired, "What happened?" My reply was, "A hippo attacked us! Do you have a stretcher?" Vic leaned down, placed his ear next to Rob's chest and intently listened. After about a minute, he turned and with dismay shook his head.

A couple of staff members brought a large, flat board with hand-holds on either side. This would serve as a stretcher. However, no one would touch Rob nor help me remove his lifeless form from between my legs, out of the mokoro and onto the "stretcher". They insisted upon first finding and donning some rubber gloves. The fear of AIDS is a reality in this part of the world!

We eventually carried Rob's lifeless body into the shade of a nearby hut and covered him with a sheet. I kept insisting a mokoro should be sent – "Immediately!" – to retrieve the others. After what seemed to be an interminable wait, this finally was done. With the radio inside the lodge, Vic contacted the airport in Maun and requested that a medical officer and others be sent to Delta Camp - "as soon as possible!" In turn, he was told, "A medical examiner and investigating officers will be sent as soon as possible."

Up until then the shock of what had happened did not bother me. Suddenly I was haunted with, "What should we have done to try to save Rob? Should we have tried to take him to shore, rather than return to Delta Camp? What about the others? Will the hippo also attack them?" These and other thoughts coursed through my mind. It was a nightmare!

An airplane eventually roared overhead and then landed at the nearby landing strip. A Land Rover shortly delivered a medical doctor, who said his name was Mark. He then introduced us to his lady medical assistant and two sharply-dressed black police officers. At approximately the same time, three mokoros appeared on the river in front of the Camp. One contained Nikki, Ziggy and Mox, another Jay, Ken and Mpula, and the third only the lone staff officer that had been sent from Delta Camp. What a relief to see all were safe!

I met the mokoros at the shore. I could not believe the hippo had not completely demolished the mokoro in which Rob and Ken had been riding. Although the mokoro had been sunk and the gear strewn about in the water, there were only a couple of marks on the wooden canoe that had been hewn by hand out of the trunk of a "sausage" tree. It was unbelievable!

I then learned that, somehow - even though she was only a few feet away - Ziggy had not witnessed the hippo attack upon Rob. She wanted to know, "Where is Rob? How is he? Is he OK?" Her inquiries were met with silence and downcast eyes. No one would tell her that her new husband was dead. Ziggy then persisted with, "Let me see Rob! What's wrong? Why won't anyone talk to me?"

Kim, one of our tour guides, and Aysel, a staff member from Oddball's, arrived at Delta Camp about the same time as those in the three mokoros. When apprised of what had happened, Kim broke into tears and tried to put her arms around Ziggy. Still, no one would tell Ziggy the terrible news. Finally, Aysel pointedly stated, "I'm sorry, but your husband is dead." Ziggy's immediate retort was, "No! No! It's not true! He's my life! This is all a terrible dream." She then insisted upon seeing Rob, even though we attempted to convince her that, "It's better if you don't see him now."

As we tried to console Ziggy, Nikki became almost hysterical. She sobbed as if her heart was broken and kept saying over and over, "What would I do if it had been Ken? What would I do? It's all so terrible!" I likewise thought, "What would I do if it had been my son Jay?" I still wonder!

I accompanied Mark in his medical examination of Rob. I explained to him what had happened and how we did not even know there was a hippo in that area prior to its attack. I also queried him as to what we could have done to prolong Rob's life. His reply was, "Even the damage to the left leg could have been fatal without immediate medical attention." And, "The damage in the groin area of his right leg is so severe that – even with medical aid – there's a good chance he would have bled to death within minutes."

Following completion of the medical doctor's examination, the native staff members insisted that they be permitted to form a circle around Rob's lifeless body to offer a prayer and to pay their last respects. The police officers, a prim, young woman and a slightly older man, then insisted upon taking statements from our three guides, as well as from each of us that had witnessed the tragedy. As to my best recollection, I told them, "We were about thirty minutes out from Delta Camp when we encountered a cow hippo and calf. Thereafter, it was about another fifteen minutes before we were attacked by a large hippo that we had not previously seen. Five to ten minutes thereafter, Rob died in my arms, during our approximately thirty-five-minute journey back to Delta Camp. The rest of our group finally arrived at Delta Camp about an hour after Lucas and me."

Another plane eventually arrived at the nearby landing strip and Rob's body; Ziggy and Nikki were transported by Land Rover to the plane and then flown back to Maun. While we waited, Ken and Jay related how – after the hippo had gone up into some bushes – they and Mpula had retrieved the mokoro from the bottom of the marsh. After they emptied the water out of it, Mpula insisted that they try to find and retrieve ALL of their gear from off the bottom of the marsh.

This was despite both Nikki's and Ziggy's repeated pleas of "Let's get out of here!" Furthermore, the hippo, which had retreated onto a small, brush-covered islet, kept snorting and grunting and they did not know whether or not it was going to attack again. It was a frightening situation, but they somehow managed to retrieve all of the gear from the marsh and stash it on the mokoro.

Ken and Jay were both wearing walking shorts. The coarse grass and reeds, through which they waded while up-righting the mokoro and retrieving the gear, severely cut and scratched their bare legs. Jay's legs looked almost like raw hamburger. However, upon our return by Land Rover to Oddball's Camp, Kim retrieved some antibiotic salve from her medicine kit and, except for a few scars, Jay's legs were almost completely healed by the time we returned home two weeks later.

We were greeted by a group of six tourists when we arrived at Oddball's. They had just returned from a "three-day campout in the bush". Included in the group was a young couple from Adelaide, Australia, a young fellow from Budapest, Hungary, a Swede, and a young German girl. They insisted upon our recounting details about the tragedy in which we'd been involved. Although they'd observed many wild animals during their three days in the "bush", they claimed they had not observed a single hippo or crocodile. I guess one never knows what to expect in the Okavango!

Another plane arrived while we were eating lunch. Ken, Jay and I flew back to Maun in this plane and then were taken to a compound on the outskirts of town. After getting settled in a room next to one occupied by Ziggy and Nikki, we retreated to the nearby swimming pool. There, I lounged next to the pool and tried to record the horrendous happenings of the day in my journal and Jay soaked his festering legs in the water of the pool. While we were thus occupied, a tall (six-foot-six inches!), good-looking young man approached us and introduced himself as Mark. He had heard about our terrible experience and wanted us to relate details about it to him. Thereafter, he also began to relate experiences he'd had during his life and especially since coming to Africa.

Mark was from Klamath Falls, Oregon and had come to Africa only six months previous. Besides being a "would-be writer" he also was an employee at Oddball's. He recounted, "I've witnessed a number of deaths during my stay in Botswana." He then proudly displayed a bracelet on his wrist, which he claimed he'd retrieved from the stomach of a large crocodile they'd shot after it attacked and killed a native woman. He told how he had had an on-going vendetta with and had been attacked by marauding baboons at Oddball's. Also, how the rising water from the recent rainy season had concentrated wildlife and especially snakes upon the remaining high ground in the Delta. As a result, he had removed two spitting cobras from his tent in a single day. He further claimed, "I've encountered too many puff adders to even count!" On and on Mark related almost unbelievable experiences he'd had during his six-month sojourn in Botswana. He then retrieved from his nearby room some draft articles he'd written about these experiences and proffered them to me to read and comment upon. Africa truly can be an exciting place!

After Mark's departure, Ziggy eventually joined me at the edge of the pool. I told her how, insofar as I could tell, Rob never suffered after the hippo attack and how I was thankful for the opportunity to become acquainted with her and Rob. She, in turn, told me about how she and Rob had met and then courted for some years before getting married. She claimed, "We were the perfect love! We never quarreled. We agreed upon everything. Everyone told us our love was too good to be true. They claimed it could never last." We discussed many things and I tried to assure her that Rob's death did not necessarily end their marriage. God's plan for our happiness provides a way for our marriage and family ties to be eternal.

Ziggy persisted in stating, "Somehow, I don't know how, Rob will let me know if he's Ok. He won't leave me without letting me know he's alright." I pondered deeply about her faith and as to how this might happen. Then, the next morning, she told me how she'd received her confirmation as to Rob's well-being. Rob's camcorder, which he wanted to use to photograph the cow hippo and calf at closer quarters, had been retrieved from off the bottom of the marsh at the site of the hippo attack. It was completely water logged and inoperable. Nevertheless, Ziggy had laid it on a table next to her bed.

Then, in the middle of the night, the light on the camcorder went on and the camcorder started running. Furthermore, it kept running until she picked it up! "This," she claimed, "is how Rob was letting me know he is alright." She then emphatically stated, "No one can persuade me otherwise!"

We spent almost three days in Maun. These were spent arranging for Rob's body to be shipped back to Melbourne, Australia for burial. This entailed having a mortician come from Johannesburg to embalm the body, visiting numerous government offices and personnel, filling out innumerable legal forms, obtaining a casket, etc. Following this seemingly interminable ordeal, I was ready to "bag " the rest of our trip through Namibia, the Kalahari Desert, down to the Skeleton Coast, along the Orange River and then to Cape Town. However, Ken and Nikki claimed, "You'll get over what we've gone through quicker IF you continue on with us." Thus, after bidding Ziggy farewell, Jay and I continued on with Ken, Nikki, and our guides Jacques and Kim.

A few days later, while we were camped in a dry streambed in the Kalahari, I was awakened by the banging of pots and pans. This ruckus was caused by some feral cattle that had invaded the kitchen area at the back of our truck/bus. I exited the tent and started shouting to drive the cattle off. Suddenly, a black cow with long, sharp horns charged me. I grabbed her horns, which encircled my waist, and desperately struggled to keep her from goring me. I also started to scream at the top of my voice. Fortunately, Jay heard my cries and quickly grabbed a shovel and beat off the cow. All I could think was, "I survived the hippo attack, but now I'm going to be killed by a darn cow!" What an anti-climax!

During my more than thirty-year career as a wildlife biologist, I've had a tigress literally roar in my face, after George Schaller and I unexpectedly encountered her in the tall grass in central India – where he was studying deer and tiger. On nine occasions, I was charged by Indian one-horned rhino, while conducting a survey of this species in eastern India and central Nepal. I've also been "bowled over" by bighorn rams and "jousted" by Himalayan tahr and other species of wild sheep and goats, while attempting to capture and/or obtain blood samples from them for genetic studies. I've also been repeatedly kicked and chased by "American" elk and deer, while studying these species. And, I've been bitten too many times to count by rats, mice, prairie dogs and other wild animals. I also was bitten by a vampire bat in the Amazon River Basin, while accompanying some herpetologists on a collection expedition and sleeping in a bamboo hut. Thereafter, I anxiously waited for a couple of weeks to see whether or not the bat had transmitted rabies to me. Nevertheless, our encounter with a hippo on the Okavango perhaps is my most memorable wildlife experience.

On numerous occasions throughout my life I've been miraculously protected from serious harm and even death. Why, I do not know. I can only surmise the Lord yet has something important for me to do. I hope this is true and that I can accomplish what I am supposed to do.

PRIZED POSSESSIONS

It has taken almost a lifetime for me to realize that families are the most important thing in life. As stated by L. Tom Perry (April 2015 General Conference for The Church of Jesus Christ of Latter-day Saints) "Family is the center of life and the key to eternal happiness."

During a Sunday School class early in 2014, our teacher passed out slips of paper and asked each class member to: "List your five most prized **material** possessions". After briefly pondering the question, I listed the following: 1. Home, 2. Food Storage, 3. Land, 4. Water and 5. Books. I had no inkling whatsoever at this time that what I considered to be my "most prized possessions" essentially would be gone prior to the end of the year.

Reasons for listing what I did include:

1. HOME: During an extended period of time out family lived around the world. For example, we lived in six countries (Ecuador, India, Chad, Mexico and Australia) and a like number of states (Colorado, Utah, Wyoming, Maryland, Texas, and Idaho). Although we lived in more than 30 residences and even purchased five of the houses in which we resided, it was not until we purchased the family farm from my father and, thereafter, built "our dream home" on it that I felt we were truly living in "our home". The family farm, which we called "The Ranch", was where I spent much of my youth and where I always longed to be. It was here that I planned to spend the rest of my life.

    The house we built on "The Ranch" was not overly extravagant, but it included almost everything we envisioned or wanted in our "home"; it's more than 3,300 square feet of living space and 17 rooms provided ample room for our family, as well as the many souvenirs and possessions we had accumulated while 'vagabonding" around the world.

2. FOOD STORAGE: The principle of "being prepared" has been instilled in me ever since I can remember. While living in places like Calcutta, India and Chad, Africa, we witnessed – first hand – the dire effects of malnutrition and starvation. This further instilled in me a desire to try and avert such a calamity ever befalling members of our family. Thus, we attempted to always maintain an ample supply of food and other basic commodities – sufficient to maintain both us and our extended family for at least a year. We were blessed by so doing. For example, by purchasing in quantities and while desired items were on sale greatly reduced our food budget. Furthermore, when I accepted a two-year assignment in Chad, Africa, we were allowed to ship 3,000 pounds of consumable goods. We did not have sufficient funds to purchase such a large amount, but we solved our problem by simply crating and shipping the food supply we already had in our storeroom.

3. LAND: In 1896, my great-grandfather (James William Spillett) purchased an extended parcel of some of the original irrigated homesteads in the Rockland Valley of southeastern Idaho. These he turned over to my grandfather (James Edward Spillett or "Ted") and two great uncles (Benjamin Joseph and George Walter) to jointly operate. This they unitedly did until around 1910 when the Valley was opened to dry-land homesteading. They then equally divided the irrigated land, which was their inheritance, and each built a residence adjacent to their holdings. Thus, each homesteaded an additional 160 acres of dry land. My grandfather subsequently died and his brother (my "Uncle Ben") married my grandmother. The dry land homesteads subsequently were lost during the "Great Depression" and my father (James Oren Spillett) eventually purchased "The Ranch" from Uncle Ben. Then, in 1981, I purchased "The Ranch" from my father.

I considered "The Ranch" as a legacy and envisioned it remaining in our family for perpetuity. Furthermore, I considered it as a place of refuge or where my family members could always come to get away from the perils or troubles of the world, while being able to at least eek out a living. I realized "The Ranch" (being only 120 acres) was not large enough to provide an adequate living for a family. But I thought it would at least provide a place to live and the basic necessities for life could be gleaned from it. I also thought the planting of an apple orchard would bolster its value and productivity. Thus, we planted a 900-tree apple orchard and diligently worked for almost 30 years to maintain and improve it.

4. WATER: In much of the western United States the availability of water determines both the value and the productivity of the land. "The Ranch" has water rights in the 3rd and 8th oldest deeded ditch water rights in the Rockland Valley. However, these do not provide sufficient water to irrigate the entire 120 acres – ever when flood irrigation is converted to sprinkle irrigation. Thus, upon acquiring the property from my father, the first thing I did was apply to the State Department of Water Resources for a permit to develop an irrigation well large enough to sprinkle-irrigate all of our 120 acres. I knew that whatever I might do to try and improve or make more efficient use of my ditch water would be protested by Farold Nelson, who controlled more water rights than anyone in the Valley. Rather than fight him, I'd simply use well water to irrigate our entire property. However, after considerable expense, we found the well we developed would irrigate only about half of our land. Thus, in order to irrigate our entire property, we'd also have to use our ditch water. This resulted in my requesting a permit to change the point of diversion for my ditch water rights and then pumping directly out of the South Fork of Rock Creek to sprinkle irrigate. As expected, Mr. Nelson took me to court and I spent more than 20 years and many thousands of dollars fighting to maintain and make better use of my deeded water. Fortunately, I finally won. This is why I considered our deeded water rights to be one of my "prized possessions".

5. BOOKS: Books have been dear to me throughout my life. Some of the fondest memories of my youth are about my sitting with my father on the steps of the old log house on

"The Ranch" and him reading memorable books to me. Books such as: "The Call of the Wild", "Baree Son of Kazan", "Tom Sawyer", "Huckleberry Finn", "Big Smoke Mountain", "Girl of Limber Lost", and so on. I also remember my reliving (in my mind) many of the stories read to me. Perhaps because of these choice memories, I have been an avid reader and book collector throughout my life. Even when funds were scarce, which was common during the early part of our marriage and especially during the many years I was a university student, I somehow usually managed to regularly purchase books of special interest to me. And, I closely guarded these.

During much of my life I've probably averaged reading at least two books per month. Besides technical books or those relating to wildlife biology, I am drawn to biographies of famous people who have succeeded by overcoming adversity. Travel or books on geography, as well as those depicting wild animals also are special for me. Virtually all of my books are non-fiction. It seems to me that real happenings usually are more dramatic and interesting than are fiction or "make-believe". As a result, the walls of our home (especially those in the basement) were lined with loaded bookshelves and there were stacks of boxes filled with precious books in our storeroom. In short, I've collected thousands of books.

Within what seemed to be a relatively short time, my wife Carol and I were hit with a "double whammy". Because of dementia, she no longer could take care of our home. And, because of lung problems, I no longer could take care of our apple orchard or even the yard and garden. None of our children were interested in the family farm or orchard. They also claimed they could not find suitable employment to support them and their families in or near the Rockland Valley. Thus, it appeared our best alternative was to sell the farm. Oh, how this hurt! My hopes and plans, not to mention all of the time and effort we'd spent over many years, seemed to be for naught. I then began to more fully realize we cannot take our material possessions with us – sometimes not even in this life, let alone in the life to come!

It is true that some material things are important and are needed for life; i.e. food, clothing and shelter. But, how much of our time and effort is expended in accumulating material things that are of relatively very little value or which we really do not need? As I've grown older, more and more I've realized how little I actually need of the vast array of material goods our modern world offers us. The accumulation of material things may not necessarily be wrong, but the priority used in obtaining them may be; i.e. "But seek ye first the kingdom of God, and His righteousness and all these things shall be added unto you." (Matt. 6:33)

Contemplating, "What are the truly important things in life?" I've concluded it is our relationship with others; "Do unto others as you would have them do unto you." Or "Love thy neighbor as thyself." I further believe this is especially true with respect to members of our families.

The scriptures, which are God's word, given to us through "His servants the prophets", tell us "families can be forever". Therefore, should not one of our major objectives in life be that of continually striving to improve our family relationships? Likewise, through the scriptures we learn we are the spirit children of our Father in Heaven. Thus, all mankind is God's family!

Because our Father in Heaven loves us, He has given is the opportunity to come to earth – first, to obtain a body, which is in "His likeness or image", and then to prove ourselves or gain experience in choosing between right and wrong. A part of this earthly experience is our opportunity to have children or form families – somewhat similar to Him. Through the scriptures we also learn how (because of rebellion) Satan was cast out of heaven and came to this earth to be an "opposition to all righteousness". Is it not striking how Satan does all in his power to tear down the family; through pornography, immorality, same sex marriage, etc.?

Looking back upon my life, I think one of my biggest regrets is not having spent more time with the members of my family, as well as with relatives and friends. I fear I spent far too much time striving to accumulate material possessions, many of which I did not need.

Now, virtually all of these are gone; we sold our home, land and water, donated my books to the local library, and essentially gave away our food storage, most of our clothes, souvenirs, and other goods. Carol, my wife of 53 years, passed away on April 22, 2015. But, I still have our five children and nineteen grandchildren, as well as a good number of relatives and friends with whom I can associate. They mean much, much more to me than do my former "prized possessions". And, I look forward to being with them not only during this life but forever!

POST SCRIPT

"As man now is, God once was:
As God now is, man may become."
Lorenzo Snow

Over the course of many years I have concluded:

There are no ordinary people. Each of us is unique. Because of our uniqueness, our lives present a story that may inspire others, either for good or ill – or both. I think ALL of us have a story we should share with others.

We are the spiritual children of a loving, just and merciful Father in Heaven. As sons or daughters of God we each have a "spark" of divinity within us that will lead us to truth and light. However, our mortal or physical bodies are an enemy to God. If we succumb to our carnal desires, rather than seeking after spiritual light, we will be led into darkness.

Because our Father in Heaven is a just God, a price must be paid for each of our sins or wrongdoings. But, because He also is a merciful God, He sent "His Only Begotten Son in the flesh" – Jesus the Christ – to be our Savior or to redeem us from our sins. IF we will repent and strive to do our Father's will, Christ will pay the price for our sins. Thus, we can become worthy to return to God's presence and eternally dwell with Him.

Because each of us is unique, somehow our Father in Heaven has placed us in that situation here on earth where we can best work out our salvation.

We do not have to be perfect to become instruments in God's hands to further His work. We only have to be willing to do so.

Satan or the Devil is real and will do all in his power to entice us to give in to our carnal desires and to deny the influence of our spiritual heritage. It seems he especially likes to use addictive or habit-forming enticements (i.e. drugs, alcohol, pornography and immorality) to entrap us into doing his will. Nevertheless, we have our God-given liberty to choose for ourselves. The choice is up to us!

Finally, as stated by an ancient prophet, "When we are in the service of our fellow beings, we are only in the service of our God." (Mosiah 2:17)

I hope that both you and I can always strive to choose wisely.

Copies of HAPPENINGS may be obtained by contacting:

Machelle Mitton
442 S. Center
Hyrum, UT 84319
machellerose@yahoo.com
(435)881-6702